Business and Management Practices in Greece

Business and Management Practices in Greece

A Comparative Context

Edited by

Rea Prouska

and

Maria Kapsali

palgrave
macmillan

First published 2011 by
PALGRAVE MACMILLAN

Palgrave Macmillan in the UK is an imprint of Macmillan Publishers Limited, registered in England, company number 785998, of Houndmills, Basingstoke, Hampshire RG21 6XS.

Palgrave Macmillan in the US is a division of St Martin's Press LLC, 175 Fifth Avenue, New York, NY 10010.

Palgrave Macmillan is the global academic imprint of the above companies and has companies and representatives throughout the world.

Palgrave® and Macmillan® are registered trademarks in the United States, the United Kingdom, Europe and other countries.

ISBN 978–0–230–24585–3

This book is printed on paper suitable for recycling and made from fully managed and sustained forest sources. Logging, pulping and manufacturing processes are expected to conform to the environmental regulations of the country of origin.

A catalogue record for this book is available from the British Library.

A catalog record for this book is available from the Library of Congress.

10 9 8 7 6 5 4 3 2 1
20 19 18 17 16 15 14 13 12 11

Printed and bound in Great Britain by
CPI Antony Rowe, Chippenham and Eastbourne

Contents

List of Tables and Figures

Tables

Figures

List of Abbreviations

ADECH	Athens Derivatives Exchange Clearing House
ADEDY	Confederation of Public Servants
ADEX	Athens Derivatives Exchange
ASE	Athens Stock Exchange
ASEP	Supreme Council for Human Resources Selection
ATHEX	Athens Exchange
BoD	Board of Directors
BoG	Bank of Greece
CAF	Common Assessment Framework
CAP	Common Agricultural Policy
CCP	Central Counter Party
CEC	Commission of the European Communities
GMID	Global Market Information Database
CIA	Central Intelligence Agency
CLA	Collective Labour Agreements
CLAs	General National Collective Labour Agreements
CORDIS	Community Research and Development Information Service
CPR	Cost Per Rating
CSD	Greek Central Securities Depositories
CSF	Community Support Framework
CSGR	Centre for the Study of Globalisation and Regionalisation
CSR	Corporate Social Responsibility
DEPANOM	National Health System Construction Company
DINK	Double Income, No Kids
DSS	Dematerialised Securities System
EAGGF	European Agriculture Guidance and Guarantee Fund
EC	European Commission

ECB	European Central Bank.
ECJ	European Court of Justice
EEC	European Economic Community
EGSSE	National General Collective Agreement
ELTE	Accounting and Auditing Oversight Board
ELOT	Organization for Standardization
EMU	Economic and Monetary Union
ENA	Alternative Market of the Athens Stock Exchange
EOMMEX	Hellenic Organization of Small and Medium Enterprises and Handicraft
EPEs	Limited Liability Companies
ERDF	European Regional Development Fund
ESEE	National Confederation of Greek Traders
ESF	European Social Fund
ETF	Exchange Traded Fund
ETVA	Hellenic Industrial Development Bank
EU	European Union
FDI	Foreign Direct Investment
FIFG	Financial Instrument for Fisheries Guidance
FSF	Financial Stability Fund
GAP	General Accounting Plan
GATT	General Agreement on Tariffs and Trade
CCP	Central Counter Party
GDP	Gross Domestic Product
GMID	Global Market Information Database
GSEBEE	General Confederation of Professional Craftsmen and Small Manufacturers of Greece
GSEE	Greek General Confederation of Labour
GSI	General Secretariat for Industry
GSRT	General Secretariat for Research and Technology
HCMC	Hellenic Capital Market Commission
HELEX	Hellenic Exchanges SA, the listed holding company of Athens Exchange

HRM	Human Resource Management
IB	International Business
IFRS	International Financial Reporting Standard
IKA	Social Security Institution
IMF	International Monetary Fund
IMP	Integrated Mediterranean Programme
IOBE	Foundation for Economic and Industrial Research
IS	Innovation System
ISO	International Organization for Standardization
KETHI	Research Centre for Gender Equality
KKE	Communist Party of Greece
KVS	Income Tax Legislation
KYP	Hellenic National Intelligence Service
LSDV	Least Squared Dummy Variables
MA	Managing Authority
MBO	Management by Objectives
MC	Monitoring Committees
M&Cs	Municipalities and Communities
MBO	Management by Objectives
MELRA	Ministry of Education, Lifelong Learning and Religious Affairs
MiFID	Markets in Financial Instruments Directive
MEF	Ministry of the Economy and Finance
MIAPAD	Ministry of Internal Affairs, Public Administration & Decentralization
MNC	Multinational Corporation
MoD	Ministry of Development
MTF	Multilateral Trading Facility
NATO	North Atlantic Treaty Organization
NBG	National Bank of Greece
NBS	National Business System
NIS	National Innovation System

NPL	Non-Performing Loans
NUTS2	Nomenclature of Units for Territorial Statistics
OAED	Greek Manpower Employment Organization
OECD	Organisation for Economic Co-operation and Development
OLS	Ordinary Least Squares estimator
PASOK	Pan-Hellenic Socialist Movement
PPPs	Public–Private Partnerships
RBV	Resource Based View
R&D	Research and Development
ROI	Return on Investment
ROP	Regional Operational Programme
SCP	Structure–Conduct–Performance
SEA	Single European Act
SELE	Association of Certified Accountants Auditors
SEV	Hellenic Federation of Enterprises
SF	Structural Fund
SMART	System for Money Settlement of Athex Reconciled Transactions
SME	Small and Medium-sized Enterprise
SOEL	Institute of Certified Public Accountants of Greece
SOL	Institute of Sworn-in Accountants
SPD	Single Programming Document
STI	Science Technology and Innovation
TIF	Thessaloniki International Fair
TFP	Total Factor Productivity
TQM	Total Quality Management
UNIDO	United Nations Industrial Development Organization
UCITS	Undertakings for Collective Investments in Transferable Securities
VAT	Value Added Tax
WHO	World Health Organization

Acknowledgements

The editors would like to thank all of the authors for their valuable contributions to this volume and also the publishing team at Palgrave Macmillan for their continuous support throughout the project.

Notes on the Contributors

Panagiotis Ballas holds a PhD in innovative services adoption marketing from Manchester Business School. His main research interests lie in the area of innovation adoption and consumer research. He also holds two master's degrees, one in Internal Auditing and Management and one in Accounting and Financial Management. He has work experience not only in academia, but also in banking.

Ioannis Bournakis is Lecturer in Economics at Middlesex University Business School. He holds a PhD in economics from the University of Kent. His research interests include international trade, economics and productivity growth, exporting and productivity at firm level, and industrial organization with emphasis on the analysis of market concentration and measure of mark-ups.

Joseph Butler holds a PhD in historical anthropology from the National University of Ireland (Maynooth). His research interests are the social and political history of Europe and its consequences for the contemporary world. He currently teaches modern history and politics at Hampstead Fine Arts College in London.

Constantinos Caramanis is Associate Professor of Accounting at Athens University of Economics and Business. He holds a PhD in accounting from the University of Edinburgh. His research interests include the history and current developments in the Greek auditing profession, the market for audit services and issues in financial reporting. He has published widely and has also worked in the industry as a certified auditor. He has recently served as a member of the Greek Accounting and Auditing Oversight Board and as chair of a committee on the reform of Greek accounting law. He has undertaken consultancy projects with private sector companies on financial reporting issues, as well as with the Greek Ministry of Finance on public sector accounting and auditing.

Emmanouil Dedoulis is Lecturer in Accounting at Athens University of Economics and Business. He holds a PhD in accounting from the University of Essex. His research interests include the development of the institution of auditing, the Code of Ethics and current developments in the accounting and auditing standards. He has published in reputable international journals. He has professional experience as an assistant certified auditor and is a member of the Institute of Certified Auditors in Greece.

Ioannis Gedeon is Business and Marketing Intelligence Manager at the Institute for Work-Based Learning at Middlesex University. He holds an MSc in marketing from the University of Lincoln. He has held various senior positions in sales and marketing in Greek and British firms.

Kyriakos Hatzaras is a member of the Health Management Group at Imperial College Business School. He holds an MEng in electrical and electronic engineering with management from Imperial College London, and an MPhil in European studies from the London School of Economics and Political Science. His research has been published by the European Commission, the OECD, the universities of Tokyo and Warwick, the LSE's Hellenic Observatory, and the World Council of Hellenes Abroad.

Maria Kapsali is Research Associate in the Innovation and Entrepreneurship Group at Imperial College Business School. She holds a PhD in business administration with a specialization in operations, technology and innovation management from Manchester Business School. Her research interests include innovation policy, innovation systems, policy implementation instruments, operations in innovation firms, and innovation projects in healthcare.

Ageliki Katsiyianni is an attorney at law specializing in commercial, banking and finance law. She holds a Master of Laws (LLM) from University College London (UCL).

Eirini Kokkori is legal counsel at Coral SA (former Shell Hellas SA) of Motor Oil Hellas group of companies. She has held various senior positions as a legal consultant in companies such as OTEplus SA, the affiliate of the Greek telecommunications organization OTE. Her work focuses on company, labour and commercial law. She holds a Master of Laws (LLM) from University College London (UCL) and is currently studying for a PhD in securities law at the University of Athens law school.

Athanasios Kouloridas is Visiting Lecturer in the Department of Business Administration of the Economic University of Athens. He is a partner at Athens Business Lawyers and legal counsel for the Greek Union of Listed Companies.

Nektarios Polychroniou is an attorney at law specializing in commercial law. He holds a Master of Laws (LLM) from Georgetown University.

He is currently completing his PhD, with a specialization in money laundering, at the University of Athens law school.

Efthimios Poulis is Senior Lecturer in Strategic Management at Norwich Business School, University of East Anglia. He holds a PhD from Manchester Business School. He has held positions at the Athens University of Economics and Business, Manchester Business School, Bournemouth University and Buckinghamshire New University. He is a reviewer for top international academic journals and track chair for *Dynamic Capabilities* (European Academy of Management) and *Strategic Management* (British Academy of Management).

Konstantinos Poulis is Lecturer at the University of Essex. He holds a PhD in international business from Manchester Business School and has worked in several European countries. He has published in several outlets while his work features in conference proceedings of various business academies.

Rea Prouska is Senior Lecturer in Human Resource Management at Middlesex University Business School. She holds a PhD from Manchester Business School and specializes in outsourcing HR activities. Her research interests are in HR outsourcing/offshoring, graduate employability and gender. She is co-editor of *Critical Issues in Human Resource Management*.

Alexandros Psychogios is Senior Lecturer in management and human resources, as well as Academic Research Coordinator in the Department of Business Administration and Economics in City College, International Faculty of the University of Sheffield. He holds a PhD in business administration from the University of Warwick. His research interests are associated with international HRM and business strategy, knowledge management and change, organizational learning and development, organizational theory and analysis, TQM and public services management.

Introduction

Rea Prouska and Maria Kapsali

The purpose of this book

We started this book with a need to satisfy our own curiosity to have an almost complete picture of the business system and management practices in Greece. Most of the contributors have conducted research in Greece and have knowledge of the theory and practice of management in Western European firms, and have identified key differences between the system and practices in Greek counterparts. However, we still needed a comprehensive explanation as to how the national business system functions and how management is really practised at the firm level in Greece overall. We felt that now more than ever is an appropriate time for this endeavour in the light of the recent economic crisis. We believe that the example of Greece has educational value as a case study, drawing attention to crucial issues and suggesting directions for solutions for peripheral countries that share many similarities and challenges. Therefore, our main questions are: What are the main issues of concern that one should know about in the business system and management practices in Greece? Where does the firm stand in the midst of all of this? Where do these stand in comparison with other peripheral European countries?

Our curiosity was further strengthened by the fact that academic literature on the Greek business system and management practices in firms is scarce, compared to research on these subjects in other countries, such as the UK. This is because research has focused mostly on observing 'core' or 'developed' business systems, while there is less research on semi-peripheral and even less on peripheral business systems. As a result markets, investors and business people work on assumptions based on reputation about these systems, rather than comprehensive and accurate descriptions based on evidence from in-depth research. For this reason, we chose to compare the Greek business system with those in the other peripheral EU countries (Portugal, Italy, Ireland and Spain) and the UK, which is selected as a representative of the core EU economies. The difference between the two categories is based on the definitions of the world systems theory (Wallerstein, 1974; 2000) as 'core is the developed, industrialized part of the world, and the periphery is the "underdeveloped", typically raw materials-exporting, poor part of the world; the market being the means by which the core exploits the periphery'.

This is the gap that this book is aiming to bridge: to bring together current knowledge on the Greek business system and management practices and to present these in an analytical and comparative way that would enable the reader to see them from a holistic point of view. Hence, this book is, firstly, a valuable resource to anyone doing research on or interested in research focused on Greek business and management; secondly, an excellent reference for students studying undergraduate or postgraduate programmes with a comparative or international element; and thirdly, it can provide a holistic picture for anyone interested in doing business with or investing in business in Greece.

The book is arranged in three parts, with the intention of providing a succinct outline of the business system in the first part, and the management practices of modern firms in Greece in the second part. Part I (Chapters 1 to 6) deals with the country's political, economic, financial, legal, development and innovation institutional structures, and frequently attributes management practices to them. Cause and effect relations between systemic structures and practices also appear often through Part II (Chapters 7 to 13), which looks at management practices within the firm (strategic management, international business, sales, marketing, human resource management, total quality management, accounting and auditing). The idea was to draw out these cause and effect links from both parts to reveal how the systemic structures in the first part are linked to the management practices in the second part. However, it was not a clear-cut division between systemic causes and management practices, nor should it be; therefore the chapters in Part III (Chapters 14–16) bring all the pieces together to discuss the complexity of the whole picture in the light of comparison with the other peripheral business systems. The rest of this introduction provides brief summaries of the chapters.

Summary of chapters

Part I: The Greek Business System

Chapter 1: Politics – political and economic developments through a historical perspective

The first chapter highlights the turbulent political environment since 1830 and how this formed the economic system. This period is described in three parts, separating in more or less equal time periods the 180 years of Greece's recent history as a free state. It concludes with three main themes cutting through this historical transition, which was characterized by wars, internal conflicts and economic highs and lows. These three themes are: first, a pattern of social, political and economic division; second, the way in which geopolitics, foreign relations and external powers interfere in domestic politics, contributing to these patterns of division and creating a culture of dependency of political action on exogenous systems; and third, the use of the public sector as a tool for politics. The consequences of this triad are cycles of economic deconstruction and reconstruction which are characterized by policy discontinuity, and partisan political practice, creating a vacuum in supportive business infrastructures and institutions. The business system is characterized by a majority of micro firms and a small minority of medium and larger firms and multinational corporations. The role of business is precarious; the firm is kept under the control of the owners, in a small organic form characterized by a strong entrepreneurial spirit, which is responsive, flexible and opportunistic, inhabiting markets with unstable conditions.

Chapter 2: Economics – productivity performance, determinants and future prospects

Chapter 2 highlights productivity performance. Greece's traditional area of specialization has been agriculture, a sector over-protected with the imposition of government tariffs and quotas. However, this sector shrank when the market become quite competitive after Greece's entry to the EU. The industrialization period was short, and since the 1970s the manufacturing sector has been shrinking due to the process of de-industrialization. At the same time as manufacturing and agriculture are in decline, there is a steady increase in specialization in financial, hospitality, retail, trade and water transport services. Despite the convergence of nominal macroeconomic fundamentals, the process of productivity convergence over the last 40 years has been very slow and GDP per capita is consistently less than the average in the EU and other developed countries. A major reason for the productivity gap is the fact that the Greek business system cannot undertake intensive research and development (R&D) activity due to large budget deficits and low technology uptake. Finally, there are concerns about whether the current specialization in financial services can constitute a model of sustainable development.

Chapter 3: Finance – banking and investment

Chapter 3 highlights the main developments in the Greek financial sector and the transition from the 1950s state of intervention that restricted competition and dominated the market through state-owned and nationalized players, until the early 1990s, with the modernization of regulation that led to the liberalization of the financial markets and the complete modernization of banking, which led to a boom in the industry in the late 1990s. Many state-controlled banks were privatized, mainly through listing their shares on the Athens Exchange and public offering programmes. Greek banks responded to the new conditions by undertaking mergers and acquisitions and by expanding in regional markets such as in South-eastern Europe. The banking system resisted the current global crisis because they did not employ the US credit system but difficulties started because of the public sector deficit which raised problems in liquidity.

Chapter 4: Development – the role of the public sector and firms in economic development

This chapter shows how the import of EU policy is not enough to modernize the innovation system, and provides the reasons for this. This research shows how wider public sector organizations are the ones which benefited mostly from participating in the second and third Structural Programmes (1994–2006), having marginalized the participation of private firms and restricted their role to that of sub-contracting. The role and resources of public organizations have been enhanced, while private innovative firms have had limited participation in the development process, with their potential still untapped and their entrepreneurship discouraged by bureaucracy.

Chapter 5: Innovation – the National Innovation System

Chapter 5 explores the National Innovation System (NIS) in Greece, using the Triple Helix model as an explanatory device. Innovation policy in Greece started to develop in the 1980s. The NIS appears to have most of the standard policy instruments in place, but shows disappointing performance results on several scoreboards. The NIS has a strong international supply-driven orientation, with EU funds as its main funding source. The key institutional actors are public ministries and regional public services and the private sector is a weak contributor in the creation and diffusion of innovation. The system is characterized by a lack of operationalizable policy and focuses on top-down implementation, without however establishing a strong executive institution, or having institutionalized measures to strengthen the position of firms, which are the weakest link in the system. Firms have low levels of technology absorption and adoption, and they are dominated by the public sector's regulatory and supply roles in the system. Firms have developed risk aversion and mistrust of established institutions, and they are confused about their choices due to lack of information and substantial support. More specifically, the relations and interactions between the actors in the NIS are weak, because the boundaries between policy and firms are too rigid.

Chapter 6: Law – company, tax and employment law

Chapter 6 highlights the main issues relating to company, tax and employment law. Greek company law is primarily based on French legislation and largely influenced by EU legislation. Companies can be classified into two broad categories: personal companies (unlimited and limited partnerships being the main types) and capital-based companies (principally sociétés anonymes and limited liability companies) Greek tax law has been known for its frequent changes (sometimes multiple changes within the same tax year). Greek companies are subject to income tax, value added tax, real estate tax, and social security contributions. Employment law developed later in Greece than in most European countries, due to the country's belated industrialization. Individual labour law regulates the relations between employer and employee and the rights and obligations that arise from the employment agreement. Collective labour law regulates the relationship between employers and trade unions and provides a framework for collective employee voice mechanisms.

Part II: Management Practices in Greek Firms

Chapter 7: Strategic Management

Chapter 7 explores the link between the micro-external and internal environments and the competitive and corporate strategic practices in Greek firms. Firstly, using Porter's model of the micro-external market, the firms' micro-external environment is characterized by powerful suppliers and weak buyers, with little threat of substitutes, few complementary products and low threat of entrants (with the exception of the retail market). Secondly, using a Resource-Based View perspective it is established that most firms do not possess significant resources and competences to allow them to achieve sustainable competitive advantage in the global environment (with the exception of some successful Greek multinational companies).

Consequently, there are significant differences in the way local small firms and MNCs compete. Local small firms are more risk-averse in their competitive and market strategies, do not employ management practices and rely on their local connections to create a competitive advantage. MNCs, on the other hand, use networking, employ scientific management principles and have distinctive market directions to create a competitive advantage. In terms of creating competitive advantages through the value chain, firms tend to focus on operations and marketing/sales, while support activities like logistics are ignored, and especially activities that require larger investments, such as R&D. Competitive strategies are mainly the outcome of intuition, bias, path-dependency and imitation. The most common strategy for creating competitive advantage is based on cost leadership rather than differentiation. Finally, regarding corporate strategies, most firms use some related diversification, and mostly horizontal integration, mainly through the acquisition of other competitors or companies producing substitute products. Vertical integration is rare.

Chapter 8: International Business

Chapter 8 explores the business activity of firms through the boundaries of the national business system. Firms demonstrate a remarkable presence in world markets with multinational activity stretching from the Balkans to North and South America and the Far East. Greece ranks among the top 50 countries in the world for foreign investment, and her multinationals account for almost a third of the overall turnover. Two major powerhouses of the Greek international activity are tourism and shipping. A paradox is observed here: while a significant number of sophisticated firms have followed the 'hard' road of foreign direct investment, exports are relatively lagging behind, and are not, therefore, a major contributor to the economy. The geographical and product scope of exports remains one of the lowest in the EU, because it is to a large degree regional with the majority targeting European markets.

The main structural weaknesses reflected in international practice are: first, the small size of firms which is the reason for the weakness to adjust to new forms of organization and to benefit from technological advances that generate sources of competitive advantage; second, the high degree of black market activity and the incomplete (but constantly improving) infrastructure and transport network; and third, constant changes in the corporate taxation regime and bureaucratic procedures when setting up of companies, that discourage foreign investment.

Chapter 9: Human Resource Management

Chapter 9 examines the practice of Human Resource Management (HRM) in Greece, which started to develop after the 1970s due to competitive pressures on firms (participation in the EU, the presence of MNCs and the higher educational level of professional management). Firm size directly affects the size and role of the HR department and a difference in practices between micro firms and MNCs is observed. Even though larger firms and MNCs have more formalized HR policies and procedures in place, these are usually absent in micro firms and SMEs. Key HRM activities are employee recruitment and selection, performance management, training and development and employee rewards, and there is a trend to outsource these activities to external consultants. Three critical HRM issues are identified in this chapter: the mismatch between supply and demand in skilled labour, the ageing workforce which affects pension policy, and gender equality in the workplace, particularly the current gender pay gap, working time, parenthood and sexual harassment. An additional critical issue is the power asymmetry between employer and employee and industrial action, especially in the public sector.

Chapter 10: Marketing

Chapter 10 highlights the differences in marketing practices between micro firms and larger or MNCs. Micro firms are sceptical of spending on marketing activities, primarily due to their targeting mainly local markets. Therefore, marketing is not their top priority, as they do not find contemporary marketing methods necessary. Marketing in micro firms is primarily based on personal relationships forged by sales managers who are the ones that mainly perform marketing activities, although salespeople are not formally educated or trained in marketing. Consumer research in not available, accessible or useful to micro firms: they use push-marketing and low-cost, low-risk promotional solutions, such as flyers, and they procrastinate in applying marketing promotions. Practices like e-marketing, mobile marketing and customer relationship marketing are gaining ground. Micro firms imitate marketing practices, in comparison to larger firms and MCNs that implement integrated strategic marketing plans, focus on their corporate and product image and use marketing consultants to outsource product campaigns and promote themselves to the wider market. A tension is observed between the clients and the consultants, however. The main challenge faced by marketing consultants is large companies that have marketing departments in place (and often refer to them as 'sales departments').

Chapter 11: Sales

Chapter 11 explores the sales practices in Greek firms. The role of the sales professional differs significantly between micro firms and MNCs in terms of the volume and standardization of practice. Customer relationship management (CRM) is valued by all types of firms, which emphasize customer feedback as a way of evaluating levels of customer satisfaction and demand. Knowledge and understanding of customer needs are gained through the relationships cultivated between the sales operative and the customer. CRM and sales professionals focus on building long-term relationships, rather than simply selling products and services. As a result, the sales profession has been thriving, even since the latest crisis, and it has evolved to have greater access to information, training and education than a few years ago. Inside the firm, performance management of sales professionals is based on output rather than behaviour. However, sales professionals are still considered generalists rather than product specialists or customer specialists. The e-advertising and e-sales fields are currently being developed in Greece and there are already a few good examples of organizations advertising and selling online.

Chapter 12: Total Quality Management

Chapter 12 examines the application of the Total Quality Management (TQM) philosophy in the Greek business system, taking into consideration that it is significantly different from the systems from which it originated; this fact is the cause of difficulties in its implementation. The chapter examines this argument in terms of the cultural and institutional factors in the private and public sectors.

The main cultural factor which are not conducive to the devolved, participatory practices of TQM are: the centralized control structure in firms, the autocratic/authoritative practice of senior managers and CEOs, the (mainly administrative) role of middle managers, and the trust gap within organizations due to the lack of open and clear communication. The institutional factors explain this cultural phenomenon in terms of the small size of firms, the locality of the markets, the quasi-industrial, low-process efficiency business system, individualism and the fact that people perceive TQM as synonymous with ISOs and both as a regulation rather than an improvement practice. TQM never evolved from business practice, but was rather a response to external competitive pressures.

Although larger firms created TQM departments they still perceive TQM as a peripheral function. MNCs were keener to adopt TQM; however, it is still far from being fully integrated into the production processes. Although managers understand its importance, they are not familiar as much with process quality and with TQM methods; firms emphasize product quality. On the other hand, facilitators of TQM implementation include the fact that competitive productivity has become a significant issue for managers and firms, the need for firms to implement 'hard' TQM practices (such as ISO), and the reformative cultural force which supports the modernization of the system. The public sector has tried to use TQM to improve services; however, few of them had limited success because of their complex structure, regulations and procedures.

Chapter 13: Accounting and Auditing

Chapter 13 explains how accounting and auditing practices did not emerge from a business need, but were rather imposed by state legislation in the early 1900s, and thus they were seen as an auditing tool in the service of government tax collectors. The business system did not adopt auditing practices easily, since micro firms and SMEs usually have centralized control mechanisms and did not need complicated auditing practices, which imposed restrictions on their *laissez-faire* operations. When Greece joined the EU, however, the institutional and legal framework for accounting and auditing practices changed, because there were pressures to modernize corporate legislation and adopt International Financial Reporting Standards, International Standards on Auditing and EU directives for the operation of the financial sector (banking and insurance) and capital markets. However, Greece's performance in the implementation of EU-inspired reforms has been poor, because of structural and institutional problems. State intervention was successful only after the creation of a watchdog, which dictated the status and practices of the profession. The liberalization of the auditing profession eventually took place in 1992 following an intense intra-professional struggle, which so far, has failed to produce any significant results.

The modernization of accounting practice has been undermined by the government's frequent ad hoc interventions in reporting issues. At the moment, companies implement two diametrically opposite accounting models: IFRSs (the Anglo-American model) which are market-oriented, and accounting rules (Law 2190/1920 and the General Accounting Plan – GAP) which draw on a deep-rooted, tax-oriented tradition. The EEC GAP and the transposition of EEC accounting and auditing directives were introduced in the 1980s, but have not been kept up-to-date with international developments, while it is an over-procedural and unnecessarily costly system. In the 2000s, the introduction of IFRSs helped progress accounting practice, but also revealed the weakness of local accounting standards as well as the inappropriateness of legal provisions in corporate legislation, even of those introduced in conjunction with the switch to IFRSs. The chapter concludes with a few recommendations: to establish a new watchdog, to create a new tax system for accounting standards for unlisted companies, and to create new corporate and tax legislation.

Part III: Conclusion: Summary, Comparison and Suggestions

Chapter 14: The Business System and Management Practices in Greece

The first conclusion chapter provides a summary of management practices and the business system, by bringing together all the causal factors from the business system which explain certain types of management practices. The discussion describes the situation in typical firms (micro firms and SMEs), with references to larger counterparts for comparison.

Chapter 15: Systems and Practices – Peripheral Countries Compared with the UK

The second conclusion chapter completes the picture by comparing the Greek business system with, first, other peripheral countries' business systems (Portugal, Italy, Ireland and Spain) and, second, the UK (which is a representative of a core-developed business system). It is not the purpose of this chapter to compare business systems *per se*, but rather to show how the systemic factors discovered in the book exist in different business systems and how these affect management practices. We then include some statistical evidence from EU databases to illustrate them.

Chapter 16: Suggestions for Further Research on the Business System and Practices in Greece

The final chapter discusses ways forward in terms of academic research focusing on Greek business, based on the suggestions by the contributing authors.

Part I
The Greek Business System

1

Politics

Political and Economic Developments through a Historical Perspective

Maria Kapsali and Joseph Butler

Overview

This chapter describes the political history of the Modern Greek state since its re-establishment in the nineteenth century and the impact it has had on the economy and the business system. It should be emphasized that this is an outline, highlighting certain themes in Greek politics, economy and business, and not a political analysis. There is plenty of scientific literature on that (from which we draw on) because this chapter is intented to inform people that are unfamiliar with the history of Modern Greece and provide them with the background information that will help them understand the more analytical chapters later. We therefore provide a summary of the political events and the major economic and business trends that went along with them. It is a top-down picture that brings to the surface certain themes that will be referred to in later chapters. These themes derive from the intertwining of political, economic and social factors which results in a complex mix of choices and events.

At the time of writing, Greek economic difficulties are in the news. The recent global recession hit the national economy hard, the consequences making international news. European powers have been pondering 'solutions' while there has been a spate of criticism of domestic economic and public affairs which even go as far as to brand the whole country with certain characteristics. The impact of politics on business practices and the economy is now a poisoned chalice for Greek politicians, who are aware of the internal structural problems and that they are (considered to be) part of the problem (Beesley, 2010).

There are a number of themes arising from this chapter that are fundamental to understanding the other chapters. The first theme is that throughout Modern Greek history (1830 to present) outside forces have actively interfered and even intervened in political and social affairs very much in a colonial way. Greece geographically is on the south-east periphery of Europe, right at the crossroads between Western Europe, the Balkans (recently under the influence of the former Soviet Union), the Middle East (under the influence of Islamic cultures) and North-east Africa. The constant contact with this eastern Mediterranean cocktail of cultures and socioeconomic systems, which has been causing turbulent global historical events for centuries, exposes the country to levels of complexity and uncertainty verging on chaos, and the evolution of habits that it is difficult to understand without the help of anthropologists.

On a practical level, Greece's position on the southeast flank of Europe is hugely strategic, and for that reason the country is being pulled in different directions to compromise with various (and often conflicting) forces, which have often explicitly interfered, taking the role of the 'protector' or patron. In the last century alone, Greece has been affected by two World Wars, the Great Depression, a civil war, the Cold War, seven military coups, numerous 'local' wars (with the Balkans and with Turkey), the oil crisis and other economic pressures, the political and monetary integration with EEC (European Economic Community)/EU (European Union) and the latest global 'crunch'. During all these (often violent) events, the country was to be outnumbered and financially exhausted. Greek politicians have had to walk a thin line between accepting (mainly from western political sources) economic or military aid (during conflict and for recovery and reconstruction) and giving up some of their government's sovereignty by allowing interference in domestic affairs, leading to loss of internal control.

Apart from the importance of external politics in internal affairs, the second theme is how these geopolitical factors affect the type and size of the economy and business practices. For example, political events have affected the mobility, skill level and type of labour, which in turn affected the type of industrial sectors that emerged and grew and others which perished. The combination of the political instability with a large public bureaucracy has made it difficult to attract both foreign direct investment (FDI) and inwards investment. Frequent changes in regime and economic policies have led to a lack of consistent national strategy and the lack of a developed institutional base to provide guarantees for industrial investors. Firms found they needed to be small in order to be low-cost, low-investment and short-term oriented and to develop an agile, entrepreneurial attitude; this makes for a business landscape which is volatile and mercurial, with a high rate of self-employment and a micro-family structure (up to ten employees), with single ownership and management. The system as it is cannot sustain large manufacturing sectors. These elements create a uniquely unbalanced national system that is highly competitive and efficient in some sectors, especially services and smaller-scale agricultural production, and very weak in others such as manufacturing.

The development of this business system is explained in more detail in the rest of the chapter in three sections: (i) from the formation of the country until the end of the nineteenth century, (ii) the first half of the twentieth century, and (iii) the second half of the twentieth century.

Modern Greece from 1830 to 1900

The main historical events of this period were *the establishment of a government (monarchy), industry* and *successive liberation* of the country. The principal issues were: partisanship, the patronage of the Great Powers and the controversial function of the monarchy; the establishment of economic and political structures through choices such as land reforms and public bureaucracy; and social issues such as education, social disparity, the modernization of the language and ecclesiastical issues, along with the constant battle to liberate areas of Greek population that remained under occupation.

Modern political Greek history starts with the formation of a newly created state in 1830, after a war of independence from occupation by the Turkish Ottoman empire. The new country was but a fragment compared with the part that was still occupied, most of which was to be liberated in successive steps over the next 90 years. At that time, there were more Greeks living outside the new state's borders than within (Clogg, 2002). The issue of *irredenta* (national populations within other states) was, and still is, a major one in the region generally. Mazower writes, 'in the ethnic kaleidoscope of the Balkans, above all, the principle of nationality was a recipe for violence' (Mazower, 2000: 104). From the beginning there was foreign influence in Greek affairs. Lord Byron, as an envoy of the British, predicted that 'an "independent" Greece would be a colony of the sovereigns of Europe' and the British ambassador in Athens in 1841 said that 'Greece is either Russian or English and, since she must not be Russian, she must be English' (Sarafis, 1990: 124). From its very creation the country's fate was decided by the triad of 'great powers', as they were then called, Britain, France and Russia, which played an active political role even within the parliamentary processes and legislation by patronizing their own political parties. It was the Greeks themselves who had fought the war of independence but it was the Great Powers (Britain, France and Russia) that negotiated the boundaries of the country and even its sovereigns (Clogg, 2002: 39–46; Legg, 1969). The first monarch of independent Greece, who was chosen by the British, was Bavarian, and the first government was dominated by Germans (later replaced by a Danish dynasty on the throne). Greek politics were to remain dynastic up until 1974, with monarchs interfering in parliamentary politics, often using the army or the police to affirm their authority. This caused a deep division in the country (called 'the Schism') between royalists and liberals, which on many occasions led to violent confrontation resulting in several coups and causing radical shifts in economic and external relations policies, as well as two national catastrophes in 1922 and 1974.

Dynastic politics created economic and social fragmentation and conflict. The Turkish tyranny was replaced by a foreign bureaucracy, the 'Bavarocracy', which did not solve problems and had no appreciation of indigenous cultural, economic and social issues. The period following liberation was a missed opportunity to change that situation – the first government merely formalized the rule of patronage and bribery that had previously thrived under the Ottoman system. In short, the foundations of the infamous bureaucracy that still exists today were laid at that time, combining a western-oriented multi-layered centralized procedural system with the oriental system of decentralized political patronage and clientilism (the Bavarian bureaucracy did not make processes transparent). That system has changed little since then. In a sense, it is being artificially sustained because it acts as a safety net against the consequences of radical change: every time a catastrophe (economic or military) happened, the state had to pick up the pieces and essentially revive a damaged economy by creating jobs in the public sector. The system functioned through political favouritism and patronage. This inevitably led to a large public sector and some levels of corruption (Herzfeld, 1991: 289) a situation which is typical of Mediterranean countries (Zinovieff, 2004: 160–1; Legg, 1969). All political parties have relied on this system to gain and retain power (Clogg, 2002: 199–200).

This system created the cultural basis for the clientelist behaviour of politicians and civil servants, which had many consequences. First, it affects internal co-ordination: society is fragmented into small groups that can be adversarial. Second, the system functions mainly through informal channels and cliques. As a direct outcome of these, any kind of formal political structure that does not allow for this behaviour but, conversely, tries to subdue it, is simply ignored. It did not help that the first government was not sensitive to the burning social issues at the time, such as the language division and the political role of the church, which were important for progress and some sort of social cohesion (Legg, 1969). It did not help that the king ruled without a constitution and effectively delayed the establishment of civil codes of liberty and obligation, which would have rid the system of the remains of the Ottoman culture. The window of opportunity to escape the system of eastern authoritarian statism with paternalistic and particularlist allocative practices was missed (Taylor-Cobby, 2006). This situation continued after 1863 with the arrival of the new Danish king and his successors.

There were a number of consequences across the political–business axis. The economy lacked any kind of industrial infrastructure; education, law, public state, executive organs and industry had to be reconstructed from scratch. There was only a small wealthy mercantile class of Greeks living in different parts of the Mediterranean region which had inspired the independence movement and provided support (Clogg, 2002: 23–5). The population was illiterate, agrarian and untrained, ravaged by a prolonged period of occupation, siege and massacre. Greece had access to 36,000 km^2 of land expropriated during the War of Independence. Land reform was the first challenge for the new kingdom. The countryside was devastated, depopulated and hampered by primitive agriculture methods and marginal soils; poor communications prohibited wider foreign commerce until the late nineteenth century (Moffett, 1889). It took several decades of redistributive land reforms to create a class of free peasants among veterans of the War of Independence and the poor, and by 1870 most Greek peasant families owned about 20 acres. The Law for the Dotation of Greek Families of 1835 extended low-cost loans of 2,000 drachmas to every family to enable them buy a 12-acre farm at auction. These farms were too small, but signalled the social goal of equality for all Greeks. The Turkish *tsifliks* (very large estates cultivated by tenant farmers) were abolished and the class rivalry between land owners and peasants was reduced. This pattern of small ownership continues to the present, even with the huge shrinking of the agricultural industry in the last two decades.

The Modern Greek state spent the nineteenth century trying to establish itself, but remained in debt to the London financial institutions (including Rothschilds Bank), which had financed the independence war. The state taxed heavily to raise the repayments, but little remained to invest in developing an industrial infrastructure. The economy remained agrarian and poor; the peasant classes, which were the majority, unable to benefit from proper education, turned to emigration to the USA. Piperopoulos (2009) quotes Agriantonis (1991, 1986) on the characteristics of industrialization during this period: lack of specialization in production capabilities, industrial production was chosen at random and production processes were basic. With a lack of specialization in the supply chain activities and vertical integration, industrialization emerged more from the initiatives of a few entrepreneurs and remained so since there was no strategically planned policy taking advantage of industrial infrastructures and since the middle classes did not have influence or resources to invest. The majority of the labour force still depended on agriculture. Services, such as marine trade, and small-scale industries, such as weaving, became the main business activities (Liberakis, 1991; Agriandonis, 1986). Industry was therefore marginalized in the economy from the start. It did not complement the other types of production, and did not develop the critical mass needed to develop industrial clusters; their emergence was mainly opportunistic. For example, in 1850 problems with silk cultivation in France increased the demand for silk thread and the first Greek industry emerged (Demiris, 1991; Limberakis, 1991). However, successful growth was observed; the port of Piraeus expanded to become by 1879 the country's most important harbour, while an industrial landscape developed around it (Kabouroglou, 1985).

Non-industrialized sectors such as trade and commerce which produced a quicker, lower-risk profit dominated the economy at the expense of industrial production. This was another reason why the public sector grew disproportionally large, since it tried to absorb the surplus of unspecialized labour. But the war was still on, the fortunes of the new state were still uncertain and large amounts of funds were spent on military equipment for defence. However, productivity in the areas that did benefit from investment (commerce and agriculture) expanded rapidly, and the railway infrastructure rapidly developed, showing that the country had high capacity for growth, albeit insufficient to overcome deficit. Effectively the country was formally declared insolvent in the 1890s.

Modern Greece from 1900 to 1950

The main historical events of this period were, in order: *the Balkan Wars, World War I, the Great Depression, National Schism, the Asia Minor campaign and Greek genocide, a dictatorship and thirteen coups, World War II and the Civil War.* Among the principal issues during this period were the constant civil unrest of the Schism between the royalist and liberal factions and the resultant instability in policies; the military disaster with Turkey which resulted in the genocide of the Greek population in Smyrna; a huge wave of immigration creating a crushing economic burden; and several coups that severely affected business investment. Another is the triad of economically and socially devastating international events, the Great Depression, the World Wars and the Civil War, which left the country in urgent need of reconstruction, not only economically but, most importantly, socially, with frequent uprooting and resettling of populations leaving little margin for stability and growth.

Greece's strategic geographical location has meant little security for her borders. Between 1912 and 1922 Greece was involved in the Balkan Wars and later sided with the *Entente* Allies (Britain, France and Russia; later Italy, Portugal, Japan, Serbia, Romania and Belgium) against the Central Powers (the German, Austro-Hungarian and Ottoman empires and the kingdom of Bulgaria) in World War I. After the war Greece was encouraged by Allied promises of the Greek-populated land in Turkey, but was left on her own in the middle of a military campaign after France and Italy withdrew their support and the rest of the Allies declared their neutrality. Without backing in the middle of a military progression, it became a disaster culminating in what became known as 'the Catastrophe', when the Turkish nationalist offensive against the Greek army turned on the indigenous population. The Greek minority in Turkey was uprooted, slaughtered or deported (along with the Armenians and other Christian minorities). Under the terms of the Treaty of Lausanne (1923) Turkey renegotiated the Treaty of Sevres with the Allies, who decreed an exchange of the remaining populations (1,400,000 Christians on Turkish land for 500,000 Muslims on Greek soil). Almost 1.4 million refugees swelled the existing population of 5 million native Greeks (Pallis, 1929; Black, 1948). These population exchanges did make the populations of both countries more homogeneous (Mazower, 2000: 107), but they came at a tremendous human cost, and with huge economic implications for Greece which could not handle the country's population suddenly increasing by a quarter.

The period of recuperation after the Catastrophe was not smooth. After a decade of war and the resettlement of the refugees, Greece was unable to secure or to pay back any loans from abroad to finance the war with Turkey. The Finance Ministry declared the dichotomization of the drachma: the value of drachma was halved in 1922 (and again in 1926). Half of the drachma's value would be surrendered by the government in exchange for a twenty-year 6.5 per cent loan. This led to large revenues for the state, but deflation resulted, interest rates rose and investment decreased as people began to stop holding cash and began holding real goods (Freris, 1986). The economic devastation caused by World War II would ensure that these loans would not be repaid, but it is doubtful that the government would have been able to repay them anyway. On the other hand, industries such as textiles and ammunition grew to supply the military. Catastrophe refugees contributed significantly to the boost in business and banking, as many of them were well-educated and entrepreneurial (Lampsidis, 1989; Issawi, 1984), especially in urban areas where the majority settled (Hirschon, 1989). The population exchange also affected the agricultural sector since refugees settled on abandoned estates. The reshuffling among the other powers had some positive effects. After the disintegration of the Ottoman empire, Britain saw Greece as the ideal means of keeping the Dardanelles and the Suez Canal under its control (Goldstein, 1989) and provided capital and loans for the construction of a public and commercial transport system (Mouzelis, 1978).

The Great Depression hit Greece particularly harshly in 1932, as a poor country dependent on agricultural exports and with emigration to the USA, the escape route from rural poverty, closed off. The Bank of Greece adopted deflationary policies but these failed because the drachma was pegged to the dollar and the country had large war debts and a trade deficit. Remittances from abroad declined sharply, the value of the drachma plummeted and the foreign exchange reserves were almost wiped out. The economy went off the gold standard, and Prime Minister Venizelos was forced to default on Greece's national debt in 1932 and declare a moratorium on all interest payments. The protectionist policies which were adopted then, however, allowed domestic industry to expand, and by 1939 industrial output exceeded that of 1928 by 79 per cent. In spite of everything the growth rate was, on average, 3.5 per cent from 1932–39 (Freris, 1986), and the economy entered a capitalistic phase, with, selectively, high levels of investment in industry, tax allowances and protectionism, and the emergence of monopolies. To support inefficient business taxes were imposed on low and middle-class incomes. Even this, however, did not reduce the gap between the primary and tertiary sectors on one hand and the secondary on the other, or the gap between small- and medium-sized enterprises (SMEs), which were in the majority, and larger organizations (Piperopoulos, 2009; Tsouflidis, 2003; Kostis, 1999). The most significant problem, however, was that education restructuring was halted due to the lack of any strategic direction to support an industrial infrastructure. Any change in government or ministerial leadership resulted in changes to educational practices, leading to unstable labour markets detrimental to a developing society that wants to industrialize (Iakovidis, 1998).

Just before World War II, the regime had changed to a dictatorship which was backed up by the monarchy and the government tried to remain neutral in order to deal with internal dissatisfaction, but also to sustain the trend towards economic growth that was finally achieved after 1932. The country was dragged into war by Mussolini, who tried to invade but was defeated in 1940. Hitler invaded in 1941 in support of Mussolini; the country succumbed and was split into three occupied zones, Italian, German and Bulgarian. The strong resistance movement that followed led to savage German reprisals against civilians: 2,000 villages were burnt and 70,000 people were executed (Beevor, 1992). Privation in the guise of a full-scale famine was inflicted by the Germans, who appropriated most agricultural production and banned fishing; industry was halted for lack of raw materials and two-thirds of the Greek mercantile fleet was sunk (Carabott and Sfikas, 2004). As a result, Greek industries, such as tobacco, lost their foreign markets. Due to appropriations, and because the British blockaded foreign relief from the Red Cross to Greece, 300,000 people starved to death in 1941–42, and thousands were sent to camps along with the Jewish communities which resided mainly in the north. It is estimated that the Greek population was reduced by 7 per cent (Sedgwick, 1948). Forced loans imposed by the occupying Axis powers severely devalued the drachma and Greece experienced the third severest hyperinflation in recorded economic history, compared only to Germany's after World War I and Hungary's after World War II (Freris, 1986). In 1943, prices were 34,864 per cent higher than in 1940; in 1944, prices were 163,910,000,000 per cent higher than 1940 (Carabott and Sfikas, 2004; Clogg, 2002).

The Greek resistance, which had a number of successes against the occupation, was ideologically inclined towards communism, but supported the Allies' (and Churchill's) plans. After the war, however, Churchill and Stalin divided the Balkans into 'areas of influence' and Greece was to be in the British zone. The resistance came to be considered a threat by Britain and the new governments, including the king, whom she supported. Eventually the two sides came into conflict, resulting in a five-year Civil War (1944–49). When the British government was no longer able to maintain their support for the 'democratic' side in the Civil War (Marr, 2008), the mantle of safeguarding Greece was passed to the Americans (Weiner, 2007: 24-5), who were never overly concerned with the 'democratic credentials of their 'client states' during the Cold War, as long as they were anti-communist. The Civil War ended with the military defeat of the left in 1949. The Communist Party of Greece (KKE) was outlawed. The Civil War resulted in 100,000 deaths and caused catastrophic economic disruption. In addition, at least 25,000 Greeks and an unspecified number of Slavs living in the Greek region of Macedonia were either voluntarily or forcibly evacuated to Eastern block countries; many of them emigrated. To make matters worse, there were now 700,000 displaced persons in the country (Clogg, 2002; Collard, 1990). Apart from the human cost and the disruption to supply and demand in the economy, the Civil War extended the tradition of the Schism: the division between royalists and liberals-centralists was now added to that between capitalists and communists, creating a literal cultural schism, socially and politically.

During this 50-year period, national sovereignty was either obsolete or under constant threat. Economic disruption came either from conflicts within or from external shocks, and made the country unable to sustain any consistent economic and business growth, as the basic layers of its institutional fabric had to be reconstructed several times. Nevertheless business seemed resilient and periodically achieved high levels of growth (Polizos and Panagiotopoulos, 1998). and to further this, governments chose either to accept debt or to follow protectionist or devaluation policies. However, no matter how much they borrowed, it is naive to assume that a system which is so fragmented, its structures conflicting with each other, would be magically restored to a functional whole just by the injection of cash. The economy during these fragmented periods resembled that of underdeveloped capitalism, with low agricultural production; bureaucratic public administration; control of most deposit accounts; direct or indirect management of the insurance sector and SMEs (through the National Bank of Greece and the Commercial Bank of Greece); ever growing services; and an industrial sector unable to invest and grow (Piperopoulos, 2009; Choumanidis, 1990). Inward and direct investment was mainly state- derived and the frequent resettlement of populations meant an unstable labour supply which discouraged investment even further. In an unstable environment business depended more and more on entrepreneurship and small business. For these reasons industrialization was slow and the vast majority of business consisted of family SMEs competing without the advantages of larger firms to invest in modernization. This situation was pervasive in all sectors, primary, secondary and tertiary. Due to the inability of Greek SMEs to collaborate in co-operatives or clusters, as in Denmark and Italy, the gap between them and the small proportion of politically connected and oligopolistic larger firms remained and grew (Piperopoulos, 2009). Education remained a low political priority (especially technical education), and thus a lack of specialized labour was added to the lack of investment in industrialization.

Modern Greece between 1950 and 2010 and the roots of the debt crisis

The main historical events of this period in were, in order: *recovery from the period of conflict through joining international alliances such as NATO, the Marshall plan, the Cold War and the continuation of the socio-political divisions culminating in the military dictatorship, the restoration of parliamentary democracy and the end of monarchy, the turn towards redestributionary politics to mend social divisions, joining the EC and the EU monetary union, and the upturns in the economy that led to the current crisis.*

In 1947, the USA formulated the Truman Doctrine and began to actively support a series of authoritarian governments in Greece, Turkey and Iran, in order to ensure that these states did not fall under Soviet influence (Miller, 2009, 1998). Through the Marshall plan, the North Atlantic Treaty Organization (NATO), the General Agreement on Tariffs and Trade (GATT), the World Bank and the International Monetary Fund (IMF) the USA began to foster economic, military and political integration, The Central Intelligence Agency (CIA) (Weiner, 2007; Pelt, 2006) began to work closely with the Greek military, the newly-founded and US-backed Hellenic National Intelligence Service (KYP) and the LOK Special Forces (Mountain Raider Companies). This collaboration was especially strengthened after Greece joined NATO in 1952 since she is a vital link in the NATO defence arc (Pelt, 2006; Ganser, 2005). The controversial and unstable relationships mainly with the then communist Balkans (Hatzivassiliou, 1995) and with Turkey, which has always been a source of friction (Koliopoulos and Veremis, 2007), combined with the need for reconstruction of industry and infrastructure after World War II and the Civil War, were the major incentives to be part of this partnership. This partnership was characterized by high levels of interference in government ministries and domestic policies, much as the Great Powers did in the previous century (Legg, 1969).

After the end of the Civil War the economy was in an extremely poor state. According to Maddison (1995), Greek purchasing power compared to French fell from 62 per cent in 1938 to about 40 per cent in 1949. However, an impressive rate of economic development was achieved from the early 1950s to the mid-1970s due to a combination of factors such as the Marshall Plan, a drastic devaluation of the drachma, price and import controls, reduced interest rates, developments in the chemical industry, tourism and the services sectors and massive publicly-funded infrastructure reconstruction (particularly the road network). The Fordist model of industrial production was partially implemented in Greece, principally geared towards export production and achieving a modest peripheral form and level of integration within the international economy (Vasiliadis, 2008). The average rate of economic growth was 7 per cent, second only to Japan's during the same period. Growth rates were highest during the 1950s, and exceeding 10 per cent for several years, mostly in the 1960s. This resulted in an 'urban renewal' that encouraged migration from the rural areas to the urban centres, and especially Athens. Despite improvement in the economy though, the basic conditions of the 1940s (widespread poverty, illiteracy, shortage of foreign exchange, repressive and ineffective government) remained within the 1960s, leading to a series of constitutional crises and to a particularly brutal and backward military dictatorship. The Marshall plan was not implemented well, in the sense that there was no balanced development of infrastructure throughout the country because the government used the resources mainly in the urban centres, causing massive migration and urbanization (which led to a temporary growth of certain sectors like construction) and creating a business sector dependent on state funds, without establishing institutions for supporting entrepreneurship and technological progress. Industrial production and agriculture were marginalized and services (mainly shipping, trade and tourism) started to dominate the business sector.

However, the theme of political and social division that was initiated by the Schism mutated after the Civil War into a division between conservatives and leftists, with the military-king-conservatives and central-liberal political trends fighting for power (Jesse, 2007). After the Catastrophe, the military had gained political significance that lasted from 1922 until the end of the 'Colonels' dictatorship' in 1974, and was involved many times in coups, always using the 'communist threat' to intimidate the population. However, it was the last king of Greece, Constantine II, who triggered a course of events that led to a dictatorship that ruled the country from 1967 to 1974.

The young king wanted to play an active role and exercise power like his predecessors, so he dismissed the centralist Prime Minister Papandreou in 1965, creating a constitutional crisis that finally led in April 1967 to a dictatorship beyond his control. In December 1967 he went into exile after his unsuccessful counter-coup.

The Colonels' dictatorship caused Greece to become an international pariah and interrupted her process of integration into the EU at an incalculable cost of lost opportunity (Coufoudakis, 2002; Stern, 1975). The worst thing, however, was that when internal divisions occurred among the heads of the regime (the Colonels) a counter-coup (organized in December 1973) by one of them tried to legitimize itself by intervening in Cyprus, thus providing Turkey with the opportunity for invasion and occupation of northern Cyprus, a tragedy that continues until today. The historical repercussions of the dictatorship were profound and are still felt to this day.

Although it is common knowledge that the US government actively supported the coup d'état of 1967, there is no direct evidence to support such claims (Kassimeris, 2006; Moseley, 1999). It is, however, likely that the US military was informed of the coup by Greek liaison officers (Miller, 1998) and it is a fact that the junta gave financial support to the White House (Weiner, 2007: 282–7) which officially remained 'neutral'. In 1999, however, US President Bill Clinton apologized on behalf of the US government for supporting the military junta in the name of Cold War tactics, as did Ambassador Nicholas Burns in 1998 (Hunt, 1999). This situation led to the rise of anti-American feeling in the population, which treated any subsequent attempts to interfere with suspicion.

In contrast to the political aspect, the regime managed to sustain high rates of economic growth, low inflation and low unemployment during 1967–73, mainly by encouraging FDI. GDP continued to grow from the 1950s on, driven by investment in the tourism industry, public spending in significant infrastructure development, and pro-business incentives that fostered both domestic and foreign capital spending and investment by international companies. Although capital flowed from private US companies such as Esso, Reynolds Metal, Dow Chemical, Coca Cola and Chrysler, large sections of the economy were effectively controlled by US capital and the financial health of the country remained precarious. Economic growth started to decline by 1972, when public dissidence and internal infighting in the regime made the country unattractive investment-wise, and when the Bretton Woods system collapsed. The collapse of the dictatorship in 1974 was followed by a major annual contraction in GDP (about 5 per cent), the worst recorded in Greece's post-war history (OECD, 2009). Marginal GDP contractions were also recorded in the 1980s. In total, the Greek GDP grew for 54 out of the 60 years following World War II and the Civil War (Bairoch, 1976).

However, after the fiasco in Cyprus, senior military officers withdrew their support from the junta, which collapsed. The ex-prime minister,

Kostas Karamanlis, who fled into exile in Paris before the coup, returned to establish a government of national unity until the elections which he won in November 1974 with his newly organized conservative party, New Democracy.

With the Third Hellenic Republic, a period of unobstructed parliamentary democracy began for the first time, after the monarchy was abolished with a referendum in 1974, essentially putting an official end to the bitter division and conflict that had plagued the country. Societal transformation started to take place on a large scale: the peasantry disappeared, Greece began to receive immigrants and participatory democracy became embedded in the political culture. Karamanlis worked to defuse war with Turkey and also legalized the Communist Party, offering reconciliation between different political factions and a new constitution (Clogg, 2002). On 1 January 1981, Greece became the tenth member of the EU. Membership of the EU has been desirable, not just for economic, but also for strategic reasons. The risk of military conflict remains; Greece was almost embroiled in the Balkans conflict of the 1990s and in 1996 nearly went to war with Turkey over the Imia islands. Military fiscal commitment remains high, largely as a result of tensions with Turkey (Beesley, 2010) with severe effects on the economy since expenditure on defence were proportionally the highest among NATO countries during the 1990s (Clogg, 2002: 224). Clogg (2002) writes that one of the reasons that Karamanlis had been so determined to gain entry for Greece into the EEC was to prevent future military takeovers.

In 1981 the first socialist government was elected when the Pan-Hellenic Socialist Movement (PASOK) won, led by Andreas Papandreou. The next three decades were characterized by successive governments between the conservative party (New Democracy) and socialists (PASOK). After two rounds of parliamentary elections in 1989 and weak coalition governments, New Democracy won in 1990, to be succeeded by PASOK again three years later. In 2004, New Democracy won, remaining in power until 2009 when PASOK took over again. The coming to power of centralists-socialists had both positive and negative implications politically. The PASOK governance of the 1980s entailed a wholesale renovation of the nation's power structure, with vital consequences. The part of the right-wing establishment created during World War II and the military junta that determined the allocation of resources and public sector jobs was overthrown. Essentially, the gap between the poor masses and the rich right-wing establishment was reduced massively and a large middle class emerged, where conflicts (at least of the violent type) were infrequent. But this came at a price.

The price was the slowing down of the high levels of economic growth which was achieved since the 1950s due to the redistribution policies, which were contrary to good economic practices, and which were used extensively by the socialist governments to achieve a less fragmented society. This was to be the Achilles' heel for the economy. It initiated a series of shocks in the 90s that led to the current crisis.

The story goes like this: These policy shocks, according to Alogoskoufis (1995), resulted from the political change in the early 1970s from a controlling authoritarian regime to a series of both conservative and socialist governments. Before 1974, the political regimes were (sometimes extremely) autocratic with negative social effects. However, their fiscal and monetary policies were tightly controlled (fulfilling the requirements of Bretton Woods), and had established a steady and quite high growth in the economy and trust from external funders. Greece was considered a high-performing newly industrialized economy amongst the OECD countries before the 1970s (rapid growth, high investment and low inflation). This economic regime, however, broke down after 1974. Subsequent governments failed to sustain the commitment and co-ordination mechanisms that guaranteed high returns to capital. The post-1974 governments created market distortions (radical socialist policies that led to a steep increase in labour costs; semi-regulated financial system; public monopolies; nationalizations and subsidies; enlargement of public administration; and a supply-driven system based on investment grants and EC transfers). These market distortions not only discouraged private investment, but also caused a reduction in the return on the investment undertaken. The reason was the social unrest about redistribution, one of the principal objectives of government policies. Successive governments had relatively short lives and did not develop continuity of strategic direction either in industrial policy or in governance structures. And even if they did, the implementing institutions function through the bureaucratic system, rendering attempts to establish transparent accountability systems and unity of action (or even intention) very difficult.

Another cause of economic deterioration is the lack of the institutions to absorb the tremors of these economic and social 'shocks' (Alogoskoufis, 1995). Vasiliadis (1998) attributes this to the lack of institutions supporting relations between the government, the labour system and credit. The struggle for redistribution between various socio-economic groups after 1970 left governments in the middle trying to satisfy the conflicting objectives of re-election, growth, redistribution and social harmony. Eventually, the state ended up being a negotiator between rival groups in society without having the power to enforce real change in the structure of their relationships. Governments have tried to introduce formal procedures for social dialogue, but the 'social partners' perpetuated the culture of partisanship, corporatism and polarization, and failed to agree on policy reform (Petmezidou, 2000), making industrial relations highly costly and leading to political inertia (Venieris, 2003). The resulting disequilibrium was unsatisfactory, but resolution through political means was displaced by using the EU transfers that temporarily provided relief from its consequences. The problem both then and now for politicians who attempt to tackle these issues is the cost in votes and the reaction from the electorate who perceive these reforms as another wave of autocratic policies. For example, after 1985 PASOK initiated a series of reforms designed to tackle these economic problems. The party discouraged imports, cut public expenditure and attempted to increase government revenues. The result was limited success, a wave of strikes and a swing to the opposition in municipal elections (Clogg, 2002). For similar reasons, all subsequent attempts to modernize industrial policies have not been extremely successful. Nonetheless, by 1999 a dramatic improvement was achieved in inflation, budget deficit (below 3 per cent) and growth rate (an average of nearly 4 per cent), meeting the criteria for Greece's entry into the Eurozone (Oltheten *et al.*, 2003), mainly due to the 'hard drachma policy' employed since 1995, under which the exchange rate was used as a nominal anchor. Despite these reforms and measures, however, the structural problems remained (Pirounakis, 1997).

The economic growth continued albeit slower and discontinuous, with some stagnation during the 1980s, however the annual growth consistently outperformed most European nations. This high performance made Greece an advanced economy, with an income per capita close to that of France or Germany (IMF and World Bank, 2008). However, three key landmarks can be identified in the evolving politico-economic landscape: the slowdown of economic growth after 1974; the deterioration in the balance of payments; and the failure to control inflation in the 1980s when inflation fell sharply elsewhere in the OECD (Organisation for Economic Co-operation and Development) countries (Alogoskoufis, 1995). There are several reasons for these. Expansionary fiscal policies tripled the debt-to-GDP ratio from 34.5 per cent in 1981 to triple figures in the 1990s, and by 1991 interest payments on public debt reached 12 per cent of GDP. The budget deficit peaked at 9 per cent in 1985 and the 'black economy' emerged during that time. Inflation rose as a result of populist policies, so politicians pursued stabilization programmes to cut inflation from 25 per cent in 1985 to 16 per cent in 1987.

The Greek public sector became one of the largest among OECD countries. Within the Greek economy there was, and still is, a large 'black economy', which produces corruption, which in turn raises the need for a highly regressive taxation system much encouraged by the public sector, and high public sector deficits. Therefore, low performance cannot be correlated with low productivity. Greece has the highest percentage of employers and self-employed people in the EU, while worker productivity has been rising significantly (Timmer *et al.*, 2007). However, labour costs increased rapidly during the 1980s and industry could not invest to modernize due to a lack of finance (Oltheten *et al.*, 2003). Performance is more linked to the hydrocephalic structure of the business sector (huge service sector, low agricultural and weak industrial sector) which defines the demand for certain types of labour (Piperopoulos, 2009), combined with the loss of protectionist and monetary policies after the adoption of the Euro, which in turn raised costs and reduced investment. The major challenge, therefore, was to decrease the large debt, while increasing economic growth. In November 2009 the new PASOK government admitted that the debt and deficit were too high and revealed an estimated deficit of 12.7 per cent of GDP for 2009, which was far greater than initial estimates. It was alleged that this was due to the fact that the previous government had hired Goldman Sachs to hide the debt (Schwartz and Dash, 2010). The new budget proposed by the government was projecting total debt to raise from 113.4 per cent of GDP in 2009 to 121 per cent in 2010, while the Stability and Growth Programme was aiming to cut deficit from 12.7 per cent in 2009 to 2.8 per cent in 2012. European leaders resolved to protect the Euro through approving a US$ 100 billion bailout plan (Frayer, 2010), backed Greece's Stability and Growth Programme and urged public sector restructuring to cut the wage bill. The programme aimed at implementing a combination of public sector wage cuts and tax increases which would generate €4.8 billion in savings. However, the government warned that the borrowing costs were too high to make this programme a success. Despite this, by April, the government announced that the deficit was reduced by 39.2 per cent for the first quarter (Vima, 6 April 2010). The news were ignored by the main financial media and therefore markets were not informed of this development. In May, the government announced the fourth round of austerity measures to meet the terms of the EU agreement and also announced that the deficit had been reduced by 41.5 per cent for the first quarter of the year, but the news was again ignored by the main financial media.

It seemed that being a member of the Eurozone had limited the policy options available to Greece to resolve this crisis. In the 1950s and up until the 1980s, the economy could be stimulated with monetary policies, but now the government's sole option was to cut costs. Before joining the Eurozone, Greece could print new money and inject it into the system by purchasing outstanding debt, but this is no longer an option. It is for this reason that economists consider the possibility of Greece exiting the Eurozone to be a good solution (Hankel *et al.*, 2010).

The austerity measures led to protests, clashes with police on the streets of Athens and general strikes (*The Guardian*, 24 April 2010). There is a spirit of popular resistance among the Greeks (Boyes, 2010) because citizens perceive the new policies as driven by outside interests-which is not far from the truth. The crisis is seen as a justification for imposing fiscal austerity on the population in exchange for European funding. Democratic accountability in public sector structures is in dispute, but not only in Greece, since the truth is that the western world was and still is unprepared for the level of corrupt dealings that brought a world recession in the name of liberal capitalism (a term which can be interpreted in many ways). Stiglitz (2010) criticized the EU for being too slow and insufficiently supportive of the government, too deferential to bond rating agencies and lacking the willpower to establish 'a solidarity and stabilization framework' like Bretton Woods (Alogoskoufis *et al.*, 1996). The fact that the actions of many financial actors is beyond the control of the law is obvious from the reactions of heads of state. Spanish and Greek Prime Ministers and the German Chancellor accused speculators and hedge funds of worsening the crisis (O'Grady, 2010; Stevenson, 2010). Chancellor Merkel stated that 'institutions bailed out with public funds are exploiting the budget crisis in Greece and elsewhere' (Donahue, 2010), implicating Goldman Sachs in the Greek bond yield increases (Connor, 2010; Schwartz and Dash, 2010).

These politico-economic and social phenomena have significant effects on the economic situation, because they affect the form and implementation of policies and the institutions which are their basis. Alogoskoufis (1995) argues that policy regimes and their institutional underpinning are crucial to the investigation of the causes of the current politico-economic situation. The phenomenon is reproducing itself in a cycle. If this infrastructure was actually established, eventually social practices would be acculturated into a new mode of operating business (Clogg, 2002). It is this before/after comparison that shows how political practices and institutions have formed business and how they can help achieve growth at the levels that were once.

Summary

This chapter summarized key political and economic events from 1830 until the present day. The scope of the timeline was wide but the presentation allowed us to identify the patterns of behaviour and their causes. To sum up, three recurring themes throughout this politico-economic history affect the business system: division, structure and policy.

The most common theme historically is that of, as Jesse (2007) eloquently puts it, a pattern of socio-political division that repeatedly strikes throughout the country's political history, leading to partisanship: divisions over foreign patronage (e.g. the Great Powers), divisions between royalists and liberals since the Schism, communists and fascists/-centralists, conservatives and socialists, supporters of foreign allies (the USA, the EU etc.) and opposition, and so on. It seems that in every conflict, especially where foreign interference was involved, divisions formed which collided, creating a highly volatile environment. The phenomenon is not unlike that observed in other countries: continuous infighting for power that leads to the search for effective structures based on social negotiation and compromise. This is a social phenomenon in all societies; it is only that in the case of Greece, because of the higher occurrence of dynamic events than in other parts of the western world, this fight is more intense and frequent, and the effects and people's reactions more dramatic.

This pattern of division is mirrored in the public sector which has been used as a tool for more politics rather than for the implementation of policies. This again is not a unique phenomenon, but it is observed at a high level, because of two phenomena: first, the public sector plays several socioeconomic roles: a token for votes; a safety net for business and employment during economic shocks; and an anchor to impose some kind of order in a highly volatile environment where social groups lack an institutionalized 'negotiating space'. Second, because the boundaries of the public sector are very strong since they were made for controlling political opposition based on the control and the distribution of state resources in the economy; public administration is not designed to provide infrastructures for business and industry or to (formally) collaborate with private economic actors. As a result, institutions to regulate the actors in the business system (government, credit, labour) or the innovation system (government, academia, business at firm level), and the infrastructure to support the function of such a business system are only partially in place or not well developed.

A third pattern is the political choices and their implementation through those absent or patchy institutional and infrastructural frameworks.

Geopolitics has created a political 'culture of dependency', upon mainly westernised organizational and political structures and economic systems which however contradict local practices. In this way, interference leads to internal divisions and loss of internal control as has been manifested so often. Symptoms of this attitude are military conflicts, civil unrest and the expensive weapons race (the other source of public debt). Therefore, the imitation and importation of policies from other systems has not been a successful recipe for the growth of the business system.

The business system is also affected by divisions and the policy structure. The constant change and conflict created discontinuity in policy, a loss of strategic direction and this weakened implementation. For example, the successive social divisions wounded society so much that governments after the 1970s were forced to use unsuitable redistributionary policies in ineffective attempts to reduce social and economic inequalities, damaging business development and inflating public debt. The policies are mostly imitations of foreign models. However, these do not fit the Greek business system, so they were not implemented correctly. In addition, the legacy of electional politics has forced contemporary governments, which genuinely try to modernize, to make tough choices through a public machine whose structure is archaic.

Where does the business world stand in the midst of all of this? Most firms are micro firms, family-type concerns which are trying to stand on their own feet, not having much institutional support or access to resources like investment, finance, markets or technology, trying to respond flexibly to changes in the market and very much controlled by the state machine. There is a strong entrepreneurial spirit, which is responsive, flexible and opportunistic. It is very much an organic form of organization with all the advantages and disadvantages this entails. Actually this seems to have worked well as it kept the business sector alive even in tough circumstances, but it really needs to be supported if the economy as a whole is to grow sufficiently to raise productivity and tackle the current and future crises.

References

Agriantonis, C. (1986) *The start of industrialization in Greece in the nineteenth century*. Athens: Historical files of the Commercial Bank of Greece.

Agriantonis, C. (1991) 'Hellenic industry in the 19th century, prospects and problems of integration', in Dertilis G. and Kostis, K., (eds), *Modern Greek History Themes (18–19th Centuries)*. Athens: Tipothito.

Alogoskoufis, G., 1995. The Two Faces of Janus: Institutions, Policy Regimes and Macroeconomic Performance in Greece. *Economic Policy*. 10(20): 149.

Bairoch, P. (1976) 'Europe's GNP 1800–1975', *The Journal of European Economic History*, 5(2): 273–340.

Barker, E. (1987) 'Yugoslav policy towards Greece, 1947-1949', in Bærentzen, L., Iatrides, O., Langwitz, O. Smith J. (eds), *Studies in the History of the Greek Civil War, 1945–1949*. Copenhagen University: Museum Tusculanum, p. 263.

Beevor, Antony (1992) *Crete: The Battle and the Resistance*. London: Penguin Books.

Black, E. C. (1948) 'The Greek Crisis', *The Review of Politics:* 10(1): 84–89.

Carabott, P. and Sfikas, T. D. (2004) *The Greek Civil War: essays on a conflict of exceptionalism and silences*. Aldershot: Ashgate Publishing.

Choumanidis, L., (1990) *Economic History of Greece:* Volumes I and II. Athens: Papazisis.

Clogg, Richard (2002) *A Concise History of Greece* (2nd ed.) Cambridge: Cambridge University Press.

Collard, Anna (1990) 'The Experience of Civil War in the Mountain Villages of Central Greece', in M. Sarafis and M. Eve (eds), *Background to Contemporary Greece*: Volume 2, pp. 223–55.

Connor, K. (2010) 'Goldman's Role in Greek Crisis Is Proving Too Ugly to Ignore', 27 February, *Huffington Post*. http://www.huffingtonpost.com/kevin-connor/goldmans-role-in-greek-cr_b_479511.html.

Coufoudakis, V. (2002). 'Recent Perspectives on Cyprus', *Journal of Modern Greek Studies*, 20(1): 143–146.

Demiris, K. (1991) *The Greek weaving industry: historical and typogical exploration*. Athens: Cultural and Technological Foundation ETBA.

Donahue, P. (2010)' 'Merkel Slams Euro Speculation, Warns of "Resentment", *BusinessWeek*, 23 February. http://www.businessweek.com/news/2010-02-23/merkel-slams-euro-speculation-warns-of-resentment-update1-.html.

Frayer, L. (2010) 'Europe Tries to Calm Fears Over Greek Debt Crisis', *AOL News*, 8 May. Retrieved 9 May 2010 from. http://www.aolnews.com/2010/05/08/europe-tries-to-calm-fears-over-greek-debt-crisis/.

Freris, A. F. (1986). *The Greek Economy in the Twentieth Century*. New York: St. Martin's Press.

Frierson, B., Hay A., (2010) 'Reuters – Fed's Balance Sheet Liability Hits Record' 14 January. http://www.reuters.com/article/idUSTRE60D5WK20100114.

Ganser, D., (2005) *NATO's secret armies: Operation Gladio and Terrorism in Western Europe*. Routledge, p. 216.

Goldstein, E. (1989) 'Great Britain and Greater Greece', *The Historical Journal*, 32: 339–56.

Hankel, W., Nölling, W., Schachtschneider, K. A. and Starbatty, J. (2010) 'A euro exit is the only way out for Greece', *Financial Times*, 25 March. *Referencing:* http://www.ft.com/cms/s/0/6a618b7a-3847-11df-8420-00144feabdc0.html. (Accessed 2 May 2010).

Hatzivassiliou, E. (1995) 'Security and the European Union: Greek Foreign Policy 1952–62', *Journal of Contemporary History*, 30(1): 187–202.

Herzfeld, M. (1991) *A Place in History: Social and Monumental Time in a Cretan Town*. New Jersey: Princeton University Press.

Hirschon, R. (2003) *Crossing the Aegean: an appraisal of the 1923 compulsory population exchange between Greece and Turkey*. Oxford, UK: Berghahn Books.

Hunt, T. (2008) 'Clinton concedes regret for US support of Greek junta'. *Topeka Capital-Journal*, 18 August.

Iakovidis, G.I. (1998) *Technical and Professional Education in Greece, A Comparative Approach between the Greek and German System.* Athens: Gutenberg.
IMF and World Bank 2008 April data *Referencing*: http://www.imf.org/external/datamapper/index.php.
Issawi, C. (1984) *The Economic History of the Middle East and North Africa* Columbia University Press.
Jesse, N. (2007) 'Greece (1944–1949)', in DeRouen, K. and Heo, U., (eds), *Civil Wars of the World, major conflicts since WWII.* ABC-Clio.
Kabouroglou, P. (1985) *The history of Piraeus from 1833–1882: general situation, trade, shipping and industry.* Athens: Karavias. Kassimeris, Christos (2006) 'Causes of the 1967 Greek Coup', *Democracy and Security,* 2(1), 61–72.
Koliopoulos, J.S. and Veremis, TM. (2007) *Greece: The Modern Sequel: From 1821 to the present* (2nd ed.) London: Hurst & Company.
Kostis, K. (ed.) (1999) *Modern Banking in the Balkans and West – European Capital in the Nineteenth and Twentieth Centuries.* Aldershot: Ashgate.
Lampsidis, G. (1989) *The refugees of 1922: their contribution to the development of the country.* Thessaloniki: Kiriakidis bros. Legg, K.R. (1969) *Politics in Modern Greece.* USA: Stanford University Press.
Liberakis, A. (1991) *Flexible specialization: crisis and reconstruction in the small industry.* Athens: Gutengerg. Maddison A. (1995) *Monitoring the World Economy 1820–1992.* OECD.
Marr, A. (2008) *A History of Modern Britain.* London: Pan MacMillan.
Mazower, M. (2000) *The Balkans.* London: Weidenfeld & Nicolson.
Miller, J.E. (2009) *The United States and the Making of Modern Greece.* Chapel Hill: University of North Carolina Press.
Moffett, W.H. (1889). *Garden and Forest* 2(95): Garden and Forest Publishing Co., Tribune Building, New York.
Moseley, R. (1999) 'Thousands decry US in streets of Athens', *The Chicago Tribune* 17 November.
Mouzelis, N.P. (1978) *Modern Greece: Facets of Underdevelopment.* London: Macmillan.
OECD (2009) StatExtracts. *Country statistical profiles 2009: Greece.* Retrieved from: http://stats.oecd.org/viewhtml.aspx?queryname=18154&querytype=view&lang=en.
O'Grady, S. (2010) 'Soros hedge fund bets on demise of the euro'. *The Independent,* 2 March. http://www.independent.co.uk/news/business/news/soros-hedge-fund-bets-on-demise-of-the-euro-1914356.html (Accessed 11 May 2010).
Oltheten E., Pinteras G. and Sougiannis T. (2003) 'Greece in the European Union: policy lessons from two decades of membership', *The Quarterly Review of Economics and Finance,* Winter.
Pallis, A. (1929) 'The Greek Census', *The Geographical Journal,* 73(6): 543–8.
Pelt, M, 2006. Tying Greece to the West: US-West German-Greek relations 1949–1974. Museum Tusculanum Press.
Petmesidou, M. (2000) 'Social protection in Greece in the nineties: reforming the "weak" welfare state', in Mitsos. A. and Mossialos, E., *Contemporary Greece and Europe.* Aldershot: Ashgate, pp. 330–80.
Piperopoulos, P. (2009) 'Economics, business and society in Greece: towards a national innovation system', *International Journal of Economics and Business Research.* 1(3): 277–90.

Pirounakis, N.G. (1997) *The Greek Economy*, London: Macmillan.
Polizos, G., Panagiotopoulos, B. (1998) *Historical industrial equipment in Greece.* Athens: Odysseas. Sarafis, M. (1990) 'Contemporary Greek History for English Readers: An Attempt at a Critical Analysis', in M. Sarafis and M. Eve, (eds), *Background to Contemporary Greece: Volume 1*, pp. 123–52.
Sarafis, M. and Martin, E., (eds) (1990) *Background to Contemporary Greece: Volumes 1 and 2*, London: Merlin Books.
Schwartz, N.D. and Dash, E. (2010) 'Banks Bet Greece Defaults on Debt They Helped Hide', *The New York Times*, 24 February. http://www.nytimes.com/2010/02/25/business/global/25swaps.html?_r=1&dbk.
Sedgwick A. C. (1948) 'The Plot against Greece', *Foreign Affairs*, 26 (3): 486–96.
Stern L. (1975) 'Bitter Lessons: How We Failed in Cyprus', *Foreign Policy*, 19: 34–78.
Stiglitz, J. (2010) 'A principled Europe would not leave Greece to bleed' *The Guardian*, 25 January. http://www.guardian.co.uk/commentisfree/2010/jan/25/principled-europe-not-let-greece-bleed (Accessed 25 January 2010).
Taylor-Gooby, P. (2006) 'The Greek Welfare Reform in the European Context', in Petmesidou, M. and Mossialos, E. *Social Policy developments in Greece.* USA: Ashgate Publishing Company.
Timmer M.P., O'Mahony, M. and van Ark, B. (2007) *EU KLEMS Growth and Productivity Accounts: Overview November 2007 Release*, Groningen Growth and Development Centre, University of Groningen, University of Birmingham.
Tsouflidis, L. (2003) *Economic History of Greece.* Thessaloniki: Macedonia University Press.
Vasiliadis, L. (2008) 'How Greece and Ireland Have Been Positioned in the World Developments Since 1945: A French Regulation Approach', *Journal of Social Sciences*, 4 (1): 42–55.
Venieris, D. (2003) 'Social Policy in Greece: rhetoric versus reform', *Social Policy and Administration*, 37(2): 133–47.
Vimaonline, (2010) 'To Vima: Greek deficit reduction for Q1'. http://www.tovima.gr/default.asp?pid=2&artid=324738&ct=3&dt=09/04/2010 (Accessed 9 April 2010).
Weiner, T. (2007) *Legacy of Ashes: The History of the CIA.* London: Penguin Books.
Zinovieff, S. (2004) *Eurydice Street: A Place in Athens.* London: Granta Books.

2
Economics
Productivity Performance, Determinants and Future Prospects

Ioannis Bournakis

Overview

In a period of economic recession, the primary focus of a government is to ensure that the economy will soon return to the long-term path of economic development. Most of the policies designed to achieve of this goal can be characterized as either stabilization or stimulus. Although some fiscal injections are needed as a matter of urgency, the fiscal stimulus itself is unable to generate sustainable growth effects in the long term.

Recently, the Greek economy has attracted an excess of attention due to the exceptional circumstances of its public sector finance. The inability of the Greek government to find the required funds to finance public debt makes for the likelihood of bankruptcy, casting further doubts over the stability of the whole eurozone. The newly elected government is beginning to implement a stabilization programme focusing on reducing spending and increasing revenue from taxation. The contractionary fiscal policy appears to be a single solution for the consolidation of public finances, but without public investment it is very likely to cause a deeper recession in the economy. For policy makers, the issue is to decide which activities public resources should be devoted to, and more importantly, how these activities benefit the economy. For example, if resources are directed only towards unemployment and similar benefits, then only consumption is triggered without any productive benefit to the economy. On the other hand, public investment in production capabilities and infrastructure might serve as an important engine of economic development in the long term.

The economic policies that impact on development prospects explicitly influence competitiveness and productivity. When a country experiences increased productivity, economic activity is stimulated again, so it becomes much easier to escape from recession. Under conditions of economic expansion, it is easier for the government to reduce debt, avoiding critical problems of social cohesion and welfare that can be caused by the use of extensive contractionary policies. Note that productivity improvement is not the solution for any short-term rigidity that has appeared in the economy – for the latter, fiscal policy intervention remains more effective. While a certain amount of time is required to improve productivity, this effort is always valuable as it ensures sustainable economic growth.

This chapter consists of three sections. The first section examines productivity in Greece in various sectors. The second section tests whether Greece has converged to the level of the European frontier. The third section identifies the determinants of productivity shifts.

A conceptual definition of productivity

Productivity is a measure that reflects different aspects of economic performance. At the macroeconomic level, productivity is directly associated with a country's economic welfare. Countries from the developed world experience high levels of GDP per capita, reflecting the high living standards of those countries. When each worker produces more for a given amount of effort, that worker is expected to have more real income to spend. At a firm and industry level, productivity captures competitiveness (Bournakis, 2009a). Higher productivity indicates optimal use of the existing resources, with a reduction in both cost and prices. From the consumer point of view, lower prices mean higher real income and thus higher welfare.

The role of productivity in the public agenda is not always very clear. In this section, the use of the term 'productivity' is clarified and some misconceptions addressed. One of the most common productivity drivers is research and development (R&D), a time-consuming activity involving some uncertainty before the final outcome. This suggests that if one considers productivity policies influence short-term variables such as inflation, then the final outcome of this activity is ambiguous. This confirms the standard Keynesian notion that monetary and fiscal tools are definitely more effective in controlling short-term economic fluctuations.

As Krugman (1993) emphasizes, the terms 'competitiveness' and 'productivity' are sometimes used incorrectly, particularly by those who do not realize that countries operate within income constraints with limited resources available to meet their needs. According to the fundamental principles of economics, nations cannot be productive in all activities, as this would lead to a mercantilist approach in which trade is viewed as a chance to exercise international dominance. Instead, idiosyncratic reasons and/ or country characteristics dictate the sectors in which countries can perform relatively better than others. Therefore, productivity cannot be viewed as an indicator of economic strength; instead it is a measure that exhibits the international specialization which promote international trade, making all the countries involved better off. There are certainly cases of countries which use appropriate policies to drive specialization towards new and more dynamic sectors. The execution of this decision is time-consuming, which also implies that specialization in new activities cancels comparative advantage in other traditional sectors of the economy.

Another misconception is the inverse relationship of productivity with unemployment. Historical data for advanced developed economies such as the USA, the UK and Germany (Baumol *et al.*, 1994) show that this negative effect has not occurred because when a country experiences high rates of productivity growth, equilibrium mechanism in the economy creates new jobs in other sectors to replace those lost from high productivity performance.

Although productivity impacts on a society's living standards, it also substantially affects the trade sector. In an integrated European economic environment without traditional trade barriers, trade activity is no longer influenced by tariffs and exchange rate fluctuations. Instead, relative productivity in various sectors determines how well countries perform in international markets. European countries do not only compete with their counterparts in the rest of the EU, but in some industries the important competitors are overseas countries such as India and China (where many manufacturing activities are outsourced due to cheap labour costs). The phenomenon of outsourcing explains to a great extent why many European countries are shifting their specialization away from less productive manufacturing to new dynamic services activities. Such a shift in the pattern of specialization has been observed in the UK economy following the implementation of the necessary structural reforms.

Turning to the Greek case, it is difficult to identify its position in the rapidly changing European environment for many different reasons. A traditional area of specialization for Greece was agriculture, which has been over-protected with the imposition of government tariffs and quotas. The establishment of the European single market has changed these conditions, creating a more competitive environment in agriculture. The role of the Common Agricultural Policy (CAP) was to help countries adapt to the new competitive environment by providing subsidies. This sort of policy only has a short-term effect, however, as in the long run farmers need to develop new crops with high demand in EU markets without relying on subsidies. In addition, Greece's public administration has various rigidities making the operation of the public sector inefficient. The absence of a competitive business environment in the public sector affects all economic activity, with the state remaining an important player in many different respects.

Competitiveness is crucial issue on the agenda of most political parties in Greece. Increased competitiveness is mainly achieved via improvements in productivity leading to intensive international trade activity. The productivity–trade nexus is a vital path for the Greek economy as it can contribute to the growth of domestic industries. The many benefits of international expansion include larger-scale production generating new jobs and reducing unemployment, and trade networks with other countries bringing Greek producers into contact with international best practices, diffusing knowledge spillovers.

The Greek economy 1995–2005

This section outlines the areas of specialization in the Greek economy. Table 2.1 shows sectoral shares of GDP and total employment in 1970 and 2005. Manufacturing output accounted for almost one-third of overall production in 1970 while 2005 shows a substantial decline of almost 43 per cent in. Similarly, manufacturing employment declined almost 44 per cent in the same period. These figures demonstrate that a strong trend towards de-industrialization has occurred in the last four decades. De-industrialization can be seen even more clearly by observing the increased output and employment shares of the financial sector. The percentage of the Greek labour force employed by the financial sector has increased from 4.6 in 1970 to 10 per cent in 2005, an increase of 116 per cent. The agricultural sector has substantially shrunk over the same period in terms of both output and employment. The dramatic decline of the employment share in agriculture reflects, to a great extent, the migration of a large share of population from rural to urban areas, while tourism (hotels and restaurants) and retail trade sectors have experienced an expansion during the period under study.

Figure 2.1 helps us to better understand Greece's relative position in terms of aggregate productivity, measured by GDP per capita. There is a

Table 2.1 Employment and output shares of various sectors 1970 and 2005

Sector	Output share			Employment share		
	1970	2005	Change	1970	2005	Change
Manufacturing	34.91%	19.90%	–42.99%	27.68%	15.52%	–43.94%
Finance and business services	12.52%	15.25%	21.73%	4.63%	10.00%	116.21%
Construction	10.85%	9.53%	–12.11%	15.07%	9.83%	–34.73%
Wholesale and retail trade	9.96%	13.52%	35.74%	5.12%	9.38%	83.31%
Agriculture	9.62%	5.12%	–46.70%	11.84%	2.99%	–74.77%
Community social services	9.22%	17.46%	89.39%	20.32%	37.51%	84.58%
Hotels and restaurants	5.57%	8.54%	53.27%	2.38%	4.61%	93.31%
Transport	5.28%	8.46%	60.28%	9.88%	7.84%	–20.63%
Public administration and defence	3.65%	6.98%	91.19%	7.92%	12.57%	58.77%
Health and social work	2.27%	4.37%	92.82%	4.06%	7.72%	89.89%
Education	1.63%	3.04%	86.97%	5.05%	10.12%	100.66%
Other community services	1.58%	2.76%	74.74%	2.66%	4.19%	57.38%
Electricity, gas and water supply	1.48%	1.72%	16.51%	1.61%	1.74%	8.13%
Private households	0.10%	0.31%	217.94%	0.70%	2.86%	308.56%

Source: Compiled by author, based on EUKLEMS Database, www.euklems.net.

clear upward trend for Greece over the period 1970 to 2005, but a widening gap with the GDP per capita of the EU-15 average is evident. More interestingly, Greece has performed relatively worse than other European economies which experienced a similar level of GDP per capita in 1970. For instance, Ireland and Greece started from the same point in 1970, but Ireland's GDP per capita was one of the highest in Europe in 2005, even exceeding Germany's. One can infer from this that while Greece has taken some firm steps towards development, convergence with the productivity levels of developed (or otherwise 'frontier') countries is slow.

The de-industrialization process in Greece and manufacturing productivity

Table 2.1 indicates that a process of de-industrialization occurred in the period 1970–2005. There are a large number of possible reasons for this

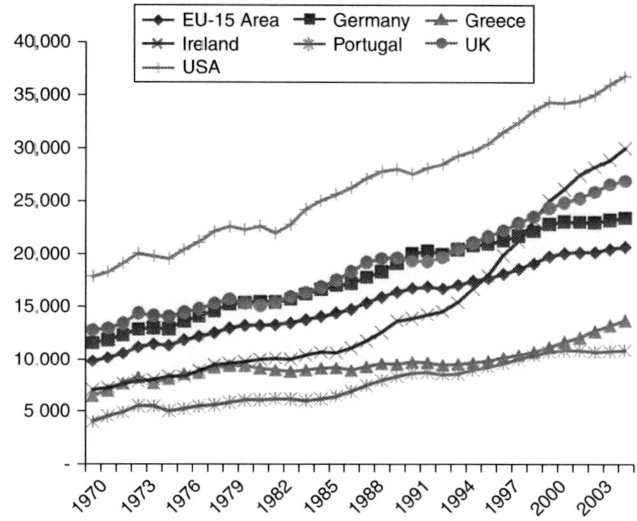

Figure 2.1 GDP per capita 1970–2005 (constant 2000 US$)
Source: Author's calculations with data obtained from EUKLEMS database, www.euklems.net.

phenomenon, including both economic and sociological approaches. The increased participation of women in the labour market is one factor that justifies why resources have shifted from manufacturing to finance. The female labour force cannot undertake the heavy manual tasks of traditional industrial jobs, so it becomes more convenient for female workers to find employment in the services sector (for a further discussion on this see Bournakis and Vecchi, 2010).

The analysis in this chapter focuses mainly on whether productivity plays a role in the de-industrialization process. Note that it is not always clear whether productivity is a cause or a consequence of de-industrialization. In addition, it is not always possible to know if resources are driven from manufacturing to services because the latter sector is more productive so higher wages are on offer. The reverse scenario is likely to be true so the steady shift of resources towards the services sector has made the remaining resources in manufacturing more productive. A similar scenario is valid for the marked shrinking of the agricultural sector. The industrialization process after the end of World War II was accompanied by a rise in agricultural productivity. Industrialization associated with the rise in agricultural productivity suggests, to a great extent, that the remaining agricultural workforce became more efficient. The impact of various determinants on productivity performance is investigated later in this chapter. The analysis begins by looking at labour productivity behaviour of various sectors of the Greek economy.

Figure 2.2 shows labour productivity trends in five main sectors of the economy between 1970 and 2005. Manufacturing follows an upward trend over the period, while the agricultural sector's productivity, which starts from a relatively lower point, grows faster, managing to converge and even exceeding manufacturing's productivity by the end of the sample period.

After the 1990s, the financial sector exhibits a downward trend in labour productivity. Tourism and retail trade behave similarly, experiencing a productivity downturn in the second half of the 1980s and recovering slowly in the second half of the 1990s. This preliminary evidence shows that the de-industrialization process of the 1990s has forced an increase in productivity in the manufacturing sector, while the large shift of employment resources towards the financial services sector has negatively affected its productivity. The upward trend observed in manufacturing is explained by the efficient utilization of resources, but the impact of advanced technological assets, such as machinery and equipment, on productivity also needs to be investigated. In other words, has capital deepening in the manufacturing sector (associated with the use of advanced production techniques) increased output, compensating for the diverting of resources towards the financial sector?

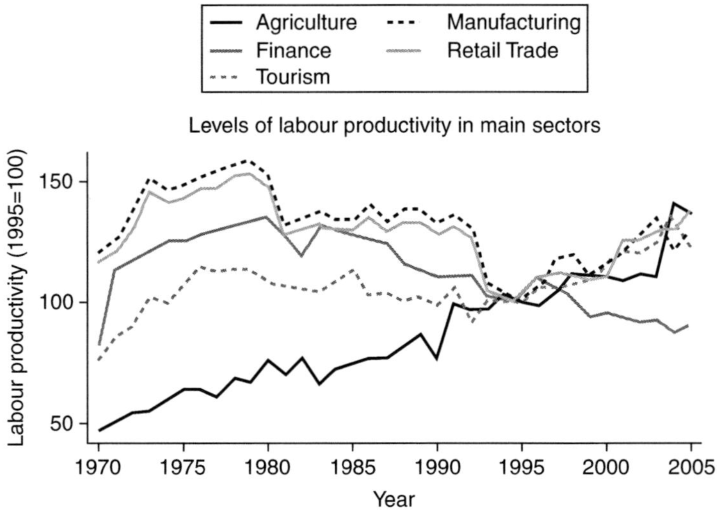

Figure 2.2 Labour productivity in Greece 1970–2005
Source: Author's calculations with data obtained from EUKLEMS database, www.euklems.net.

Although the Greek economy follows a pattern of de-industrialization, the manufacturing sector still remains large both in absolute and relative terms. The fact that productivity levels shows an upward trend over time prompts an investigation of productivity performance in disaggregate manufacturing industries. Table 2.2 shows that the manufacturing sector grew at a rate of 2 per cent over the period 1970–2005. This rate is close to those found in Germany and the UK (O'Mahony and Wagner, 1996) for a sub-sample of the current period. Greece performed relatively well in the coal and chemical industries while it maintained relatively high productivity in some traditionally low cost- based industries such as basic metals, rubbers and plastics and tobacco. In the

Table 2.2 Average labour productivity growth 1970–2005

ISIC sector code	Manufacturing industry	Labour productivity
15	Food and beverages	2.965%
16	Tobacco	2.624%
17	Textiles	0.229%
18	Clothing; dressing and dyeing of fur	0.863%
19	Leather and footwear	0.272%
20	Wood and products of wood and cork	–1.044%
21	Paper and paper products	3.360%
22	Printing, publishing and reproduction	3.606%
23	Coke, refined petroleum and nuclear fuel	5.785%
24	Chemicals and chemical products	4.218%
25	Rubber and plastics	2.723%
26	Other non-metallic minerals	2.937%
27	Basic metals	2.842%
28	Fabricated metal	2.608%
29	Machinery	0.966%
30	Office, accounting and computing machinery	–1.406%
31	Electrical machinery and apparatus	1.990%
32	Radio, television and communication equipment	3.402%
33	Medical, precision and optical instruments	1.567%
34	Motor vehicles, trailers and semi-trailers	1.215%
35	Other transport equipment	0.772%
36	Other manufacturing	1.997%
	Summary statistics	
	Sample average	2.022%
	Standard deviation	0.122
	Minimum	–41.125%
	Maximum	74.278%

Source: Author's calculations with data obtained from EUKLEMS database, www.euklems.net.

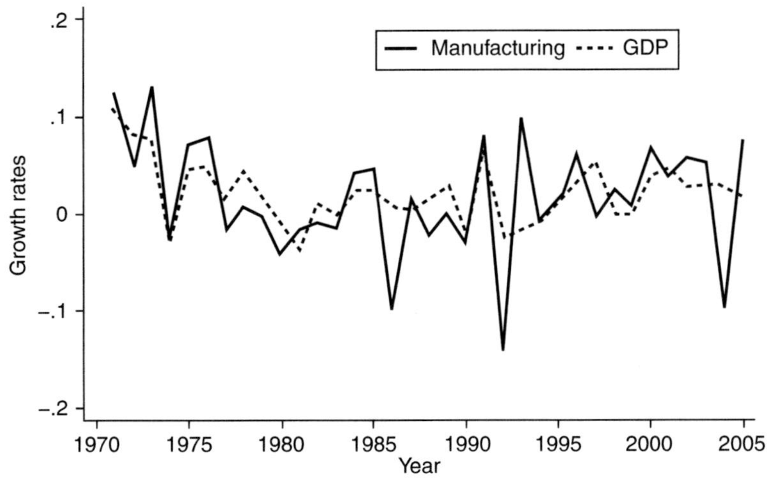

Figure 2.3 Manufacturing labour productivity growth and GDP growth
Source: Author's calculations with data obtained from EUKLEMS database, www.euklems.net.

so-called heavy industry, such as motor vehicles and machinery, Greece exhibited below average growth rates, while only wood and office machinery experienced a negative growth rate over this period.

Manufacturing productivity is a pro-cyclical variable, the strength of which depends on the business cycle movements of the total economy. Figure 2.3 confirms that GDP growth rate and manufacturing productivity follow a very similar pattern. This supports the claim that not all movements in productivity growth reflect structural reforms. Instead, when the economy is in an expansionary phase with high aggregate demand, then workers work overtime, resulting in an occasional increase in productivity. Conversely, when the economy faces a recession with low demand, before starting redundancy proceedings firms adopt a strategy of under-utilization of the existing resources, resulting in lower productivity.[1] In the following sections, an econometric analysis of the factors that significantly influence productivity is presented.

Does Greece's productivity equal levels in the rest of the EU?

Greece is a peripheral country of the EU with a GDP per capita consistently less than the EU average and that of other developed economies.

The question of whether Greek manufacturers manage to meet the productivity level of their advanced European counterparts is now examined. Neoclassical growth theory states that developing countries initially fall far behind the frontier and they tend to grow faster, converging in the long run to the productivity level of the frontier. This proposition relies on the assumption that because capital exhibits diminishing returns, countries are unable to benefit infinitely from capital deepening. Consequently, it is possible for developing countries to close the productivity gap separating them from their developed counterparts.

In this analysis, the convergence hypothesis for Greece over the period 1970–2005 is investigated, selecting Germany, a country widely accepted as a European productivity leader, as the frontier economy. Table 2.3 shows clearly that Greece was a productivity outlier in all manufacturing activities at the beginning of the sample. The data in

Table 2.3 Relative labour productivity of Greece and Germany 1970–2005

Sector	Industry	1970	2005
15	Food and beverages	0.028	1.200
16	Tobacco	0.029	0.325
17	Textiles	0.084	0.691
18	Clothing; dressing and dyeing of Fur	0.095	0.786
19	Leather and footwear	0.112	0.686
20	Wood and products of wood and cork	0.086	0.608
21	Paper and paper products	0.016	0.520
22	Printing, publishing and reproduction	0.032	1.172
23	Coke, refined petroleum and nuclear fuel	0.051	1.180
24	Chemicals and chemical products	0.026	0.334
25	Rubber and plastics	0.022	0.607
26	Other non-metallic mineral	0.037	1.190
27	Basic metals	0.103	0.869
28	Fabricated metal	0.030	0.799
29	Machinery	0.091	0.359
30	Office, accounting and computing machinery	0.128	0.221
31	Electrical machinery and apparatus	0.112	1.678
32	Radio, television and communication equipment	0.218	1.551
33	Medical, precision and optical instruments	0.084	0.604
34	Motor vehicles, trailers and semi-trailers	0.069	0.508
35	Other transport equipment	0.119	0.676
36	Other manufacturing	.	0.777
	Average	0.075	0.788

Source: Author's calculations with data obtained from EUKLEMS database, www.euklems.net.

Table 2.3 can be interpreted as follows: a typical Greek manufacturing industry has 7 per cent of the productivity of its German counterpart in 1970, while this proportion has increased to 78 per cent in 2005. The poor productivity performance of Greece in 1970 has improved over the 35-year period, but in 2005 Greece still falls behind Germany in most of the activities. Exceptionally, Greece's performance is superior to Germany's in food beverages, printing and publishing, other non-metallic, and electrical machinery and apparatus. Table 2.3 also displays the average growth rates of manufacturing industries in both countries. Germany maintains on average a higher rate of labour productivity growth than Greece, making the convergence process of the latter even harder.

Greece becomes relatively more productive than Germany in the food and printing and publishing industries. Those are industries in which Greece has experienced on average a higher rate of labour productivity growth, enabling convergence to occur. In chemicals and rubbers (and plastics), Greece has a labour productivity growth rate above the sample average, but still falls behind because Germany maintain a similar or even higher growth rate.

The standard modelling of β-convergence as suggested by Barro and Sala-i-Martin (1991) is followed here. The regression used for testing the convergence hypothesis takes the following form:

$$\Delta \ln LP_{GER,t} = a_0 + \beta\left(\frac{LP_{GER,1970}}{LP_{GRC,1970}}\right) + u_{i,t} \quad (1)$$

The dependent variable in equation (1) is Germany's (*GER*) growth rates of labour productivity while the explanatory variable is Germany's relative productivity level compared to Greece's (*GRC*) in the first year of the sample (1970). The sign of the estimated parameter β is expected to be negative, confirming the proposition that the higher the initial level of relative productivity, the lower the rate of productivity growth. Equation (1) is also augmented with a disturbance term of zero mean and constant variance. Instead of assuming that parameter β is the same for the whole period, we estimate (1) for different time sub-samples checking whether the speed of convergence is the same over time.

Table 2.4 shows the estimated results from equation (1). Column 1 refers to estimates from the whole sample revealing a negative β coefficient. Overall, German industries with high relative productivity in 1970 experience lower growth rates of labour productivity in the

Table 2.4 Regression results for the convergence hypothesis in Greece

Variables	1975–2005	1970–1980	1980–1990	1990–2005
RLP_1970	–0.01*	–0.01	–0.01	–0.02**
	(–1.79)	(–1.00)	(–1.65)	(–2.09)
Constant	0.08***	0.06***	0.05***	0.10***
	–3.82	–4.04	–3.89	–3.99
Observations	665	153	153	325
R-squared	0.005	0.006	0.01	0.005

Notes: Raw data for the regressions of this table are taken from EUKLEMS database. The dependent variable of the regressions is the growth rate of Germany's labour productivity as appeared in equation (1). t-statistics are displayed in parentheses, level of significance is as follows: *** 1%, ** 5%, * 10%. Estimates are consistent for heteroscedastic standard errors.

following years, enabling Greek industries to catch up. Although the sign of the estimated parameter is always negative, the significance level of the coefficient varies across different periods. These results suggest that Greece's convergence process is weak in the 1970s and 1980s while it becomes stronger in the 1990s. Comparing the rate of convergence in Greece with benchmark results in the convergence literature, the overall speed of convergence can be said to be somewhat lower than the one documented in Barro and Sala-i-Martin (1991) (i.e. which is in the neighbourhood of 2 per cent). A rate of convergence of 2 per cent is documented in Greece only from 1990 onwards which can be characterized as the most effective period in closing the productivity gap with Germany.

The sources of labour productivity growth

The results from Table 2.4 reveal the existence of a convergence process in Greek manufacturing for the period 1970–2005. A corollary of the above finding is to identify which factors play an important role in the convergence process. Research into the determinants of labour productivity often attracts the attention of policy designers.

Capital intensity is the first variable under consideration. According to Solow's (1957), growth model, capital is subject to diminishing returns, implying that after a certain point capital services are exhausted so they no longer lead to faster rates of economic growth. This feature of capital allows poor countries to converge, closing the gap that separates them from rich ones. Capital stock is generated through the accumulation of investment flows, which in turn are derived from the rates of saving as a proportion of income. In an inter-temporal context, to keep the same growth rate of capital stock per worker, a consistently higher saving rate is required, which in turn has an inverse effect on consumption.[2] A core implication of the neoclassical theory of growth is that at more advanced stages of economic development countries should rely on other engines in order to sustain economic growth.

Wolff (1991) claims that US productivity leadership in the previous century is the result of a very high rate of growth in the capital–labour ratio, while the loss of high productivity positions for countries such as the UK coincides with very low rates of investment. Nonetheless, the high rates of economic growth for the US economy persist even after the savings rate declines. This finding is highlighted in the endogenous growth approach in which capital is not subject to diminishing returns (see models of Lucas, 1988, and Romer, 1990). This model stresses the role of capital deepening in embodying technical progress via the purchase of technologically advanced capital assets. While both neoclassical and endogenous approaches to growth emphasize the importance of technology for growth, the latter approach links technological effort to a country's development level. For advanced countries what really matters is to boost the technological frontier with the development of new ideas, products and processes, while for less developed countries what matters is technology catch-up, which is the effective adoption of techniques already used in advanced economies. The latter role describes accurately the needs of Greece as already suggested in Bournakis (2009). In the empirical section of this chapter, the hypothesis of whether capital–labour ratio is associated with the level of labour productivity is tested, further exploring the contribution of technological progress and capital intensity to labour productivity growth.

Abramovitz (1986) attributes fast rates of convergence after World War II to 'social capability' factors. Social capability includes, among other things, the educational attainment of the workforce. The idea here, obviously, is that a skilled worker is more efficient than an unskilled one. The main reason for including a human capital measure in an empirical model of productivity is that education is a variable greatly affected by policy-making choices. There are also strong empirical grounds for the selection of this variable as Mankiw *et al.* (1992) find that omitting a human capital variable from the Solow model explains why the growth rate depends so much only on population and savings rate. Augmenting Solow's model with a variable that captures human capital with cross-country data provides a much better explanation, justifying why some countries are richer than others.

There is a great deal of research that establishes a positive relationship between R&D and productivity. R&D represents innovative activity whose outcomes are likely to result in higher either technical or economic efficiency. In any case, labour productivity is positively associated with R&D activity. A typical quantitative effect of R&D on various measures of productivity, ranging from 2.5 to 3.5 per cent, is given by Griliches and Regev (1995). We can interpret these values as follows: a 1 per cent increase in the R&D measure leads to a 2.5 per cent increase in productivity. This estimate is usually referred to as the social return to R&D, as there are always knowledge spillovers which benefit not only the parties conducting R&D but the whole economy. The fact that R&D has a social character raises the question of its funding. Although it is quite rare to have a complete data series with the funding origins of R&D and discovering if the latter generate substantial knowledge externalities then governments should make larger funding contributions than private industries.

In reality, the latter consideration becomes more complicated if one takes into account that many European countries that lag behind in productivity terms run permanent large budget deficits, like Greece, so it costs even more to undertake intensive R&D activity. A costless option is to adopt a policy frame (usually through tax exemptions) that provides the private sector with incentives to intensify R&D. Similarly. government policy needs to simplify the ways that R&D outcomes of other countries can spread to Greece. Improving absorptive capacity must be a top priority when the home country lacks resources to fund its own R&D efforts.

Finally, it is often acknowledged that international trade generates productivity gains. Nonetheless, the set of gains is usually restricted to those related to the shift of a country's production possibility curve. More importantly, international trade in commodities is a transmitter of knowledge and ideas that contribute to the gains accumulated by the less developed country. This type of dynamic gain is also known as trade-induced gain and affects the recipient country's productivity performance. Exporting enhances learning effects as it brings domestic producers into contact with international best practice, while with importing, they have the chance to use more sophisticated raw materials. Linking this argument to R&D activity, it can be argued that trade in commodities yields trade in ideas and techniques used for the production of these commodities. For example, Greece gains from bilateral trade with Germany not only because it can consume products which it is unable to produce itself, but also because German products facilitate intensive R&D effort whose outcomes can be disseminated in the Greek economy.

An econometric model for the sources of labour productivity

The above discussion, specifying labour productivity, can be summarized as a function of the following variables :

$$LP = f(CI + TR + RD + HC)$$

where *CI*, *TR*, *RD* and *HC* stand for capital intensity, trade, research and development and human capital, respectively. The empirical validity of the above arguments can be assessed by transforming the productivity function into two econometric specifications:

$$\ln LP = \alpha + \beta_1 \ln CI_t + \beta_2 \ln TR_t + \beta_3 \ln RD_t + \beta_4 \ln HC_t + u_{i,t} \qquad (2)$$

$$\ln LP = \alpha + \gamma_1 \ln CI_t + \gamma_2 \ln TR_t + \gamma_3 \ln RD_t + \gamma_4 \ln HC_t + \eta_i + \lambda_t + u_{i,t} \qquad (3)$$

The dependent variable *LP* is the level of labour productivity, defined as the ratio of output per worker, while β and γ are coefficients to be estimated. To capture the degree of heterogeneity at the industry level as well as to account for economy-wide macroeconomic effects, (2) is augmented by a set of industry η_i and time dummies λ_t Table 2.5 presents the results of estimating specifications (2) and (3).

The data used for the estimation are taken from UNIDO. This database has been chosen in preference to EUKLEMS because UNIDO has a longer data series for investment in capital assets. EUKLEMS information about capital assets in Greece starts from 1995 while in UNIDO the data availability goes back to 1963. However, there is another data limitation, the availability of R&D series. OECD-STAN is the only source with information about R&D and the series is initiated in 1987. Given these data constraints, specifications (2) and (3) have been estimated for the period 1987–99. Appendix 2.1 summarizes statistics for the data and the variables used in this section.

Specification (2) is estimated with OLS (Ordinary Least Squares estimator). The marginal effects are shown in the table so the reported coefficients can be interpreted as elasticities. A 10 per cent increase in

Table 2.5 Determinants of labour productivity 1987–99

Variables	**OLS**	**LSDV**	**OLS**	**LSDV**
	Spec. 1	**Spec. 2**	**Spec. 3**	**Spec. 4**
Exports	–0.006	–0.002	–0.054***	–0.026**
	(1.298)	(0.388)	(4.7)	(2.219)
Imports	–0.002***	–0.001***	–0.003***	–0.002
	(7.502)	(3.076)	(4.45)	(1.272)
CI	0.43***	0.18***	0.549***	0.511***
	(13.29)	(6.569)	(10.86)	(12.88)
RD	0.03***	0.01**	0.034***	0.0008
	(9.417)	(2.057)	(2.746)	(0.049)
HC			0.06***	0.05***
			(3.696)	(3.024)
Constant	6.028***	8.85***	3.475***	4.463
	16.48	24.55	(8.607)	(8.18)
Industry dummies	No	Yes	No	Yes
Year Dummies	No	Yes	No	Yes
Observations	234	234	57	57
R-squared	0.67	0.94	0.91	0.98
F(11,198)		19.49		
		(0.00)		

Notes: t-statistics are displayed in parentheses. Level of significance is as follows: *** 1%, ** 5%, * 10%. Estimates are consistent for heteroscedastic standard errors. OLS shows estimates from equation (2) and LSDV shows estimates from equation (3).

capital intensity raises labour productivity by 43 per cent. Similarly, a 10 per cent increase in R&D per worker increases labour productivity by 3 per cent. As noted earlier, the latter coefficient can be viewed as the social return from R&D. In the LSDV (Least Squared Dummy Variables) estimates from specification (3), the size and the magnitudes of capital and R&D intensity becomes 18 per cent and 1 per cent, respectively. This cut in the size and magnitude is justified largely by the inclusion of industry and time dummies. The F-statistic indicates whether the estimated coefficients of industry and time dummies are jointly significant equal to zero. This hypothesis is rejected suggesting that there is unobserved heterogeneity in our sample that should be accounted for. This sort of unobserved effect might refer to managerial and organizational practices that play an important role in labour productivity but it is very difficult to measure precisely in econometric terms.

Turning to trade variables, none of them has a positive impact on productivity. This finding lends no support the idea trade-induced learning. More importantly, the coefficient of import share is negatively signed and statistically significant, implying that Greece's dependence on imports affects productivity performance adversely.

Columns 3 and 4 in Table 2.5 present results from specifications including human capital. Note that the length of the sample that includes human capital is reduced due to data unavailability for the whole set of industries, but the qualitative picture of the results remains unchanged. Human capital is revealed to be an important driver of labour productivity while capital intensity and R&D maintain their positive role. In column 4, the positive coefficient of R&D vanishes, leaving capital intensity and human capital as the only statistically significant coefficients.

The analysis of this section suggests that among the factors investigated, capital intensity has quantitatively the strongest impact on the level of labour productivity. The economic intuition behind this result is that as the means of production becomes more automated with the introduction of advanced and sophisticated machinery, the labour force also manages to improve productivity. Similarly, investing in R&D contributes to positive movements in productivity although the effect is relatively weaker in economic terms. The level of education improves employee capability, showing a positive sign as expected. The importance of trade in productivity performance requires further investigation in view of the negative sign of trade variables in Table 2.5. According to Bournakis (2009b), lagged variables of higher order appear with a statistically significant sign. Table 2.6 replicates specification (2) of Table 2.5, experimenting with higher order lags in trade variables and seeking to reveal whether learning effects from trade are implemented with hysteresis. Indeed, we find that the fourth lag of imports has a positive and statistically significant estimate at the 5 per cent level. This finding suggests that imports facilitate some knowledge effects but their diffusion in the Greek economy takes time.

Technology catch-up and productivity growth

In econometric specifications (2) and (3), we focus on the determinants of productivity level without addressing what drives the growth rate of labour productivity. As already discussed, in the neoclassical approach to growth, once the economy is in the steady state path of development then the growth rate of output per worker is only stimulated by technological progress. This proposition is equivalent to considering that capital deepening is unable to maintain high growth rates over a long-term horizon.

Table 2.6 Determinants of labour productivity 1987–99 with higher-order lags of exports and imports

Variables	LSDV	LSDV	LSDV	LSDV
L. Exports	–0.002			
	(0.357)			
L. Imports	0.003			
	(0.307)			
L2.Exports		0.006		
		(0.133)		
L2.Imports		0.059		
		(1.127)		
L3.Exports			0.024	
			(0.452)	
L3.Imports			0.063	
			(1.176)	
L4.Exports				–0.0362
				(0.835)
L4.Imports				0.116**
				(2.120)
CI	0.160***	0.157**	0.136*	0.123
	(2.714)	(2.441)	(1.870)	(1.435)
RD	0.00737	0.0053	0.00955	0.0136
	(0.880)	(0.607)	(1.034)	(1.375)
Constant	10.41***	9.234***	10.83***	9.469***
	(15.79)	(13.11)	(14.02)	(9.826)
Industry dummies	Yes	Yes	Yes	Yes
Year dummies	Yes	Yes	Yes	Yes
Observations	217	200	182	162
R-squared	0.942	0.939	0.934	0.933

Notes: The L-operator denotes lag values of variables. In our estimation the fourth lag of imports has a positive and statistical significant coefficient. t-statistics are displayed in parentheses. Level of significance is as follows: *** 1%, ** 5%, * 10%. Estimates are consistent for heteroscedastic standard errors.

In the long run only technological progress can stimulate growth. A notable difficulty with testing this proposition is the accurate definition of the level of technology. For the purposes of this analysis, technology is conceptualized within a Solow (1957) framework. This represents a residual measure implying that technological improvements are completely unconnected to the purchase of factors of production.[3] The methodology starts from the specification of an aggregate production function as follows:

$$Y_{i,t} = A_{i,t} L_{i,t}^{\alpha} K_{i,t}^{1-\alpha} \tag{4}$$

where Y, L and K are value added, labour and capital stock, respectively. Subscripts i and t indexes industry and time while α is the share of labour in the production process. Assuming constant returns to scale, then capital share is one minus the labour share. Taking logs and re-arranging produces:

$$\ln TFP_{i,t} = \ln Y_{i,t} - \alpha \ln L_{i,t} - (1 - \alpha)\ln K_{i,t} \tag{5}$$

TFP stands for total factor productivity and is a proxy for our technology measure. If factors are paid their marginal products, then output elasticity with respect to labour and capital can be calculated as the share of labour compensation to total revenue. Having said this, all variables in equation (5) are observable so we can obtain a measure of technology.

For countries like Greece that are behind in technology terms, what demonstrates particular interest is not the level of technological progress *per se* but the country's ability to adopt technological advances from the frontier country. As noted earlier, this adoption process is referred to as technology catch-up, and it boosts the rate of labour productivity in the steady state. As with the convergence hypothesis, the case of Germany can again be used to testing whether Greece has the potential to increase the rate of labour productivity growth via technology transfer:

$$\Delta \ln LP_{i,t} = \gamma_1 CI_{i,t} + \gamma_2 \frac{\ln TFP_{i,t}^{GRC}}{\ln TFP_{i,t}^{GER}} + u_{i,t} \tag{6}$$

Table 2.7 presents results from specification (6) showing relative TFP between Greece and Germany and reflecting the technology catch-up between the two countries. The sign of the estimated parameter γ_2 is expected to be positive. The estimate of the capital intensity is negative while technology catch-up affects productivity growth positively. The results remain the same even after using higher order lags of capital intensity. This finding confirms the role of technological progress as an important engine of productivity growth in the long term. Based on this, the main concern of policy makers should be the identification of those channels that allow for a faster technology catch-up. Trade has been proved to be one of those important channels as it transmits the R&D effort conducted in the more advanced country to the one that is behind.

Summary

This chapter analyzed the productivity of Greek manufacturing. Productivity is a key welfare measure determining the level of

Table 2.7 Technology catch-up and labour productivity growth

Variables	LP Growth	LP Growth	LP Growth	LP Growth
RTFP	0.006**	0.037***	0.04***	0.0225
	(2.057)	(3.106)	(3.704)	(1.655)
CI	–0.0021			
	(1.052)			
L.CI		0.0008		
		(0.410)		
L2.CI			0.0005	
			(0.288)	
L3.CI				–0.0001
				(0.101)
Constant	0.039**	–0.00824	–0.0072	0.00374
	(2.128)	(0.417)	(0.408)	(0.223)
Observations	96	82	71	60
R-squared	0.448	0.433	0.515	0.447

Notes: The L-operator denotes lag values of variables. t-statistics are displayed in parentheses. Level of significance is as follows: *** 1%, ** 5%, * 10%. Estimates are consistent for heteroscedastic standard errors.

competitiveness and living standards. It is clear that the industrialization period in the Greek economy has been short, with the manufacturing sector shrinking since 1970. This reallocation from industrial activities to service sectors resulted in the growth of manufacturing productivity by an average of 2.2 per cent for the period 1970–2005.

A popular discussion in the economic agenda of the 1990s was Greece's 'convergence' with the macroeconomic measures of other EU countries. Although there has been a nominal convergence in basic macroeconomic terms, the process of productivity convergence over the last 40 years has been very slow. Some crucial drivers of labour productivity, such as capital intensity, are strictly related to the broader economic architecture, which is, in turn, determined by global trends, so there is little room for individual intervention. On the other hand, econometric analysis reveals much heterogeneity, suggesting individual industrial effects in productivity movements. This set of characteristics is very likely to reflect organizational practices adopted by individual firms and/or various institutional rigidities related closely to efficiency levels. Rigidities of this sort are chronic in nature and associated with the existence of bureaucratic procedures or the lack of performance incentives, especially in the public sector.

The current economic crisis has massively affected traditional sectors of specialization in Greece, such as maritime trade and tourism, and raised many concerns as to whether specialization in financial services can constitute a model of sustainable development, given the existing characteristics of the Greek economy. Based on the experience of East Asian countries, including China, it can be argued that specialization in manufacturing offers a relatively less vulnerable business environment, moving economic development into a more sustainable path. A subsequent important issue for a peripheral European country like Greece is to develop those strengths necessary to compete successfully in international markets.

To identify a pattern of specialization under conditions of free trade and outsourcing activities towards countries with cheap labour is a challenging task, not only for Greece, but for the whole of Europe. Other European countries, such as the UK, have over time moved their focus towards services, replacing traditional industrial activities. This shift is to a great extent an admission that with outsourcing to East Asian countries available, where many manufacturing commodities can be produced more cheaply, European countries need to look for new areas of comparative advantage. The Lisbon Treaty (2007) sets out clearly that Europe's future is in new technologies, the so-called 'knowledge economy' implying that Europe must expand production in areas where advanced skills and human capital are required.

Ultimately, Greece needs to follow this EU directive and focus on the manufacturing of high technology products and services. The current unsustainable structure of the Greek economy along with other stylized facts of international competitiveness suggest that only by focusing on those sectors can Greece look forward to a certain prospect of sustainable development. This is no easy task, but Greece has the resources and capabilities required to adopt the production of high technology goods and services. What Greece lacks is the efficient means of using these resources.

This discussion does not mean that Greece should not make a painstaking effort to enhance productivity horizontally in a number of neuralgic domains such as public, business and institutional. Improving productivity in these sectors presupposes the removal of chronic rigidities such as bureaucracy and lack of meritocracy to ensure that the adoption of a new production model in Greece is feasible. In other words, a structural reform of all parts of economic life is a prerequisite of injecting funds into specific sectors.

Appendix 2.1 Data summary

Variable	Source	N	Mean	Std. Dev.	Min	Max
LP	UNIDO	252	78892	0.50	24401	373200
Export share	UNIDO	252	0.22	0.73	0.01	1.22
Import share	UNIDO	252	0.85	0.93	0.03	5.98
CI	UNIDO	252	20142	0.62	3246	105316
RD	OECD -STAN	234	20.41	1.72	0.11	1386.63
HC	EUKLEMS	252	0.08	2.90	0.03	0.13

Variables definition

Output: Gross output in constant 1995 USD.
Imports: The ratio of imports to total output. Imports are expressed in constant 1995 USD
Exports: The ratio of exports to total output. Exports are expressed in constant 1995 USD
CI (Capital intensity): The ratio of capital stock per employee. Capital stock is generated by using the inventory perpetual method as follows: $K = (1-\delta)K_{t-1}+I_{t-1}$ where δ is the physical depreciation rate of capital assumed to be 15% and I denotes investment in assets of Gross Fixed Capital formation expressed in constant 1995 USD.
RD: The ratio of R&D expenditure per employee. R&D is expressed in constant 2000 USD.
HC: The ratio of employees with a degree from tertiary education to total number of employees.

Notes

1. Hall (1990) refers to the cyclical behaviour of productivity as the invariance property of the Solow residual. This consideration suggests that if the short-run cyclical influences are not extracted from total factor productivity (TFP) of the Solow model, then TFP measures tend to be upward-biased. In other words, TFP is biased in booms and downward-biased in recessions.
2. In a closed economy context, income can be devoted only to consumption and saving with the identity I=S (i.e. investment=savings) to hold in the long run.
3. This exogenous formulation of technology is also called 'manna from heaven', or/and a measure of ignorance. In other words, technology is whatever contributes to output increases but it is unobserved.

References

Abramovitz, M. (1986) 'Catching Up, Forging Ahead, and Falling Behind', *Journal of Economic History*, 46 (2): 385–406.

Barro, R. and Sala-i-Martin, X. (1991) 'Convergence across States and Regions', *Brooking Papers on Economic Activity*, 1991(1): 107–82.

Baumol, W., Blackman, S. and Wolff, E. (1994) 'Long Run Growth in the US Productivity: Is there a Slowdown?', In *Productivity and American Leadership: The Long View*. Cambridge: MIT Press.

Bournakis, I. (2009a) *Competitiveness Trade and Productivity: With Special Reference to Greece*. Germany: VDM Verlag.

Bournakis, I. (2009b) 'Does Greece Learn from Germany? Technological Catch-Up and the Channels of Productivity Growth in the Greek Manufacturing Sector', *Journal of World Economic Review*, 4 (2): 105–24.

Bournakis, I. and Vecchi, M. (2010) 'Intangible Capital and the Pattern of Specialisation in the EU', *Review of Economics and Institutions*, 1(2).

Griliches, Z. and H. Regev (1995) 'Firm Productivity in Israeli Industry 1979–1988', *Journal of Econometrics*, 65(1): 175–203.

Hall, R. (1990) 'Invariance Properties of Solow's Productivity Residual'. In P. Diamond(ed.), *Growth Productivity Employment, Essays to Celebrate Robert Solow's Birthday*. Cambridge: MIT Press.

Krugman, P. (1993) 'What Do Undergrads Need to Know about Trade?', *American Economic Review*, Paper and Proceedings, 83: 23–6.

Lucas, R. (1988) 'The Mechanics of Economic Development', *Journal of Monetary Economics*, 22(1): 3–42.

Mankiw, G., Romer, D. and Weil, D. (1992) 'A Contribution to the Empirics of Economic Growth', *The Quarterly Journal of Economics*, 107(2): 407–37.

O'Mahony, M and Wagner, K. (1996) 'Anglo-German Productivity Performance since 1973'. In D. Mayes(ed.), *Sources of Productivity Growth*. Cambridge: Cambridge University Press.

Romer, P. (1990) 'Endogenous Technological Change', *Journal of Political Economy*, 98: 71–102.

Solow, R. (1957) 'Technical Change and the Aggregate Production Function', *Review of Economic and Statistics*, 39(3): 312–20.

Wolff, E. (1991) 'Capital Formation and Productivity Convergence over the Long-Run', *American Economic Review*, 81(3): 565–79.

3
Finance
Banking and Investment

Athanasios Kouloridas

Overview

This chapter provides an insight into finance regulation and financial practices and developments in Greece. For the last decade the main thrust of changes at finance level has been the implementation of European legislation, in the context of the financial services action plan, in addition to the modernization of the finance and business environment in line with international practice. However, the international financial crisis and the subsequent deterioration in Greek public finances set a new course for the Greek financial sector which now faces new challenges and different priorities.

The chapter is organized in four main sections. The first section serves as an introduction and provides the broader context by mapping the main economic outlook and its impact on the financial sector as well as the characteristics of the Greek financial sector. The second section presents the main legal and regulatory developments at the banking level, while the third section presents them at financial markets and financial services level. Finally, the fourth section seeks to identify the main challenges that the Greek financial sector faces at regulatory and market level.

The economic outlook and the financial sector

Until the early 1990s, the Greek financial sector operated under a strict state intervention system of rules and regulations that restricted competition and market development, and was dominated, at least in the banking sector and in market infrastructures, by state-owned and nationalized players. However, over the last twenty years, the financial sector in Greece has undergone important institutional and operational changes. These adjustments were the result of a number of factors such as the liberalization of financial markets; the modernization of financial regulation at EU level and the implementation of financial services action plan; rapid technological progress in information technology (IT); and the increasing integration of European money markets and clearing services through the operation of Eurosystem, which was significantly promoted by the introduction of the euro (Bryant *et al.*, 2001). In the light of this changing financial environment, the adjustment required by adoption of both the spirit and letter of EU legislation, alongside traditional legal texts, such as the Civil Code, has been a major challenge in Greece. It has brought about significant reforms both in financial practices, financial regulation and the organizational structures of market players such as banks, insurance companies and investment firms, and in the business conduct of such regulated entities. In addition financial markets, financial services law and banking regulation have been completely modernized.

The impact of all this on the market has been considerable: the Greek banking system has been gradually liberalized and this has led to significant competition among market players. Greek banks responded to these new conditions by undertaking mergers and acquisitions (Athanasoglou and Brissimis, 2004; Mylonidis and Kelkinova, 2005). Also, in the same period, many state-controlled banks were privatized, mainly through listing their shares on the Athens Exchange and public offering programmes (see for example Tsionas *et al.*, 2003; Halkos and Salamouris, 2004; Eichengreen and Gibson, 2001).

Furthermore, Greek banks have been expanding in regional markets (mainly in South-eastern Europe) (Athanasoglou *et al.*, 2008). During the last ten years the Greek banking system has enjoyed a favourable macroeconomic environment, in both Greece and in South-eastern Europe. Lending access to fast-growing markets combined with easy borrowing access to European interbank markets and substantial liquidity provided by Eurosystem have contributed to healthy profitability, rapid loan portfolio growth, wide net interest margins and high-yield lending to borrowers (Rezitis, 2006; Asimakopoulos *et al.*, 2008). In addition the implementation of new IT technologies expanded Greek banks' access to the market and permitted the creation and marketing of new financial products and services (for example, internet and telephone banking) (Noulas, 1997).

The above factors, in conjunction with the negligible exposure of Greek banks to US sub-prime assets and other complex structured products, considerably mitigated the financial fallout from the first wave of the recent global financial crisis. While the international financial crisis took its toll in a number of EU countries, severely affecting financial systems invested deeply into sophisticated financial products (structured products and derivatives), it had, at least initially, a lesser impact on Greek banks. Before the burst of the Greek-specific fiscal crisis, Greek banks appeared relatively sound in terms of profitability and capital adequacy (Bank of Greece, 2010). In addition, the Greek banks maintained a low level of non-performing loans (approximately 7.2 per cent of total loans) and a relatively low loan-to-deposit ratio (Bank of Greece, 2010). In sum, the Greek banking system escaped from the sub-prime crisis in a generally robust condition and suffered less than some other EU member states. This was mainly attributed to the banking sector's investment focus on Greek public debt and on neighbouring countries' private sectors. However this investment strategy means that it is unlikely Greek banks can remain immune from the recent difficulties in Greek public finances. Moreover, the impact of economic and financial problems in some of Greece's neighbours is also a concern.

In the aftermath of the global financial crisis that started in 2007, the macroeconomic and budgetary situation has deteriorated markedly during 2010 and Greek public finances have worsened much beyond what could have been expected as a result of the downturn. These developments are largely due to national factors that have developed over the longer term, resulting in a deterioration of the net lending position of the Greek economy and high and persistent external imbalances, mirroring a large-scale loss of competitiveness and a marked deterioration of the fiscal position (Bank of Greece, 2010). National policies for the conduct of fiscal policy, the efficiency of public administration and lack of structural reforms have contributed to poor economic and fiscal performance. This primarily fiscal crisis affects the financial sector, and especially banking, in a number of ways.

With the deteriorating fiscal results came the downgrading of government bonds by rating agencies, and investors started withdrawing from Greek bonds, driving up their yields. Furthermore, it is clear that the deep macroeconomic and structural problems, combined with inevitable strong fiscal adjustment over the medium term, will depress activity for some time. For banks these factors translate into low business growth, increased loan quality problems and continued pressure on margins. Although Greek banks are well capitalized with an average capital adequacy ratio of around 12 per cent, they have been squeezed by slower economic growth and rising provisions, which reached 7.7 per cent of total loans outstanding last year (Bank of Greece, 2010).

More specifically, in the course of 2009 the quality of the loan portfolio declined, resulting in an increase of the NPL (non-performing loans) ratio (on a solo basis) to 7.2 per cent in September 2009 (from 5.0 per cent in December 2008), albeit at a decelerating rate. The NPL ratio increased for all types of loans, but the increase was more pronounced for consumer loans (September 2009, 11.7 per cent; December 2008, 8.2 per cent). The NPL ratio for mortgages reached 6.9 per cent (from 5.3 per cent at the end of 2008) and for corporate loans reached 6.4 per cent (from 4.3 per cent at the end of 2008) (Bank of Greece, 2010).

On account of those higher provisions, and partly because of trading losses related to their large portfolios of Greek government bonds, Greek banks recently reported mostly disappointing fourth quarter earnings. These included a surprise €87 million loss at the National Bank of Greece (NBG), the country's largest lender by assets. In addition, the loss of market confidence in the Greek economy meant that the Greek banking sector has experienced difficulties in accessing liquidity on wholesale markets, leaving it substantially reliant on Eurosystem lending. To be more precise, Greek banks have lost wholesale market access to fund their operations since the end of 2009 (Bank of Greece, 2010). Maturing inter-bank liabilities have not been renewed, or only at high costs, and some moderate deposit outflows were noted during the first months of 2010, which has put additional pressure on the liquidity position of many Greek banks. As a result, the banks have increasingly relied on Eurosystem credit operations. The effects of the fiscal and macroeconomic crisis on the Greek banking sector were recently realized as cuts in financial strength and deposit and debt ratings.[1] Nevertheless, and despite the heightened challenges that the Greek banking system faces, it retains a relatively strong solvency position. The system's equity base was substantially strengthened in 2009, jumping from €24 to €33 billion, including €3.8 billion of capital injection from the government, capital increases from the owners, and retained earnings. In addition all banks are complying with the capital adequacy requirement of 8 per cent, and the average capital adequacy ratio rose to 11.7 per cent at the end of 2009 (Bank of Greece, 2010).

Trends in the investment services sector and securities market are similar. The liberalization of services and modernization of infrastructures created a boom in the industry in the late 1990s. However, insufficient regulation and supervision led to the first collapse of the market by the end of the 1990s. With European integration at financial level, the implementation of the financial services action plan, and global economic growth, came concrete profitability for Greek listed companies and increased confidence of domestic and foreign investors in the Greek securities market. The international financial crisis halted business once more, and when there were signs that the Greek securities market and investment services sector was about to return to positive performance, the lack of confidence caused by the budgetary crisis, considerable liquidations of long positions, short selling pressures, and slim prospects for economic growth sent the Athens Exchange general index (ATHEX) to a 15-month low.[2] Losses since the start of the year have reached 32.39 per cent, while the FTSE/ATHEX 20 blue-chip index has fallen to its lowest point in the last decade.[3]

Financial regulation: the banking sector

During the last twenty years Greek banking law and regulation have changed dramatically. The major changes in the Greek banking systemoccurred after 1992 when interest rates were liberalized, and various credit rules and capital movement restrictions were abolished. Law 2076/1992 also transposed into Greek law the Second Banking Directive of 1989. Banking regulation, including any administrative rules, is currently based, firstly, on Law 3601/2007 which transposed onto Greek banking legislation the provisions of Directives of the European Parliament and of the Council Nos. 2006/48/EC relating to the taking up and pursuit of the business of credit institutions[4] and 2006/49/EC on the capital adequacy of investment firms and credit institutions,[5] and secondly, on the Constitution of the Bank of Greece.

Greek banks are supervised by the Bank of Greece. The Bank of Greece is a very old institution. It was established in 1927 by an Annex to the Geneva Protocol and started operations in May 1928. The Bank of Greece is incorporated as a *Société Anonyme,* its shares are listed in the Athens Exchange and its primary role is to act as the central bank of the country. Since January 2001 the Bank of Greece has been an integral part of the Eurosystem. The Bank of Greece is responsible for implementing the Eurosystem's monetary policy in Greece and safeguarding the stability of the Greek financial system. In the performance of its tasks, the Bank enjoys institutional, personal and operational independence and is accountable to the Greek parliament. The Bank of Greece is engaged in other non-regulatory activities including the operation of the government bond market,[6] the clearing and registry system for government bonds[7] and the cash settlement of the transactions entered in the Athens Exchange.[8]

The Bank of Greece has the power to grant to banking institutions the requisite licence. Licencing is subject to compliance with certain statutory conditions[9] including minimum capital requirements, fit and proper tests for major shareholders and management, and operational and organizational requirements. In addition the Bank of Greece has the power to revoke a banking licence for the reasons specifically set out in the law, including, *inter alia*, the failure of the institution to comply with the authorization requirements and capital adequacy requirements on an ongoing basis. The Bank of Greece is also responsible for the continuing prudential supervision of banking institutions. The scope of prudential supervision encompasses both the domestic operations of credit institutions domiciled in Greece and their branches in other EU member states and banks' managerial and accounting arrangements, the efficiency of their internal control systems and compliance with applicable capital adequacy and liquidity requirements (Hadjiemmanuil, 2008).

The Bank of Greece is also entrusted by Law 3601/2007 with rule-making powers[10] to regulate the organization and operation of banks subject to its supervision. Such rule-making powers are exercisable for prudential and economic policy purposes, and for conduct of business purposes. However, regulation on conduct of business, including transparency and the business terms under which the banks transact with their client, is very limited and until now those issues were left to be regulated either *ex post* under civil law through the case law issued by the Supreme Court (Areios Pagos) on the legality of various terms and practices implemented by banks, or through the application of consumer law 2251/ 1994 as currently in force, including the directive on transposition of consumer credit,[11] supervision and enforcement of which, however, lies with the Ministry of Economy, Competitiveness and Shipping. Apart from consumer credit, rules of conduct in the provision of banking services and banking products are not as detailed as the ones applicable to the provision of investment services and financial products, pursuant to implementation of the Markets in Financial Instruments Directive (MiFID) into Greek law. This regulatory disharmony leaves little room for a level playing field in cases where banking services or banking products can be offered as substitutes for investment products and services (for example, fixed-term structured deposits, cash management or unit-linked products). Finally, the Bank of Greece has enforcement powers, and can impose sanctions in cases of non-compliance with the legal and regulatory requirements governing the operation of credit institutions.

While liberalization and modernization have for the past twenty years been the driving forces of Greek banking regulation developments, the recent global financial crisis required extraordinary measures to be taken. In late 2008, the previous Conservative government had passed a €28 billion support package that consisted of a mixture of loan guarantees, direct capital injections and special liquidity measures to boost the Greek banking system. Law 3723/2009 provides for three types of state aid: 1) state participation in the share capital of each bank by virtue of redeemable and convertible preference shares in exchange for a contribution in kind (government bonds);[12] 2) provision of a state guarantee to credit institutions of up to €15 billion for loans given until 31 December 2009;[13] and 3) private placement of Greek state bonds to credit institutions.[14] The law was fiercely opposed by academics as it contained various provisions that not only introduce dubious exemptions from the general rules of company law (2190/1920) and capital market law but also do not conform to superior constitutional and EU Community law rules. The incompatibility with company law directives is in the mandatory abolition of existing shareholders' pre-emption rights with regard to the issue of the preference shares,[15] and dividend distributions which are only allowed in cases of profits. Article 1, para. 3 of the law provides for a fixed-return right of the preference shares issued at 10 per cent interest, irrespective of profit.[16]

However, European Court of Justice (ECJ) case law leaves little room for deviation from the application of EU company law directives. More precisely, the Court has already stated on many occasions that rules that replace decisions of the company organs are against EU law (2nd Directive), even in cases where they are designed to ensure the reorganization and continuation of a credit institution which is in an exceptional situation by reason of its debt burden.[17] State intervention intended to protect investors or avoid bank runs is not in itself a satisfactory justification for compulsory measures which bypass resolutions made by the organs of the company under EU company law.[18] In addition no such deviation from EU company law directives can be remedied by any approval of the reorganization programme by the European Commission, since such an approval covers only state aid law aspects of the reorganization of companies that are in distress according to Article 87, para. 3, point c of EC treaty and not the application of company law directives.

While only part of the aid was used by Greek banks (Bank of Greece, 2010), the effects of the Greek fiscal crisis required an extension of the banking assistance package. The Greek authorities prepared the necessary detailed legislation in June 2010, as required in the Memorandum of Economic and Financial Policies signed by Greece and the International Monetary Fund (IMF), the European Commission (EC) and the European

Central Bank (ECB). Anticipating that banks' profits may decline further, possibly impacting their equity position, the government's plan included the establishment of a fully independent Financial Stability Fund (FSF). The primary purpose of the FSF is to preserve the financial sector's soundness, and thus its capacity to support the Greek economy, by providing equity support to banks as needed. Whenever supervisory assessments conclude that a bank's capital buffer might fall below adequate levels, the shareholders will be required to immediately bring additional capital or take bridging capital support from the FSF. If banks are then not able to expeditiously raise additional capital on their own and repay the FSF, a restructuring process will take place under the leadership of the FSF, in line with EU competition and state aid requirements. The Fund is established as a private law legal entity and its legal structure allows for private participation. The equity is provided in a way similar to that used for the previous state aid, mainly in the form of preference shares to credit institutions authorized to operate in Greece under licence from the Bank of Greece. The preference shares are convertible into ordinary shares under certain conditions specified in the legislation establishing the Fund. Participation in the Fund is mandatory, based on a trigger linked to the minimum required level of capital adequacy requirements, as established for specific credit institutions by the Bank of Greece in its capacity as the competent supervisory authority, if no private solution has been found. The FSF is fully funded by the government in the amount of €10 billion from the resources available under the EU-IMF programme for this purpose. The agreement reached with the IMF, the ECB and the EC includes detailed provisions as to organizational issues, for example, governance of the fund, participation, organizational and financial independence, and semi-annual reporting to the Greek parliament, the powers of the Fund and the condition upon which aid will be received by requesting banks (Bank of Greece, 2010).

In order to fulfill its purposes the Fund enjoys certain powers over credit institutions receiving capital from the Fund, to be exercised following consultation with the Bank of Greece. These powers are without prejudice to the supervisory powers of the Bank of Greece, and include, without limitation, the following powers:

- to appoint a member of the Board of Directors of a credit institution;
- to require a credit institution to present a restructuring plan;
- to veto key decisions of a credit institution (e.g., business strategy, dividend distributions, salary caps, liquidity and asset liability management, etc.);

- to call a general shareholders' meeting for a credit institution in accordance with Greek company law;
- to require conversion of preference shares into ordinary shares insofar as a credit institution fails to meet (1) the minimum required level of capital adequacy requirements established for credit institutions generally under applicable regulatory requirements, or (2) certain financial conditions to be established in the restructuring plan for the credit institution (Bank of Greece, 2010).

To alleviate some of the concerns described above regarding the interaction of the aid rules with European company law provisions, the legislation establishing the Fund specifies an objective procedure to be followed in establishing a market-based conversion price, taking account of the impact of the Fund's intervention, the rights of shareholders under Greek law and EU state aid requirements. The same applies to any restructuring plan which also needs to be approved by the European Commission by virtue of a decision. In addition, the conditions applicable to any capital increases should be aligned with the Commission Decision of 19 November 2008.[19] Under this decision, the granting of equity capital is made, among other conditions, subject to the credit institutions paying a market-oriented, non-cumulative remuneration depending on the risk profile of the credit institution and the quality of the capital. In addition, the credit institutions will not pay dividends or coupon on hybrid capital, unless they are legally obliged to do so, which is typically the case when a credit institution reports profits.[20] Finally, preference shares will be repurchased by the credit institution for an amount equivalent to the amount originally invested in the credit institution. After five years the shares will be repurchased or be remunerated at penal rates. If they cannot be repurchased because the capital adequacy requirements are not fulfilled, the preference shares will be converted into ordinary shares.

Although financial stability and prudential matters are expected to be the main focus of Greek financial regulation in light of the current financial crisis, it should be remembered that the cornerstone of sustainable economic growth is the ability of banks to facilitate credit intermediation between savers and investors and to provide the critical services consumers and firms obtain from banks to run their daily lives and business. It should not be forgotten that some of the reasons behind the recent financial crisis were the pro-cyclical amplification of risks. A second set of rules must therefore address either banks' reluctance to inject money they receive as support, or the effects of lack of access to refinancing services may have on certain individuals or companies.

A draft law on debt arrangements for over-indebted individuals draws on similar legislation in other member states and fills a significant gap in Greece's current insolvency legislation. In particular, it introduces procedures to enable over-indebted physical persons (not legal entities), who are not merchants for the purposes of the existing bankruptcy framework and who have a proven and continuing inability to service pecuniary debts to credit institutions and other creditors, to seek to repay such debts with more favourable conditions and to obtain debt relief where there are no assets available for the repayment of such debts or where their current and expected income is not sufficient for that purpose. The draft law also contains special provisions, such as enabling debtors to request the exclusion of their primary residence from realization of their assets, and the possibility of a judicial settlement without debt relief where a debtor is temporarily unable to service their debt.[21] However the proposed framework needs to be clear in providing the right incentives for debtors falling within its scope to service their debts appropriately. It should also contain sufficient safeguards to avoid moral hazard, as this could have serious adverse consequences on banks' capital and liquidity positions, as well as on the overall cost of financing. The current proposal for a personal debt restructuring law will be in line with international best practice to ensure that credit discipline is maintained, that creditor and consumer rights are protected, and that relevant information concerning borrowers' track records is preserved.

In addition, Law 3816/2010 on restructuring of business and professional debts owed to credit institutions seeks to introduce one-off temporary measures intended to enhance liquidity in the market by supporting, in particular, business, professional and agricultural activities. The law is aimed at enabling people engaged in these activities who are in financial difficulties to restructure their overdue debts towards banks, thus providing liquidity support and ensuring the viability of their activities under the current adverse economic circumstances. The law is an interim measure providing for a limited period for people that have already entered into loan or credit agreements with banks to apply to have their debts restructured if such debts have become overdue before the application of the law. Moreover, on the basis of specific criteria, the law also provides for one-off repayment arrangements in relation to debts that have not become overdue (performing debts).[22] Furthermore, the law amends the existing legal framework on the recording and processing of credit bureau data in an attempt to strike a balance between the availability of information on debtors, which is necessary for accurate assessment of credit risk, and the unwarranted exclusion of debtors from access to credit necessary for the pursuit of economic activities.

Financial regulation: investment services

In the late 1990s the investment sector underwent major changes both in terms of privatization of available markets and infrastructures[23] and the implementation of new electronic systems and markets.[24] Those structural changes were completed in 2003 with privatization of the Athens Exchange, the transfer of the Greek state's remaining stake to seven Greek banks and the transfer of supervisory responsibilities to the Hellenic Capital Market Commission (HCMC). Those structural changes were followed by a complete modernization of capital markets and investment services law, mainly due to the implementation of the EU financial services action plan. Between 2004 and 2007 all major financial services directives, including the UCITS directive (current EU legislation for investment funds),[25] Market Abuse Directive,[26] Prospectus Directive,[27] Transparency Directive[28] and MiFID,[29] with their implementation measures, were transposed into Greek law.

The Hellenic Capital Market Commission is responsible for monitoring compliance with the provisions of investment law. The objectives of the HCMC are to ensure the integrity of the market, to mitigate systemic risks, and to protect investors by increasing transparency. The HCMC is a public body enjoying operational and administrative independence. It supervises, among others, brokerage firms, investment firms, mutual fund management firms, portfolio investment companies, real estate investment trusts and financial intermediation firms. It also oversees compliance of Athens Stock Exchange (ASE) listed companies with capital market legislation. The HCMC is responsible for the approval of prospectuses, as far as investor requirements to receive complete information during public offerings and the listing of securities in organized markets is concerned. Entities and organizations subject to supervision by the HCMC also include regulated markets, clearing houses and their administrators, such as the Athens Stock Exchange and Hellenic Exchanges, the entity responsible for the clearing and settlement of transactions on securities and derivatives, as well as investor indemnity and transaction security schemes, such as the Common Guarantee Fund and the Supplementary Fund. The Commission is endowed with the authority to impose administrative sanctions (suspension and revocation of licence, trading halts, imposition of fines) on any supervised legal and physical entities that violate capital market law. Finally, the Capital Market Commission enjoys comprehensive regulatory powers, which encompass both prudential and conduct-of-business matters. However, while the responsibilities of the HCMC are broadly similar to those of the Bank of Greece (BoG) in relation to banks, it should be noted that the former is much more heavily concerned with conduct-of-business matters, while the latter focuses on prudential issues. This difference in regulatory approach was further emphasized with the implementation of MiFID, which provides for extensive regulation of the conduct of business of investment firms and credit institutions when providing investment services, while no such detailed rules exist with regard to banking services.[30]

2007 was a turning point for financial markets and investment services regulation with the transposition of MiFID into Greek legislation by means of Law 3606/2007. Under Law 3606/2007 the Commission issued nine regulations, which incorporate the executive measures laid out by MiFID and include:

a) the code of conduct for investment firms
b) the minimum organizational requirements for investment firms;
c) the evaluation of qualifying holdings;
d) the fitness test applied to managers and directors of entities licensed under Directives in the financial field;
e) the registration of tied agents in the public register;
f) the exemptions from the transparency requirements;
g) the transaction disclosure and information recording obligations;
h) the conditions for the authorization of regulated markets; and
i) the bookkeeping obligations of financial intermediation firms.

The incorporation of MiFID into Greek law also closed a noteworthy gap in the HCMC's regulatory powers which concerns credit institutions offering investment services. Under the new rules HCMC supervises credit institutions when providing investment services. However, HCMC powers are only limited to conduct of business rules, while ongoing supervision of organizational matters related to the provision of investment services by credit institutions remains with the BoG.

Another significant step made was the transposition into Greek legislation of EU Directives 2006/48/EC and 2006/49/EC on the capital adequacy of credit institutions and investment firms, by means of Law 3601/2007. Under Law 3601/2007, the Hellenic Commission issued six regulations, which incorporate the Directives' executive measures and establish the operating rules for the calculation of the capital adequacy requirements of investment firms.

With the implementation of MiFID, the last barriers to the entry of remote members to the Athens Exchange were removed. In addition, although MiFID's scope does not extend to post-trading activities, it acknowledges as a key component of market integration the abolition of any such barriers by establishing a right of access for all intermediaries, including remote members, to a Central Counter Party (CCP) clearing and settlement system of their choice for the finalization of their transactions in an organized market, provided that certain prudential requirements are met. [31] MiFID abolished the previous monopoly under which post-trading activities in Greece's securities and derivatives markets were only open to Greek Central Securities Depositories (CSD) and to Athens Derivatives Exchange Clearing House (ADECH) respectively.[32] The new regime is based on the principle of licence. However, this liberalization has not yet resulted in new players entering the game, and HELEX group still has a monopoly in post-trading.

The effects of MiFID legislation on Athens Exchange markets are similar. Market operators need to be licenced by HCMC, and the legal monopoly of Athens Exchange gave it the roles of authorization and prudential supervision regime for market operators. Again, this liberalization did not result in new players entering the game, and HELEX group still provides monopolistic services in market services, in shares, corporate bonds and derivative products.[33] This monopolistic approach can, among other reasons, be attributed to the fact that Greece operates a direct holding system for securities in listed companies. Securities are dematerialized, and are recorded by HELEX to individual accounts for each investor, while no omnibus accounts are recognized by the system. Similarly, clearing and settlement in derivatives is performed at an investor level with the latter being the counterparty of HELEX to the derivative contract, which acts for that purpose as a CCP. However, as far as the latter is concerned, with the incorporation of MiFID into Greek law, no investors can be counterparties in a central counterparty system.[34] This means that the structure of the current system may be found to be incompatible with EU law. Moreover, the relevant rules of Law 2533/1997 were abolished in February 2009, when the interim period for the enactment of the new derivatives regulation had expired.[35] No such regulation has been issued yet, which means that for the time being there is a legal gap and there is no legal basis for the present clearing and settlement system on derivatives.

Finally, a major development over the past few years, at least in terms of infrastructures, has been the enactment of the framework for the operation of other financial products such as Exchange Traded

Funds (ETFs) and structured products, which, however, have seen little success to date. In addition market infrastructures and the security of transactions were reinforced through continuous improvements in the rulebook of the ASE markets and the regulation for the clearing and settlement of transactions on securities and derivatives. This has enabled the implementation of the provisions on Markets in Financial Instruments established by Law 3606/2007, through the revision of the framework governing the operation of the Supplementary Fund for Clearing. The main purposes of this are to rationalize member contributions, the method for calculating customer order limits, the management of the Fund's cash reserves, and the size of the Common Guarantee Fund, in a manner that does not burden supervised firms with increased operating costs. In addition the alternative market of the Athens Stock Exchange (EN.A) was granted a licence to operate as a Multilateral Trading Facility (MTF). This new non-regulated market is not subject to the strict admission and ongoing requirements that apply in regulated markets. The EN.A Rulebook is notified to the HCMC, which is responsible for supervision, particularly on issues concerning market abuse, public offerings and prospectus requirements.

Both the global financial crisis and the new wave of Greek budget crisis caused HCMC to redefine its approach on short selling with, in 2007, the abolition of the tick rule, and the considerable slackening of the obligation to borrow in advance the securities sold short. Short selling had been fully liberalized until the first wave of the global financial crisis when HCMC, like other regulators around the world, temporarily banned it. Short selling bans were recently lifted,[36] only to be re-imposed following the Greek budgetary crisis.[37]

Prospects – the way forward

With Greece experiencing the first domestic recession since the early 1990s and with a considerable lack of confidence in the Greek economy, a rather subdued private sector credit expansion and a public sector trying to address chronic fiscal imbalances, the medium-term outlook for the financial sector looks challenging. For the financial sector, reliant on international finance markets, the current difficulties mean that financial institutions must revise their strategies to ensure quality in lending and investment activities. In addition the current budgetary crisis will undoubtedly be the main driving force for changes in financial regulation. This means that financial sector policies need to maintain stability. Supervisors and the government will need to further strengthen and clarify the key elements of Greece's supervisory and financial crisis framework to assist the financial system through this period of lower growth and limited access to foreign markets. However such extraordinary measures cannot override the application of normal EU company law and must respect the Greek constitution.

The immediate challenge for the financial sector is to manage carefully the current tight liquidity conditions. For supervisors this means intensified supervision including, but not limited to, faster and more frequent data reporting, and further development of a comprehensive framework for regularly stress-testing financial institutions. However, attention should also be given to the lack of an adequate set of rules on the conduct of business in the provision of financial services other than investment services. The division of regulation between investment and banking services does not seem to be an appropriate way to regulate institutions that provide cross-sector services. One way to mitigate this problem and also achieve the necessary economies of scale and scope to increase the resources dedicated to financial supervision, is to opt for a single financial authority, as is the case in the UK or Germany. Another approach would be to follow recent developments and divide supervision between two cross-sector supervisors (Hadjiemmanuil, 2008): a) a prudential supervisor (for example, the Bank of Greece) who would be responsible for supervising the financial and organizational soundness of financial institutions; and b) a conduct-of-business supervisor (for example, HCMC with additional powers at this level) who would be responsible for the protection of users of financial services (investors, borrowers, etc.). In addition HCMC would still act as the listing authority.

Notes

1. On 30 April nine Greek banks including National Bank of Greece SA, the country's largest lender, had their credit ratings lowered by Moody's Investors Service, three days after Standard & Poor's cut their debt to junk.
2. 11 July 2010.
3. 709.20 points (11 July 2010).
4. OJ L 177/30.6.2006.
5. OJ L 177/30.6.2006.
6. Electronic Secondary Market for Securities°(HΔAT).
7. System for Monitoring Transactions in Book-Entry Securities.
8. SMART (System for Money Settlement of Athex Reconciled Transactions).
9. Set out in law 3601/2007.
10. Mainly through Acts of Governor.
11. 2008/48/EC L 133, 22 May 2008.
12. Art. 1 of the law.

13. Art. 2 of the law.
14. Art. 3 of the law.
15. Art. 40, para. 1 of the second Company law directive (77/91/ EEC) requires a qualified majority in the form of an extraordinary resolution.
16. Art. 15 of the same directive (Art. 44a of Law 2190/190).
17. *Pafitis and others* v *Trapeza Kentrikis Ellados A.E.* (C-441/93), para. 40.
18. See also ECJ judgments C-367/96, *Alexandros Kefalas and others* v *Elliniko Dimosio (Greek State) and Organismos Oikonomikis Anasygkrotisis Epicheiriseon AE (OAE)* of 12 May 1998; C-381/89, *Syndesmos Melon tis Eleftheras Evangelikis Ekklissias and others* v *Greek State and others* of 24 March 1992; C-134/91 and C-135/91, *Kerafina-Keramische-und Finanz Holding AG and Vioktimatiki AEVE* v *Hellenic Republic and Organismos Oikonomikis Anasygkrotissis Epicheirisseon AE* of 12 November 1992; C- 19/90 and C 20-90, *Marina Karella and Nicolas Karellas* v *Minister for Industry, Energy and Technology and Organismos Anasygkrotiseos Epicheiriseon AE* of 30 May 1991.
19. N 560/2008 support measures for the credit institutions in Greece.
20. However, the credit institution should not be allowed to use reserves to book a profit.
21. Articles 9 and 10 of the draft law.
22. Such measures include: i) a one-year period of grace with a respective extension of the contractual term of the loan and capitalization of interest on expiry of the period; (ii) a two-year suspension of repayments of outstanding capital with a respective extension of the contractual term of the loan and payment of interest over the suspension period in accordance with the interest periodicity provided for in the agreement; or (iii) a three-year extension of the contractual term of the loan. In accordance with Article 2(4) of the law, applications for debt repayment must also be submitted within a specific time period.
23. During 1997 to– 1999, the Athens Exchange was partly privatized.
24. In 1999 the Integrated Automated Trading System (OASIS) along with Dematerialised Securities System (DSS) was implemented while, during the same year, the Athens Derivatives Exchange (ADEX) and the Athens Derivatives Exchange Clearing House (ADECH) began operation.
25. Law 3281/2004.
26. Law 3340/2005.
27. Law 3401/2005.
28. Law 3556/2007.
29. Law 3606/2007.
30. See above.
31. See Arts 34 ss of MiFID and Arts 72 ss of Law 3606/2007 which transposed the relevant MiFID provisions.
32. Now both have been merged with Hellenic Exchanges SA (HELEX), the listed holding company of Athens Exchange.
33. Apart from ASE the only other organized market in Greece.
34. Art. 75 of Law 3606/2007
35. Art. 85, para. 6 of Law 3606/2007
36. Decision 1/509/15.5.2009, HCMC, which also provided a number of additional requirements in terms of market disclosure and HCMC notification of uncovered positions, etc.
37. Decision 548/28.4.2010 HCMC.

References

Asimakopoulos, I.G., Brissimis, S.N. and Delis, M.D. (2008) 'Efficiency in the Greek banking system and its determinant factors', *Bank of Greece Economic Bulletin*, 30: 7–34 (in Greek).

Athanasoglou, P.P. and Brissimis, S.N. (2004) 'The impact of M&As on the efficiency of banks in Greece', *Bank of Greece Economic Bulletin*, 22: 7–34 (in Greek).

Athanasoglou, P., Georgiou, E. and Staikouras, C. (2008) 'Assessing Output and Productivity Growth in the Banking Industry', *Bank of Greece Working Papers*, no 92.

Bank of Greece (2010) *Greece - Memorandum of Economic and Financial Policies*, 3 May 2010.

Bryant, R.C., Garganas, N.C. and Tavlas, G.S. (2001) *Greece's Economic Performance and Prospects*, Bank of Greece and the Brookings Institution, pp. 43–95.

Eichengreen, B. and Gibson, H.D. (2001) 'Greek Banking at the Dawn of the New Millennium', in R.C. Bryant, N.C. Garganas and G.S. Tavlas (2001) *Greece's Economic Performance and Prospects*. Bank of Greece and the Brookings Institution, pp. 545–97.

Hadjiemmanuil, C. (2008) *Organisational structure of supervision of the Financial Sector: an international debate. A single supervisory authority for financial sector.* Athens: Nomiki Vivliothiki (in Greek).

Halkos, G.E. and Salamouris, D.S. (2004) 'Efficiency measurement of the Greek commercial banks with the use of financial ratios: a data envelopment analysis approach', *Management Accounting Research*, 15: 201–24.

Mylonidis, N. and Kelkinova, I. (2005) 'Merging Activity in the Greek Banking System: A Financial Accounting Perspective', *South Eastern Europe Journal of Economics*, 1: 121–44.

Noulas, A. (1997) 'Productivity growth in the Hellenic banking industry: state versus private banks', *Applied Financial Economics*, 7: 223–8.

Rezitis, A.N. (2006) 'Productivity growth in the Greek banking industry: A nonparametric approach', *Journal of Applied Economics*, 9(1): 119–38.

Tsionas, E.G., Lolos, S.E.G. and Christopoulos, D.K. (2003) 'The performance of the Greek banking system in view of the EMU: results from a non-parametric approach', *Economic Modelling*, 20: 571–92.

4
Development
The Role of the Public Sector and Firms in Economic Development[1]

Kyriakos Hatzaras

Overview

The EU's cohesion policy has supported the development of its peripheral member states and regions through multi-annual national Community Support Frameworks (CSFs) co-financed by the EU and national governments. The Integrated Mediterranean Programmes (IMPs), the Single European Act (SEA) and subsequent reforms of cohesion policy regulations were the basis for collaboration on economic and development social policies for Europe's regions with EU, national and sub-national government and examine partner organizations. In this multi-level governance framework, the mobilization of business actors and the development of sub-national governance were identified as key priorities. Co-operation between government and private entrepreneurship has been understood as essential in promoting national and regional economic growth. At the time of the recent economic crisis in Greece, twenty-five years after the IMPs and the SEA, the earlier dominant role of the state in economic development appears transformed as central and sub-national government and wider public sector organizations emerge as the principal recipients of funding, programme and project management experience, having a leading role in the development process stimulated by cohesion policy. By contrast, private firms have had a fragmented participation in the process, mainly as contractors in the implementation of specific projects. Based on quantitative data from Greek national and regional programmes of the second (1994–1999/2001) and third (2000–2006/2008) EU programming periods, this chapter examines the leading role of public organizations in development. On this basis, it suggests that the earlier dominant role of the state in the Greek economy has now been transformed, and concludes with recommendations.

More specifically, this chapter looks at the trajectory of Greece's economic development from a longitudinal, inter-temporal perspective. The main aim is to explore an area which has thus far eluded policy makers and scholars looking at countries of the European periphery, that of the transformation of the state's role in the pursuit of economic growth. Based on an institutional economics approach and interpretation of quantitative data from Greek cohesion policy programmes, this chapter puts forward the premise that this transformed role of the state is reflected in formal and informal constraints in governance, the economy, society and culture. The chapter discusses how the earlier dominant role of the state from post-WWII until the 1980s has been transformed as facilitated by the EU cohesion policy, and on the implications of this new role.

Socio-economic cohesion has only recently emerged as a key policy area of the EU. The Structural Funds (SFs) predate the formulation of an integrated structural, regional or cohesion policy. The European Social Fund (ESF) was established in 1957 with a focus on human resources development, and the European Regional Development Fund (ERDF) was created in 1975 to support infrastructure projects. The Cohesion Fund, available to less developed member states of the EU, was established in 1994; the European Agriculture Guidance and Guarantee Fund (EAGGF) and the Financial Instrument for Fisheries Guidance (FIFG) were launched in 1962 and 1992 respectively, and they no longer fund EU cohesion policy programmes. The co-financing of national and regional multi-annual programmes termed national Community Support Frameworks (CSFs) by SFs and national funds constituted an institutional innovation in the provisions of the Single European Act (SEA) of 1987, and the new policy delivery framework established in 1988. The SEA established socioeconomic cohesion as an EU policy objective, implying a process of convergence based on higher economic growth on behalf of member states and regions lagging behind. The 1988 review of the SF regulations provided for the joint involvement of EU, national and sub-national authorities in policy making, and doubled available finance for the second programming period of 1994–1999/2001. These policy initiatives drew attention to cohesion policy programmes supporting economic and social development carried out in several EU member states and regions during the 1990s.

Additionally, cohesion policy objectives and financing were further highlighted in the debates on the EU budget after 1999 due to the EU's eastern enlargement. The pre-accession strategy for the fifth enlargement of 2004 drew on three funding instruments aimed at the improvement of the socioeconomic infrastructure of ten new member states. As well as the inclusion of most regions of these states, the Lisbon goals were also introduced in the framework of cohesion policy for the fourth programming period of 2007–13, highlighting the importance of knowledge and employment generation for Europe in the modern era of global competitiveness. These developments led cohesion policy expenditure to become second only to that of the Common Agricultural Policy (CAP), and placed cohesion firmly on the EU policy-making agenda. The inclusion of the formerly centrally-planned economies of the east in the EU's economic system has brought to the fore a long-standing question for Europe's underdeveloped areas: has the state been in retreat before further economic modernization and the necessarily ultimate aim of cohesion policy, that of economic and social development?

It is also important to consider the relative lack of attention that has been paid to these issues in relevant publications by leading senior scholarship and international organizations active in this field. At best, analyses highlight the importance of private sector engagement and the growth of private capital mobilization in the implementation framework of national CSFs, nationwide sectoral or regional programmes (see for example Nanetti, 1996:66–7; Leonardi, 2005; CEC, 2001; OECD, 2002:175–8; CEC, 2004). However, as we shall see, private capital mobilization is not synonymous with balanced participation by the private sector in the pursuit of economic growth in the national or regional context. Nonetheless, in fairness to the European socialists, one point needs to be advanced in this brief account of the reasons for lack of attention to a transformed role for the state. In 1986, the European Commission (EC) under Jacques Delors established a new regional policy framework on the basis of the SEA, through which the provisions of the Treaty of Rome on the reduction of 'differences existing between the various regions and the backwardness of the less favoured regions' and, further, the 'harmonious development of economic activities, a continuous and balanced expansion' (Dunford *et al.*, 2001:1) would be pursued. This policy was intended as a solidarity cushion for underdeveloped regions against the imminent adverse consequences of the Single Market and Economic and Monetary Union (EMU), and a support for socioeconomic convergence, regional governance and local democracy across the periphery.

The chapter's argument proceeds as follows. The next section sets out the earlier dominant role of the state in the economy of countries at the European periphery, and discusses the nature of its transformation, namely the enhancement of central and sub-national state structures. Empirical data on cohesion policy co-financed programmes illustrate how central and sub-national public organizations have taken advantage of funding and expertise through their appointed roles in the cohesion policy delivery framework since 1988. These data further exemplify how, in the Greek case, these organizations have played a leading role in the national and regional development process, in contrast to the lesser role of a fragmented private sector.

The economic role of the state in the periphery of Europe

Between the early 1950s and the mid-1970s, countries at the European periphery pursued Keynesian national economic policies to attain economic growth and development. The key and common feature has been a centralized (totalitarian in Spain, Portugal and in Greece after 1967) governance system that harnessed production and resource allocation through a plethora of regulatory instruments such as grants, loans and subsidies, investment control and approval, national policies involving subsidies to regional business and the creation of industrial development poles.[2] After the mid-1970s, the crisis of the national macroeconomic management model in these countries was met by a growth of the welfare state and associated public expenditure, notably in Italy and Greece. At its extremes, extensive and constitutionally irreversible nationalization of enterprises took place in Portugal on the restoration of democracy (Roccas and Padoa-Schioppa, 2001:40–5). Entrepreneurship and private initiative were hindered by being subject to state favouritism and control by a large bureaucracy, while the extensive role of the state in the economy enlarged the scope for inferior public service delivery and clientelism until the mid-1990s (Roccas and Padoa-Schioppa, 2001:40–5; Amato, 1996: 158–60). Notwithstanding the somewhat different example set by Spain, where an export-led growth model and successive reforms pursued by the Spanish socialists in the 1980s created the foundations for rapid convergence with the European core, this extensive state economic dominance has had implications for the macro-economy and competitiveness into the 1990s for countries at the periphery like Greece and Portugal that needed to embark on major modernization programmes towards the attainment of the Maastricht criteria and EMU.

This earlier state-led economic growth paradigm in the periphery occurred in the global context of the Fordist model of production, where demand and supply grew in a managed manner through the pursuit of national Keynesian macroeconomic policies. In each domestic context, policies redressing adverse regional socioeconomic outcomes were managed within the confines of the nation state. The incentive for the internationalization, or 'Europeanization', of regional policy in the EU and its advancement thereafter was provided by the crisis of Fordism that ensued across the western world in the 1970s. Western Europe was lagging behind the US and Japan in economic performance after a decade of monetary and fiscal policies adopted single-handedly by individual governments in their attempts to remedy their national macroeconomic and competitiveness issues. It was thought that growth challenges in the post-Fordist era would be better tackled if the EU decisively embraced the completion of its internal market and monetary union. At the same time, these advanced forms of economic integration were seen as posing a risk of potential socioeconomic depletion through migration to underdeveloped member states and regions. Moreover, successful post-Fordist growth paradigms entailed new forms of industrial organization based on skill and flexibility in production, and were now spatially delimited in regions and localities. Product and service innovation based on knowledge creation, networking among small and medium-sized firms (SMEs), and local governance supplying a range of collective public goods conducive to the success of networked, knowledge-based firms were seen as significant new features of regional growth and recognized as new developmental determinants (Ottaviano and Puga, 1996:19–21, 25; Asheim and Dunford, 1997:449; Garmise, 1998; Maskell and Malmberg, 1999a:5–8, 1999b:11–16; Fujita and Thisse, 2002:8–9).

Cohesion policy was first 'europeanized' with the creation of the European Regional Development Fund (ERDF) in 1975. This had been a purely intergovernmental initiative involving the aggregation of finance at EU level, its re-distribution among member states and use at the discretion of each national government. In its first ten years, the ERDF was a remedial instrument for the short-term alleviation of shocks to specialized regional industrial production associated with further economic integration, operating largely irrespective of the attributes of specific regions (see Nanetti, 1996:62–4; Leonardi, 2005:34, 40–8, 65–6). However, two further developments served to underline the need for a more elaborate form of regional policy to be pursued at EU level. The increasing competitive pressures on European business due to the unremitting internationalization of production and the southern enlargement of the EU with Greece in 1981and Spain and Portugal in 1986, led to the first experimental trials of multi-dimensional programmes in Belfast, Naples and Lozere, to the launch of IMPs benefitting Greek, southern Italian and Mediterranean French regions and ultimately, to the SEA. Among other forms of institutional innovation, such as the timetable for the completion of the Single Market, expansion of the role of the European Parliament, and majority voting, the SEA formally endorsed cohesion as a political aim of the EU to be pursued through the use of the SFs (Nanetti, 1996:59–64; Leonardi, 2005:40–8).

The review of SF regulations in 1988 set out the delivery framework for EU cohesion policy.[3] This involved a re-organization of priorities for regional aid and the introduction of the new principles of *partnership* and *additionality*. A regional classification was put together by the EC according to regions' purchasing power and key aspects of their production structures. Geographical delimitations of the NUTS2 area (Nomenclature of Territorial Units for Statistics, 2nd level) taxonomy and income per capita less than 75 per cent of EU average were assigned the status Objective 1, while regions facing industrial decline, youth or long-term unemployment, or rural development challenges were classified as Objectives 2, 3, 4 and 5 respectively. In the cases of peripheral countries where the whole or large parts of the territory were classified under Objective 1, Single Programming Documents (SPDs) constituted the national CSF of that member state. Through the CSFs, cohesion policy was to be implemented nationwide and in individual regions in an integrated manner over specified periods,[4] reflecting the initial experimentation of multi-dimensional programming through synergy among SFs.[5] Moreover, the notion of *partnership* referred to the potential for collaboration which the policy delivery framework offered to central and sub-national government, business associations and other socio-economic organizations in member states (Leonardi, 1992:2). These actors were invited to become involved in the design of policies of immediate relevance to their sectoral or local constituencies. The new regulations required that development programmes be prepared by the central government of each member state in the form of single programming documents (SPDs), based on consultation with sub-national governance, economic, social and cultural organizations, and the EC. *Additionality* in funding reflected the tripartite new collaborative structure, in that these programmes were to be financed through a combination of SF, member state[6] and private sector funds.

The principle institutional innovation introduced by cohesion policy has been the significant role of regions as units of area *and* governance. As the earlier dominant role of central state government machinery managing the national macro-economy declined due to the growth of international business, successful new paradigms of industrial production were seen to be regionally delimited, hingeing on the growth of SMEs, and based on the provision of collective goods such as education and training, finance, business restructuring and export support (Dunford and Perrons, 1992).[7] By 1990, it was thought that sub-national governance would be best suited to undertake this role of collective goods provision in the regional context (see Leonardi and Garmise, 1992:265–9; Nanetti, 1996:70–3). The enhancement of regional and local self-government was thus seen as contributing to economic efficiency and the promotion of democratic governance, and was regarded as the primary catalyst of economic growth and social development in Europe. It has been on this rationale and, crucially, on the basis of the partnership principle, that cohesion policy has promoted *regionalization* in the European periphery. Cohesion policy created opportunities for new formal and/or informal powers to be directly delegated or contested on behalf of existing sub-national regional governments, and for the creation of new administrative and planning organizations. This institutional re-organization favouring the regions has been a common experience across cohesion countries, and has formed part of the wider framework of European integration. It led to a re-ordering in member states of the previous institutional framework between national and regional levels in the three distinct fields of public life, namely governance, the economy, society and culture (see Rokkan and Urwin, 1983:1–17). Scholars who pioneered this new policy approach conceptualized an economic and social development path for European regions and localities stemming from their earlier social and historical backdrop. This path, illustrated in Figure 4.1, centred on institutional decentralization and the transfer of powers to regions, the diffusion of entrepreneurship based on new forms of industrial organization favouring the growth of SMEs and, crucially, on the interplay between the two (Nanetti, 1988, 1996:72–3; Leonardi and Garmise, 1992; Leonardi, 1995).

This policy approach emphasized the important role of the private sector from the start. A notable example was the Palermo ministerial conference organized by the 1988 Italian EU Presidency, where the empowerment of sub-national socioeconomic actors, a plan to study[8] the regional situation *vis-à-vis* existing EU policies and the advent of the Single Market were discussed. Private business actors, such as entrepreneurs, financial organizations, professional associations, trade unions and so on, were seen as the vital socioeconomic forces' that would ultimately determine 'the success or failure of development initiatives in peripheral areas' (Leonardi, 1992:5–6). Furthermore, the report on a preferred strategy for social and economic cohesion in Europe after 1992, which the European

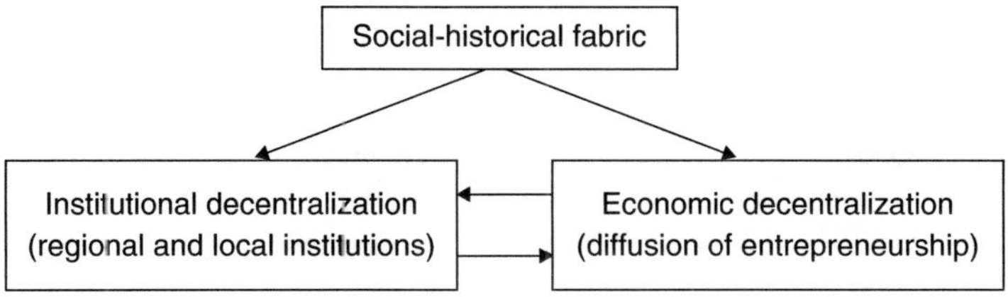

Figure 4.1 Model of local development
Source: Adapted from Nanetti (1988).

Parliament commissioned from the National Institute of Economic and Social Research in London, stressed the importance of the direct involvement of the private sector in the implementation of cohesion policy (Begg and Mayes, 1991:94, 97). Another example has been the emphasis on the uneven participation of the private sector in peripheral countries in the development process stimulated by the first CSFs (Nanetti, 1996:73–9). However, a prominent role was still ascribed to sub-national governance. Regional governments were seen as having scope to act in various concurrent roles in the regional and local development process, for example, as facilitator, stimulator, contributor and co-ordinator of economic activity; no grounds were seen for the assumption of such roles either by non-governmental organizations or the private sector (Nanetti, 1996:73–85). Moreover, the weak capacity of municipalities and communities to participate in the development process stimulated by cohesion policy (see, for example, Nanetti, 1996:86; Hatzaras, 2005:12), led to regional governments often becoming the primary point of reference for implementation of cohesion programmes (see, for example, Morata and Muñoz, 1996:212–7; Hatzaras, 2005).

Evidence from developed EU countries and regions suggests that partnership between sub-national governance and private business organizations has fared well from 1985 to the present period of 2007–13, notably in Britain and Germany (see Roberts, 2000:289–91; Thielemann, 2002:53). By contrast, it has been highly problematic in the EU periphery (Papageorgiou and Verney, 1992:144–7; Ioakimidis, 1996b:353; Morata and Muñoz, 1996:206–8; Nanetti, 1996:75–6).[9] During the second programming period of 1994–99/2002, the mobilization of private capital as part of the total CSF expenditure in each member state has seen a substantial increase compared to 1989–93. Private funds expended as part of CSFs totalled €8.9bn between 1994 and 2002, compared to €1.1bn during 1989–93. Across eligible areas, private capital mobilization increased from €33.2bn to €111.5bn; the highest increases were noted in Germany, Spain and Italy, while Ireland and Portugal witnessed a more modest increase to private capital mobilization than Greece (Leonardi, 2005:55–9). However, these increases alone cannot confirm the attainment of an economic development process featuring an equitable role for business in peripheral economies. Hence the important questions with regard to economic growth and social development pursued by cohesion policy in the EU periphery remain: what has been the exact nature of the private sector's involvement in the tripartite governance structure and partnership for development that was put in place in 1988? Has the state been in retreat before further economic liberalization in the EU periphery? Given the earlier economic structure of peripheral countries, these are important questions for the aims and delivery framework of cohesion policy.

The literature that has looked at cohesion policy implementation in EU peripheral regions since the IMPs and fieldwork research for this work carried out in Greece suggest a negative response to these questions. Overall, regional policy and associated expenditure are seen to have contributed to efficiency gains and convergence by peripheral regions through regionalized interventions, that is, targeting resources at the appropriate level of area and governance (CEC, 2001:xx–xxii; CEC, 2004:xvii–xxiii; Leonardi, 2005:104 6). However, the recent economic crisis in the EU periphery, exemplified by the difficulties of Greece and Spain, suggests a mismatch between the intent and contribution of cohesion policy, and an economic and social development process linked to higher national and regional competitiveness. The evidence of two regional and two national programmes implemented in the period 1994–2010 confirm the following. In serving the cohesion policy strategic aim of mobilizing and involving sub-national social and economic actors and realizing the tripartite development partnership, these programmes have strengthened central government, sub-national state and wider public sector organizations, such as central and sub-national state agencies, state education and research, state-supported professional organizations and others. These organizations had long been the key potential partners in the periphery, created out of the earlier state-led growth and development trajectory. Since 1985, they have been the entities that have acted as national and regional programme beneficiaries. As we shall see, they have benefited extensively in terms of finance, policy expertise, and programme and project management experience through their substantial role in and exposure to cohesion policy delivery and through their visibility as modern organizations anchored in the EU policy context and implementing key initiatives at the national and sub-national levels (see CEC, 2004:xvii).

By contrast, the private sector has only seen private investments co-financed through the cohesion policy delivery framework. At the sub-national level, business organizations have taken the role of contractor/implementer of prescribed set-piece programmes, sub-programmes, projects and actions. Viewed from an institutional perspective, the private sector in Greece has had a secondary role in the pursuit of growth and development. This has taken place in a domestic context where a key aspect of the institutional framework is the norm of looking to the state to provide goods which have long been perceived as 'public', and of which the state has long been the sole provider. The Greek political and economic institutional framework is often described as 'statist': the state as a provider of goods and facilitator of economic exchange has long been a key of the mental construct of citizens in relation to their political, economic, social and cultural activity (see Ioakimidis, 2001:76–9). At the end of the first period of 1989–93, private sector involvement in the development process was already noted as low (Nanetti, 1996:86). As shown in Figure 4.2, the development trajectory in Greece has entailed a secondary role for business and has largely been one of central and sub-national state

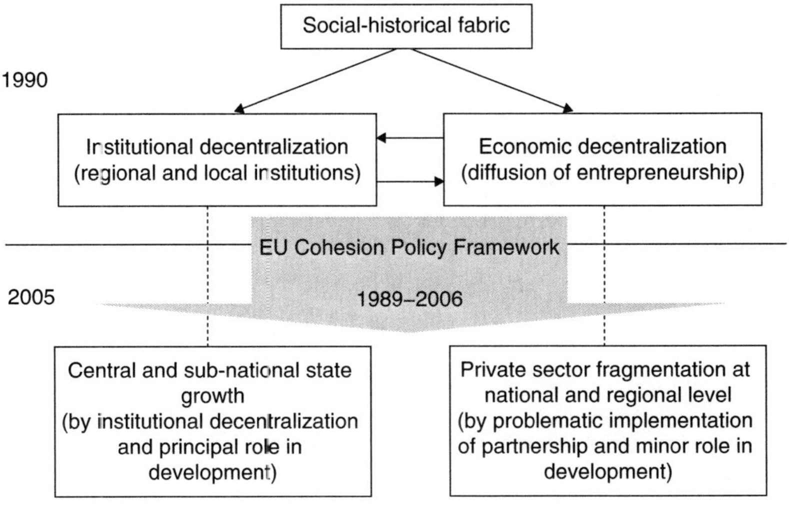

Figure 4.2 The socioeconomic trajectory of Greece

growth, facilitated by the EU cohesion policy delivery framework of the period 1985–2008.

The empirical reality

Evidence in support of the above hypothesis has been visible on the ground in earlier policy implementation periods than those relevant to our fieldwork research. The reality that private business actors needed to engage with the cohesion policy framework as much as EU member states' administrations was already apparent during the first programming period of 1989 –93. Involvement of business initiative in regional development was limited during this period across the periphery, due to the small size and loose organization of the private sector (Nanetti, 1996:75–6). By contrast, the state was already consolidating and expanding its earlier role in the pursuit of economic growth, as central and sub-national government organizations put together development plans focused on delivering infrastructure projects, often at the expense of other and new determinants of socioeconomic development. In some cases, SF grants would be made available solely to public sector organizations, for example, the 1989–93 SME programme in central Macedonia (Morata and Muñoz, 1996:206–8; Nanetti, 1996:78). The two subsequent reviews of cohesion policy and SF regulations in 1993 and 1999, ahead of the second and third periods respectively, focused on budgetary control, transparency and delivery, and therefore did not alter the macro-level development trajectory of the European periphery shown in Figure 4.2. The discussion that follows on two regional and two sectoral programmes implemented in the Greek context during the second and third programming periods illustrates the main features of this trajectory.

Greece and its thirteen regions have been classified as Objective 1 territories under cohesion policy. The entire country had had an average income per capita of less than 75 per cent of EU average ever since it became an EU member in 1981. Before accession, European leaders were heralding the inclusion of the mother of European civilization inside the European family, while domestic political discourse saw animated debates on the orientation of Greece between East and West, the alleged intervention in the nation's affairs by the latter in the seven-year military junta and the conflict in Cyprus in 1974. The challenges and actuality of EU membership were hardly discussed. At the same time, pre-accession offered Greece a chance to stabilize its restored democracy, an early *rapprochement* of its administration with European institutions, and a frame of reference for its foreign policy (Ioakimidis, 1996a:36).

Greece's system of government has traditionally been highly centralized, featuring two local government tiers of (a) municipalities and communities (M&Cs) and (b) prefectures or districts (*nomoi*). A regional government tier was introduced in 1986, as the domestic response to the IMPs and cohesion policy. Further minor modifications in subnational governance and the cohesion policy implementation structure have not compromised the long-standing *status quo*, with the Hellenic Republic remaining a highly centralized politico-administrative system. The capital area of Attica is the seat of central government, the parliament, the judiciary, most of the public administration and wider public sector organizations and, as a result of the state-led growth trajectory since WWII, has developed a predominant position within public life in Greece. The 1980s was a decade of policy experimentation to the detriment of the Greek macro-economy and competitiveness (Alogoskoufis, 2000:133–45; Ioakimidis, 1996a:36; Pagoulatos, 2001:193–4; Roccas and Padoa-Schioppa, 2001:57–9). A short interval of conservative government that followed saw a forceful, and thus failed, approach to reforms needed to limit the role of the state in the domestic economy, which had evolved into an over-centralized entity of gigantic proportions (Ioakimidis, 1996a:40, Alogoskoufis, 2000:141–2; Ioakimidis, 2001:76–9; Roccas and Padoa-Schioppa, 2001:52, 57–9). Greece began the second EU programming period in 1994 with a persistent divergence of income and competitiveness from the rest of the EU, and domestic macroeconomic instability.

Greece's second CSF (CSFII) was therefore seen as a significant policy instrument for growth and development across its national territory. CSFII was expected to form a cornerstone in the quest for the reversal of economic decline and nominal and real convergence with developed EU areas (CEC, 1994:18–20). The CSF strategic plan sought to address several key features of Greece's underdevelopment: structural weaknesses and macroeconomic deterioration; deficiency in basic infrastructures; and the long period of underinvestment in human capital and regional disparities among Greek regions. Total funding (CSFII complemented by the Cohesion Fund) availability for the period was set at €32.8bn, while total funding earmarked for the thirteen Regional Operational Programmes (ROPs) was €7.4bn (CEC, 1994:99–108). The following section looks at two ROPs, parts of Greece's CSFII, in two northern border regions. These are (i) Central Macedonia, an urbanized region with a relatively diversified economy centring on the regional capital Thessalonika, second largest urban centre in the country, and (ii) Epirus, a relatively isolated rural regional economy. The third CSF (CSFIII) of 2000–08 was of even higher significance for the economic future of the country. It was designed at a time when Greece was preparing for entry to EMU, its ambitious financial scope greater than ever before. A total of €54.5bn became available for a period of seven years, of which €31.8bn and €11.2bn were to be provided by the EU and Greek government respectively; private capital mobilization was estimated at €11.5 million.[10] Annual GDP in 2000 was €136.3bn, therefore the equivalent of 40 per cent of the country's GDP was made available initially to 2006, then until 2008. These figures suggest that the third CSF has represented an even greater economic development opportunity for Greece to improve competitiveness and converge further with the EU's developed economies. In 2000, the state still had a rather dominant role in the domestic economy, while the Greek private sector was fragmented, business networking was scarce and export activity weak.[11] Total government expenditure as a percentage of GDP was then at 46.7 per cent while Greek intra- and extra-EU trade balance was minus (−) €23.5bn.[12] The research for this period focuses on two national (also known as 'sectoral') programmes), Information Society and Competitiveness.

The key attributes of the CSF implementation structure for both periods have been the following. Monitoring was to be carried out at the levels of both the entire CSF and individual programmes by their Monitoring Committees (MC), the MC of the CSF and those of each programme forming part of the CSF. These committees met twice a year for a detailed review and assessment of progress in programme implementation and management. The work of each programme's MC was based on data collection relating to the financial, physical and socioeconomic indicators by the Managing Authority (MA) of each programme. It also involved the formal participation of all actors in the multi-level governance structure, namely the (appointed representatives of the) EC, central governance and sub-national organizations, that is, local government institutions, professional and other socioeconomic organizations and groups. In accordance with the CSF regulations, the MC was to be assisted in its review and assessment work by independent assessors and would report to the CSF Monitoring Committee (see CEC, 1994:111–12, 114–15).

Regional programming implementation in Greece, 1994–2002

In the case of regional programmes, implementation and management were to be carried out by sub-national government and state field administration services. In each of the thirteen regions the ROP General

Secretariat, part of the regional government tier structure, was responsible for day-to-day programme implementation and project management and was thus working closely on a daily basis with other sub-national government organizations, such as regional technical services, the Prefectural Programming Units (Directorates), and M&Cs. In each region, decision making with regard to project inclusion in the ROP was facilitated by the operation of the Regional Council that also convened twice a year, prior to sessions of the ROP MC. All sub-national government organizations that sat on the MC were also members of the Regional Council. The General Secretary of the region chaired the Regional Council and the ROP MC, and has thus been seen as the key actor in the process of regional growth and development stimulated by EU cohesion policy implementation in Greek regions. Lastly, finance was to come from three main sources. For each region, these were the prefectural funds, the regional fund created by the EU cohesion policy, and central government funds. These three sources were used to finance approved projects that were then categorized by funding source, that is, funded by prefectural, regional or ministerial funds (*SANA*, *SAEP* and *SAE* respectively), in accordance with related legislation passed on the so-called 'collective decisions' on project financing.

The ROP tables of projects funded by *SANA*, *SAEP* and *SAE* are maintained and published by the prefectures and the region, the MA and the Greek Ministry of the Economy and Finance (MEF). These have been obtained and evaluated in terms of their impact on the regional economy as part of this research. Specifically, projects were firstly categorized according to their association with infrastructure build, a legacy instrument of economic development, which local and regional governments in southern peripheral regions had long been familiar with (Papageorgiou and Verney, 1992:145–6, Nanetti, 1996:78).[13] Subsequently, projects were aggregated in terms of those consisting only of infrastructure build (category *I*), those delivering infrastructure and leading directly to new and invariant (not seasonal) employment generation in the sector concerned (category *IE*), and those not related to infrastructure but to new and other determinants of development (*N*, or *Nc* for cultural projects).[14] Finally, all projects were categorized in terms of their final beneficiary, that is, the organization responsible for project implementation and receipt of associated funding.[15]

Central Macedonia

The tables that follow reveal the extent to which state structures and their role in development have been strengthened at the sub-national level, and lead to a set of observations relating to policy efficacy in these two regional contexts. Table 4.1 depicts data of programme expenditure incurred by Central Macedonia's regional fund. The introduction of the regional fund has been a key innovative feature of cohesion policy in the period 1994–2002; the point to note is that the Central Macedonian regional government has rather monopolized it. The greater part of the €145.3 million granted to the regional fund has been utilized by the region in the pursuit of 29 infrastructure projects over the period. Nine of these relate to public social service provision, that is, building of new hospitals, disability care units and related projects, thus contributing to the growth of employment in the regional welfare state sector. Projects connected with new developmental determinants account for only 34; half of them have formed the technical assistance to the programme's implementation and have been of limited significance in terms of budget and impact. The rest relate broadly to the multi-dimensional, endogenous development paradigm; most of these projects have offered continuous professional training on behalf of SMEs and the industrial workforce, the international promotion of tourism, or the alleviation of social exclusion. There were also a handful of infrastructure projects that have been managed by M&Cs, prefectural services and wider public sector utility agencies, whilst implementation by central government and/or the wider public sector has been insignificant. A crucial and recurrent attribute, as further illustrations confirm, is the absence of any form of business organization in the ownership and delivery of policy and programme content supported by the regional fund.

Table 4.2 illustrates expenditure incurred by the seven prefectural funds in Central Macedonia. Prefectural authorities have dominated this strand of programme finance, largely following the legacy approach to development centring on infrastructure. The majority of these projects have delivered small and medium-sized road building, space re-design,

Table 4.1 ROP Central Macedonia *SAEP* expenditure

Beneficiary category / **Project category**	**M&Cs**	**Prefectures**	**Regional government**	**Wider public sector (of which state education)**	**Central government**	**Private sector**
I	5	1	20	4	0	0
IE	0	1	9	1	1	0
N	0	0	34	1(1)	0	0
Nc	0	0	0	1	0	0
Total funding (€ million)	3.17	5.01	133.08	4.03 (0.06)	0.56	0

Table 4.2 ROP Central Macedonia *SANA* expenditure

Beneficiary category / **Project category**	**M&Cs**	**Prefectures (of which Prefectural Technical Services)**	**Regional government**	**Wider public sector (of which state education)**	**Central government**	**Private sector**
I	0	456 (106)	2	0	0	0
IE	0	107 (30)	0	0	0	0
N	0	1(0)	0	0	0	0
Nc	0	25 (23)	0	0	0	0
Total funding (€ million)	0	222.22 (15.33)	1.00	0	0	0

electrification, water supply, irrigation and sanitation works. Projects of the *IE* category have mostly been concerned with building primary and secondary school facilities. Around a fourth of *I* and *IE* projects were directly delegated to prefectural technical services. The *Nc* row shows that culture was favoured in this case, as most prefectural fund projects relating to other determinants of development have been about the construction of new provincial cultural centres, sports facilities and improving access to archaeological sites. The single non-cultural *N* project has been the completion of the new production organizations' centre in Pieria. Prefectural funding was not utilized by either central or regional government, M&C or private organizations.

Table 4.3 presents data on the largest part of the Central Macedonia ROP expenditure, projects financed by central government funds. This reveals how M&Cs and firms founded by local authorities dominate project work relating to locally significant infrastructure works, such as provincial road building, urban space redesign, water, sewage and waste management network extensions and maintenance. In a very few cases, these have involved setting up small teams to operate new facilities, for example, new biological sanitation stations in tourist areas, which make a limited contribution to local employment growth. M&Cs have also managed forty-two cultural heritage projects (new municipal culture centres, sports grounds and conservation of old buildings) and a handful of *N* projects related to the development of human resources, use of new technology in delivering services to citizens, and business networking among handicraft firms.

This table also includes isolated examples of projects realized by a range of public organizations. Implementation of 27 *N* projects by prefectures,

Table 4.3 ROP Central Macedonia *SAE* expenditure

Beneficiary category / Project category	M&Cs (of which enterprises founded by M&Cs)	Prefectures	Regional government	Wider public sector (of which state education)	Central government	Private sector
I	611 (15)	8	21	18 (5)	35	0
IE	15 (2)	2	5	18 (12)	2	3
N	9 (4)	27	2	2 (0)	10 (ROP:4)	4
Nc	42 (1)	0	0	3 (1)	34	0
Total funding (€ million)	95.15 (2.08)	14.94	101.92	121.36 (32.73)	76.06	65.85

most relating to agritourism, and the realization of nineteen *I* and *IE* projects by public sector organizations (for example, the Thessaloniki International Fair (TIF), the Hellenic Industrial Development Bank (*ETVA*), and the national health system construction company (*DEPANOM*) are also of note. The private sector appears once again with a marginal share of participation in the development process. Specifically, three major projects have been realized within the ROP2 for Central Macedonia through collaboration with private actors: a major hospital constructed by the Papageorgiou Foundation, an international press centre by the Union of Daily Newspaper Reporters of Macedonia and Thrace, and the education and training centre of *PASEGES*,[16] which have all been based in the region's capital.[17] Moreover, the four *N* category projects have been about the use of information technology in support of SMEs. These have been implemented by the Development Union of Macedonia or *ANEM*, a private organization founded by the Union of Industries of Northern Greece that later merged with the public Centre for Entrepreneurial and Cultural Development or *KEPA* to form *KEPA-ANEM*, an organization heavily supported by EU cohesion funding. Lastly, central governance field administration (mostly the services of the Ministry of Agricultural Development and Foods) has been responsible for realizing 35 infrastructure projects, while the Ministry of Culture alone has managed the completion of 34 cultural projects in the region.

Epirus

Central government led the implementation of the ROP of the agrarian region of Epirus in a politicized manner, largely because local organizations had low levels of technical competence and capacity to jointly participate effectively in the development process (see Hatzaras, 2005). The Epirus regional fund was launched at the very end of the programming period and supported only one road building project implemented by one prefecture. Prefectural fund (*SANA*) and central government expenditure (*SAE*) breakdown, illustrated in Tables 4.4 and 4.5, imply a programme with a focus on transport and service infrastructure build. The four prefectures of Epirus completed 144 and 41 projects in *I* and *IE* categories respectively, supported by regional technical services as and when the need arose for a further ninety-five projects. Epirus M&Cs have made a marginal contribution, while central field administration and the private sector have had no role.

Central government expenditure incurred as part of the ROP underscores the leading role of prefectural and regional technical services in the realization of the programme. With thirty-nine and fourteen projects in *I* and *IE* categories respectively, and thirty projects on new developmental determinants, mostly cattle genetic improvement

Table 4.4 ROP Epirus *SANA* expenditure

Beneficiary category / **Project category**	**M&Cs (of which enterprises founded by M&Cs)**	**Prefectures**	**Regional government**	**Wider public sector (of which state education)**	**Central government**	**Private sector**
I	9 (0)	144	95	0	0	0
IE	7 (0)	41	0	3 (1)	0	0
N	4 (0)	3	9	1 (1)	0	0
Nc	1 (0)	2	3	0	0	0
Total funding (€ million)	10.73 (0)	97.62	46.80	3.11 (1.89)	0	0

Table 4.5 ROP Epirus *SAE* expenditure

Beneficiary category / **Project category**	**M&Cs (of which enterprises founded by M&Cs)**	**Prefectures**	**Regional government**	**Wider public sector (of which state education)**	**Central government**	**Private sector**
I	23 (1)	39	280	9 (3)	2	0
IE	1 (0)	14	28	11 (3)	0	0
N	4 (0)	30	43 (ROP: 23)	7 (5)	11	2
Nc	3 (0)	0	22	3 (0)	3	0
Total funding (€ million)	11.24 (0.003)	65.72	91.25	35.67 (14.90)	6.38	5.29

programmes across the four prefectures, the Epirus prefectures come out as the principal beneficiaries of programme implementation experience and funding with a total sum of approx. €163 million. Regional services have also played an important role, as they absorbed a higher share of central government funding for the implementation of 280 forestry, small road works between communities, irrigation and water supply projects. The region administered twenty centrally funded *N* projects, mostly related to professional training, integrated tourism planning, and industrial modernization. Lastly, wider public sector utility companies and education organizations had a small share in implementing other parts of the programme.

National programming implementation in Greece, 2000–06

The two programmes implemented during the third programming period that this work has drawn upon are the Information Society and Competitiveness national programmes of the Greek CSFIII. The Information Society programme has aimed at advancing the use of new information and communication technologies for the exploitation, dissemination and documentation of knowledge through digitization.[18] The programme has been structured on four axes of intervention, in education and culture, public service to citizens, development and employment, and communications and technical assistance, with a total initial budget of €2.99bn.

The research presented in this chapter draws on two points in time during this programme's implementation, late 2005 and late 2010. In late 2005, the third programming period in Greece still had one year of publicity and tender invitations, and three more years of implementation until the end of 2008. The data illustrated in Table 4.6 must hence be understood as a snapshot of the programme carried out up till that time.

In December 2005, €0.63bn €2.99bn budgeted had already been spent; public expenditure was at €0.55bn, while private capital mobilization stood at €0.08bn. This represents absorption of 21 per cent in the first six years of a seven-year programme. Table 4.6 shows the same beneficiary categorization for each of the 1,223 projects implemented until the start of 2006 and demonstrates clearly the overwhelming emphasis of this programme on working with the wider public sector and state education organizations in particular in its first six years. Greece's wider public sector, notably secondary and higher state education, appear to have benefited the most, through programmes and projects relating to their operations and fund

Table 4.6 Information Society programme beneficiaries, December 2005

Beneficiary category	M&Cs (of which enterprises founded by M&Cs)	Prefectures	Regional government	Wider public sector (of which higher & secondary state education)	Central government	Private sector
Number of beneficiaries	382 (54)	33	14	621 (543)	105	47

management. The Aristotle University of Thessaloniki, the Universities of Crete, Ioannina and Patras and the National Network for Research and Technology have taken the lead in acting as project beneficiaries, each in five sub-programmes. Other public higher education institutions were awarded at least two projects within the education and culture axis. The rest of approximately five hundred projects are smaller in scale, related to measure 2.4 on 'regional GIS and innovative actions' that has mainly been about technical equipment provision and upgrades for numerous primary and secondary schools around the country. The Information Society organization managing the programme has itself acted as beneficiary in seventeen projects. Further, 382 projects were awarded to municipalities, communities and firms founded by these; most are associated with measure 2.3 on 'electronic governance and citizen services'. The municipalities of Ioannina and Trikala in the regions of in Epirus and Thessaly respectively top the list, benefiting from four programmes each. 33 prefectures launched a total of 42 projects; nine among them (Thessaloniki, Kilkis and Pieria in Central Macedonia and Thesprotia in Epirus) were appointed project beneficiaries twice, within measures 4.2 ('development of local access infrastructures') and 2.4. Further, each of the thirteen regions gained programme management and implementation experience from measure 2.1 on 'electronic governance and citizen services, planning, studies and pilot projects', with the exception of Epirus where two projects, in measures 2.1 and 4.2, were managed by the Epirus region. Central ministry organizations managed 105 projects across programme axes, with the Ministries of the Economy and Finance, Foreign Affairs, Interior, Development and Merchant Navy dominating the scene. Additionally, 47 private sector organizations acted as programme and project beneficiaries until December 2005. These have been non-profit organizations governed by civil law, mostly arts and sciences foundations, undertaking projects in measure 1.3 on the 'documentation, exploitation and exposition of Hellenic culture'.

At the end of 2006, despite apparently increased interest by beneficiaries, the programme budget was revised downwards. While the approved projects total was nearing €3.30bn, available budget stood at €2.85bn in November, and was revised to €2.68bn in December of that year. By December 2008, programme beneficiaries had absorbed €1.93bn (budget absorption of 72 per cent), while the approved projects total increased to €3.59bn. The programme drew to a close in October 2010 when, with reference to a €2.68bn budget, the approved projects total was revised to €3.07bn and absorption was at €2.88bn. This funding had been allocated to a total of 4,407 beneficiary organizations participating in the programme since 2000. Figures 4.3 and 4.4 illustrate the total approved funding per type of beneficiary, and the number of organizations per type of beneficiary. They show how funding for this programme came to be largely absorbed by central government and wider public sector organizations: €2.64bn was allocated to 325 state entities managing the largest projects of new business information systems, communication networks and internet portals, mostly between €1 million and €5 million

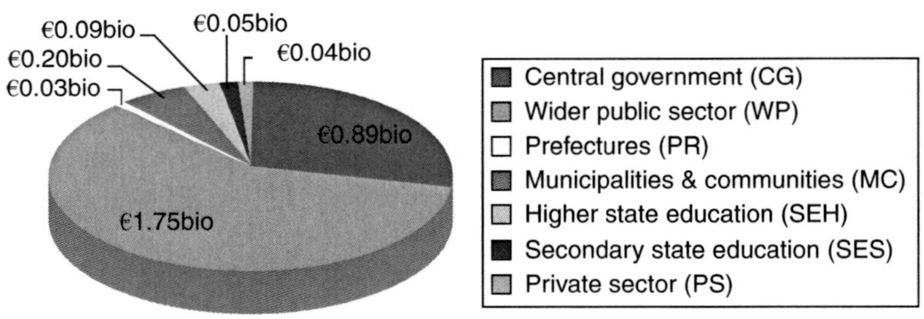

Figure 4.3 Information Society approved funds by beneficiary type

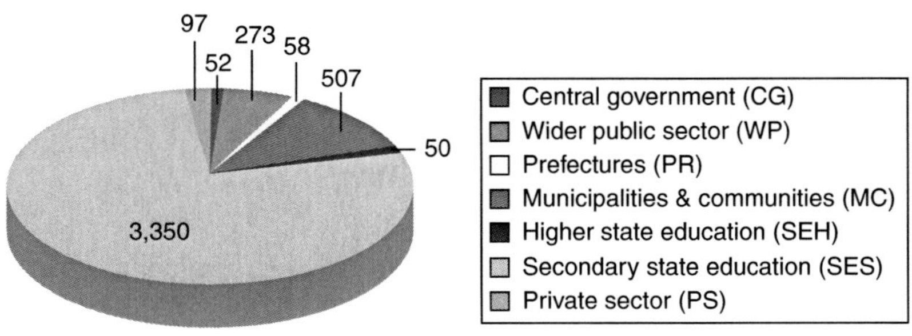

Figure 4.4 Information Society beneficiaries by type

each. Further, 507 M&Cs were awarded €0.20bn for IT projects ranging in budget from €100,000 to €500,000. An interesting feature is the focus on providing IT for schools: 3,350 schools across the country benefited from small IT projects budgeted between €20,000 and €150,000. Lastly, 97 private sector entities in the form of non-profit foundations and associations of the arts and sciences benefited from a total project budget of €0.04bn between 2000 and 2010. Although they are non-profit and rather limited in number, this is considered a positive implementation feature, as it is through the activity of such organizations that a social development process may be enhanced.

Finally, Table 4.7 presents beneficiary data on the CSFIII Competitiveness programme that has aimed at the enhancement of entrepreneurialism in key sectors of the Greek economy such as energy, industry and services, research and development, tourism, commerce and retail and human resources, with an EU and national state budget of €3.35bn, mobilizing another €3.32bn of private capital.[19]

These data reveal that the implementation of this programme has focused on sub-national government, the wider public sector and central government. All fifty-three prefectural authorities of Greece benefited, and many collaborated with M&Cs in establishing and operating local development firms acting as beneficiaries, once the appropriate legal framework was put in place in 2000. Rural development, support to SMEs and other actions on new developmental determinants have been implemented by these as part of the programme. SME support programmes featured recurrent cycles of projects providing financial support to SMEs through a competitive process involving preparation, submission and assessment of individual business plans; there was no explicit emphasis on facilitation of business networking as part of these. Regions have largely been absent in the implementation of Competitiveness, while examples of private sector entities being responsible for project delivery were limited to three cases, one example being the Greek Development Agency led by the Federation of Greek

Table 4.7 CSFIII Competitiveness programme beneficiaries

Beneficiary category	M&Cs (of which enterprises led by M&Cs)	Prefectures (of which enterprises led by prefectures)	Regions	Wider public sector (of which State Research)	Central government	Private sector
Number of beneficiaries	13 (13)	78 (25)	1	41 (29)	20	3

Industries. Some of the local development firms' operations reflect the EU cohesion policy local development paradigm as originally intended, in that they have promoted networking between sub-national governance and local entrepreneurial and industrial business organizations. Their establishment has been based on the initiative and participation of sub-national government actors, with the prefectures or M&Cs themselves taking the lead; however, in many cases these organizations rely on their continued inclusion in programmes and absorption of EU and national funding to sustain their operations.

In addition, twelve ministerial agencies and 29 public research institutions have acted as programme beneficiaries throughout the period. A notable initiative has been the establishment of the first business clustering facilitator organization based in Athens, hosted and managed by a public research organization. Preparatory work for its launch, and the selection of the micro-electronics and embedded systems industrial sector for carrying out a pilot clustering programme, were completed in March 2006. In January 2007, the Micro-electronics Innovation Centre was launched in Maroussi, Attica, and an agreement was signed with the Sophia Antipolis Foundation, the support organization of the Sophia Antipolis ICT business park in France. Since then, the facilitator has been awarded further EU funding within the current period of 2007–13, as well as international and domestic awards for its activity.[20]

Summary

The empirical exposition provided in this chapter illustrates the premise with which it began. The earlier role of the state in economic development in Greece, a peripheral member state, has been transformed through successive phases of EU cohesion policy implementation. This transformation is observed in the growth as strengthening of central government and wider public sector organizations, and the empowerment of sub-national government organizations. These have both been attained through a recurrent absorption of large parts of funding, experience and exposure to programme management in each programming period since 1985. The two regional programmes reviewed here had a strong emphasis on infrastructure build, with most projects delivered by technical services of regional, prefectural and municipal authorities. In the case of Information Society, the dominance of its implementation by public organizations seems to have stifled its progress and compromised the timing and scale of its impact. The Competitiveness programme has been taken up by central and sub-national government actors who have managed the flow of investment financing to small firms and produced modest outputs in the form of business networking and government – business collaborations. It would be necessary to obtain data from other member states in order to ascertain the validity of these observations elsewhere in the periphery. Moreover, the specific impacts of these projects in the business sector would need to be ascertained and assessed, in order for the argument of this chapter to be qualified further. However, the financial magnitude, wide range and totality of projects that central government and wider public sector organizations have managed, underlines the dominant role of the central and sub-national state machinery in the pursuit of economic development.

The recent fiscal crisis of the Greek government, its debt refinancing through the International Monetary Fund, and widespread private sector tax evasion further suggest that the impact of these programmes in terms of inducing collaboration between sub-national government and business, enhancing innovation capacity and export growth on behalf of private and public sector organizations alike has been limited. This seems to contradict the purpose of cohesion policy, that is, convergence between well-developed member states and regions and those lagging behind. The post-1988 reformed cohesion policy has been an integral part of regulated capitalism, a programme that has centred on a diverse pan-European interest coalition, has shaped the course of European integration and created the so-called European model of a social market economy since the start of the 1980s. These have been brought about through successive policy initiatives in support of competition and market growth, such as the Single Market, EMU and the Europeanized cohesion policy itself (Hooghe and Marks, 1999:75).

The principal result of the implementation of cohesion programmes in the case of Greece is that the previous institutional framework, which was regarded as stifling business growth, harbouring low competitiveness and impeding economic and social development, has hardly changed. The role of public organizations in the domestic economy has been enhanced through their assimilation of funding, policy and programme management experience, while the participation of businesses in development has been marginal. Consequently, policies and programmes have not produced their anticipated benefits to the fullest extent possible, the potential of networking and synergies among actors remains untapped, and firms and entrepreneurs are stifled by the dominance of public organizations that are weak in their capacity to pursue policies aimed at growth and development. As long as employment growth and business networking are not actively supported within the private sector, needed regional market growth, integration of regional economies and their inclusion in international exchange and trade networks remain intermittent at best.

In the era of heightened global business competition and declining public finances, business and other private sector actors need to become an integral part of national and regional growth and development processes. Organizations in the public and private spheres need to work together in new modes that help induce a balanced and equitable growth process, which in turn produces the required outputs, such as knowledge, research, innovation, new products and services and export growth. Recent changes in the cohesion policy approach and framework underscore the importance of business, knowledge and research for European regions. The preceding analysis is suggestive of a key implication for Greece, in that unless the balance between state and business and their roles in economic development is redressed, and new modes of collaboration in securing and appropriately utilizing available funding are found, it is likely that the economic future of the country will continue to be at risk.

Notes

1. Earlier versions of this work were presented at the second Anglo-Japanese Academy workshop 'Globalisation, Regionalisation and National Policy Systems', organized by the universities of Tokyo and Warwick at the Centre for the Study of Globalisation and Regionalisation (CSGR), University of Warwick, January 2006.
2. A prime example has been the *Cassa per il Mezzogiorno*, a special fund designed to assist the Italian south with economic modernization. The performance of the *Cassa* has been controversial; see Leonardi (1995:159–63), Grote (1996:274–7).
3. For a concise account of Europeanization theory, see Börzel and Risse (2003).
4. These have constituted the so-called first, second, third and fourth programming periods of 1989–93, 1994–99/2001, 2000/2002–06/2008 and 2007–13 respectively.
5. These cohesion policy features, the availability of substantial funding and gradual enhancement of the roles of the European Parliament and the European Court of Justice, have given rise to what has been observed as a mode of governance unique to the EU, namely 'multi-level governance' (Marks, Hooghe and Blank, 1996).

6. The notion of state or public funding here refers to funds administered by central government in EU member states.
7. These have been regions in the Third Italy (for example, Tuscany), the German Laender and others (Dunford and Perrons, 1992; Cook, 1992). These regions have been studied individually and their cases have further been highlighted through convergence analysis (Leonardi and Garmise, 1992:258–67; Leonardi, 1995:86–119; on Tuscany see Leonardi, 1998). It is doubtful whether this collective goods provision has been a direct result of the existence or performance of empowered sub-national governance. Whereas this has been documented as holding in the case of Tuscany, regional cases in Germany suggest that it has been the existence of a nationwide multi-actor and co-operative governance framework, where regional governance and polity are included, that has yielded success in the post-Fordist era. It would thus appear that a combination of (a) offensive restructuring, (b) effective regional governance and (c) a consociational national governance framework have been the keys to regional paradigmatic success in the post-Fordist era (see Dunford and Perrons, 1992; Hall and Sockice, 2001).
8. This study was subsequently commissioned by the EC from the European University Institute of Florence (see Leonardi, 1992:1–6).
9. See Ioakimidis (1996b:357) for an exception to this in the case of Greece's preparation of the second CSF in 1993.
10. These details are available at the website of the EC DG Region at http://ec.europa.eu/regional_policy/funds/prord/document/chapter3_en.pdf (accessed 4 November 2010).
11. Micro, small, and medium-sized enterprises (SMEs) have traditionally accounted for 99 per cent of all firms in Greece (Maggina, 1992:88; Tsoulouvis, 1994; CEC, 2009); their contribution to GDP in 1992 was estimated at 38 per cent (Maggina, 1992:88).
12. Statistical data referred to have been extracted from the Eurostat database at: http://epp.eurostat.ec.europa.eu/portal/page/portal/statistics/search_database (accessed 4 November 2010).
13. A similar approach has been employed by Mitsos (2001:316). Reference must also be made to the fact that the growth of the construction sector in Greece has been one of the key impacts of CSFII during 1994–99/2002. During the period, the focal point of this construction sector activity has progressively been the capital region of Attica due to preparations for the 2004 Olympic Games in Athens. In the absence of any significant sectoral export activity, the employment growth induced was short-lived and this sector experienced a deep crisis in late 2004 (TEE, 2005a:5, 8–9, 2005b, 29–30).
14. This categorization has been based on standard engineering project management knowledge. In cases of difficulty, project content was verified with either the MA or the external evaluators of each programme.
15. These quantitative data for Central Macedonia and Epirus were first acquired by the Programming Directorates of prefectures in the two regions and by the regions of Central Macedonia and Epirus. They were then verified with the management evaluation consultants working on the programmes, ensuring as minimal errors as possible.
16. *PASEGES* is the Panhellenic Union of Agricultural Co-operatives.

17. These collaborations occurred on an *ad hoc* basis as there has been no prior facilitation or culture of public–private partnerships (PPPs) in Greece. The relevant legal framework was put in place as late as spring 2005, shortly before the visit of the DG REGIO Commissioner Danuta Huebner to Athens. In the fourth programming period of 2007–2013, PPPs are expected to form a major instrument to overhaul and expand public social services in regions (CEC, 2005:11–12).
18. All information and data related to the programme have been extracted from www.infosoc.gr, accessed December 2005 and October 2010.
19. All information and data related to the programme have been extracted from www.antagonistikotita.gr, accessed December 2005 and November 2010.
20. More information on the activity of this organization is available at www.corallia.org/en/about-corallia/historical-background.html (accessed 7 November 2010).

References

Alogoskoufis, G. (2000) 'The Greek Economy and the Euro', in Mitsos, A. and Mossialos, E. (eds) (2000) *Contemporary Greece and Europe*, Aldershot: Ashgate, pp. 131–55.

Amato, G. (1996) 'The impact of Europe on national policies: Italian anti-trust policy', in Mény, Y., Muller, P. and Quermonne, J. L. (eds) (1996) *Adjusting to Europe*, London: Routledge, pp. 157–74.

Asheim, B. and Dunford, M. (1997) 'Regional Futures', *Regional Studies*, 31(5) 445–55.

Begg, I. and Mayes, D. (1991) *A New Strategy for Social and Economic Cohesion after 1992*, Directorate-General for Research, European Parliament, Luxembourg, Official Publications of the European Communities.

Börzel, T. and Risse, S. (2003) 'Conceptualising the Domestic Impact of Europe', in Featherstone, K. and Radaelli, C. (eds.), *The Politics of Europeanisation*, Oxford: Oxford University Press, pp. 57–80.

Commission of the European Communities (1994) *GREECE Community Support Framework 1994–1999 Objective 1: Structural development and adjustment of regions whose development is lagging behind*, Office for Official Publications of the European Communities, Luxembourg.

Commission of the European Communities (1995) *Development Prospects of the Central Mediterranean Regions (Mezzogiorno – Greece)*, Regional Policy and Cohesion series (1995), Office for Official Publications of the European Communities, Luxembourg.

Commission of the European Communities (2001) *Second Report on Economic and Social Cohesion*, Office for Official Publications of the European Communities, Luxembourg.

Commission of the European Communities (2004) *Third Report on Economic and Social Cohesion*, Office for Official Publications of the European Communities, Luxembourg.

Commission of the European Communities (2005) Communication from the Commission, Cohesion Policy in Support of Growth and Jobs: Community Strategic Guidelines, 2007–2013, COM (2005) 0299, 5 July 2005.

Commission of the European Communities (2009) *SBA FACT SHEET GREECE*, European Commission DG Enterprise and Industry. http://ec.europa.eu/enterprise/policies/sme/files/craft/sme_perf_review/doc_08/spr08_fact_sheet_gr_en.pdf (accessed 7 November 2010).

Cooke, P. (1993) 'Regional innovation networks: an evaluation of six European cases', in Getimis, P. and Kafkalas, G. (eds) *Urban and Regional Development in the New Europe*, Athens: TOPOS, pp. 155–84.

Dunford, M. and Perrons, D. (1993) 'Regional inequality as a cause and consequence of slower growth', in Getimis, P. and Kafkalas, G. (eds) *Urban and Regional Development in the New Europe*, Athens: TOPOS, pp. 9–35.

Dunford, M., Hall, R., Smith, A. and Tsoukalis, L. (2001) 'Introduction', in Hall, R., Smith, A. and Tsoukalis, L. (eds) *Competitiveness and Cohesion in EU Policies*, Oxford: Oxford University Press, pp. 1–28.

Fujita, M. and Thisse, J.F. (2002) 'Agglomeration and Economic Theory', in Fujita, M. and Thisse, J.F. *Economics of Agglomeration: Cities, Industrial Location and Regional Growth*, Cambridge: Cambridge University Press, pp. 1–22.

Garmise, S. O. (1998) 'Convergence in the European Community: The Case of Tuscany', in Leonardi, R. and Nanetti, R. Y. (eds) *Regional Development in a Modern European Economy: the Case of Tuscany*, London: Pinter, pp. 29–48.

Grote, J. (1996) 'Cohesion in Italy: A View on Non-Economic Disparities', in Liesbet Hooghe (ed.) (1996) *Cohesion Policy and European Integration: Building Multi-Level Governance*, Oxford: Oxford University Press, pp. 256–93.

Hall, P. and Soskice, D. (2001) *Varieties of Capitalism: The Institutional Foundations of Comparative Advantage*, Oxford: Oxford University Press.

Hatzaras, K. S. (2005) *Multi-level Governance, Europeanisation and the Poorest EU Region: Epirus and the Hellenic CSF II*, 2nd LSE PhD Symposium on Modern Greece, 10 June 2005, Current Social Science Research on Greece, London, LSE Hellenic Observatory WWW site.

Hooghe, L. and Marks, G. (1999) 'The Making of a Polity: The Struggle Over European Integration', in Kitschelt, H., Lange, P., Marks, G. and Stephens, J. D. (eds) *Continuity and Change in Contemporary Capitalism*, Cambridge: Cambridge University Press.

Ioakimidis, P. (1996a) 'Contradictions Between Policy and Performance', in Featherstone, K. and Ifantis, K. (eds) *Greece and the European Union: Between European Integration and Balkan Disintegration*, Manchester: Manchester University Press, pp. 33–52.

Ioakimidis, P. (1996b) 'EU Cohesion Policy in Greece: The Tension Between Bureaucratic Centralism and Regionalism', in Hooghe, L. (ed.), *Cohesion Policy and European Integration: Building Multi-Level Governance*, Oxford: Oxford University Press, pp. 342–63.

Leonardi, R. (1992) 'The Role of Subnational Institutions in European Integration', in Leonardi, R. (ed.) *The Regions of the European Community*, London: Frank Cass, pp. 1–13

Leonardi, R. (1995) *Convergence, Cohesion and Integration in the European Union*, London: Macmillan.

Leonardi, R. (1998) 'Introduction: The Role of Tuscany in the European Union', in Leonardi, R. and Nanetti, R. Y. (eds), *Regional Development in a Modern European Economy: the Case of Tuscany*, London: Pinter, pp. 3–28

Leonardi, R. (2005) *Cohesion Policy in the European Union: The Building of Europe*, London: Palgrave Macmillan.

Leonardi, R. and Garmise, S. (1992) 'Conclusions: Subnational Elites and the European Community', in Leonardi, R. (ed.) (1992) *The Regions of the European Community*, London: Frank Cass, pp. 247–74.

Maggina, A. G. (1993) 'SMEs in Greece: Toward 1992 and Beyond', *Journal of Small Business Management*, 30(3): 87–90.

Malmberg, A. and Maskell, P. (1999a) 'Guest Editorial: Localised Learning and Regional Economic Development', *European Urban and Regional Studies*, 6 (1): 5–8.

Malmberg, A. and Maskell, P. (1999b) 'The Competitiveness of Firms and Regions: 'Ubiquitification' and the Importance of Localized Learning', *European Urban and Regional Studies*, 6 (1) 9–25.

Marks, G., Hooghe, L. and Blank, K. (1996) 'European Integration from the 1980s: State-Centric *v.* Multi-level Governance', *Journal of Common Market Studies*, 34 (3): 341–77.

Mitsos, A. (2001) 'The Community's Redistributive and Development Role and the Southern European Countries', in Gibson, H. D. (ed.) *Economic Transformation, Democratisation and Integration into the European Union: southern Europe in Comparative Perspective*, Basingstoke: Palgrave, pp. 306–42.

Nanetti, R. Y. (1996) 'EU Cohesion and Territorial Restructuring in the Member States', in Hooghe, L. (ed.), *Cohesion Policy and European Integration: Building Multi-Level Governance*, Oxford: Oxford University Press, pp. 59–88.

OECD (2002) *OECD Territorial Reviews: Tzoumerka, Greece*, Paris: Organisation for Economic Co-operation and Development.

Ottaviano, G. and Puga, S. (1996) 'Agglomeration in the Global Economy: A Survey of the "New Economic Geography"', London: Centre for Economic Policy Research Discussion Paper Series (International Trade), Paper no. 1699, pp. 1–40.

Papageorgiou, F. and Verney, S. (1992) 'Regional Planning and the Integrated Mediterranean Programmes in Greece', in Leonardi, R. (ed.) *The Regions of the European Community*, London: Frank Cass, pp. 139–61.

Roberts, P. (2000) 'European Union Regional Programmes – Lessons for Practice and a Review of Future Options' in Shaw, D., Roberts, P. and Walsh, J. *Regional Planning and Development in Europe*, Aldershot: Ashgate, pp. 277–300.

Roccas, M. and Padoa-Schioppa, T. (2001)'Economic Change and Democratisation in Southern Europe', in Gibson, H. D. (ed.), *Economic Transformation, Democratisation and Integration into the European Union: Southern Europe in Comparative Perspective*, Basingstoke: Palgrave, pp. 31–74.

Rokkan, S. and Urwin, D. W. (1983) *Economy, Territory, Identity*, London: Sage.

TEE (Technical Chamber of Greece) (2005a) *Kitazontas Exo Apo ta Sinora* (Looking Outside the Borders), *Enimerotiko Deltio TEE (*Technical Chamber of Greece Newsletter*)*, Issue 2340, Athens: TEE.

TEE (Technical Chamber of Greece) (2005b) *Economike Diplomatia me te Symmetohe tou TEE* (Economic Diplomacy with the Participation of TEE)

Enimerotiko Deltio TEE (Technical Chamber of Greece Newsletter), Issue 2342, Athens: TEE.

Thielemann, E. (2002) 'The Price of Europeanization: Why European Regional Policy Initiatives are a Mixed Blessing' *Regional and Federal Studies*, 12(1): 43–65.Tsoulouvis, L. (1994) 'Urban and Regional Restructuring in Northern Greece and the Single European Market', in Hardy, S. (ed.), *An Enlarged Europe: Regions in Competition?*, London: Jessica Kingsley.

5
Innovation
The National Innovation System

Maria Kapsali

The Triple Helix model – a tool for analysis of national innovation systems

Innovation was initially considered by traditional economic models as an exclusively internal organizational activity, where actors were coming together to fix prices, pool finance and set up their marketing strategies. However, recent research reveals how innovation actors align their production capabilities to manage their knowledge flows and broaden their knowledge bases and innovation repositories. Seen in this light, innovation is understood as a knowledge-intensive process.

The definition of innovation, once the application of an invention, has shifted to the operation at an interface bringing together users, producers, entrepreneurs and policy makers in a 'transaction space' where problems and possibilities can be considered in tandem, without necessarily a consensus, through discourses that previously took place within separate institutional spheres. Evolutionary innovation paradigms, such as the Triple Helix, better explain innovation as a non-linear, interactive learning process (Kaufmann and Tödtling, 2000; Malecki, 1997; Dosi, 1988). The Triple Helix (see Figure 5.1) is a spiral model capturing multiple reciprocal relations at different points in the production of innovation, by describing how the three main sub-systems (government, academia and industry) relate to each other through processes of mutual adjustment in order to produce innovation (Leydesdorff and Etzkowitz, 2001). The three subsystems, also understood as the domains of 'policy', 'science' and 'business', function and interact under different rules of interpretation, decision rules, objectives and specific communication standards (Kaufmann and Tödtling, 2000: 8, 10). The Triple Helix provides a snapshot of the configuration of actors (government institutions, university and firms) in a spiral of relations and collaboration networks along the paths of industrial innovation and policy making (Casia *et al.*, 2009). This recurring interaction is what makes innovation systems evolutionary; they do not reach equilibrium since they are in constant flux and there is no optimal system to compare them with. The basic idea is that everything interacts with everything else (Padmore *et al.*, 1998), although these interactions and relations are researched from a macro level. Innovation and technology policies therefore are more an outcome of these interactions, rather than a unique policy function (Viale and Etzkowitz, 2005).

During relationship-building, actors' boundaries open up allowing for emergent interdisciplinary multi-actor exchange to produce collaborations (Etzkowitz and Leydesdorff, 2000). In this phenomenon the catalysts are the interconnections between knowledge producers and users of research; the emergence, spread and convergence of communications technology; and the consequent transition from vertical to lateral and multi-media modes of co-ordination. Institutions and actors are expected to assume multiple roles and functions, not only within their own institutions, but also within their new hybrid-boundary organizations (such as industrial liaison offices in universities or strategic alliances among companies, accompanied by network-based integration mechanisms), whereas previously the roles of institutions and actors were pre-defined or forced upon them under functionalist innovation policies (Leydesdorff and Etzkowitz, 2001). Actors operate on an axis of their new roles as well as their traditional functions. Thus, academia is now a place for spin-off firm-formation in addition to its traditional role as a provider of trained human resource and research ideas. Government traditionally provided the regulatory environment for firms to produce, but it now also invests through public venture capital. Industry adopts the role of the university in developing training and research within firm operations, sometimes at the same level of quality as universities. The creation of boundary spaces and relations is of major importance (Lepori, 2003: 19) and results in the need for intermediary-boundary agencies (Etzkowitz, 2003) which intervene in a variety of institutions and organizations, cutting across institutional boundaries. Boundary agencies position themselves in the relevant environments using network co-ordinators that translate between different domains and promote this role-substitution. These co-ordinators possess inter-organizational and interpersonal skills; they rise to higher levels in universities and companies; they increasingly form their own interface organizations; and they become knowledge brokers.

Communications among the actors is not complete, since it can be disrupted by institutional interests, by market forces and by unexpected innovations. All participants develop a partial perspective, and they are reflexively aware of doing so (Leydesdorff and Etzkowitz 2001).

Research on National Innovation Systems (NIS) has been conducted in a relatively small number of countries; in general, the innovation system varies across countries. This is because of the instability of system actors and their relations, which leads to high levels of complexity resulting in the system becoming non-linear, evolutionary and synergistic (although it very much depends on deconstruction, conflict and competition as well). The innovation system is in a constant state of decomposition, of becoming, of emergence, and self-organizing, peaking at the edge of chaos. Research into this systemic paradigm, however, attaches importance to all parts of the innovation system, and does not focus on the power asymmetries in systemic relations between actors.

In other words, innovation intensity depends on the interaction between private sector strategies and public sector policies, producers and users-markets, and the mediatory role of institutions co-ordinating their interaction. These co-ordinated interactions between the public and private sectors create a favourable, or otherwise, environment for innovation.

The following two sections analyze the application of this concept to the Greek business system and the systemic structure in terms of the

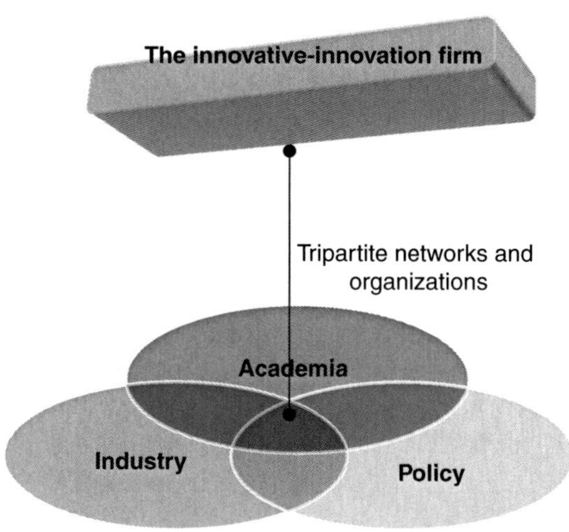

Figure 5.1 The Triple Helix model and the innovation firm

function and relation of the Triple Helix elements and the policy function in the Greek innovation system.

The structure and performance of the Greek National Innovation System

We will first provide a snapshot of the structure of the Greek NIS: the allocation of power and responsibility between the actors in the system and their roles. This is an important first step before describing the interaction between the actors and the implementation of innovation policies in the Greek NIS that follows in the next section.

The key institutional structure of the Greek NIS, according to Deniozos (2004), Sotiropoulos (2006), Komninos and Tsamis (2008), Tsipouri and Papadakou (2005) and Cogan and McDevitt (2003: 24–5, 65–6) is as follows. In the Ministry of Development (MoD) the key actors for innovation are the General Secretariat for Industry (GSI) and the General Secretariat for Research and Technology (GSRT). MoD and GSRT control both the design and implementation of policy. A variety of regional development agencies, such as research institutes, incubators, technology parks and a selection of programme implementation tools, act merely as support mechanisms under the supervision of MoD. Evaluation mechanisms are not established and most schemes have not gone through a formal evaluation (TrendChart, 2006). Deniozos (2004) claims that the GSRT is led by a strong academic lobby pushing for support for their research. Lack of continuity in GSRT policy is a common occurrence leading to lack of industry confidence in the research system and consequently to policy which marginalizes private innovators and investors.

The Ministry of Education, Lifelong Learning and Religious Affairs (MELRA) is responsible for the development of human capital at all levels; and runs the operational Programme for Education and Initial Vocational Training, which was launched in the framework of the third Comminity Support Framework (CSF) (2000–06). MELRA determines, supervises and spends the most significant part of innovation funds (50 per cent) at the eighteen public universities and polytechnics, which are surprisingly independent, since their management is not actually accountable for their performance to MELRA. These institutions are the only source of formally accredited education and knowledge creation through academic research, and they are bound by a strict legal framework, public sector homogeneous structures and decision-making procedures. MELRA has a centralized cabinet and its civil servants do not have the think-tank capacity to produce elaborate operational policies and assist MoD and GSRT in their strategic plans. Changes in the university structure by central government therefore have been made very slowly and universities continue to operate as very loose institutions where academics are free to pursue their research initiatives as long as they successfully contest appropriate funding (from the EU and other sources). Links between academia and industry are not considered necessary, so that applied research initiatives are fragmented. Instead, innovation from other western countries is an important influence and plays a significant role in the import-orientation of firms (Balzat and Pyka, 2005). The result is a tertiary education and lifelong learning system which are remote to innovation practice.

The Ministry of Labour, Social Affairs and Equal Opportunities is responsible for the Operational Programme for Employment and Vocational Training, and for the Community Initiative EQUAL, both launched during the third CSF (2000; 2002–2006; 2008) along with MELRA. This has been one of few examples of policy taking account of some of the needs of the business sector (see ESFCMA, 2008).

The business sector is the weakest component of the innovation system. Deniozos (2004) attributes this to low levels of technology absorption and use by entrepreneurs, the dominance of the public sector's regulatory and supply roles in the business system, combined with a low demand for educated labour and plentiful supply of highly educated labour. More specifically, according to Deniozos (2004) and Balzak and Pyka (2005), despite the large pool of educated young labour micro firms can only afford to hire staff with lower educational qualifications, and cannot afford to support employee professional development, resulting in poor levels of life-long learning and mediocre quality of services. Because most production is by micro firms in selective, short-term-profit service sectors, firms do not feel a need to develop innovation; there are no intrinsic incentives, since there is no market to demand for their development and absorb innovation outputs. Greek firms have therefore developed an aversion to the risks of innovation, because there is no demand for it and they can avoid major long-term investment. Besides, the dominance of state and wider public sector organizations in the absorption of funds for innovation initiatives (see Hatzaras, Chapter 4 in this volume) has resulted in the business sector developing conformism and mistrust of established institutions. In addition, Greek firms often do not seem to be familiar with the practice and use of innovation, since there is confusion about the choices they have to make, partly due to misinformation about policy and lack of practical support at the individual firm level. Because of the limited interaction between actors involved in the innovation system the business sector is isolated from the latest developments in research and is usually dependent on the import of technology from other systems.

Structural links between the different parts of the Greek innovation system, such as incubators and techno-parks, are only recently established (dating from the 1980s) and immature, in that they are not intensely focused towards innovation. They are also characterized by frequent shifts of roles and responsibilities around the same central agencies. It seems that the institutional structure (starting from the public organizations which hold the funding down to the firm level) is top-down clout and does not encourage emergent co-operation between and amongst the parts of the system. Greece's R&D intensity is below EU average (overall R&D investment 0.91 per cent of GDP) (WHO, 2004; CORDIS, 2004a, b). The Greek NIS tends to have a high degree of internationalization, as it is resourced by international funds (significantly above EU average) with EU funds constituting the major funding source. Most of this funding is allocated to public sector organizations (municipalities and administrative public bodies and publicly monitored agencies) and higher education and government research organizations. Finally, Greece has the lowest R&D expenditure per researcher in the EU-15, in both public and private research, leading to a skill shortage in this area. The lack of a system for competitive funds or systematized allocation inhibits the development of both basic and applied research (Nature, 2001: 545). The research system is dominated by the universities (50 per cent) and public research institutes (25 per cent) with business occupying the remaining 25 per cent (Tsipouri and Papadakou, 2005). The largest share of private sector R&D is covered by industry funds, while government funds account for only 1.2 per cent (WHO, 2004; CORDIS, 2004a, b, c, d). There is also inequality of resource allocation amongst the dominant funded actors. There are 35 public research organizations of which the five most active manage close to 60 per cent of the total funds. However, the business sector is the least important actor (in terms of participation, resources and production) of the three and a comparably weak contributor of innovation outputs.

The most striking observation about the behaviour between actors within the system is the low level of collaboration between the three domains, policy, academia and industry. Initiatives have been adopted by the government, with support coming mainly from the Structural Funds, to develop *intermediary agencies* for improving the administrative context and dissemination of public R&D investment. However, that led to legally quasi-private institutions which nonetheless operate within public service organizations that themselves have limited power. Intermediate bodies and advisory committees emerge from political and legislative initiatives but operate under a 'private law' regime. This autonomy in the system threatens their effectiveness and can cause infighting. They either fail to become financially self-sufficient and may discontinue, or fall into inertia and hibernation.

The consequence is that operational policy is not coordinated or implemented properly due to these structural imbalances. Financial co-ordination (controlled by MEF) is the only channel of interaction between institutional actors in the Triple Helix through the medium of programmes. What is unusual is that the right decisions are often taken through unusual processes or for the wrong reason and often a successful programme has been based on the individual efforts of professional champions or motivated beneficiary organizations (see Komninos and Tsamis, 2008).

We will now turn to describe the policy and the interactions between the actors in the system, in order to complete the picture and conclude on the main points and areas for improvement.

Innovation policy and politics within the system

The Greek NIS appears to have most of the standard innovation policy instruments and other actors in place, but repeated disappointing results on several scoreboards (World Economic Forum, European Competitiveness Report, World Competitiveness Scoreboard, and Science, Technology and Industry Scoreboard) show that policy implementation is not achieving the desired objectives. Scholars have criticized the lack of clear policy vision and focus from the top, compounded by the absence of a strong executive agency to implement policies, the lack of encouragement for business to invest in innovation (Cogan and McDevitt, 2003: 24–5, 65–6), and strong monitoring whose remit stretches beyond financial control of programmes.

For historico-political reasons (Collins and Pontikakis, 2006) the whole-hearted introduction of an innovation policy in Greece did not happen until the latter part of the twentieth century, but still in an incomplete way, since the designers of the system did not account for the structural problems discussed previously. The description on the structure of the Greek NIS revealed inequalities between the allocation of power – in terms of access to resources and decision making – between the actors and different levels of participation in the planning and production and use of innovation. These structural problems have affected the both the content and process of policy content and implementation. The interests and needs of the actors are as always diverse, but they do not negotiate and there are no formal policy implementation mechanisms to co-ordinate their interaction (Kapsali, 2008). There is no horizontal co-ordination due to the weak capacities of the MoD and GSRT, or any evidence of a multilateral longer-term and systematic consultation on the agenda setting process (Bartzokas, 2005; Tsipouri and Papadakou, 2005). The secretariats have insufficient resources and they are supported by agencies which do not perform effectively as co-ordination mechanisms. Political actors, of course, seem to be aware of all these as they have been trying for the past 25 years to establish policies, albeit in a fragmented and timid way, to progress from an academic, supply-led system into a more inclusive, interactive Triple Helix model. Too much, too soon, led to rushed policy initiatives that did not rely on the emergence of a demand-led system. This in turn led to a dependence on top-down implementation schemes, with the unsatisfactory results described above.

Therefore one root cause is that the policy objectives are vague and represent mostly the objectives of the most powerful stakeholders who receive most of the available funding. The Greek government has not elaborated an overall Science and Technology policy with clear and continuous vision and agenda (such as a Strategic Plan or Multi-annual Programme as indicated in Law 1514/85). In addition, the Lisbon strategy and its targets were taken into account in planning and implementation of STI policy in the CSF framework only after 2005 (CEC, 2010). The R&D policy objectives are a combination of objectives set by different Ministries, mainly the MEF and the MoD. MELRA plays the most decisive role in promoting research and supporting human research potential priorities during policy design, since it consumes the greater part of the budget and has the most significant influence socially, leading to a strong lobby. The second most influential, the MEF, is mainly responsible for the management of CFSs and plays a crucial role in the administrative implementation of CSF nationwide sectoral (or thematic) and regional programmes.

Some inefficiencies and omissions can be identified in the content and objectives of innovation policy and in its shifting priorities (see Figure 5.2 for the policy trajectory since 1981). The current strategic plan for science and technology 2007–13, produced by GSRT (2007), presents innovation policy priorities and strategy and a framework for the achievement of its objectives, addressing the issues by thematic or sectoral priority. The policy aim, outlined in the plan, is to provide tax incentives and direct grants to encourage business to become involved in research and hire researchers. The document also mentions attracting investors to incubators and technology parks and encouraging researchers to undertake entrepreneurial activities. However, the infrastructure and processes to support these stated aims do not seem to be effective enough. The need for an electronic infrastructure and intellectual property rights is mentioned, but on the research system – universities and public organizations (note also that business is not included in this part of the policy) – the document states that academics should focus on collaborating with foreign research centres and bid in EU programmes. The selective development of research units is primarily to support the educational purposes of new researchers and create reference points for international research. Exploitation (applied research) is emphasized, but it is not clear how it may be supported, given the fact that the system does not produce enough basic research for it to be applied or commercially exploited (Nature, 2001: 545). In any case, in order to stimulate and orientate applied research, funds are directed towards business in priority sectors which are considered of major importance to the national economy. There is also a reference to improving administration in order to support research.

Therefore, policy objectives and priorities are, to a considerable extent, formulated at the national level in an abstract way and this is because the implementation side of the system structure is weak. Bartzokas (2005) found three challenges to the implementation of innovation policy: First, the major challenge for both the Greek NIS and the local production system is technology diffusion and adoption. Because of procedures, deadlines and regulations in their programmes, policy makers have to introduce instruments supporting technology diffusion with a set of incentives in a market where the local production and consumption of knowledge is marginal. The policy makers are not tackling the real problem: the weakness of absorptive capacity at firm level and this can be attributed partly to the fact that participation by firms in the policy design stage is minimal. Policy priorities are chiefly designed by public actors, while lobbying by powerful organizations representing employers and firms centres on the advancement of their sectoral economic interests; innovation is not on their agenda. The private sector is dominated by micro firms that do not have the resources, systems and understanding to create and develop or invest in innovation. Their perception of technology is limited to adopting it, often

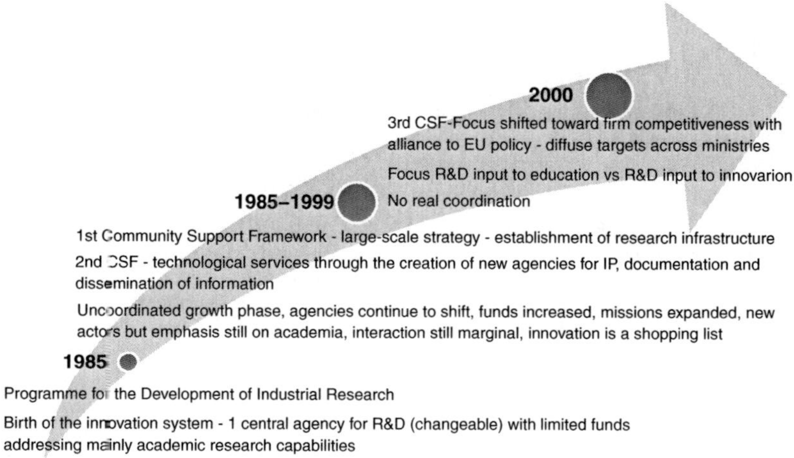

Figure 5.2 The evolution of the Greek innovation policy
Source: Based on Tsipouri and Papadakou (2005).

through importing it from overseas, if it is cost-effective and simple. These micro-firms, historically, are non-adopters or creators of innovation (Pontikakis *et al.*, 2006), since they operate in an environment with scarce resources, limited access to information, markets or networks or decision making, and there are few rewards for risk-taking behaviour, so they have a very conservative attitude and have become risk-averse. Their (usually service) operations are basic, and they often do not need to use sophisticated technology to produce, sell and make a profit. Since this situation is endemic, there is not much competition and therefore no demand, and the products themselves are simpler. Policy usually assumes that the main cause of low development and absorption of innovation at firm level is limited capital but of course this is only part of the reason. Low innovation production and absorption is also related to firms' output and productivity capacity.

This leads directly to the second challenge, which is the restructuring of the production system (Bartzokas, 2005). The Greek economy, as we have seen, is not innovation-driven. Productivity remains low, the contribution of technology-intensive sectors is marginal and they are only mobilized by productivity, the macroeconomic environment and opportunities for profitable activities abroad. Bearing in mind that entrepreneurial activity faces many institutional and bureaucratic obstacles, investment occurs in sectors with either a short-term high rate of return or with very low risk. This environment is not conducive to the optimum utilization of skills, competence and other social capital which are being accumulated in the NIS. The system has not developed the critical mass of local technological capabilities, which industrializing countries need to 'catch up'. Innovation-related activities have always been very low priorities for Greece in terms of both policies and practices, except when it comes to the final allocation of each Community Support Framework (CSF). Investment in R&D and innovation has always remained below 5 per cent of the aggregate flows of CSF despite the fact that other components of the Greek NIS, including accumulation of human capital, fixed capital investment, ICT infrastructure and firm-level investment processes, have received the lion's share of funds in the CSF framework. The bulk of technological infrastructure remains underutilized since local firms lack both effective selection processes and their corollary, carefully crafted solutions. Resources are thus diverted and underutilized. Any modern and dynamic firms which are willing to invest in innovation appear apprehensive by this situation and unwilling to participate in new ad hoc efforts of co-ordination.

The third challenge is the outward-oriented, supply-driven R&D system. In R&D systems driven by market forces, a mature market for ideas emerges and develops its own incentives and investment allocation rules. In supply-driven systems, on the other hand, institutional inefficiency is overlooked when there is a continuous flow of resources. Over 25 years, Greece developed an extensive network of institutions, actors and interests in the area of *knowledge development* in universities and government-financed institutions. Researchers and academic experts, who are key power holders in the research system, emphasize that this provision is always the government's responsibility (and lobby for maintaining existing capacity). The real problem in this supply-driven R&D system, therefore, is that the actors respond not to market incentives but to funding opportunities. The availability of funds drives the system and, because these funds are externally sourced, the system has outward orientation. This imbalance in the Triple Helix in favour of academia and other public sector organizations leads to institutional inertia, mistrust and ineffective collaboration among actors. Therefore, reform of the R&D system, primarily addressing universities and public research organizations, is a pre-condition for the restructuring of the innovation system and the successful implementation of any policy objectives designed to support a productive Triple Helix. Greek policy makers realize this problem; however, periodic attempts by government to reform the higher education system have met with strong opposition from academics themselves, who have both successfully lobbied the government to re-think their plans and significantly influenced the legitimization of their social and union agenda on the Greek public opinion.

The problem with top-down implementation and centralized policies is their linear design: a series of logical steps based on rational choice and control that ignore power politics and control of resources and influence. The structure of the organization in the innovation programmes reflects the weakness of the central authority to control powerful actors and devolve power effectively, which lies at the heart of policy implementation failure, not only in the design but also at the operational level (Kapsali, 2008). Katehakis *et al.* (2002: 26–9, 38–9, 49, 57, 64) and Pangalos and Angelidis (2003: 33–6) criticize this kind of determinism as well, and argue that social inclusiveness is the correct solution for policy planning. Pangalos and Angelidis add that the budget and time frames are too unrealistic to fit a reality where the supply chain is expensive and slow; for example, the government seems to think that introducing basic administrative control systems will compensate for the lack of crucial medical infrastructure such as IT. But the most important aspect is that no consideration seems to be given to the systemic effects of introducing too much, too soon, supported by too few resources. It fails to match operational realities and may seriously damage parts of the system (an example is the underdeveloped primary mental health care services; see Hatzaras, 2010). Examples such as this confirm that the controlling power structure of the state leads to institutional void, poor infrastructure and alienation among actors.

Summary

The Greek NIS is an aspiring innovation system, which is dependent on external funding –, therefore supply-driven – and has specialized in the administration of this external funding. At the same time there have been attempts to use this funding both to cover gaps in the existing ICT infrastructure and to catch up with innovation in other systems by trying to implement policy frameworks set up in those systems. At first glance, the remedy for this situation would seem to be the empowerment of the private sector through investment and more direct participation in policy design and implementation, which may in turn generate trust and collaboration with academic actors who are more business-oriented. In addition, the development of clusters of innovative firms collaborating in fragmented production systems would represent a major step forward. Although the EU policy frameworks actively target this aspiration, public administration is not used to acting as a mediator creating rules for the conduct of institutions. A closer look shows that structural inefficiencies within the Greek system prevent this type of policy being implemented because the Triple Helix system was developed for mature markets which can absorb innovation and firms with investment and absorptive capacity for developing and using innovation. The Triple Helix also works in an environment which has developed a system of basic research which can be turned into applied technology through collaborations between academia and business. Finally, emphasis on interaction mechanisms is essential if the Triple Helix is to work. In Greece, a variety of factors seem to defeat the purpose of inter-systemic collaboration: insufficient institutions governing business networks; the irrelevance of innovation to domestic market demand and SMEs' lack of innovative capacity; the silos between academia and business stemming from the asymmetric power structure of the national policy system; and the lack of a basic research system.

The good news is that gross domestic expenditure in innovation is expected to rise to 1.5 per cent of GDP in 2010 from 0.20 per cent in 1980 and 0.68 per cent in 1999. Thus there is some recognition of the need for more internal investment by domestic institutions and resource allocation for research, rather than a reliance on competition for funds from foreign institutions. However, this figure still remains one of the lowest in the EU/OECD for dedicated expenditure on innovation. However the structural characteristics of the institutions need to guarantee the rational distribution of this resource. This investment, encouragingly, seems to have had positive effects: during the periods of even small increases in expenditure, the volume of scientific publications and exports of high-tech products has also increased. Whilst the latest increase in expenditure might also be expected to have a similar effect, it could be more and it could be directed towards building absorptive capacity in the system and breaking down the silo-boundaries between institutions, rationalizing (and not bureaucratizing) processes of resource allocation. It is not enough to remove the barriers between the research system and other national systems; internal barriers between academia, business and policy structures are the ones that inhibit the dynamism a Greek innovation system could achieve. This achievement will arise not from programmes and other administration tools or funding availability, but from embedding new practices into the routines of current institutions and actors. A system that understands the needs of the micro-entrepreneurial firm and the markets within which it is situated is essential to support their innovation capacity; policy should be designed to fulfil these needs. Programmes and projects alone will not create innovation production and capacity unless they correspond to these needs. To this end, policy design decisions need to be inclusive, with strong support for entrepreneurship and leadership. Innovation policies need to support champions embarking on risky paths to profitability, policies tailored to the innovation options available to micro firms. These are some of the ways forward towards including the business sector in policy design and implementation, and ultimately towards the emergence of a demand-led innovation system. We resolve then, that the Greek NIS awaits its champions.

References

Balzat, M. and Pyka, A., (2005) 'Mapping National Innovation Systems in the OECD Area', Beitrag Nr. 279, University of Augsburg (Germany), Department of Economics.

Bartzokas, A.,(2005) 'Monitoring and analysis of policies and public financing instruments conducive to higher levels of R&D investments The "POLICY MIX" Project Country Review Greece UNU-MERIT.' United Nations University - Maastricht Economic and social Research and training centre on Innovation and Technology Maastricht University, 23 December 2005.

Bosworth, B. and Kolintzas, T. (2001) 'Economic Growth in Greece: Past Performance and Future Prospects', in Bryand *et al.* (eds), *Greece's Economic Performance and Prospects*, Bank of Greece.

Bourantas, D. and Papadakis, V. (1997) 'Greek Management, Diagnosis and Prognosis', *International Studies of Management and Organization*, 26(3): 13–32.

Cassia, L, Colombelli, A. and Paleari, S. (2008) 'Regional transformation processes through the universities-institutions-industry relationship', *Industry and Higher Education* 22(2): 105–18(14).

Commission of the European Communities (2010) *Final Report of the Ex-post Evaluation of the European Social Fund (2000–2006)*. available at: http://ec.europa.eu/regional_policy/sources/docgener/evaluation/tech_en.htm http://ec.europa.eu/regional_policy/sources/docgener/evaluation/expost2006/wp11_en.htm http://ec.europa.eu/social/main.jsp?catId=701&langId=en& internal_pagesId=616&moreDocuments=yes&tableName=INTERNAL_PAGES.

Cogan, J. and McDervitt, J. (2003) 'Science, Technology and Innovation Policies in Selected Small European Countries', *VATT-Research Reports*, 96, Helsinki.

Collins, P. and Pontikakis, D. (2006) 'Innovation Systems in the European Periphery: the Case of Ireland and Greece', *Science and Public Policy*, 33(10): 757–769.

CORDIS (2004a) Welcome to CORDIS FP5web Your Gateway to FP5 Information and Services, http://cordis.europa.eu/fp5/ (accessed 14 February 2004).

CORDIS (2004b)FP5 Management – Legal and Financial Issueshttp://cordis.europa.eu/fp5/management/home.html (accessed 14February 2004).

CORDIS (2004c)Greece: Overview – New Research Policy Developments, CORDIS Erawatch – Research Inventory, http://cordis.europa.eu/erawatch/

index.cfm?fuseaction=ri.content&topicID=7&countryCode=GR&parentID=4 (accessed 1 June 2004).

CORDIS (2004d)'R&D and Innovation in Greece', Greek Research and Innovation Information Service, http://cordis.europa.eu/greece/rd_policies.htm (accessed 6 November 2004).

Deniozos, D., (2004)'A National Science and Technology Policy Overview: Greece 2004', in Kobal, Edvard and Radoasevic, Slavo, *Modernisation of Science Policy and Management Approaches in Central and South East Europe*, IOS NATO Series.

Dosi, G. (1988) 'Sources, Procedures, and Microeconomic Effects of Innovation', *Journal of Economic Literature*, 26(3) :1120–71.

ESFCMA/EYSEKT (2008) 'Annual Meetings of ESF Operational Programmes: A review of interventions of the European Social Fund per policy field during the period of implementation of the 3rd Community Support Framework', Athens, 8–10 December 2008.

Etzkowitz, H. (2003) 'The Triple Helix of University–Industry–Government Implications for Policy and Evaluation', *Social Science Information*. 42(3): 293–337.

Etzkowitz, H. and Leydesdorff, L. (2000) 'The dynamics of innovation: from National Systems and "Mode 2" to a Triple Helix of university–industry–government relations', *Research Policy*, 29: 109–123.

Hatzaras, K.S. (2010) 'Programme Design and Continuity of Healthcare Reform: the Case of Greek Mental Care. Better healthcare through better infrastructure'. 3rd Annual Conference of the Health and Care Infrastructure Research and Innovation Centre proceedings, pp. 42–54.

Katehakis, D.G., Tsiknakis, M. and Orphanoudakis S.C.(2001/2) 'A Healthcare Information Infrastructure to Support Integrated Services over Regional Health Telematics Networks', Health IT Advisory Report, Medical Records Institute, Vol. 4, No. 1, pp. 15–18.

Kaufmann, A. and Tödtling, F. (2000) 'Science-Industry Interaction in the Process of Innovation: The Importance of Boundary-Crossing between Systems', 40th Congress of the European Regional Science Association, Vienna.

Komninos, N. and Tsamis, A. (2008) 'The System of Innovation in Greece: Structural Asymmetries and Policy Failure', *International Journal of Innovation and Regional Development*, 1(1): 1–23.

Leydesdorff, L. and Etzkowitz, H. (2001) 'The Transformation Of University-industry-government Relations Electronic', *Journal of Sociology* ISSN: 1198 3655.

Malecki, E. (1997) *Technology and economic development: the dynamics of local, regional and national competitiveness*, Longman.

Nature, 1 February 2001. 'Greece should abandon a short-sighted policy'.

OECD (2005a), *Governance of Innovation Systems, Volume 1: Synthesis Report*, Paris: OECD.

Pontikakis, D., Lin,Y., Dermibas, D. (2006) ,History matters in Greece: The adoption of Internet-enabled computers by small and medium-sized enterprises', *Information Economics and Policy,* 18: 332–358.

Sotiropoulos, D.A. (2006) 'The Remains of Authoritarianism: Bureaucracy and Civil Society in Post-Authoritarian Greece', *Cemoti*, 20 – Medias d'Iran et d'Asie Centrale, http://cemoti.revues.org/document1674.html (accessed 27 June 2006).

Souitaris, V. (2002) 'Firm-specific competencies determining technological innovation: a survey in Greece' *R&D Management*, 32(1): 61–76.

Tsipouri, L. and Papadakou, M. (2005), 'Profiling and Assessing Innovation Governance in Greece: Do increased funding and the modernization of Governance co-evolve?' *Governance of Innovation Systems, Volume 3: Case Studies in Cross-Sectoral Policy,* Paris: OECD.

Viale, R. and Etzkowitz, H. (2005) 'Third Academic Revolution: Polyvalent Knowledge: The "DNA" of the Triple Helix', 5th Triple Helix Conference, Turin.

WHO (2004) 'Highlights on Health, Greece 2004', World Health Organisation, Regional Office for Europe, <run on>http://www.euro.who.int/eprise/main/who/progs/chhgre/system/20050314_1 (accessed 3 March 2004).

6
Law
Company Law, Tax and Employment Law

Eirini Kokkori, Ageliki Katsiyianni and Nektarios Polychroniou

Overview

The Greek system of governance is based on the principle of separation of powers and the state therefore has three branches: the legislature, the executive and the judiciary (Panezi, 2008). The legislative branch consists of the parliament and the President of the Republic, with the main legislative power assigned to parliament. The executive branch consists of the government (Prime Minister and ministers) and the President of the Republic. It is important to note that it is the government and not the President of the Republic that is politically accountable. The judicial branch relates to courts, and these are divided into administrative, civil and criminal courts.

There are two main sources of law: private and public law. Private law is based on the Civil Code and contains five chapters: general principles, contract law, property law, family law and hereditary law. In addition, there are three other main legislative texts relevant to the Civil Code which include additional provisions and these are: the Code of Civil Procedure (court procedures relating to civil trials), Commercial Code (legislation relating to corporations), and legislation regarding labour issues (Panezi, 2008).

Public law consists of constitutional law, administrative law (regulating administrative process and relevant issues), administrative procedure (regulating the function of lower administrative courts and the State Council, criminal law (dealing with criminal acts and their legal consequences), public international law (including general international law, customary law and treaties which Greece is party to) and European law (Panezi, 2008).

The purpose of this chapter is to highlight legal issues concerning the operation and management of firms in Greece. Although it is not possible to examine all legal issues relating to corporations, this chapter will shed light on some of the main issues in company law, tax law and employment law.

Company law

Greek company law is principally based on French legislation. However, it is significantly influenced by EU legislation, since company law and regulations in member states have been substantially harmonized, in the context of establishing a single market for financial services. Various European directives and regulations contain provisions affecting the operation of companies and regulating corporate issues.[1]

Although commonly perceived as part of commercial law, Greek company law is a separate division of law, inasmuch as it regulates all types of companies, irrespective of whether they have commercial capacity or legal personality or whether their goals are non-profitmaking or profit-seeking.

It is important to note that only specific types of companies are recognized by Greek law (*numerus clausus*). Public entities are not considered to be companies. In addition, unions[2] are not companies in the strict sense[3] and are subject to special legislation (for example, Farmers' Associations,[4] Labour Unions[5] and so on).

Under Greek law, commercial firms can take a variety of legal forms (see Table 6.1). Overall, companies can be classified into two broad

Table 6.1 Legal form of Greek commercial enterprises

Legal Form	Number	Percentage
Sole proprietorship (personal company)	721,504	79.9%
General partnership (OE)	78,020	8.6%
Limited partnership (EE)	13,115	1.4%
Limited liability partnership (EPE)	20,319	2.2%
Sociétés anonymes (AE)	30,459	3.8%
Joint venture	15,810	1.7%
Co-operative	5,671	0.6%
Shipping and ship-owning	1,846	0.2%
Other	15,887	1.8%
Total number of enterprises	*902,631*	

Source: Based on National Statistical Service of Greece (2009).

categories: *personal companies* and *capital-based companies*. These two types (and their sub-categories) are discussed in more detail in the next two sections.

Personal companies

Personal companies are so called because of the personal involvement, of partners in the operation, administration and management of the company, and also because of the fact that at least one partner must bear unlimited personal liability for the company's debts. The two most important types of personal companies are *unlimited partnerships* (OE) and *limited partnerships* (EE).[6]

Both unlimited and limited partnerships have legal personality, that is, they have their own property, which is separate from the property of their partners, a company name and seat, and they are bearers of rights and obligations. Their legal personality is maintained even throughout the liquidation period. They have one or more specified commercial objectives.

In order for such companies to be incorporated, a written contract between two or more partners is necessary, containing the articles of association, that is, provisions regarding the company name, seat, duration, objectives, management, company assets contributions, distribution of profits, dissolution, liquidation and so on. A notary deed is not mandatory. The corporate name must be approved by the appropriate chamber of commerce. The articles of association, after validation by the chamber of commerce and the tax authority, must be submitted to the First Instance Court in order to be published. Filing with the relevant chamber of commerce and tax authority is also necessary.

In unlimited partnerships, all partners are personally liable towards the creditors of the partnership for all company debts, jointly and severally (unlimited partners). Their liability is unlimited and continues even after the dissolution of the company. By contrast, limited partnerships consist of at least one partner with unlimited liability (unlimited partner) and at least one partner with limited liability (limited partner), whose liability does not exceed the value of his own contribution to the company, whether this is money, goods or services.

Partners in both unlimited and limited partnerships may be legal or natural persons. All partners (unlimited and limited) have a right and obligation to participate in the management of the company and to take part in the decision making, through their voting rights. However, only unlimited partners have the right to represent the company to third parties. All partners are obliged to pursue the objectives of the company and bear a fiduciary duty towards the company and each other, which includes a duty to protect the partnership's interests, a duty of confidence and prohibition of competition. They have the right to be personally informed on all company issues and to check the books and financial data. The partnership's internal organization is freely determined by the partners (only specific Civil Code provisions regarding partnerships are compulsory). Unless otherwise stipulated in the company contract, partners exercise their powers of administration and representation collectively and a unanimous decision is necessary to bind the company towards third parties, with the exception of urgent cases that call for immediate action. However, partners may agree that majority decisions suffice *or* that each partner individually may act on behalf of the company *or* that administration is delegated to specific partners, the administrators, which is common practice in multi-member partnerships. Administrators are fully liable towards their co-partners for their acts and omissions. Partners who are not administrators bear liability towards each other only to the extent of their diligence regarding their personal affairs.

Unless otherwise stipulated in the articles of association, all partners (unlimited and limited) have the right to participate in the profits and the liquidation product of the company, according to their so-called 'participation right', which is equivalent to the value of their contribution to the company. Contributions are obligatory in order to become a partner of the company, and unless otherwise agreed, they are of equal value. The sum of contributions and everything acquired through the administration of the company constitutes the property of the company. A partner's 'participation right' in the company is not transferable, unless otherwise provided in the articles of association or agreed unanimously by the partners. Claims against partners are not transferable, except claims regarding participation in the company's profits or the product of liquidation and administrator's claims.

The company name in both unlimited and limited partnerships consists of the name of one or more unlimited partners and the initials OE or EE, respectively. Furthermore, unlimited partners are considered by law as traders. However, partnerships themselves acquire commercial capacity if they actually engage in commercial activity as legal persons.

Other types of personal companies include:

(i) *Civil partnerships,*[7] which strictly speaking have no commercial purpose or capacity, although their objective may be financial, as in partnerships established by professionals.[8] Certain types of civil partnerships are subject to special legislation, for example, law firms[9] and consortiums.[10]

(ii) *Co-partnerships*, which have financial purpose, commercial capacity, and aim at the financial, social and cultural development of their members and the improvement of their quality of life in a common enterprise, especially in the fields of production and consumption of goods, supply of goods/services, credit, transport and tourism, with the exception of rural activities.[11]

(iii) *Dormant or silent partnerships*,[12] whereby only one or more partners transact with third parties who ignore the dormant or hidden partner's connection to the company.

(iv) *European Economic Interest Groupings (EEIGs)*.[13]

Dissolution of personal companies

Personal companies are dissolved in case of:

(i) fulfilment of their objective or impossibility of fulfilment;
(ii) expiry of duration, in case of limited duration partnerships, unless they continue operating, thus becoming of indefinite duration;
(iii) notice of early termination by any partner, due to a material reason (such as material breach of contract by a partner) in personal companies of definite duration;
(iv) notice of termination at any time and for any reason by any partner, subject to an obligation of compensation in case of untimely and unjustified termination, in companies of indefinite duration;
(v) death, bankruptcy or subjection of partner to judicial support.

In case of events mentioned above under (iii), (iv) and (v), the articles of association may provide that the company will continue with the rest of the partners. Liquidation is carried out by all partners collectively or by a liquidator appointed by unanimous decision. Claims against third parties are satisfied first, then claims of partners against each other, then contributions (money/objects, or their equivalent in money) are returned to their initial owners, and if any company assets remain, they are distributed among partners in proportion to their participation right.

Capital-based companies

Capital-based companies (corporations) are so named because they are fully and exclusively liable to redeem their debts by means of their own assets (capital), and lack the personal nexus that exists between personal companies and their partners. For this reason, the protection of creditors demands that minimum capital requirements are satisfied at all times. They are open-type companies, with legal personality and *ex lege* commercial capacity, that is, existing irrespective of their objectives and actual activity. Their capital is divided by shares of equal nominal value, freely transferable.

Establishment of such companies by only one person (legal or natural) is allowed. Conclusion before a Greek notary public of a notary deed containing the articles of association is compulsory and requirements regarding registration, filings and initial and ongoing publicity must be fulfilled.

The most important types of capital-based company are *sociétés anonymes* and *limited liability companies*. Other types are *joint ship ownerships,*[14] which are a hybrid type of company with features appertaining to both limited liability companies and limited partnerships, and *limited by shares companies,*[15] which in practice are rare in the Greek economy.

Sociétés anonymes (AE)

Sociétés anonymes are regulated principally by codified Law 2190/1920, the cornerstone of the relevant legislation, which was extensively reformed in 2007 to incorporate Directive 2006/68/EU.[16] Particular types of sociétés anonymes are regulated by specific legislation: for example, credit institutions,[17] investment companies,[18] insurance companies,[19] venture capital and mutual guarantee companies,[20] Greek shipping companies,[21] factoring companies, and leasing companies which are licensed and prudentially supervised by the Central Bank of Greece.[22] Corporations whose shares are listed on a stock exchange are also subject to special regulation and legal requirements. The analysis below only refers to sociétés anonymes which are not subject to special legislation.

The incorporation of sociétés anonymes, besides a notary deed containing the articles of association, entails reservation and approval of the corporate name by the appropriate chamber of commerce, granting of a licence of establishment by the relevant prefecture, an initial registration with the Sociétés Anonymes Registry kept by the Ministry of Development in the prefecture, publication of a summary of the articles of association in the government gazette and filing with chamber of commerce and tax authorities. If the share capital does not exceed €3,000,000, the prefecture's licence of establishment and the approval of amendments to the articles of association, are not required. The articles of association must include provisions regarding the company name, objective, registered office, duration, share capital and shares, board of directors and general meeting, accountants, shareholders' rights, annual financial statements, distribution of profits, dissolution and liquidation.

Sociétés anonymes must also comply with on-going filing and publication requirements regarding important corporate issues and decisions, such as annual financial statements, amendments of the articles of association, increase and decrease of capital, formation of the board of directors and powers of representation, merger, conversion, dissolution of the company, appointment of liquidators and so on. Sociétés anonymes of other EU member states must comply with ongoing filing and publication requirements regarding their branches established in Greece.

The minimum share capital of sociétés anonymes is €60,000, fully paid up. The share capital is divided into common shares of equal nominal value, granting equal rights to their holders. Common shares represent holders' right to vote at the shareholders' general meeting, to participate in the corporation's profits (dividends) and liquidation proceeds and to exercise minority shareholders' rights (such as convening the general meeting, provision of corporate information, audit of the company and so on). Besides common shares, a company may issue privilege shares, which do not grant voting rights, but grant privileges in respect of the receipt of dividends and of the proceeds of liquidation. The nominal value of shares may range from a minimum of €0.30 to a maximum of €100. Shares are freely transferable. They may be issued as either tangible or intangible, registered or bearer shares. The increase or reduction of share capital is, in principle, decided by the general meeting and there are publication requirements. Unless otherwise stipulated by the articles of association, common shares grant pre-emptive rights to shareholders in case of a capital increase. Sociétés anonymes may acquire their own shares under specific circumstances and after compliance with procedures and requirements set by law.

Bodies of sociétés anonymes. The constituent bodies of sociétés anonymes are: (i) the Shareholders' General Meeting, (ii) the Board of Directors (BoD), and (iii) the Auditor(s).

The Shareholders' General Meeting is the superior body of the company, having general authority to decide on any corporate issue. It is held at least annually (in principle at the company's registered office) in order to approve the annual financial statements, to absolve the board of directors and accountants from any liability to indemnify the corporation regarding the performance of their duties during the previous financial year and to elect its accountants for the period until the next general meeting Besides the above, the general meeting is by law the only body competent to decide, according to certain quorum and majority conditions, on important corporate issues specified by law, such as the election of the BoD, amendments of the articles of association, the increase or reduction of the share capital (exceptions apply), the allocation of profits (issue of dividends), the issue of convertible bonds, the conversion of the corporation to another company type, its merger or division, its dissolution and so on. The general meeting is convened by invitation of the BoD, in accordance with certain time limits and publication requirements. An invitation is not needed if all shareholders of the company are represented at the meeting, and no one objects to its convention.

The *Board of Directors* (BoD) represents the company legally before the courts and extra-judicially, and has the power to decide on any issue connected with the everyday management of the company, its financial administration and the pursuance of its objective in general, except in cases where the law or the articles of association have explicitly reserved exclusive authority to the general meeting. The BoD is elected by the general meeting and comprises at least three members. The articles of association may provide that legal persons can be appointed as members of the BoD. It may not serve for more than six years; however it may serve up to the date of the next general meeting. Members can always be re-elected and are freely revocable by the general meeting. The BoD elects its chairman and vice-chairman. It is common practice, but not mandatory, that the managing director of the company is also a member of the BoD. The BoD may delegate the exercise of specific authorities to certain of its members or other persons to the extent allowed by the articles of association. It can make binding contracts with third parties, even if publication requirements have been met regarding restrictions of its powers, unless proven that the latter knew or should have known that such actions exceeded the objective of the company or the BoD's powers. The BoD usually delegates extensive powers of management, business decisions and representation to the managing director; however the law does not prescribe the existence of such an office as obligatory. The BoD convenes whenever prescribed by the law and the articles of association or when necessary on the invitation of the chairman stating the topics on the agenda. A minimum of two members acting together have the right to request that the BoD convenes. Unless otherwise provided by the law or the articles of association, at least half of the members plus one have to be present at the BoD meeting and a majority decision suffices. The members of the BoD and their delegates are fully liable towards the company for acts or omissions regarding the company's management, unless they prove that they acted as reasonably diligent businessmen.

There is a three-year limitation period for negligence claims. They are also bound by a duty of trust, non-competition and non-conflict of interests. Minutes of the general meeting and the BoD's meetings must be kept, and for this reason a company secretary is usually appointed.

Auditors are elected by the general meeting. They have to be certified in case of corporations fulfilling certain financial criteria, such as initial share capital of over €3,000,000. Auditors audit the annual financial statements, monitor the company's logistical and administrative state of affairs during the financial year, are fully liable to the company regarding the exercise of their duties and have the power to request an extraordinary general meeting.

Dissolution of sociétés anonymes. If the assets of the company are reduced to half of the share capital, the general meeting must decide either to dissolve the company or to take appropriate measures. The corporation is also dissolved in case of (i) expiry of its duration, following decision of the general meeting, (ii) bankruptcy, or (iii) a judicial decision upholding a petition made by shareholders representing a third of the share capital and demanding the dissolution due to a material reason, or a petition of whoever has a legal interest therein, in specified cases.

Liquidation follows dissolution. The company continues to exist, but only for the purposes of liquidation. Liquidators (receivers) are appointed by the general meeting. Their appointment causes the immediate cessation of the BoD's powers. Liquidators make an inventory of all company assets, and then proceed to their liquidation and the compilation of claims in order to pay off the company's debts. The liquidators prepare and submit to the general meeting for approval the initial and final financial statements, at the beginning and at the conclusion of the liquidation, as well as annual financial statements during the period of liquidation. Claims by creditors, such as staff, the state, secured or unsecured subordinated debts, and claims by bond-holders are satisfied first from the proceeds of the liquidation according to an order determined by the law. If the proceeds suffice, they are distributed first to holders of privileged securities, then to holders of common securities, according to the number of shares that they own.

Limited liability companies (EPE)[23]

In order for a limited liability company (EPE) to be incorporated, a notary deed is required, containing the articles of association, which must include the partners' names, residence and nationality, the company's type, name, registered office, objective, duration and capital, the goods contributed and extent of participation by the partners, and the shares. The notary deed is filed with the relevant First Instance Court (which keeps a Limited Liability Companies Register) and published in the government gazette. Founders of the company bear unlimited and several liability for all debts incurred before the completion of the incorporation.

EPEs must comply with ongoing filing and publication requirements regarding amendments of articles of association (including increase and decrease of company's capital), appointment of administrators or liquidators, annual financial statements, dissolution and so on. Only decisions and information which have been published at least fifteen days in advance can be used against third parties.

EPEs are subject to a minimum capital requirement of €4,500, fully paid up. The partners' participation (contribution) in the company is represented by one or more shares of equal value. Each share represents one voting right in the general meeting. An EPE cannot issue shares in the form of securities. Unless otherwise provided in the articles of association, each share is freely transferable by means of a notary deed and after making the relevant entry in the company's partners' book. Any change regarding the company's partners and number of shares must be published. The value of each partner's participation cannot be less than €30 or multiples of this amount. The company can never acquire its own shares.

Bodies of the EPE. The main constituent bodies of the EPE are (i) the general meeting of partners, (ii) the Administrator(s), and (iii) the Accountant(s).

The *General Meeting of Partners* is the supreme body of the company and is entitled to decide on any company issue. It is convened by written invitation by its administrator(s), at least once a year. An invitation is not needed if all partners are present and have no objection. The general meeting has exclusive authority to decide on amendments of its articles of incorporation, the appointment, absolution from liability and revocation of service of administrators, the filing of suits against the company's administrators, accountants or partners, extension of duration, merger, dissolution and appointment of liquidators. The quorum required for decisions consists of voting rights representing at least half of the company's capital and a majority decision suffices, though in order to decide an amendment of the articles of association, a higher quorum (three-quarters) and majority (three-quarters) is required, and a unanimous decision is required in case of change of the company's nationality and reduction of rights/increase of obligations of partners.

Administrator(s): Unless otherwise agreed, all partners, acting collectively, administer and represent the company. However, the articles of association or general meeting's decision may provide that one or more persons may be appointed as administrators, which is common practice. Administrators are fully liable towards the company and any partner or third party. Their liability is several if they acted collectively. Administrators represent the company and their actions are binding on the company towards third parties, unless proven that the latter knew that the administrators exceeded the objective of the company or their proper powers. They are under a duty of trust and non-competition. Once a year, administrators make an analytical inventory of all assets and liabilities and draft the financial statements based on the inventory. Minutes of the decisions of the general meeting and the administrators are kept.

Accountant(s): The provisions regarding the accountants of EPEs are similar to those in respect of the accountants of sociétés anonymes.

Dissolution of the EPE. The articles of association may include provisions regarding partners' right to exit the company. Partners may exit the company for a material reason following a decision of the First Instance Court. The same court may exclude a partner from the company if so decided by the general meeting. Each partner has a right to participate in the allocation of the company's profits in proportion to the value of his or her own contribution to the company.

The company is dissolved, in any case stipulated by the law or the articles of association, by a decision of the general meeting taken by at least three-quarters of the partners, representing at least three-quarters of the capital, or by a decision of the court for a material reason, following a petition of partners representing one-tenth of the capital, or due to bankruptcy. If the capital is reduced to less than half, the general meeting must convene in order to decide either the dissolution or the reduction of the capital (at a level not less than the minimum capital requirement). After dissolution, the company enters into liquidation, which is carried out by the administrators, unless otherwise decided by a meeting of partners. The principles of liquidation as described with respect to sociétés anonymes apply similarly to EPEs.

Tax law

This section will highlight some main issues relating to tax law. It is important to note that the information provided here, although correct at the time of writing, is subject to constant revision and change in light of the Greek government's austerity measures to respond to the current economic crisis. In addition, tax law has always been known for its constantly changing nature (sometimes frequent changes on a yearly basis). Nevertheless, this section will explore the taxing of Greek firms, types of tax and tax returns.

Taxing businesses

Taxes are intended to collect revenues in order to establish a prosperous environment for economic growth. Companies doing business in Greece are subject to *corporation tax, value added tax (VAT), real estate tax,* and *social security contributions*. Tax Law 3775/2009 introduces new tax rules on the transfer pricing documentation of inter-company transactions between associated companies as well as thin capitalization rules. Legal entities subject to income tax are separated into two categories: (i) legal entities which are for-profit organizations, and (ii) legal entities of the public or private sector, either Greek or foreign, of a not-for-profit nature.

Companies registered in Greece are subject to corporation tax on their worldwide income and capital gains. Non-resident companies having a permanent establishment in Greece are subject to corporation tax on income and capital gains derived through the permanent establishment.

A financial year comprises twelve months and usually coincides with the calendar year. The financial year of a company in which a foreign enterprise has at least 50 per cent stake may coincide with that of the foreign enterprise. Tax exemptions under the Greek taxation system include proceeds from the sale of shares traded on the Athens Stock Exchange, income from ships and shipping, dividend received from a Greek company and capital gains from the sale of a business between family members.

Tax rates

The basic principles are laid down by Law 2238/1994. The tax rate for both corporations and limited liability companies is 25 per cent, also applicable to foreign companies and non-profitmaking legal entities. The tax rate for general and limited partnerships is 20 per cent. An additional tax for legal entities which acquire income from property is imposed on the total net income. This tax is calculated at the rate of 3 per cent on total gross income from property. Additional tax cannot exceed the amount of the main income tax corresponding to total taxable income of the legal entity. Consequently, if no income tax is payable due to losses, there is no additional tax regardless of the amount of income arising from property.

Tax basis

Corporations and limited companies are taxed on total annual profits before any distribution. Non-resident companies are taxed only on income arising from Greek sources. Resident corporations are taxed on net income earned in Greece and abroad. Net income is calculated by deducting expenses from gross income. Tax legislation determines non-deductible expenses, tax-free income and other income subject only to withholding tax.

Group taxation is not permitted. Each company in a group is taxed on its own accounts. However, groups of listed companies with a balance sheet value of €3.7 million, turnover of €7.4 million and 50 employees must report consolidated earnings for accounting purposes, including those from companies abroad in which they have a controlling interest.

Use of losses

In the case of losses arising at the end of the financial year that are not covered by profits gained during previous accounting periods, the following provisions apply: (i) if there are no profits, the full losses are carried forward for offset, and (ii) if profits are insufficient, the balance of the losses is carried forward to the next five successive financial years. Negative income from foreign sources can only be offset against the taxpayer's positive income arising abroad.

Types of tax

Dividend tax

Dividends are subject to 10 per cent dividend tax. Domestic dividend income is not included in the annual taxable income of the recipient entity. Dividend tax is withheld and paid in addition to corporate tax by the distributor. Income from foreign dividends is taxed under the general provisions and foreign tax is tax deductible.

If dividends are received by a resident parent company from a foreign subsidiary, the aggregate amount of any tax paid as corporation tax and as a tax on dividends, both at subsidiary level and at any other lower subsidiary, to the same or another country, is deducted from the amount of the dividends according to articles 105 and 109 of Law 2238/1994.

According to Article 54, paragraph 1 of Law 2238/1994, there is a withholding tax exemption and domestic entities are not subject to deduction of 10 per cent tax on dividends that they distribute to entities of other EU member states, in compliance with the provisions of Article 11 of Law 2578/1998, which requires (i) minimum participation of

10 per cent in the share capital of the Greek company, (ii) the foreign company (shareholder) must participate in the capital of the Greek company for at least two consecutive years with a minimum of 10 per cent, and (iii) the foreign company must be a legal entity of Appendix A1 of Law 2578/1998. In any other case the double taxation treaties (DTT) are applicable. If the domestic rate of 10 per cent is less than that of DTT, then the domestic rate is applicable.

Value added tax (VAT)

The value added tax (VAT) system was introduced by Law1643/1986 as a total or partial replacement for many other indirect taxes. The basic principles are laid down by the *Value Added Tax Code* as ratified by Law 2859/2000 and amended by Law 3833/2010, the *National Customs Code* as ratified by Law 2960/2001 and amended by Law 3815/2010 and Law 3833/2010, and finally by the *Measures to Implement the Mechanism to Support the Greek Economy by the Euro Zone Member States and the International Monetary Fund* passed on 6 May 2010. VAT is payable when any person engaged in independent economic activity supplies goods or services in Greece or imports goods into Greece.

Tax is imposed on the following: a) supply of goods and services; b) import of goods; c) intra-community acquisition of goods; and d) intra-community acquisition of goods subject to excise duty. Tax is imposed on any person or entity, national or foreign, or association of persons, provided they are engaged in independent economic activity. The Greek state and other public entities are not considered taxable persons in respect of goods and services provision in the performance of their duties.

Transactions are divided into categories according to the applicable rates: (a) standard rate (21 per cent) which applies in general, and (b) reduced rate (10 per cent) which applies to certain goods and services such as food or pharmaceutical products, medical equipment, public transport, catering in restaurants and similar firms, products and services relating to agriculture and so on. Special consumption taxes are applied to cars, tobacco products, alcoholic beverages, liquid petroleum fuels and lubricating oil products.

Article 4 paragraph1 of *Measures to Implement the Mechanism to Support the Greek Economy by the Euro Zone Member States and the International Monetary Fund* modifies Article 12 of Law 3833/2010, and increases the standard rate of VAT from 21 per cent to 23 per cent and the reduced rate from 10 per cent to 11 per cent as of 1 July 2010. Article 5 imposes a special levy at rates from 4 to 10 per cent on the total net income of certain legal entities, where the total net income exceeds the amount of €100,000. Paragraph 12 imposes excise tax of 20 per cent on the value of television advertisements.

Certain categories of transactions (such as medical services, postal services and so on) are exempt from VAT, while there are special provisions for small firms, farmers and travel agents.

A taxable person not established in Greece but resident in another EU member state, is in principle obliged, when carrying out a taxable transaction in Greece, to register and account for VAT in Greece. For this purpose, it is possible to appoint a VAT representative or to obtain a Greek VAT number and pay by electronic means.

Stamp duty

Stamp duty is imposed on transactions stipulated by the Stamp Duty Code, at rates depending on the type of transaction. Stamp duty is payable only on documents and not on their subjects. There is no obligation to pay stamp duty if there is no document, with a few exceptions such as loans proved by entries in company books.

Types of stamp duty are: a) proportional stamp duty, calculated as a percentage of the cash value stated on the document, and b) fixed stamp duty, payable at a fixed rate regardless of the value stated on the document.

Property taxes

In all cases where rights to property located in Greece are transferred for a consideration, transfer tax is due. The rate is 7 per cent on the market value of the property up to €15,000 and 9 per cent on any excess. The taxable value is calculated according to rates set in official tables based on specific factors (type of building, location, district, floor area, age, co-ownership and so on). In the few districts for which there are no official tables, these criteria are used to calculate the market value. Transfer tax is also payable when a ship under a Greek flag is transferred.

Annual land and property duty

Until to 2007 an estate tax was imposed on the total value of land and property, according to Law 2459/1997. Under Law 3634/2008 it was replaced by the annual property duty, which is applicable to any natural or legal person for property held in Greece in the relevant tax year, regardless of nationality, residence or headquarters.

In order to calculate the flat rate for legal persons, the total value of land and property and proprietary rights is taken into account as at

1 January for every tax year and calculated according to the objective value system.

Property is taxed separately. Regarding natural persons, a duty of one per thousand on the total value of the property is imposed. The normal annual property duty rate for legal entities is 0.1 per cent on the value of buildings used for own purposes and 0.6 per cent on the value of all other property. The 0.1 per cent rate also applies to immovable property owned by mutual property funds. Exceptionally, the value of immovable property owned by legal entities that pursue a commonwealth, religious or educational purpose is taxed at 0.3 per cent.

Capital gains tax

Capital gains derived from the following activities are taxed at a flat rate of 20 per cent: a) sale of any right relevant to the operation of an enterprise or to a profession, and b) sale of a commercial or other enterprise in its entirety or of the firm's name, trademark, goodwill, and so on.

Sociétés anonymes and limited liability companies can offset this tax against their income tax. Capital gains derived from the transfer of shares which are not listed on the Athens Exchange are liable at 5 per cent on the selling price of the shares. Transfer of shares listed on the Athens Exchange is liable to 1.5 per cent tax on the selling price.

Withholding tax

Several withholding taxes are imposed: on income from dividends of listed or foreign companies, on income from interest and royalties, third party fees (20 per cent), BoD member fees (35 per cent), payroll tax and self-employment tax (20 per cent). No withholding tax is imposed in Greece in relation to royalties and service fees payable to resident companies. There is no tax on interest derived by non-resident companies without permanent establishment in Greece. However, 10 per cent tax is deducted from interest on bank deposits in Euros and 25 per cent tax is deducted from any other type of interest.

Tax returns

Sociétés anonymes and limited liability companies are obliged to file their tax returns by the tenth day of the fifth month following the end of their accounting year. General and limited partnerships as well as joint ventures maintaining double-entry books are required to file within three and a half months following the end of their accounting year. If a tax return is filed but the appropriate tax is not paid, it is considered as not having been filed. In cases of non-compliance, either because of late filing or non-filing, tax penalties and fines are imposed according to Administrative and Criminal Penalties in Tax Law (Law 2523/1997).

Income tax is normally deducted from employees' gross pay monthly by the employer and paid to the tax authorities. This settles the employee's income tax liability. Any remaining balance owed or to be refunded becomes due after an assessment has been completed and issued by the tax authorities. Tax is payable in three instalments. A discount of 1.5 per cent is allowed for electronically submitted income tax returns.

Individuals liable to pay tax and public entities conducting business subject to taxation are obliged to submit a periodic VAT return every month to the Tax Department. The periodic tax return for every fiscal period must include the value of taxable supplies of goods and services, the value of intra-community service transactions and the value of exempt transactions as well as discounts and tax differences arising. The annual VAT return includes the data of all the periodic statements. Any tax credit in respect of the annual VAT return is refunded, since it cannot be transferred to the next financial year.

Employment law

Employment law developed later in Greece than in most European countries, due to its belated industrialization. The first employment laws (regarding individual employee/employer relationships, employment of females and minors, accidents at work, labour disputes and unions), were enacted at the beginning of the twentieth century. Union law and collective work agreements developed after the First World War. Significant modernization of employment law took place following the 1975 Constitution and especially in the 1980s. Extensive harmonization of employment laws among EU member states has been achieved and the development of the law in Greece was influenced in particular by French and German legislation.

The Greek Constitution recognizes and protects the right to employment and social security, to equality and non-discrimination among workers, the freedom to belong to a union and the right to strike, the latter subject to specific exceptions and restrictions. It prohibits any type of compulsory work, allowing the requisition of personal services only for specified emergencies, such as war, national defence needs and urgent social needs resulting from natural disasters or danger to public health. The Constitution also provides that general working conditions are determined by law, supplemented by collective labour agreements concluded through free negotiations and, if these fail, by rules determined by arbitration. Employment law consists of *individual employment law* and *collective employment law.*

Individual employment law

Individual employment law regulates the relations between employer and employee or labourer and the rights and obligations that arise from the employment agreement. This section will highlight some issues relating to the types of work relations and classes of employees, the recruitment process, and terms and conditions of work.

Types of work relations and classes of employees

The employment agreement is distinguished from the contract for services. An essential feature of the employment agreement is the employee's legal and factual subordination to the employer ('dependent' employment agreement). This means that employees rely on a single employer for their income and that the employer exercises managerial prerogative over them. The managerial prerogative consists of the employer's right unilaterally to determine such terms as the nature, place and performance of work, hours of work and so on, within the limits of the individual contract of employment, the personnel regulations, the applicable collective labour agreement and the law, by giving orders and instructions to the employees, as well as the right to organize, supervise and control employees' work performance, as the employer deems appropriate for the operation of the enterprise. Employment law applies only to dependent employment agreements.

The contract for services lacks the feature of dependency. It also entails provision of services for a wage, irrespective of the outcome of the services; however the service provider is free to provide its services to more employers and organize its work in terms of place, time and performance within the limits of the contract. This type of work contract is regulated by articles 648–680 of the Civil Code, which offer a lower level of protection to the service provider than do employment law provisions to the employee; for example, contracts for services of indefinite duration can be terminated by fifteen days' notice in writing, without compensation. Article 1 of Law 2639/1998 (as amended recently by Law 3846/2010) sets out an 'evidence rule' whereby a contract for services or a works contract is deemed to conceal an agreement of dependent employment if the services are provided in person exclusively or mainly to the same employer for nine consecutive months.

The general category of employees is divided into a) *labourers*, who offer physical labour, are entitled to a minimum rate of pay and have significantly lesser rights in terms of notice period and compensation, b) *employees*, who offer intellectual work, and c) *senior management officials*, who are excluded from certain protective legal provisions, such as overtime. Civil servants, who work for the central and local government and for public law legal persons, are subject to special public law terms and conditions (the most significant of which are recruitment through successful participation in a competitive examination held by an independent body [ASEP], a two-year probation period, security of tenure, and special allowances).

The recruitment process

Each employer, whether an individual or enterprise, must register with the Social Security Institution (IKA) and acquire an Employer's Registration Number (Article 6 of Law 2972/2001). Unless the employee is subject to a special social security organization, the employer must register him/her in IKA's record of newly hired employees from the first day of his/her employment (Article 2 of Law 2556/1947 and Article 10 of Law 3232/2004). Employers must submit regular (three-monthly) detailed statements to IKA regarding employees employed during the relevant term (Article 1 of Law 2972/2001). The employment must be disclosed to the Greek Manpower Employment Organization (OAED) within eight days of its start (Article 1, Legal Decree 763/1970) and within twenty days from recruitment, the basic terms of employment must be communicated in writing to the employee. If the employer does not comply with these obligations, administrative penalties (mainly fines) are imposed. Part-time contracts must be concluded in writing and disclosed to the Labour Inspectorate within fifteen days from the date of recruitment, otherwise an 'evidence rule' that they are concealing full-time employment applies (a Article 2 of Law 2639/1998). A probationary period of reasonable duration may be agreed, at the end of which the employment may be discontinued, if the employee fails the evaluation.

Lending (the services of) an employee to another employer is allowed, by means of a three-party contract, whereby, with the employee's consent, the indirect employer undertakes to pay the wages and insurance contributions and to fulfil the relevant legal obligations to public authorities, whereas the direct employer exercises the managerial prerogative over the employee. Direct and indirect employers are jointly liable for the payment of wages.

However, only specially licensed Companies of Temporary Employment are allowed as an objective to lend employees and act as recruitment agents (Law 2656/2001, as recently amended). An employer is entitled to hire employees through such companies, only in order to meet temporary or extraordinary or seasonal needs. The working term of employees lent by a Company of Temporary Employment cannot exceed twelve months in total, otherwise they are considered to be employed indefinitely by the indirect employer.

Where the contract of employment is null and void, for example in the case of an employee with no valid health card or a non-EU national with no work permit, undue enrichment provisions apply to the employee's compensation claims for earned wages.

Special legal provisions apply in certain categories of employees requiring increased protection, such as women (with respect to pregnancy and maternity issues), minors, unionists, people with disabilities, families with three or more children and so on.

Terms and conditions of work

Employees are required to offer their services to their employer, as fiduciaries, diligently and according to the latter's instructions. All employees are entitled to equal treatment and non-discrimination on grounds of sex, race, ethnic origin, political, ideological and religious beliefs and so on.

Employers are liable to pay the agreed wages to the employees, which cannot fall short of the minimum wages and allowances prescribed by the applicable collective labour agreements and the law. They are also liable to pay the required social security contributions and apply at the workplace the minimum health and safety measures stipulated by law.

Employers cannot unilaterally change the agreed employment terms, to the detriment of their employee. In such cases, the employee may either demand adherence to the agreed terms or accept implicitly or explicitly the new terms. The employee also has the right to consider such a change either as a valid 'irregular' termination of the labour contract, in which case the compensation prescribed by law can be demanded, or as an invalid dismissal, in which case overdue wage payments can be claimed for as long as the employer does not accept his/her services.

Regular annual wages used to include an extra month's salary as a Christmas bonus, half a month's salary as an Easter bonus and half a month's salary as a leave of absence allowance (a fourteen-month annual salary). These allowances have now been partially suspended in respect of public employees as part of the Greek government's austerity measures to deal with the current economic crisis. Several allowances prescribed by law or collective labour agreements, such as family, marriage, use of a foreign language, university degrees or unhealthy working environment allowances, constitute part of the minimum wage, while others are granted by the social security organization, and apply only to special circumstances (for example, maternity and sickness allowance). Other benefits are granted voluntarily by the employer, and may be assessed as part of the salary, if so agreed explicitly or implicitly (for example, by their regular payment over a long period of time).

Contracts of employment are either fixed-term or of indefinite duration. On the expiry of fixed-term contracts, the employment is discontinued without further compensation to the employee. Such contracts can be concluded in order to satisfy temporary or extraordinary needs of the employer and can only be terminated in writing for a very significant reason. If the employer is responsible for the early termination, the employee has a right to indemnification. Indefinite duration contracts concluded more than two months previously can be terminated by the employer only after serving a written notice and giving special compensation to the employee. Both the amount of compensation and the notice period depend on the duration of employment, the maximum compensation being twelve months' pay (provided that the notice period is adhered to). If the notice period is not observed, the compensation doubles ('irregular' termination). Recently, due to the financial crisis, the law changed and the period of notice of termination was curtailed. The employee is not entitled to compensation only if he or she has committed an offence against the employer or is leaving the job of his/her own accord. The employer does not have to provide any reason for the termination, but is prohibited from abusing this right by, for example, proven unjustified prejudice against an employee. Only in cases of redundancy is the dismissal subject to the observance of socioeconomic criteria specified by law regarding the selection of the employees to be dismissed. Employees must also give prior notice in order to terminate the employment, otherwise they are liable to compensate the employer.

Employers are allowed to dismiss an employee when pregnant and for a year after the birth only if they prove the existence of a very significant reason for the dismissal, which has to be unconnected with the pregnancy. Termination or discontinuation of employment for any reason has to be reported to OAED within eight days.

Collective dismissal (regulated by Law 1387/1983, as amended especially by Law 3863/2010, which increased the number of employees that can be dismissed before the special provisions regarding collective dismissal apply) covers the dismissal in one month of more than six employees for firms with 20 to 150 employees, or more than 5 per cent of the workforce or more than 30 employees (whichever is less) for firms with more than

150 employees. Collective dismissal requires written notification and discussions with the employees' representatives in the enterprise, as well as the reporting of the result of such discussions to the relevant Prefecture. If the discussions do not lead to an agreement, the Prefect has the authority not to approve some or all of the dismissals.

The retirement age was raised in 2010 to 65 years for both women and men, though certain interim arrangements apply during the introduction of the new provisions. Maximum working hours are set by the Presidential Decree of 7 June 1932 at 8 hours daily and 48 hours weekly. Nevertheless, according to the National Collective Labour Agreement of 14 February 1984, which applies to all private sector employees, the working week is only 40 hours. The system of five working days per week applies to the employees of most firms (shops being a significant exception). For employees working five days per week, additional hours means work over 40 and up to 45 hours per week, and for those working six days per week, up to 48 hours per week, and is paid at 25 per cent extra.

Overtime means work exceeding the above time limits, and is paid at one and a half times the normal rate. If overtime exceeds 120 hours per year, one and three-quarters the normal rate applies. Overtime is permissible only for urgent and extraordinary needs of the enterprise and is subject to prior written notice to and approval by the Labour Inspectorate and to the lawful keeping by the employer of a special overtime record book. If those conditions are not met, or if working time exceeds 10 hours in a day, overtime is considered illegal and is paid at double time. Work at night is paid at one and a quarter time, while work on Sunday and holidays is at one and three-quarters time. Special provisions have been established regarding flexibility in annual working hours, shifts and employees who are on call.

Annual paid holiday of 20 or 24 days is given to employees working five or six days per week, respectively, with 22 or 26 days after 3 years' service. Dismissal during the holiday is invalid. Absence due to illness (and other serious reasons) is considered as working time and is paid by the employer (subject to certain maximum time limits) and by the respective social security organization as sickness benefit, according to specific legal provisions. Special absence is granted for pregnancy and childbirth, for maternity (and paternity, under certain circumstances), including childcare and breastfeeding, for marriage, attending parent–teacher conferences, illness of a dependant, death of a family member, preparation for and participation in exams, voting, blood transfusion and dialysis, AIDS, and so on.

In case of an accident occurring at work or in connection with it, including occupational illness not attributed to the employer's negligence, the employer is released from the obligation to pay any compensation (except punitive damages), if the employee is insured by the Social Security Institute (IKA), which covers all related expenses. Otherwise, the employer must pay the lump sum compensation stipulated by Law 551/1915, which corresponds to the severity of the accident (death, permanent or temporary/full or partial inability to work and so on), and must cover all of the employee's medical expenses , including hospitalization, medication and other relevant expenses. The employer's liability for accidents at work is objective (without fault). Any accident at work must be reported immediately by the employer to the police, and to the Labour Inspectorate within 48 hours and IKA within 5 days from the accident.

Finally, male employees, on completion of their compulsory military service, have the right to be re-employed in the same job.

Collective employment law

This section will highlight some main issues relating to the protection of trade union freedoms, structure and types of trade unions, collective labour agreements, mediation and arbitration, and strikes.

Protection of trade union freedoms

All employers, employees and workers have a constitutional right to establish, participate in (provided that they have been employed for at least two months) and opt out of a trade union. Mixed trade unions consisting of employers as well as employees are not allowed. Employers are not allowed to dismiss employees or treat them unfavourably in any way as a result of legitimate union activity, nor are they allowed to intervene in the operation of a union, but must use their reasonable endeavours to facilitate such activity.

Trade unions are entitled to internal autonomy, financial self-sufficiency, democratic organization, free and effective legitimate action (through collective negotiations, strikes and so on). A certain number of founders and administrators of the union (corresponding to the size of its membership) are protected against job transfer and dismissal and can be dismissed only for serious reasons stipulated by law (such as unjustified, persistent refusal to provide services, disclosure of trade or industrial secrets and bodily injury or threatening of employer), if such reasons are proven before a special committee.

Structure and types of trade unions

The constituent bodies of trade unions are 1) the General Assembly, which is the principal body of the union, having the power to decide on all issues concerning the union, and exclusive authority to decide on specific issues of major importance (for example, strike, amendment of articles of association, dissolution, election of members of the BoD); 2) the Board of Directors (BoD), the executive body which represents the union judicially and extra judicially; 3) the Audit Committee, which supervises the financial administration of the Union; and 4) representatives of the primary or second-level union to the (general assembly of) the second-level or third-level unions, respectively. Besides primary trade unions (including local branches of unions of broader regional or national coverage, and employees' associations, which have no legal personality), there are second-level unions (that is, federations of unions of the same category and regional inter-professional Labour Centres) and third-level unions (confederations of federations and Labour Centres), the most representative of which can conclude General National Collective Labour Agreements (CLAs).

The objective of a trade union is to pursue the interests of its members, by entering into collective negotiations and concluding CLAs with the employers on the improvement of working conditions, minimum wages, benefits and allowances, safety and health provisions, recruitment, promotion and termination of employment, exercise of union rights, terms and procedures of collective bargaining, mediation and arbitration, social security issues (except retirement), and the rights and obligations of employers and employees in general.

Primary trade unions have legal personality, and consist either of employees employed by firms of the same industry/sector (sectoral unions), or employed by the same enterprise (enterprise unions), or employees of the same profession/occupation (professional unions).

Collective labour agreements, mediation and arbitration

CLAs are divided into sectoral, enterprise and local or national professional CLAs, which corresponding to the trade unions which conclude them and to the category of employees to which they apply. There are also General National CLAs, which determine the minimum employment conditions (especially wages) applying to all employees of the country. If collective bargaining fails (notwithstanding the workers' right to strike or apply other kinds of pressure), the parties have redress to mediation and if this fails, to arbitration proceedings. The selection of mediators and arbitrators and the supervision of the proceedings is carried out by OMED, an independent mediation and arbitration organization.

If a contract of employment contains terms more favourable to the employee, these take precedence over the terms determined by any type of CLA. If more than one CLA is applicable in a single case, the sectoral and enterprise CLAs take precedence over professional CLAs, provided that they contain provisions regulating the specific profession. In all other cases the terms most favourable to the employee prevail.

In principle, the regulatory provisions of the CLAs apply only to the members of the participating trade unions. However, the Minister of Labour may extend them to all employees/employers of a certain industry or profession (Article 11 of Law 1876/1990) if they already apply to employers employing over 51 per cent of the employees of the industry or profession.

Strikes

Strikes are considered the last resort for the protection of the employees/workers' rights if collective negotiations have already failed. For as long as they are on strike, workers earn no wages.

Judicial functionaries and members of the armed forces are prohibited from striking, while civil servants, local government employees, public law legal persons and those employed in firms of a public nature or of public benefit, whose operation is of vital importance in serving the basic needs of society, are subject to certain legal restrictions in exercising the right to strike.

Strikes are called by trade unions only (wildcat strikes are illegal). The exercise of the right to strike and its purpose must be legal and must not pose a threat to the survival of an enterprise. Strikes are subject to specific legal conditions, such as decision of the general assembly (for primary unions) or the BoD (for second- and third-level unions), prior notice, and security personnel.

The employer is not permitted to impose lockouts, seek injunction relief or hirestrike-breakers. Strikes may be pronounced illegal by a court of law. Continuing participation in an illegal strike is a breach of the contract of employment.

Summary

This chapter has highlighted some principal issues surrounding the operation and management of Greek corporations, as specified by Greek company law, tax law and employment law. Company law provides the framework for the legal structure of firms in Greece. Companies are generally divided into personal companies (the majority – 79.9 per cent – of all registered private firms) and capital-based companies. Firms operating in Greece are subject to corporation tax, value added tax (VAT), property tax, and social security contributions. Frequent changes to the tax system are characteristic of Greek tax law, and this is an important factor discouraging investments in new or existing companies in the country. Finally, employment law is divided into individual employment law, which regulates relations between employer and employee, and collective employment law, which concerns relations between employer and trade union.

Notes

1. Such as the incorporation of sociétés anonymes and minimum capital requirements, corporate governance, accounting and auditing principles, free movement of services and capital, elimination of obstacles to cross-border activities, equal protection of creditors and shareholders.
2. Civil Code, Articles 78–107.
3. However they have characteristics pertaining to companies, since they are groupings of persons pursuing a common objective. Specifically, they are non-profit, open type, multi-member entities, with legal personality. The pursuance of their objective (for example, social, cultural, political) is assigned to a flexible administrative body, while their members meet periodically to decide on important issues. At least twenty people are needed to found a union, a petition has to be filed and approved by the First Instance Court and publicity conditions must be fulfilled.
4. Law 2810/2000.
5. Law 1264/1982.
6. In particular Articles 20–28, 38–39, 41–44, 46–50 of the Commercial Law (complementarily Articles 741–784 of the Civil Code).
7. Civil Code, Articles 741–784.
8. In civil partnerships, in contrast to unlimited and limited partnerships, the company contract need not be written or publicised, they are not obliged to own assets and their objective may be non-profitmaking. The contributions and everything acquired though the administration of the partnership constitute common property of the partners, correspondingly to their 'participation right' in the partnership. Civil partnerships may acquire legal personality, if they have a for-profit objective, and comply with publicity requirements pertaining to unlimited partnerships.
9. Presidential Decree 81/2005.
10. Consortia are commonly formed among companies especially for project implementation, as contractors. Although certain tax and accounting provisions directly refer to them (for example, Article 1§2 Tax Code), consortia are not regulated as a distinct type of company.
11. They are founded by at least 15 people, and their articles of association are subject to the magistrate's court's approval. Co-partners have either unlimited personal liability, or personal liability up to a certain amount provided by the articles of association. The co-partnership operates though the general meeting of its members, the board of directors and the supervisory council. There are restrictions on the transfer of shares and the admission, departure and exclusion of a co-partner.

12. Commercial Law, Articles 47–50.
13. Council Regulation (EEC) No 2137/85 of 25 July 1985.
14. Code of Private Maritime Law, Articles 10–35.
15. Royal Decree of 16 June 1910, Article 38 and Law 3190/1955, Article 50A.
16. Law 264/25.9.2006.
17. Law 3601/2007 incorporating Directive 2006/48/EU (L 177/30.6.2006).
18. Law 3606/2007, incorporating Directive 2004/39/EU (L 145/30.4.2004).
19. Codification of Law Decree 400/1970.
20. Law 2367/1995.
21. Law 959/1979.
22. Laws 1905/1990 and 1665/1986 respectively.
23. Law 3190/1955.

References

National Statistical Service of Greece (2009) *Statistical Yearbook of Greece 2008*. Pireas: National Statistical Service of Greece.

Panezi, M. (2008) *A Description of the Structure of the Hellenic Republic, the Greek Legal System, and Legal Research*. Hauser Global Law School Programme, http://www.nyulawglobal.org/globalex/Greece1.htm.

Part II
Management Practices in Greek Firms

7
Strategic Management

Efthimios Poulis

Overview

Today dramatic changes are occurring in the structure and operational scope of business, government and non-profit organizations. These changes originate in both the internal and external environment of the organization. The fundamental question in the field of strategic management is how firms achieve and sustain competitive advantage (Rumelt *et al.*, 1994). This chapter discusses the strategic management practices followed by organizations in Greece. Strategic management provides the link to all the different functions inside organizations which will be analyzed in the sections of this chapter. Furthermore, the chapter presents the main concepts and frameworks that are widely used in strategic management, and extends their application to the Greek business system. In order to analyze the micro-external environment, Porter's Five Forces (1980) model is used, while for the internal environment, the Resource Based View (RBV) of the firm (Barney, 1991) model and the value chain (Porter, 1985) are used. For competitive strategies, Porter's (1980) generic strategies and Bowman's (1995) strategy clock will be used. Finally, the analysis of corporate strategies refers to diversification, both related and unrelated (Thompson *et al.*, 2007).

This chapter is organized in the following main sections. Firstly, it considers the *micro-external environment,* namely the competitive environment of Greek industries/markets. Secondly, it examines the *internal environment,* which will cover the main internal characteristics of organizations in Greece. Thirdly, it looks at *competitive strategies,* namely the strategies that organizations in Greece follow in order to achieve competitive advantage in their markets. Finally, *corporate strategies* are about the overall scope of the organizations in Greece.

Information on strategic aspects of the Greek environment is scarce since it is too sensitive for organizations to disclose. This chapter therefore primarily uses information from Euromonitor International, particularly from its Global Market Information Database (GMID),[1] and the author's research (Poulis, 2008).

Micro-external environment

The competitive environment, according to Porter's Five Forces model, comprises of competitive rivalry, threat of substitutes, bargaining power of buyers, bargaining power of customers and threat of entry. Recently, a sixth force was added, that of complementary products or services. The competitive environments of organizations operating in Greece differ according to the characteristics of the industries. There are industries in Greece that are attractive, while others are less attractive, due to idiosyncrasies of these markets.

Competitive rivalry

A principal characteristic of the Greek market is that competition is fierce, although local organizations rarely employ scientific management principles and techniques (Porter, 1980; Barney, 1991) as their multinational competitors do. Multinational corporations (MNCs) operate in the Greek market using their knowledge, experience and expertise, whereas their local competitors mainly use their intuition and experience. Local organizations often lack clear vision and a specific strategic direction, while their multinational competitors plan ahead, using contemporary tools and techniques. Local competitors take advantage of their brand awareness and long-established presence in the market. Multinational competitors exploit their innovative products and services, differentiated products and market research efforts. Competition is intense, mainly in the supermarket, food and clothing industries, and has increased in some of these markets due to the large shopping centres that have recently been built and attract almost all consumer segments (Euromonitor International, 2009). However, there are industries where competitive rivalry is not particularly strong, such as the betting, electricity (energy) and furniture markets, due to the existence of public monopolies or well-established companies that are not seriously affected by competition.

Threat of substitutes

Substitutes do not present a threat in most industries, since no clear substitutes have been developed for many of the products and services offered in the Greek market. In the retail market, however, there is a serious challenge from strong substitutes in the form of kiosks, convenience stores, butchers and so on in local neighbourhoods, which have a relatively high market share compared to other countries. This constitutes a challenge for supermarkets. Finding ways to reduce the market share of these substitutes is not an easy task. One of main characteristics of the Greek market is the personal relationship that develops between buyers and owners of these convenience stores. This personal relationship makes buyers shop from these stores, regardless of higher product price.

Bargaining power of buyers

The absence of substitutes in most industries also has an effect on the bargaining power of buyers, since in many cases they are obliged to buy from a specific provider. Whilst switching costs are not necessarily high, customers lack a wide variety of choice due to their location or other factors such as familiarity, convenience, personal relationships and so on. Moreover, there are no buyers' organizations or other forms of coalition, with the result that there is no collective decision-making or action against companies that may not trade fairly.

Bargaining power of suppliers

Suppliers, on the other hand, tend to possess more negotiating power against competing firms in a market. The supply of raw materials in Greece is not straightforward process, mainly due to lack of vertical integration in Greek organizations, and because logistics is not an advanced area of business. Greek organizations are, therefore, heavily dependent on their suppliers, either to reduce their costs or to produce differentiated, superior products. The main exceptions to this are the supermarkets, which possess significant negotiating power with companies in their industry. In fact, supermarkets are usually in a position to impose their own terms on their suppliers, as is the case in almost all countries. In the Greek market, which is not well organized or monitored, these effects are even stronger. However, action is taken when the 'war' between the industry and the supermarkets becomes unfair, unethical or even illegal: several supermarkets were recently fined by the Competition Commission for price fixing.

Threat of entry

New entrants do not present a major threat, because the competitive environment of the vast majority of industries in Greece is no longer so attractive, making organizations unwilling to invest. However, there are still some industries that seem quite attractive, especially to MNCs that want to take advantage of immature or underdeveloped markets. A prominent example of such new entrants is the 'hard discounters' in the retail industry. These hard discounters, mainly German supermarkets, invested in the Greek market, targeting price- sensitive customers. They managed to acquire market share from existing competitors and are expected to grow in terms of market share over the next five years (Poulis, 2008).

Complementary products/services

Finally, the sixth competitive force, complementary products/services, does not figure strongly in the Greek market, with the exception of a few industries. Although there are opportunities for collaboration between products such as cars and fuel, taking advantage of their complementary nature, it seems that neither side is interested in developing these strategic alliances. This reduces the interrelationships developed and, thus, reduces the effect of complementary products in the market.

Internal environment

According to the RBV theory of the firm (Barney, 1991), organizations use their internal resources and competences in order to achieve competitive advantage. Porter (1985) used a different framework to analyze the internal environment, the value chain consisting of different (primary and support) activities.

Resources and competences (in RBV terms) leading to sustainable global competitive advantage pose a real challenge for Greek organizations. This is mainly due to strategic drift following a period of success in the local market. Unique resources and core competences can be observed mainly by focusing on foreign MNCs, which use best practices from abroad, with minor amendments (if any), to gain an advantage over their local or MNC competitors. Local organizations tend to exploit their knowledge of the local market and their long-established presence in the country, which provide strong brand awareness and loyalty in some cases. This allows them to either reduce their costs or differentiate in the market.

Moreover, local organizations seldom use their networks to deal with their external environment. MNCs, on the other hand, network effectively in many ways. In the same vein, it could be argued that MNCs employ scientific management principles, whereas local organizations employ more 'traditional' practices and ways of doing business in general. This characteristic has an important effect on the different approach that organizations adopt in their markets: MNCs have a distinctive direction in the market, which in most cases differs significantly from the direction that Greek organizations follow. However, Greek organizations have recently begun to realize that they do not have to 're-invent the wheel' and that they could benefit from the best practices and role models provided by foreign organizations. This has led either to imitation or to the formation of alliances with foreign companies in order to facilitate knowledge dissemination.

As far as the value chain is concerned, organizations in Greece tend to focus on operations and marketing/sales in order to add value. The role of logistics, both inbound and outbound, is largely ignored or minimized, although these two activities could offer them significant cost reductions and improved efficiency. The beneficial effects of using scientific principles of logistics are obvious in some companies, mainly MNCs, which have used logistics properly, in order to add value.

Support activities (firm infrastructure, human resource management, technology development and procurement) are often not central to Greek organizations. The only exception could be technology development for some of the industries, for example shipping, and procurement for other industries, or retail companies, especially supermarkets. Greece as a country is not investing heavily in research and development (R&D) and this is also the case for most Greek organizations (Euromonitor International, 2006). The only exceptions are companies or industries in which technological advancements are crucial and constitute the core activity in order to achieve competitive advantage. For all other industries and companies, claims of investment in state-of-the-art equipment and technological facilities reflect their aspirations more than the reality. Procurement is generally a significant activity only for supermarkets, although their relationship with their suppliers is not ideal. There are only a few local supermarkets that do not put pressure on their suppliers. All other competitors, especially MNCs, follow the lead of their headquarters and subsidiaries all over the world, where relationships with suppliers are often fraught with difficulties.

Competitive strategies

Greece is less competitive than some other countries due to, among other things, inflexible laws and bureaucracy (Euromonitor International, 2009). According to a Euromonitor International (2009) report, Greece ranked 96th out of 181 countries in the world for ease of doing business, which highlights the problem that organizations face. However, there are a few notable exceptions to this negative image.

The strategies that organizations in Greece follow in order to achieve competitive advantage in their markets are generally not the result of well-planned approaches, structured analyses and rational decision-making processes. The competitive strategies are mainly the outcome of intuition, bias, path dependency and imitation. The analysis which follows will provide insights into the competitive strategies followed by organizations in Greece, based on Porter's (1980) generic strategies and Bowman's (1995) strategy clock.

'A major question that needs to be addressed is whether strategy is derived entirely from the environmental conditions or is there a two-way fit between strategy and environmental dimensions?' (Venkatraman and Camillus, 1984:517). In most classical studies, organizations are conceived of as being required to react to the environment by adapting to it. However, it was soon realized that organizations can be proactive or interactive to their environment. The updated structure-conduct-performance (SCP) paradigm (Porter, 1981; Scherer, 1980) presents an interconnection between market structure and firm conduct. Nowadays, strategic management and organization theory have adopted Weick's (1979) view, namely that organizations enact their environments. They define their strategy and subsequently they explore the opportunities offered in their chosen path, setting new or secondary goals (Bourgeois, 1980).

Organizations in Greece are affected by several forces when developing their competitive strategies, but the principal two are a) the type of competition, namely multinational or local, and b) the macro-environmental effects, mainly the ones from economic forces. At the time of writing (2010), Greece presents some really interesting and idiosyncratic characteristics, which have seriously affected the organizations operating in this environment and, consequently, their strategies. These characteristics are presented below.

As we saw earlier, MNCs import best practices from abroad and employ scientific management principles when developing their strategies. Most of the time this makes them more competitive in their markets, although there are still examples of local organizations being the market leaders.

The main effect, however, emanates from the macro-external environment and especially the economic one. The recent credit crunch placed Greece in a financially weak position, forcing it to request financial support from its allies in the EU. The government was obliged to take very strict financial measures that had a negative impact on citizens, considerably reducing their disposable income. This affects, and is expected to affect even more in the future, the buying behaviour and preferences of customers in Greece.

Moreover, salaries are low in Greece and this is especially true for the younger generation, a group sometimes called 'Generation 700 Euros' (Euromonitor International, 2010). This reduces the disposable income of a significant segment of the market, although these young employees tend to live at home with their parents longer in order to save living expenses.

The direct effect of macro-environmental forces on the markets that organizations in Greece operate in is that customers have become price-sensitive. The market has changed considerably in most industries, favouring companies that offer their products and services at low cost and causing companies with more expensive products and services to exit the market. There are exceptions, of course, mainly due to specific industry characteristics (see, for example, the luxury goods industry case study presented below). However, there have been significant trends in the Greek market: even a few years ago, cheap products were considered to be low quality and even customers with average or below average income would not care for it to be known that they were shopping from a hard discounter. This is no longer the case; on the contrary, customers who pay attention to price differences and research the market in order to find the best deals and the cheapest products are now considered to be 'smart buyers'. This attitudinal change is evident in most markets and has seriously affected the competitive strategies of almost all organizations.

More specifically, organizations across different industries prefer to be the price leaders in the market nowadays, reducing their prices to appeal to customers, especially the price-sensitive ones. The recent credit crunch has affected the disposable income of customers in Greece, forcing them to search for cheaper options.

The main way for companies to reduce their costs is through human resources, either laying employees off or 'urging' them to work longer hours without getting paid: 'In a dog-eat-dog environment where everyone works for long hours, it's not the fear of losing your job – but the fear of not being seen as part of the team – that keeps individuals in the office longer' (Euromonitor International, 2010).

Some organizations have also attempted to reduce labour costs through flexible forms of employment, mainly distance or e-working.

However, the two main problems they have faced are: a) the infrastructure, since Greece is in one of the lowest positions in terms of its exposure to the latest technological advancements, and b) computer literacy, which once again is one of the lowest in the EU (Euromonitor International, 2010).

Organizations pursuing cost leadership are successful in several industries, but principally in the retail sector, especially supermarkets and the clothing industry. The vast majority of Greek consumers have reduced their spending on clothing and groceries, but with low-cost organizations, they are able to buy the same amount of products at lower prices.

The interesting effect here is that Greek consumers are now more conscious of what and how they spend, whether their own income has been reduced or not (Euromonitor International, 2009). This is mainly the effect of media coverage, which has publicized the fact that they spend up to almost 200 per cent more on basic food products than consumers in other European countries, even wealthier ones (Euromonitor International, 2010).

At the same time, several organizations pursue differentiation strategies, offering different products to their customers. Sometimes this differentiation is real and obvious; however, there are times when it merely reflects the perceptions and marketing efforts of organizations. One would expect that, during times of recession, fewer companies would pursue differentiation strategies. However, this is not necessarily the case in Greece. Health-related products, the food and drinks, cosmetics and toiletries sectors include companies that differentiate. Organizations tend to achieve that type of competitive strategy through marketing campaigns promoting lifestyle changes, and superiority in product development processes (Euromonitor International, 2009).

Hardly any organizations follow a hybrid strategy, that is, pursuing cost leadership and differentiation simultaneously. Local organizations are either reluctant or unable to achieve that demanding goal; MNCs are already successful in the Greek market, due to the knowledge and expertise they carry with them when they invest in the country, and consequently they do not need to follow a more sophisticated competitive strategy in order to be successful. As a result, there are only a few examples of organizations trying to pursue the hybrid strategy, and most if not all of them are multinationals in the food sector, electronics or the furniture industries.

Focused differentiation is not a commonly followed competitive strategy, especially in an environment dominated by uncertainty and financial problems. However, there are opportunities in the Greek market for organizations that pursue focused differentiation. There are customer segments that earn enough money to allow for discretionary spending (Euromonitor International, 2008). These customers are lifestyle-conscious and favour luxury brands. However, there are other segments that organizations can target, offering a differentiated product: affluent retirees, DINK (Double Income, No Kids) customers, recent graduates, managers and immigrants (Euromonitor International, 2008, 2010). These customer segments are offered products mainly in the following sectors and industries: food, alcoholic drinks, entertainment (night clubs), cosmetics and toiletries, healthcare, cars, clothing and shoes (Euromonitor International, 2009, 2010). Despite the recent financial crisis, these customers are willing and able to spend more money on these specific categories of products, which provide them with social status and recognition.

The 'no-frills' (or focused cost leadership) strategy has recently been gaining momentum in the Greek market. One of the most successful examples is that of the hard discounters, which entered the Greek market offering low-cost alternative products. They offer the bare minimum of service, with uninviting layouts and no category management. In this way, they manage to reduce costs considerably and represent an attractive option to Greek consumers.

Another successful example of the no-frills strategy is low-quality Chinese products, mainly clothes and electronics, offered at very low prices. Price-sensitive customers tend to buy these products, although they are aware of the low quality. However, some recent accidents with faulty Chinese products have reduced their popularity with Greek customers.

Although it may sound strange, failure strategies are followed by many organizations in Greece, especially small and medium-sized firms (SMEs), but also public monopolies. One of the most prominent examples is public companies, especially telecommunications and utility (electricity and water) companies. These often provide low-quality services at a standard or even high price. Greek customers have realized, however, that there is either a lack of competitors offering alternatives, or that the competition is untrustworthy or also of low quality. It should be noted, however, that private companies in these industries are not always of low quality. Some of them offer products or services of adequate quality to their potential customers, but they still need to use the infrastructure of the public companies (ex-monopolies). As is the case in many other countries, public companies create problems for the new (private) entrants, thus increasing the dissatisfaction of their customers. In this way, which is mostly neither ethical nor legal, public companies have managed to increase the switching costs for their customers considerably, exploiting their 'first-mover advantage'.

Finally, there are examples of SMEs, especially in sectors such as clothes and shoes, that offer standard products at high prices. The new shopping centres offer the same products at lower prices due to the economies of scale that they can achieve through their purchasing power. Customers have started buying these products from companies in shopping centres rather than from small companies in local neighbourhoods.

Corporate strategies

Most organizations in Greece are not diversified in terms of corporate strategies. It seems that the overall scope of the organization, which represents the focus of the corporate strategies, is not as important for organizations in Greece as the competitive strategies discussed above. Organizations seem to place more emphasis on the competitive advantage they can achieve in their market and not so much on the different markets they can invest in. This is justified by the fact that competition in most industries is intense, and companies face considerable difficulty in achieving competitive advantage in their core industry. This leaves them with fewer resources, but also less willingness to think about and implement investment plans in other related or unrelated markets. Moreover, uncertainty about the future hinders business planning.

Unrelated diversification (Thompson *et al.*, 2007) is rarely found in the Greek market. Local organizations have several difficulties in achieving competitive advantage in their market. Investing in many unrelated markets may threaten their own survival. The fact that they cannot use their existing capabilities and they have no expertise in that market makes this option a dangerous or at least an unattractive one. Some MNCs operating in Greece belong to holding companies that have pursued unrelated diversification abroad. However, the parent companies do not invest in all the different unrelated markets in Greece. Most if not all of the time, they invest in only one Greek market. In fact, even if they invest in more than one market in Greece, these markets are related.

Related diversification (Thompson *et al.*, 2007) does exist, but the preference of organizations for this type of corporate strategy is mainly limited to MNCs that diversify in the Greek market. However, not all sub-categories of related diversification are used.

Organizations in Greece use horizontal integration, mainly through the acquisition of other competitors or companies producing substitute products. Vertical integration, both backward and forward, is rare, since the idea of controlling all the different steps of the overall process tends not to appeal to them. They do not invest in the acquisition of their suppliers (vertical integration backward), with the principal exception of dairy companies that have vertically integrated through acquiring farms in Greece. Moreover, they do not invest in acquiring their customers (vertical integration forward), the principal exception being mobile network companies, which have developed their own distribution channels in the form of retail stores.

In terms of strategy development directions (Ansoff, 1957), organizations in Greece mainly use two of them. Currently, because of the financial crisis, most organizations consolidate, protecting what they already have. There are also organizations, however, that penetrate the market further, taking advantage of the financial problems that some of their competitors may face.

There remain organizations that develop new products; these are mainly MNCs operating in the food sector. These products target their existing customers, offering them more, usually cheaper, alternatives. Local organizations are affected by the crisis and they are not willing to take more risks by developing new products.

Market development is not one of the main options for organizations in Greece. There are multinationals that use Greece as their base in order to expand in the Balkans and the Middle East, and this can be regarded as market development. Greek companies mainly invest in the Balkan countries, usually in the food sector and the banking industry.

Finally, diversification, which was previously presented, is not usually selected as one of the main strategy development directions of organisations in Greece.

The methods of strategy development used by organizations in Greece vary significantly, mostly depending on the type of the organization (multinational or local), the industry it is in and finally the specific strategy development direction it wants to follow.

If they are consolidating or penetrating the market further, organizations tend to use internal resources. The same method of internal growth is used by organizations pursuing a different strategy development direction, that of product development. Organizations in all industries develop their new products internally, so as to have more control over the process and implement their own plans properly.

The preference for internal growth is not the dominant one for the two remaining directions. For market development, organizations tend to use internal growth when they invest in other areas or markets within the borders of Greece. However, they mainly use mergers and acquisitions and sometimes alliances with organizations abroad when they invest in another country. Especially when investing in the Balkans, organizations in Greece mainly acquire local companies. There are still cases though, for example in banking, where banks have invested in other countries using their own resources.

As far as diversification is concerned, organizations in Greece tend to acquire or merge with other companies. Strategic alliances are rarely formed; however there are companies, mainly multinational ones, which diversify in new markets with new products using their own resources. Greek companies use either internal growth or mergers and acquisitions (Poulis, 2008).

Summary

In conclusion, organizations in Greece are quite actively engaged in terms of competitive strategies, but at the same time they are not particularly interested in employing different corporate strategies. Organizations in Greece seem to be relatively inflexible when it comes to changing their competitive strategy, but a lot more flexible when they make the decision to change their corporate one. Corporate strategies tend to change relatively fast, when necessary, but senior managers in organizations in Greece tend to be more reluctant to change their existing competitive strategy. The selection of both corporate and competitive strategies depends mostly on the industry, which sometimes presents idiosyncratic characteristics in the case of Greece. However, that selection may also depend on whether the organizations are local or multinational.

The main conclusion that can be drawn concerns the match between the complexity of the external environment faced by organizations in Greece and the complexity of their internal environment (Poulis, 2008). Most organizations are dealing with relatively low external complexity, due to the fact that the Greek market is not very advanced in comparison to markets in foreign countries. Since these organizations are not challenged by external forces, they tend to become complacent and match their low external complexity with a low internal one. However, for some industries that are important to the Greek economy, for example shipping, external complexity is really high, since companies operate in a truly global environment. In these cases, there are modern proactive companies that innovate or simply adapt to the dynamic markets they are in, thus possessing high internal complexity. On the other hand, one can find examples of traditional companies which are satisfied with less profit but more stability in the market and thus do not match the high external complexity, having only low internal complexity (Poulis, 2008).

In addition, there are industries that have significantly changed during the last few years (for example, higher education), mainly because of changes imposed by EU directives. Consequently, the landscape in these industries is considerably altered, with existing actors required to change and adapt to new circumstances, reflecting a higher level of quality. These changes have forced complacent organizations to compete for survival and also provided opportunities for new entrants (ICAP, 2006).

As a rule, however, the more dynamic the external environment, the more innovative and adaptive the organizations will be internally. There are exceptions to this rule (for example, public higher education institutions), but they represent only a small proportion of organizations in Greece and are almost entirely local companies performing at a lower level than their main competitors.

Note

1. GMID is an integrated online information system providing key business intelligence on countries, companies, markets and consumers. GMID contains over a million hard-to-find demographic, economic and marketing statistics for 205 countries worldwide.

References

Ansoff, I. (1957) 'Strategies for diversification', *Harvard Business Review*, 35(5): 113–24.

Barney, J.B. (1991) 'Firm resources and sustained competitive advantage', *Journal of Management*, 17: 99–120.

Bourgeois, L.J. (1980) 'Strategy and environment: A conceptual integration', *Academy of Management Review*, 5: 25–39.

Euromonitor International (2006–2010) *Country Reports: Greece*. http://www.euromonitor.com/.

Faulkner, D. and Bowman, C. (1995) *The Essence of Competitive Strategy*. London: Prentice-Hall.

ICAP (2004–2008) *Industry Reports*. http://www.icap.com/.

Porter, M.E. (1980) *Competitive Strategy: Techniques for Analyzing Industries and Competitors*. New York: Free Press.

Porter, M.E. (1981) 'The contribution of industrial organisation to strategic management', *Academy of Management Review*, 6: 609–20.

Porter, M.E. (1985) *Competitive Advantage*. New York: The Free Press.

Poulis, E. (2008) 'Testing the law of requisite complexity', Doctoral thesis, Manchester Business School.

Rumelt, R.P., Schendel, D. and Teece, D. (1994) *Fundamental Issues in Strategy.* Cambridge, MA: Harvard Business School Press.

Scherer, F.M. (1980) *Industrial Market Structure and Economic Performance.* Chicago: Rand McNally.

Thompson, A.A., Strickland, A.J. and Gamble, J.E. (2007) *Crafting and Executing Strategy: The Quest for Competitive Advantage: Concepts & Cases* (15th ed.) New York: McGraw-Hill.

Venkatraman, N. and Camillus, J.C. (1984) 'Exploring the concept of "fit" in strategic management', *Academy of Management Review*, 9(3): 513–25.

Weick, K.E. (1979) *The Social Psychology of Organizing.* Reading: Addison-Wesley.

8
International Business

Konstantinos Poulis

Overview

It is difficult to trace the origins of international business (IB) activity in Greece. Fragmentation of research, lack of documented and centrally stored evidence and practical limitations do not allow us to understand exactly the 'when' and 'how' of the origins of IB activity in the country. The fact is that international trade has been an essential component of the lives of Greek people since ancient times and it has been responsible for the spread of Greek civilization to the rest of the known world. This tradition is still evident today and its greatest manifestation is in the role of Greek shipping as the main facilitator of international trade flows. Greeks are involved in international marine logistics and international trade throughout the world but it should be emphasized that the main commercial activity is trade and not industrial production. This complements the overall identity of the Greek economy as a former agricultural and increasingly service-oriented economy showing increasing signs of de-industrialization in recent decades. More specifically, it is interesting to note at this stage that more than 90 per cent of world trade is conducted by sea while the Greek-owned fleet represents almost one-fifth of world tonnage (MARISEC, 2010). It is easy to see, therefore, that international business has always been at the forefront of economic and social activity in the country.

Nevertheless, IB as we perceive it today is a recent development. For Greece, the twentieth century was definitely an important period in the development of international business when large market-seeking and resource-seeking multinational firms were investing in Greece and Greek firms were starting to internationalize their operations (primarily in the food and services sectors). However, at this point it must be noted that IB activity associated with Greece has received scant attention from academic researchers despite the fact that Greece always had an open economy. This applies to most peripheral European economies, with the majority of IB research (or research that can be of interest to international businesses) dedicated to North American and North European contexts (Loane *et al.*, 2009; Merrilees and Tiessen, 1999).

Only in the last decade or so have a number of empirical papers been published focusing specifically on Greek international business or comparing it with other developed or developing countries and the managerial practices that support international business. For example, Barbosa and Louri (2002) aimed to examine the determinants of the ownership preferences of manufacturing multinational firms established in Greece and Portugal in the 1990s. Their study observed differences between the two countries in terms of relative foreign direct investment (FDI) size, industry and ownership choices, showing that firm and industry characteristics, interacting with location, affect ownership decisions. In a similar vein, Kessapidou and Varsakelis (2002) aimed to explore the impact of national culture on the performance of foreign affiliates in Greece. Their paper, using a sample of 478 firms, demonstrated that the further the 'national culture distance' from Greece of the foreign firm's country of origin, the better the performance of the Greek affiliate. The same study also provided additional insights around the role of culture in international business in Greece. Manolopoulos *et al.* (2007) analyzed survey data on foreign firms' research and development (R&D) activity in Greece and showed that even if original development work is at significant levels, the primary aim of multinational corporation (MNC) subsidiaries' R&D activity in the country remains the adaptation of existing technologies to local conditions.

Other studies had a sectoral focus in traditional industries of the Greek economy. For example, Harlaftis and Theotokas (2004) compared the nature and characteristics of British and Greek tramp-shipping companies over the last 130 years, with interesting results. These indicate that despite the tendency of companies to adopt corporate and managerial forms, British and Greek tramp-shipping firms remained first and foremost family firms. This is of particular relevance for the Greek business system which is dominated by small to medium-sized family-owned firms and it is in line with the observation that more than half of all registered firms in the country are owner-only and almost four out of ten employ between one and ten employees. At the same time, large firms of more than 250 employees account for a mere 0.05 per cent of all registered firms in the Greek market (National Statistical

Service of Greece, 2002). Interestingly, Harlaftis and Theotokas (2004) also stressed that the strength and viability of these family firms were associated with their networking capacity at local, national and international levels and a sense of trust-building among family firms involved in international business. There has also been increased interest in more specialist non-core IB issues which nevertheless have a great influence on IB activities, such as the role of ethics. In this respect authors such as Peppas and Peppas (2000) or Tsalikis and LaTour (1995) have investigated the importance of ethics for international management with a particular focus on Greece, enhancing our understanding of attitudes towards ethical issues.

As a result of this incomplete picture, an attempt to record IB activity in the relatively 'uncharted' territory of Greece is worthwhile, since it can stimulate further investigations into the trends and characteristics of this activity and can also generate investigations for other similar countries. For the purposes of this chapter, statistical data and figures generated by colleagues in IOBE (Foundation for Economic and Industrial Research) in Greece, the National Statistical Service and the National Export Council have been of great assistance to the author. The GMID database by Euromonitor – an integrated online information system providing key business intelligence on countries, companies, markets and consumers that contains over a million demographic, economic and marketing statistics for 205 countries worldwide – also proved to be of great help. Last but not least, the International Bank for Reconstruction and Development provided significant data to strengthen the latter sections of this effort.

International business in Greece: the outward activity of Greek firms

The first part of the principal section of this chapter will be devoted to the outward activity of Greek firms which have a presence across frontiers. Despite and maybe because of the small size of its economy and internal consumption and its supposedly peripheral role in world economic affairs, Greece demonstrates a remarkable presence in world markets, with multinationals stretching from the Balkans (for example, National Bank of Greece) to North and South America (for example, TITAN, S&B, Tsakos Group) and the Far East (for example, FolliFollie). As a result, Greek multinationals are powerful agents of change and contribute significantly to prosperity and rates of employment in several countries across the world. It is not surprising, therefore, that Greece ranks among the top 50 countries for foreign investment (Papanastassiou 2009). Nevertheless, Greece's exports, which are estimated at US$ 23.7 billion in 2008 (Euromonitor International) amounted to 6.7 per cent of GDP, which remains one of the lowest in the European Union. As a result, exports cannot be seen as a major driver of the Greek economy, which can be characterized as introvert and not fully integrated with the rest of the globalized world. At this point it should be noted that there is a paradox about the international presence of Greek firms. While a significant number of sophisticated Greek firms have followed the 'hard' road of FDI, the export scene, which is the simplest form of international expansion, lags relatively far behind. Thus, despite the huge commitment of resources associated with FDI and despite the small size of the economy, large Greek firms seem to perform more satisfactorily than small and medium-sized exporters.

Structural weaknesses of the Greek economy and their effect on IB

It should be noted that structural weaknesses in foreign trade by Greek firms reflect the enduring problems of the Greek economy and the lack of skills allowing adaptation to the requirements of the international arena. Driva and Patimpouli (2004) have stressed the factors generating this structural weakness with attendant consequences for the capacity of Greek firms to trade internationally.

The first factor is the small size of business units in Greece. This generates certain disadvantages for Greek firms which cannot take advantage of economies of scale and scope either domestically or internationally. This, in conjunction with the size of the domestic market, creates inherent barriers to Greek firms' competitiveness in the international arena.

The second factor is the inability to tailor business practices and activities to new forms of competition in the international arena. This inability may be attributed to lack of relevant international experience or limited access to sources of relevant knowledge (for example, with regard to distribution structures or patterns of consumer behaviour abroad). In any case, Greek small to medium-sized firms (SMEs) find it hard to penetrate and tailor their practices to the requirements of world markets.

The third factor is the inability of firms to avail themselves of technological advances that generate sources of competitive advantage. This comes naturally as a result of the long-term lack of focus that Greek governments traditionally had with regard to research and innovation. Greece ranks poorly among European countries that invest in research-related activities, and as a result the technology sector in Greece suffers from lack of competitiveness compared to other similar countries (with the notable exceptions of leading firms and pioneering universities or specific research centres).

The fourth factor is the high degree of black market activity and corruption and the overall unstable institutional environment in the country. The size of black market activity cannot be estimated accurately. However, arguably, it represents a high proportion of the official GDP for the Greek economy. This, in conjunction with corruption and unstable legal frameworks, creates structural weaknesses which reflect on the international competitiveness of Greek firms. A manifestation of the institutional instability under which firms are expected to operate is the constant change of the corporate tax regime in the country with attendant consequences for both outward and inward business.

The fifth factor is the incomplete (but constantly improving) infrastructure and transport network (ports, railways, roads). The turning point for this has been the Athens Olympic Games of 2004, when large amounts of money were devoted to improving the country's transport and infrastructure. Nowadays, Athens boasts a sophisticated transport and road network but nevertheless, unequal development in the rest of the country needs to be addressed.

Due to these structural weaknesses, and given the elimination of protectionism and the opening up of international (for example, central and eastern European) markets, Greek firms realized the loss of their competitiveness in the international arena. This is common and well-documented across most product categories; textiles, for example, face additional fierce competition from firms in the Far East (Driva and Patimpouli, 2004). Overall, cost leadership does not constitute a source of competitive advantage for most Greek firms who have to either increase their differentiation-based advantages or move production facilities to countries where labour and production costs are low (with consequent effects on the levels of employment and prosperity in the country).

The geographical and product scope of Greek firms abroad

With regard to the geographical scope of Greek firms' international business activity, it should be noted that export activity is to a large extent regional rather than global, with almost 80 per cent of Greek exports going to European markets (Euromonitor International). Elsewhere, a big share of Greek export activity can be seen in the Middle East, USA and

Canada. Overall, much of the internationalization of Greek multinationals is based on a psychic distance pattern with gradual commitment of resources in neighbouring countries in the Balkans (along with a noteworthy presence of Greek firms in major European markets such as the UK and Germany). Low production and labour costs in the Balkans and, consequently, the opportunity to augment the competitive positioning of the firm in the Greek market have been major drivers of Greek multinationals activity in the region. This is in line with the classic Uppsala internationalization model that European multinational firms in particular have traditionally adopted (Johanson and Vahlne, 1990).

The following are among the primary Greek exports (National Statistical Service of Greece, 2010):

Food products feature as major export items, particularly olive oil and olives, honey, yoghurt, cheese, tomato products, saffron and mastic. Beverages, especially wine, and agricultural products such as cotton and tobacco follow the same pattern.

Chemicals and plastics represent a major force in the exporting capacity of the country with firms such as Neochimiki occupying a leading position in the chemicals sector in south-east Europe.

Metals with particular reference to aluminium and copper products, where large corporations such as Aluminium of Greece and Viohalco dominate the scene.

Textiles, despite recent decline due to global pressures from low-cost producers, have traditionally featured as major exports.

Mining products, which are a natural result of the soil characteristics of several parts of Greece (for example, the island of Milos). Mining giants such as S&B demonstrate a remarkable presence in the world's markets.

Additional product categories in which Greek exports perform competitively in world markets include machinery and devices, oil, vehicle manufacturing, wood and paper products and pharmaceuticals. These are the key sectors exporting their produce from Greece but there is also considerable potential in such additional product categories as construction materials (for example, marble and cement), high-technology equipment, fish products and cosmetics.

Last but not least, particular mention should be made of the two major powerhouses of the Greek economy that are inherently international, tourism and shipping. Despite their recent decline due to the global recession of 2008–10, these two outward-oriented industries generate most wealth in the country and account for a significant proportion of the nation's GDP. With regard to tourism, Greece, due to its varied landscape, pleasant climate and rich history features as one of the major destinations of the world with tourism receipts amounting to more than US$16 bn in 2009 (Euromonitor International). Some of the key players in the tourism industry include Grecotel, the first Greek multinational hotel chain, Caravel Hotels, Ionian Hotels, Lampsa and Louis Hotels. At the same time, the Greek-owned fleet is the largest in the world and is responsible for much of the transport of goods sold internationally. Major players in the shipping sector are, among others, Anangel Shipping Enterprises, the Tsakos Group, Dryships and Danaos Corporation.

Greek multinationals

Despite the structural weaknesses of the Greek economic context, significant international activity can be observed, with several Greek multinational firms having a noteworthy or even pioneering presence in world markets. The following section provides notable examples of Greek firms which excel in the international arena (information retrieved from respective corporate websites in February 2010).

Viohalco

With production facilities in Greece, Bulgaria, Romania and the United Kingdom, Viohalco's companies specialize in the manufacture of copper, aluminium, and steel products as well as cables, generating an annual turnover of more than €3 billion. Viohalco's industrial activity abroad is represented, among others, by British-based Bridgnorth Aluminium Ltd., which manufactures lithographic sheets and foilstock, by Stomana Industry SA, a steel products manufacturer in Bulgaria, Sofia Med SA, a copper and brass processing company in Bulgaria and ICME ECAB, SA, a cable manufacturer in Romania. Viohalco is strongly export-oriented and accounts for approximately 9 per cent of Greece's total exports. Products are sold in more than 60 countries worldwide, either directly or through the Viohalco companies' commercial subsidiaries in the United Kingdom, Germany, France, Bulgaria, Italy, Romania, Serbia, Montenegro and Cyprus, as well as through an extensive network of representatives.

Intracom Holdings

Intracom is one of the largest multinational technology groups in south-east Europe. The Group's main activities are telecommunications solutions and products, electronic defence systems, e-Government projects and IT systems for public administration, financial institutions, banks and large enterprises, telephony and broadband service provision, and construction. The company has been strongly established for more than 30years in Greek and international markets with subsidiaries/participations in 21 countries and exports reaching 60 countries. The international expansion of the company reveals a strategic focus on the markets of Western Europe, central and South-eastern Europe, the Middle East and North Africa where Intracom has a strong presence and commercial success.

Coca-Cola Hellenic

Coca-Cola Hellenic serves approximately 560 million people in 28 countries. It is one of the largest bottlers and vendors of The Coca-Cola Company's products in the world, and the largest based in Europe. Coca-Cola Hellenic was formed in 2000 as a result of the merger of the Athens-based Hellenic Bottling Company and the London-based Coca-Cola Beverages. Since then, the company has extended its presence through international growth. Coca-Cola Hellenic is headquartered in Athens and is currently listed on the Athens, New York and London stock exchanges.

M J Maillis Group

The group is a world leader in packaging machinery and consumables. Since 1968, M J Maillis Group has manufactured end-of-line industrial packaging solutions for every conceivable application. These include packaging, wrapping and strapping materials and the tools and machines that use them.

Vivartia

Vivartia is the leading food company in Greece and one of the largest in Europe. Its brands reach consumers in 30 countries and are expanding across the world map. 2.5 billion Vivartia products are consumed every year reaching a regional market of 1 billion people. While Vivartia innovates within the Greek market, it has transcended national borders. Thus, Vivartia can be seen as an archetypal outward-looking firm representative of the Greek yet international entrepreneurial spirit, whilst at the same time making a substantial contribution to the growth of the national economy. It was formed in September 2006, following the absorption by DELTA Holding of DELTA Dairy SA, Chipita SA, Goody's SA and General Frozen Foods–Barba Stathis SA. Vivartia now comprises four divisions: dairy and drinks, bakery and confectionery, foodservices and entertainment, and frozen foods.

Folli Follie

This is a Greek company which designs, manufactures and distributes jewellery, watches and fashion accessories. Folli Follie is active in 25 countries with more than 380 points of sale worldwide, including shops in the most fashionable streets of the world's major cosmopolitan cities: London (New Bond Street), Tokyo (Ginza area), Paris (Rue Royale), Hong Kong (central district), New York (Madison Avenue), Dubai, Athens, Beijing, Seoul and Honolulu. In Japan and China alone, Folli Follie has around 80 and 70 points of sale respectively. Apart from the flagship stores in strategic locations, Folli Follie products are also sold through stand-alone shops and shops-in-shop in famous department stores, such as Isetan and Takashimaya in Japan, Lotte and Hyundai in Korea and Corte Ingles in Spain. In addition, Folli Follie has a strong presence in the travel retail market with points of sale in numerous airport duty-free shops around the world, such as Beijing, Seoul, Athens, Vancouver, Taipei, Hawaii and Guam among others, with Folli Follie products also available in-flight on major international airlines, such as British Airways, Aeroflot, Cathay Pacific, Japan Airlines, Qatar Airways and Singapore Airlines. It is worth noting that Folli Follie has direct control of its international distribution network by vertically integrating its operations from production to retail. Thus, it clearly demonstrates its international sophistication and its capacity to compete against traditional powerhouses of the global fashion industry.

S&B

S&B Industrial Minerals SA constitutes a multinational group of companies, with a strong international presence, selling its products in more than 65 countries worldwide. The S&B group consists of subsidiary and affiliated companies, operating mines, plants and distribution centres in more than 20 countries across 5 continents (among others in Greece, Germany, France, Italy, Spain, Bulgaria, Hungary, the USA, China, Brazil, India and Korea). The company employs more than 2,000 people for its mining, processing and trading of industrial minerals and ores activities, while its products are used for various applications including foundry, steel-making, construction and building materials, metallurgy and horticulture. All of the company's divisions hold high-ranking positions in their respective markets across Europe and the world.

TITAN

The group is an independent multi-regional producer of cement and other related building materials. It is headquartered in Greece and has an impressive track record of continuous growth since its establishment 107 years ago. Currently its production and distribution operations take place in 12 countries (with various locations in the USA, Canada, Egypt, Turkey, UK and other European countries), directly employing more than 6,000 people.

Apart from specific, stand-alone examples of excellence, however, it is important to consider the bigger picture of Greek multinational firms' activity. In this respect, Papanastassiou (2009) stresses that overseas operations of Greek multinationals account for almost 33 per cent of the overall turnover of the firms, with this percentage witnessing a steady increase in the last decade. Moreover, Greek firms' investment in their subsidiaries has seen a steady growth of 69 per cent at the beginning of the new millennium with services being at the forefront of these developments. The seminal report by Papanastassiou (2009) on Greek multinationals provides the basis for some insights into the types of international activity of Greek multinational firms.

Motivation for international involvement

There are a number of reasons why firms go abroad. The international business literature suggests four major types of motivations behind a firm's international involvement, influenced by both internal and external environmental considerations (Dunning, 2002). Firms go abroad either a) seeking for new markets to sell their products, b) to gain access to locally scarce or unavailable resources, c) to increase efficiency, or d) as part of a strategic asset-seeking behaviour. Greek multinationals follow the same pattern as most western firms, their primary motivation being the search for markets. This means that the manufacturing base of Greek firms in countries other than Greece is rather limited (mostly based in the Balkans), whereas the geographical scope of international presence does not offer opportunities for a globally co-ordinated strategic asset-seeking behaviour (Papanastassiou, 2009).

Market offering

In line with this, the vast majority of subsidiaries, with the exception of the shipping industry, are business-to-consumer firms who routinely adapt their product offerings to match the unique needs of the markets they have targeted (Papanastassiou, 2009). Thus several Greek multinationals have developed a market-oriented approach in foreign markets. This market orientation allows i) generation of customer intelligence and first-hand knowledge of the needs and wants of foreign consumers, ii) inter-functional co-ordination within the firm that enhances dissemination of this intelligence across the organizational units, and ultimately, iii) a response to these needs through notable innovative products and services. This 'adaptation logic' helps Greek firms tailor their products and services to the unique needs of foreign market segments and it follows the dominant pattern of marketing activity across borders as empirically shown by many authors in the field (Vrontis *et al.*, 2009).

Organizational structure and decision-making

With regard to decision-making, Papanastassiou (2009) notes that Greek firms that operate abroad follow a mixed approach, that is, strategic decisions are the result of a centralized decision-making process at headquarters, whereas operational decisions are the result of a more flexible approach that allows the subsidiary autonomy to act locally. The generic international strategy that drives activities of the subsidiaries abroad is, therefore, predominantly generated by headquarters, but nevertheless functional tasks such as marketing-related activities are performed at the subsidiary level. The overall purpose is to protect and augment the competitive advantages of both the subsidiary and the multinational corporation (Birkinshaw and Hood, 1998).

In summary, the picture that emerges is that several Greek multinationals perform exceptionally in foreign markets, whereas others struggle to enhance their international presence, impeded by marketing, managerial and institutional constraints. Overall, the geographical scope of international expansion still seems to be limited, with most firms resorting to familiar pursuits in countries with similar institutional and/or cultural backgrounds. This activity is predominantly associated with sales, whereas manufacturing activity overseas is still at moderate levels (perhaps reflecting the overall decline in the manufacturing base of the Greek economy).

Doing business in Greece – the foreign multinational perspective

The other side of the discussion around international business in Greece is the perspective of the foreign investor who wishes to obtain a foothold in the Greek market. Long-established attitudes and structural weaknesses, as described above, generate a not-so-favourable picture for potential investors. Greece, due to its increasing affluence during recent decades, and as a member of the EU, attracted significant levels of foreign direct investment but nevertheless, inward activity in the country presents certain difficulties for foreign firms.

According to the International Bank for Reconstruction and Development report on Greece World Bank, 2010), the country is ranked 109th out of 183 economies in respect of 'the ease of doing business in a foreign country'. This demonstrates that the environment in Greece for multinational firms aspiring to invest in the country is not as attractive as Greece's position among the world's developed countries would suggest. Constant changes in the corporate taxation regime and bureaucratic procedures for the setting up of the company normally feature as major factors that discourage many foreign firms from investing in Greece.

The International Bank for Reconstruction and Development (2010) indicates that particularly problematic areas include the realms of 'starting a business', 'employing workers' and 'protecting investors'. The investor typically needs to go through 15 different procedures which will cost 10.9 per cent of income per capita in order to get a business started. These procedures include several steps such as getting approval for the company's name from the Chamber of Commerce and Industry, filing company documents with the Athens Bar Association, depositing capital in a bank, obtaining stamps and certifications from Funds, and submitting articles of association to courts, and others.

Overall, the bureaucratic structure of the Greek economy and the unstable regulatory framework within which all firms are called on to operate impede foreign investors from setting up their firms in Greece. Nevertheless, additional reasons not to invest in Greece must also be seen at a comparative level. The unwillingness of foreign firms to invest in a member of the European Union also stems from the increased competitiveness in the global arena with regard to attracting FDI as a host country. The advent of low-cost players such as China or India has resulted in the deterioration of traditional industries in Greece, such as textiles, which could not match the low-cost competitive base, for example, of the Chinese context.

Following the crisis that hit Greece during 2009–10, Greek authorities may need to consider the reality foreign investors face and possibly enhance international trade and foreign investment through an institutional framework that facilitates rather than impeding entrepreneurial activity. Such a structural change is expected to have positive spillovers to both domestic and foreign firms, and overall will present Greece as a welcoming context for international operations.

Summary

Among the issues of particular interest to international business scholars and foreign firms aspiring to invest in Greece are ownership preferences of foreign multinationals and their determinants; the role of national culture in doing business in Greece; ethical perceptions of business practices in Greece; and the role of family ties and social networks. Specialist knowledge of this kind has often helped to explain the success or failure of international firms in many parts of the world, and thus an understanding of the implications of these characteristics for IB is crucial. The reader is encouraged to consult academic journals which periodically publish such topics related to Greece and other similar countries. The serious effects of the world economic crisis of 2009–10 on the Greek economy and consequently on Greek firms' international business activity should be considered in conclusion. Reduced levels of demand and an unclear picture regarding FDI flows are expected to shrink the GDP of the country and challenge the capacity of Greek firms to meet the requirements of the international competitive game. Moreover, rumours about the country's potential bankruptcy in late 2009 and early 2010 (due to the huge national debt) severely damaged its image in the eyes of the world and caused Greece to lose all the positive connotations it had gained after the successful organization of the 2004 Olympic Games.

According to the latest report by IOBE in 2009 (Issue 03/09), all short-term figures indicate a decline in industrial production and retail sales, with tourist receipts (the traditional powerhouse of the Greek economy) also expected to decline. At the same time, unemployment is on the rise, primarily affecting the youth. All these, in conjunction with worries about the escalating public debt of the country, create a new economic and social reality in 2010 which is expected to change the status quo of the country in the years to come.

Thus the overall outlook of the Greek economy in 2010 is not promising and inherent structural weaknesses in the economic system may jeopardize the efforts of Greek firms to internationalize their operations, while at the same time they may discourage foreign multinationals from investing in the country. Nevertheless, thanks to its strategic location at the crossroads of three continents, its highly skilled workforce and the traditional entrepreneurial attitude of its people, Greece can excel in the international business field. In order to achieve this objective, however, the institutional environment in the country and long-held attitudes must change to reflect the requirements of the new global competitive arena. It seems that Greece needs to make use of the most globalized, extrovert, productive and innovative segments of its society which currently lie hidden behind rigid norms and anachronistic practices.

References

Barbosa, N. and Louri, H. (2002) 'On the determinants of multinationals' ownership preferences: evidence from Greece and Portugal', *International Journal of Industrial Organization*, 20(4): 493–515.

Birkinshaw, J. and Hood, N. (eds) (1998) *Multinational Corporate Evolution and Subsidiary Development*. London: Macmillan.

Driva, Z. and Patimpouli, E. (2004) *Study on Exports*, National Export Council.

Dunning, J. (2002) 'Location and the multinational enterprise: a neglected factor?', in Brewer, T., Young, S. and Guisinger, S. (eds), *The New Economic Analysis of Multinationals: An Agenda for Management, Policy and Research*. Cheltenham: Edward Elgar, pp.45–69.

Harlaftis, G. and Theotokas, J. (2004) 'European family firms in International Business: British and Greek tramp-shipping firms', *Business History*, 46(2): 219–55.

IOBE (2009) 'The Greek Economy, 3/09, Foundation for Economic and Industrial Research'. http://www.iobe.gr/media/engoik/econ0309.pdf.

Johanson, J. and Vahlne, J.E. (1990) 'The mechanism of internationalization' *International Marketing Review*, 7(4): 11–24.

Kessapidou, S. and Varsakelis, N.C. (2002) 'The impact of national culture on international business performance: the case of foreign firms in Greece', *European Business Review*, 14(4): 268–75.

Loane, S., McNaughton, R. and Bell, J. (2009) 'The internationalization of internet-enabled entrepreneurial firms: Evidence from Europe and North America', *Canadian Journal of Administrative Sciences*, 21(1): 79–96.

Manolopoulos, D., Papanastassiou, M. and Pearce, R. (2007) 'Knowledge-related competitiveness and the roles of multinationals' R&D in a peripheral European economy: Survey analysis of Greece', *Management International Review*, 47(5): 661–82.

MARISEC (2010) 'The Top 20 Beneficial Ownership Countries (January 2009)' http://www.marisec.org/shippingfacts/worldtrade/top-20-beneficial-ownership-countries.php.

Merrilees, B. and Tiessen J.H. (1999) 'Building generalizable SME international marketing models using case studies', *International Marketing Review*, 16(4/5): 326–44.

National Statistical Service of Greece (2002) *Register of Greek Enterprises*. Athens: National Statistical Service of Greece (2010).

Papanastassiou, M. (2009) 'Subsidiaries of Greek multinational companies and internationalisation strategies', Economic Studies Series, Foundation for Economic and Industrial Research, Greece.

Passport GMID, Euromonitor International.

Peppas, S.C. and Peppas, G.J. (2000) 'Business ethics in the European Union: a study of Greek attitudes', *Management Decision*, 38(6): 369–76.

Tsalikis, J. and LaTour, M.S. (1995) 'Bribery and extortion in international business: ethical perceptions of Greeks compared to Americans', *Journal of Business Ethics*, 14(4): 249–64.

Vrontis, D., Thrassou, A. and Lamprianou, I. (2009) 'International marketing adaptation versus standardisation of multinational companies', *International Marketing Review*, 26(4-5): 477–500.

World Bank (2010) 'Doing Business 2011 in Greece', The International Bank for Reconstruction and Development, The World Bank. http://www.doingbusiness.org/~/media/fpdkm/doing%20business/documents/profiles/country/db11/grc.pdf.

9
Human Resource Management

Rea Prouska

Overview

Greece suffers from high unemployment rates, low demand for labour, and a severe problem in creating highly skilled and new technologically-oriented jobs (Karasiotou, 2004; Staikouras, 2004; National Statistical Service of Greece, 2005). These factors precondition the Greek market to limited investment and expansion opportunities (Eurostat, 2008), while firms are characterized by their small size: 54.6 per cent of all registered firms are owner-only and 43.7 per cent employ between one and ten employees, while large organizations (250+ employees) only account for a meagre 0.05 per cent of all registered firms in the Greek market (National Statistical Service of Greece, 2002). With an average organizational size of two employees per company, firms in Greece can be characterized as very small in comparison to the EU average (Galanaki and Papalexandris, 2007). However, the Greek economy depends significantly on the operation of micro firms. Micro- firms in Greece account for 59.6 per cent of total employment, compared to an EU-27 average of 29.5 per cent, while the share in total value added to the economy by micro-firms amounts to 38.6 per cent, compared to the EU-27 average of 20.2 per cent (Eurostat, 2008). In addition, since the Greek economic environment is characterized by low levels of government and business efficiency, competitiveness, and attraction of foreign direct investment (FDI), this leads to lower levels of investment and presence of multinational corporations (MNCs) in the market (see Haritakis and Pitelis, 1998; Joumard and Mylonas, 1999; Staikouras, 2004).

This chapter explores HRM practices in Greece by, firstly, providing a brief historical overview of the HR function to enable the reader to understand the current state of HRM in Greece. Secondly, it highlights supply and demand issues in the Greek labour market in order to illustrate organizational HR structures. Thirdly, it explores the Greek HR department and HR managers so that the factors affecting the size and role of the department, as well as the level of professionalism of managers, are understood. Fourthly, it provides an overview of the core HR activities (recruitment and selection, performance management and appraisals, training and development, employee rewards and employee relations). Fifthly, the practice of outsourcing HR activities to external providers is discussed, as this is common practice for many Greek organizations. Sixthly, an overview of the use of e-HR is provided, as this is one of the latest developments in the field. Finally, two critical issues in HRM are explored; the ageing workforce and gender equality in the Greek workplace.

Historical overview

The Greek economy enjoyed an upturn in the early 1960s as a result of the association agreement of Greece to the EEC. This agreement meant the entrance of foreign MNCs to the Greek business environment, presenting an ongoing challenge for the Greek-owned companies that suddenly had to compete with these advanced foreign firms. The MNCs successfully started their operations in Greece as they had in their possession, among other things, more sophisticated HRM techniques, techniques that were unavailable and unknown to Greek-owned organizations at that time.

Research from the 1970s (Greek Management Association, 1972; Hassid, 1977; Georgoulis, 1978) showed that the HRM function was rather underdeveloped in Greece in comparison with other management functions. The application of modern HRM practices was rather limited because Greek-owned firms were either unaware of them or considered them unsuitable for the management style in place at that time. However, the situation changed in the 1980s when Greece entered the EU, as some large and more progressive Greek-owned organizations started implementing various HRM practices introduced by the MNCs. From that point on, various HRM practices were formally implemented by Greek-owned firms, for example practices concerning the selection, appraisal and remuneration of personnel (Papalexandris, 1991, 1995). Greece is currently following the EU trend towards an improved, more strategic role for HRM; however, there is a slower pace in improvements compared to the rest of the EU (Papalexandris and Chalikias, 2002). Even today, HRM practices are not implemented in a strategic manner, but rather are used as a way of providing administrative support to the organization. With the pressure on organizations resulting from the 2010 Greek economic crisis, the HRM function is bound to be faced with budget cuts and an increasing need to prove its contribution to the bottom line of the business. Nonetheless, the field of HRM has generally developed since the 1970s, making it a promising one for Greek organizations in the future.

Supply and demand in the Greek labour market

An examination of the current state of the Greek labour market, particularly the existing demand for labour, will aid our understanding of HR structures in organizations.

Research evidence by Karasiotou (2004) reveals that only 14 per cent of firms are looking for employees with post-secondary vocational education, while 15.8 per cent are looking for university graduates and 11.4 per cent for those with a tertiary non-university qualification. Additional skills required include experience, knowledge of foreign languages and IT skills. This demand for experienced employees indicates that organizations believe that skills are better acquired through experience and not through training or education. Karasiotou (2004) found that it is more difficult to recruit employees for specialist technical and similar professions (13.4 per cent), while the remaining firms believe that they have no difficulties in finding employees with the necessary skills (57.5 per cent).

Evidence of the demand for skills is rather disappointing for the Greek labour market. Karasiotou (2004: 17) notes that 'most firms ask for low-skilled employees with this demand exceeding 80 per cent in some regions'. Employers tend to be looking for salespeople, accountants and unskilled industrial workers. It is only in Attica (the region surrounding the capital) that a demand for highly skilled and more modern occupations exists, such as IT experts and marketing specialists. However, even these positions are mostly only available in large organizations or MNCs, which constitute the minority of firms in the market. Micro firms are unable to offer highly specialist jobs. The Greek economy is primarily a services economy, while other industries, such as manufacturing, are not able to offer many specialist positions. Karasiotou (2004: 18) concludes that 'these facts highlight the severe problem faced by Greek labour market in creating high-skill and new technology-oriented jobs'.

The mismatch between demand for and supply of skills in Greece is due, in part, to the fact that Greece has the highest proportion of tertiary-level students in Europe (they account for more than a quarter of those enrolled in the education system). It has one of the highest enrolment rates (over 12.5. per cent) of adults aged 18 to 39 in tertiary education (European Commission, Eurydice and Eurostat, 2007). The fact that the majority of firms in Greece are micro in size significantly affects the types of jobs they can offer. This mismatch between supply and demand has further implications for a variety of HRM practices, such as HR planning, talent management and rewards strategies.

The HR department and HR managers

Ignjatovic and Svetlik (2002) use evidence provided by the Cranet Survey in 1999 to categorize HRM policies and practices across Europe. They place Greece in the 'eastern cluster' of countries (with Bulgaria, Estonia, Cyprus, Ireland, Northern Ireland, and Turkey). One of the major characteristics of the eastern cluster is the weak position of HRM, with few written policies and strategies, an insignificant role for HR departments and HR managers, and little senior management involvement in HR and the creation of HR strategies. In addition, employees are not involved in HRM and HR policy-making is centralized.

These findings should be considered, however, alongside the size and role of the HR department. The Greek business environment is dominated by the presence of micro firms and SMEs (National Statistical Service of Greece, 2002), which directly affects the size and role of the HR department in these firms. Research conducted by Prouska (2006) found that micro firms and SMEs generally have a small HR department in place (between one and five people). The size of the HR department increases and varies in larger organizations. Small firms do not have a formal HR policy in place, although some HR activities, such as recruitment, training and payroll, are informally performed either by the owner, or by another manager or employee. By contrast, medium-sized and large organizations boast a more organized HR department that has a formal written HR policy and performs a variety of HR activities, such as HR strategies, HR planning, performance management, employee relations, reward management, training and development, and recruitment.

The management ability of personnel managers depends on a range of qualities, skills and characteristics. These include experience, knowledge of HR and business issues, social and negotiation skills, personality, and interest in the job and people. Papalexandris (1995: 116) notes that 'such criteria indicate even more the need for special training in both personnel matters and in human skills development'.

The role and professionalism of HR managers in Greece is a factor that greatly influences the efficiency of the HR function. Research on this issue conducted in the early 1990s by Kanellopoulos (1990) and the Price-Waterhouse Cranfield Project (1993) shows that the HR department is considered to as important to the organization as other management functions such as production, finance and marketing. HR managers report directly to the head of the organization, or in some MNCs to the parent company's headquarters abroad. The majority of HR managers have a satisfactory level of education, although those who studied economics and business before the 1980s usually lack academic knowledge of HR issues, since HRM was not included in university curricula before that time. Due to the fact that the concept of HRM has only recently been established in Greece, HR managers have hitherto mostly had a legal background, been retired military officers, or had no related university education, but had acquired their position through promotion from lower levels in the hierarchy. However, Papalexandris (1995) notes that nowadays, business-oriented educational qualifications are increasingly required for entry to the HRM field, a positive sign for HRM in Greece. Nowadays, the majority of personnel managers are university graduates with an economics or business administration background, with fewer having an academic background in social sciences, law or technical subjects, or having previously served in the armed forces. Many of them have also participated in executive seminars and speak at least one foreign language (Papalexandris, 1995).

Furthermore, most HR managers have acquired their position after an average of 13 years' service in their field. Many of them have worked in other functions within the organization, as well as in other firms. This reflects the underdevelopment of HRM in recent decades, as well as the predominantly small size of firms in Greece. When HRM started developing in Greece, a number of people were promoted from various other functions within firms to the HR department. Furthermore, the predominance of small-scale firms reduced the chances of promotion within the organization, resulting in high mobility within different functions and firms (Kanellopoulos, 1990; Price-Waterhouse Cranfield Project, 1993).

HR practices

This section will highlight key points relating to managing HR in Greece, in terms of recruitment and selection, performance management and appraisals, training and development, employee rewards and employee relations.

Recruitment and selection

Until the late 1980s, few Greek firms had formalized systematic recruitment and selection policies for managerial posts (Papalexandris, 1986, 1988). During the mid-1990s, the policy of most large Greek firms and all MNCs was to recruit young university graduates with potential for internal promotion (Papalexandris, 1995).

Recruitment practices in Greek firms vary according to the size and ownership of the organization. Large Greek organizations and MNCs use advertisements, recruitment consultants and personal connections as their main source for recruiting staff (Prouska, 2006). Especially for senior management positions, MNCs have the option of transferring managers from the organization's offices abroad, as well as attracting managers from other organizations. In addition, large firms with a good reputation in the market benefit from receiving large numbers of individual applications for employment. On the other hand, small Greek firms mostly use personal connections and newspaper advertisements (Papalexandris, 1995).

Greek firms often use intuitive and subjective methods of selecting new employees, for example, interviews, CVs and personal recommendations (Eleftheriou and Robertson, 1999). Interviews, written examination and psychological tests are perceived by HR professionals to have the highest validity in terms of predicting future job performance, while application forms, references and personal recommendations are the least valid (Eleftheriou and Robertson, 1999).

Both large Greek firms and MNCs define selection criteria through detailed person specifications. The selection decision is mostly made according to experience and references, as well as relevant university education in the specific field (Papalexandris, 1995). For skilled workers, references are an important selection criterion, while for administrative and managerial positions the selection criteria include initial CV screening by the HR manager, the managing director or consultants. For more senior posts, consultants are used to provide organizations with specialized psychometric tools and personality tests (Prouska, 2006). For such posts, although the final decision lies with the managing director, candidates undergo a series of interviews with the HR and departmental/divisional managers before a decision is made (Papalexandris, 1995). On the other hand, small Greek firms take seriously and favour employee referrals (Prouska, 2006), provided however that the recommended candidates are in other ways comparable to other candidates. Employee selection in these cases relies heavily on family connections and personal contacts (Prouska, 2006; Papalexandris, 1995).

Performance management and appraisals

Papalexandris (1995: 118–9) notes that 'originally, the most widely used method of performance appraisal in Greek firms, even of larger size, was the supervisor/manager making some sort of unstructured judgement of the subordinate. Appraisal later became more formalised and comprised (in most cases) part of the routine job of the personnel department.' Performance appraisal typically consisted of 'the routine measurement of employee characteristics, using checklist forms and giving grades for various character traits such as initiative, reliability, personality, and so on' (Papalexandris, 1995: 119).

Performance appraisal processes now focus more on evaluating the employee's performance in his/her duties, rather than evaluating his/her personality and character. Processes are becoming increasingly sophisticated, particularly where performance appraisal for managerial posts is concerned, and the problems relating to this kind of performance appraisal are increasing. Some common problems encountered are the selection and measurement methods of performance evaluation criteria, as well as the impartiality of the appraiser (Papalexandris, 1986, 1995).

In most firms, the criteria used to evaluate employees are subjective, including, for example, loyalty to the organization, integrity, hard work, theoretical knowledge and communication skills. In some cases, depending on the nature of work involved, more objective criteria are used, such as meeting deadlines in preparing financial statements or completing orders on time (Papalexandris, 1986).

In the case of small Greek firms, which are primarily family-owned, formal appraisal procedures are not deemed to be necessary. Even larger Greek firms have a limited use of appraisal procedures due to 'the existence of close personal relationships and the difficulty in setting precise targets, as a result of frequent changes in the external environment of firms' (Papalexandris 1995: 120).

MNCs in Greece, on the other hand, have a complete appraisal system in place (Papalexandris, 1995). Performance appraisal processes involve the immediate supervisor, the personnel manager and the department manager, and the appraisal is based on management by objectives (MBO) or target setting, depending on the nature of work and the specific department involved.

Training and development

According to the European Foundation for the Improvement of Living and Working Conditions (2007), the levels of employee training in Greece hardly reach 20 per cent, as is the case in Spain, Hungary, Portugal and Romania. This is by comparison with northern European countries which have more than 50 per cent of workers receiving training at work.

Papalexandris' research (1986) on management development practices in manufacturing firms in Greece showed that organizations did have a specific training policy in place. Training was generally linked to appointment to management positions and to business plans. Later surveys by Papalexandris in 1990 and 1993 (Papalexandris, 1995) showed this percentage increasing. Papalexandris (1995: 121) found that 'there was a significant relationship between company size and foreign ownership and the sophistication of training offered'. According to this study, an in-house training function was found to exist in larger Greek organizations and MNCs, but not in smaller Greek firms. Papalexandris' findings therefore suggest that only MNCs and large Greek firms use systematic training and development policies.

However, Prouska's research (2006) found that although an internal training and development function did not exist in micro or medium-sized firms, training and development was one of the HR activities most commonly outsourced to external providers. Small-sized firms outsourced the training and development function on a project basis and as training needs arose. In addition, Xirotiri-Kufidu's (1993) research suggests that even MNCs do not always apply training and development practices systematically.

Employee rewards

According to the Price-Waterhouse Cranfield survey (1993) on HRM practices in Greece, organizations implement group and individual bonus schemes especially for clerical, technical and manual positions, and mostly use performance-related pay schemes as the principal way of rewarding employees. However, it is important to note the general wage levels currently present in the country, as these also affect the types of employee rewards available in the market. According to the European Foundation for the Improvement of Living and Working Conditions (2007), the lowest 10 per cent of wage earners in Greece received less than €450 in net wages per month, while the highest 10 per cent received more than €1,500. Employers often use performance-related pay and bonus schemes as a way of motivating employees. Especially since the financial crisis of 2010, which saw many firms cutting budgets and employee pay, employers find offering a lower salary and more opportunities for performance-related pay and bonuses a more attractive option.

Employee relations

In small Greek firms, which are primarily family-owned, employee relations do not exist in a formal way. The relationships between management and employees resemble those of a small family, with senior management available and able to handle any employee problems, complaints or misunderstanding.

Employee relations are an especially important HR function in large Greek firms and in the public sector. Larger employers are also more inclined to follow the law and be unionized (Psychogios and Wood, 2010). According to the European Industrial Relations Observatory (EIRO, 2009), the current system of collective bargaining has been in force in Greece without any changes or amendments since 1990. What has changed, however, is the development of this field, which has had to adapt to an intensive schedule of privatizations, mergers and acquisitions, downsizing of the public sector, and pressure to decentralize the collective bargaining system.

On one side, the Greek trade unions are represented at the highest level by two confederations (EIRO, 2009). Firstly, the Greek General Confederation of Labour (GSEE), which includes all trade unions covering employees under private employment law in the private and broader public sector. Secondly, the Confederation of Public Servants (ADEDY), which includes public administration trade unions, where public law employment relations apply (EIRO, 2009).

On the other side, three high-ranking employer organizations play a crucial role in the national industrial relations system in Greece. Firstly, the Hellenic Federation of Enterprises (SEV), which represents various industries, services and big companies in general. SEV plays an important role in the bargaining pertaining to the National General Collective Agreement (EGSSE) and some 100 other sectoral and occupational collective agreements. Its chosen strategy since the 1990s has been to prioritize dialogue at all levels. SEV represents 5,000 companies with a total of about 500,000 employees. Secondly, the National Confederation of Greek Traders (ESEE) represents trading firms. Thirdly, the General Confederation of Professional Craftsmen and Small Manufacturers of Greece (GSEBEE) represents the interests of handicraft professionals and small manufacturing companies (for example, booksellers, shopkeepers, café owners and hairdressers) (EIRO, 2009).

Since the financial crisis of 2010, some of the main causes of industrial action relate to the austerity measures introduced by the Greek government to reduce its public deficit to less than 3 per cent by 2014. In May 2010, the public deficit stood at 13.6 per cent. The proposed measures, which have caused major protests and strikes, are pay cuts, pension reform, tax reform, and plans for privatization (BBC News, 2010).

Outsourcing HR activities

Greek organizations outsource a number of HR activities to external providers (mainly management consultancies), but to a lesser extent than other western economies (Galanaki and Papalexandris, 2007). According to Prouska's research (2006), the most commonly outsourced HR activities are training, selection, health, safety and welfare, coaching and counselling, recruitment, and payroll. Micro firms, having a less sophisticated HR function in terms of activities performed to cover business needs, outsource fewer HR activities than medium-sized and large organizations. Furthermore, they have limited financial resources to afford HR services, compared with medium-sized firms and large organizations. It is also important to note that micro firms account for 99.69 per cent of the total registered private firms in Greece (National Statistical Service of Greece, 2002). Since the percentage of micro-firms with no employees or fewer than ten is so great, it is natural to find that these firms will not have their own HR department in place and so outsource even more HR activities. Furthermore, most HR activities are outsourced partially and on a project basis. This means that organizations, regardless of their size, are mostly outsourcing a specific aspect of the HR activity and only as the need arises.

The majority of organizations that participated in Prouska's research (2006), regardless of their size, perceived *access to external expertise and skills* as the main rationale behind their outsourcing decision. Micro firms emphasize *predictable costs/effective cost control,* which is also important to medium-sized organizations. Medium-sized firms agree with large organizations in perceiving *reduction in lost time* as a major benefit of HR outsourcing. Large organizations emphasize *flexibility in adapting to changing needs,* while micro firms are also concerned with the fact that through HR outsourcing they have *no need to hire/train highly skilled specialists* and that they can *increase the focus of management effort.*

Prouska's research (2006) suggests an operational rationale for HR outsourcing in Greece. Such a rationale is further supported by the extent and frequency of outsourcing (including the types of activities currently outsourced). Consequently, the HR outsourcing model implemented by Greek firms is of a conventional (or a tactical/pragmatic) nature (see Hampson, 2003; Corbett, 2004). This means that operational decisions to outsource HR activities are made primarily in order to access skills and capabilities not available in-house. This is underlined by the fact that HR management consultancies in Greece provide standardized services whose scale and scope is narrow (Galanaki and Papalexandris, 2005). This operational/conventional HR outsourcing model apparent in Greek organizations is a direct result of the small size of the HR department within firms and its operational role. These two factors in turn affect the extent and frequency of HR outsourcing (partial outsourcing, project basis), as well as the actual types of outsourced activities (mainly recruitment, training and payroll).

e-HR

One of the latest developments in the field of HRM is the introduction of e-HR, or electronic-HR, meaning conducting HRM transactions using the internet or an intranet (Lengnick-Hall and Moritz, 2003). E-HR slowly began to be adopted by Greek firms in the 2000s. It is important to mention that it was not until the late 1990s that modem internet connections for domestic and commercial use were introduced in Greece, while faster DSL internet connections became available around 2001. It is therefore not strange to find Greek organizations lagging behind in the adoption of e-HR. One of the most recent studies in this field (Panayotopoulou *et al.,* 2007) found that most Greek companies use e-HR for publishing information (one-way communication from the company to the employees/managers through the intranet) and automation of transactions (replacing paperwork by electronic input through the use of intranets and extranets). Panayotopoulou *et al.* (2007) found that the critical success factors for implementing e-HR are, firstly, an organizational culture that is supportive of its use, secondly, updated information technology (IT) skills for employees, and thirdly, a good degree of collaboration between HRM and IT to ensure successful integration of technology into HR processes. Panayotopoulou *et al.*'s (2007) study concludes that through e-HR the role of HR can be seen to be upgraded, as its adoption benefits the company's image and achieves goal alignment and cost reduction. Irrespective of these positive signs of technology adoption in HRM, the use of e-HR is not as widespread in Greece as in other countries. However, it is expected that Greek organizations will increasingly adopt e-HR technologies in the future as the need for competitiveness will continue to increase.

Critical HRM issues

The purpose of this section is to highlight critical challenges relating to employment and HRM that the Greek government, employers and trade unions would need to consider for economic growth in the future.

An ageing workforce

The ageing population, and hence ageing workforce, of the EU has become one of the central priorities for policy makers. This demographic shift has possible implications for the sustainability of pension systems and Europe's labour supply, and Greece is no exception to this. According to the EU Labour Force Survey in 2000, approximately 12 per cent of men and 4 to 6 per cent of women aged 65 and over remained in employment in Greece. Over a third of those aged 65 and over had an income which put them at risk of poverty (Winqvist, 2002). According to a Eurofound report (European Foundation for the Improvement of Living and Working Conditions, 2008) on the working conditions of an ageing workforce highlights the issues that need to be addressed: ensuring career and employment security, maintaining and promoting the health and well-being of workers, developing skills and competencies, and the work–life balance. In addition, there is a need to reconsider and restructure the current pension scheme which faces significant difficulties and is projected to collapse in the years to come, as is the case in other EU countries.

Gender equality in employment

According to a 2005 study conducted by the Research Centre for Gender Equality, Greece still has one of the largest gender gaps in its employment rate when compared with other EU member states (Tikos, 2007). Seniority is considered the most relevant factor accounting for the gender gap in Greece (European Foundation for the Improvement of Living and Working Conditions, 2010). In 2006, there was a 28.2 per cent gap, with an employment rate of 48.2 per cent for women compared with 76.4 per cent for men (Tikos, 2007). Even though a series of measures have been introduced aimed at boosting women's employability and at reconciling family and working life, gender equality in employment still remains a challenge.

The current market and employment structures do not allow for great flexibility when it comes to work-life balance provision, as it is not one of the priority issues in EU social partner negotiations. Although trade unions are aiming for the reduction of the working week, employers are in favour of adjustment and flexibility (EIRO, 2009).

The statutory working week is 40 hours, but the actual working time per week is estimated at 42.6 hours (EIRO, 2009). This is due to low wages, with workers trying to work longer hours or take on a second job to earn more money. It is also down to employer policy; for cost reasons, employers prefer overtime work to hiring new workers. It is important to note that there are cases of employers who, despite employment legislation, do not pay for overtime. Such cases are not uncommon and can be traced to the current high rate of unemployment (12.7 per cent in July 2010) and overall economic conditions. According to the OECD (EIRO, 2009), until 2004 Greece had one of the highest levels of real working hours in the world, while the National Statistical Service of Greece reported that in 2005, the proportion of employees working over 48 hours a week was 20 per cent (EIRO, 2009).

Some provision is made to support parenthood, but in many respects this needs further improvement. Maternity leave stands at 119 days (56 days pre-natal and 63 days post-natal leave), while paternity leave stands at 3 days (Law 2874:§11).

Efforts to address sexual harassment in the workplace have only recently resulted in the implementation of legislation. The first survey on sexual harassment in the workplace was carried out in April 2004 by the Research Centre for Gender Equality (KETHI), a centre supervised and funded by the General Secretariat for Equality of the Ministry of the Interior, Public Administration and Decentralization. This survey found, among other things, that victims of sexual harassment at work are frequently younger women (up to the age of 25), that the majority of reported perpetrators are men (97 per cent) in higher positions (managers, immediate supervisors and so on), and that most cases of sexual harassment (72.5 per cent) take place during the women's first two years in employment. Most worryingly, the survey found that 78.3 per cent of the women who are sexually harassed at work subsequently stop working in the specific workplace (86.2 per cent resign and 8.5 per cent are dismissed) (Stamati, 2004).

Summary

Developments in the field of HRM in Greece in recent decades are largely due to external environmental factors that have put pressure on organizations to become more competitive. Such factors include participation in the EU, external competition, the higher educational level of professional management, and the presence of MNCs in the market. This chapter has illustrated, however, that the HRM function is still developing.

Greek firms are characterized by their small size. This factor directly affects the size and role of the HR department in organizations. Although larger organizations and MNCs have more formalized HR policies and procedures in place, these are frequently absent from small and medium-sized firms. Recruitment and selection, performance management and appraisals, training and development, employee rewards and employee relations are key activities performed by Greek HR departments. There is also a trend towards the outsourcing of HR activities to external consultants, an option particularly attractive to smaller organizations which do not have clearly defined HR departments in place. Greek workplaces have also recently started using technology (e-HR) for the publishing of information and automation of transactions.

This chapter has also highlighted two critical issues in HRM. The ageing workforce was discussed, with particular reference to the consequences of this phenomenon for the sustainability of the Greek pension system and labour supply. Gender equality issues, in particular the current gender pay gap, working time, flexibility in the workplace to support parenthood, and sexual harassment at work were also explored.

The impact of the financial crisis of 2010 is still affecting Greece (and it will continue to do so for the foreseeable future). The austerity measures imposed by the Greek government have brought many changes to the workplace and have put pressure on employers and employees to increase productivity and performance, while minimizing costs. Under these economic conditions, the HRM function will continue struggling to prove its value to the business. Although the Greek HRM function has developed significantly since the 1970s, it still has a long way to go in order to be able to compare itself with HRM in more advanced economies.

References

BBC News (2010) 'Greece's Austerity Measures', 5 May 2010. http://www.bbc.co.uk/news/10099143.

Corbett, M.F. (2004) *The Outsourcing Revolution: Why it Makes Sense and How to Do it Right*. USA: Dearborn Trade Publishing.

EIRO (2009) *Greece: Industrial Relations Profile, European Industrial Relations Observatory*. http://www.eurofound.europa.eu/eiro/country/greece_3.htm.

Eleftheriou, A., and Robertson, I. (1999) 'A Survey of Management Selection Practices in Greece', *International Journal of Selection and Assessment*, 7(4): 203–8.

European Commission: Eurydice and Eurostat (2007) *Key Data on Higher Education in Europe* (2007 ed.) Brussels: Eurydice.

European Foundation for the Improvement of Living and Working Conditions (2007) *Fourth European Working Conditions Survey*. Luxembourg: Office for Official Publications of the European Communities.

European Foundation for the Improvement of Living and Working Conditions (2008) *Working Conditions of an Ageing Workforce, European Foundation for the Improvement of Living and Working Conditions*. Luxembourg: Office for Official Publications of the European Communities.

European Foundation for the Improvement of Living and Working Conditions (2010) *Addressing the Gender Pay Gap: Government and Social Partner Actions*, Ireland: Eurofound. http://www.eurofound.europa.eu/pubdocs/2010/18/en/2/EF1018EN.pdf.

Eurostat (2008) *Europe in Figures-Eurostat Yearbook 2008*. Luxembourg: Office for Official Publications of the European Communities.

Galanaki, E., and Papalexandris, N. (2005) 'Outsourcing of Human Resource Management Services in Greece', *International Journal of Manpower*, 26(4): 382–96.

Galanaki, E., and Papalexandris, N. (2007) 'Internationalization as a Determining Factor of HRM Outsourcing', *The International Journal of Human Resource Management*, 18(8): 1557–67.

Georgoulis, V. (1978) 'A Comparative Management Study of Selected Greek and European Multinational Manufacturing Firms Operating in Greece', PhD Thesis, University of Bath.

Greek Management Association (1972) *Management of Greek Firms*. Athens: Greek Management Association.

Hampson, G. (2003) 'Transformational HR Outsourcing', *HR Asia Pacific*, March, pp. 1–10.

Haritakis, N., and Pitelis, C. (1998) 'Privatisation in Greece', in Parker, P. (ed.), *Privatisation in the European Union: Theory and Policy Perspectives*. London: Routledge, pp. 123–35.

Hassid, J. (1977) *Greece and the EEU: Comparative Study of Industrial Structure*. Athens: Institute of Economic and Industrial Research.

Ignjatovic, M., and Svetlik, I. (2002) 'European HRM Clusters', paper presented at the Cranet Conference, 17–18 October 2002, Athens.

Joumard, I., and Mylonas, P. (1999) 'Reforming Greece's Public Enterprises', *Organisation for Economic Cooperation and Development-The OECD Observer*, 216: 10–12.

Kanellopoulos, C. (1990) *Personnel Management and Personnel Managers in Greece*. Athens: Greek Productivity Centre.

Karasiotou, P. (2004) *Identification of Skill Needs: Projects and Actions for Greece*, Cedefop Panorama Series no.84. Luxembourg: Office for Official Publications of the European Communities.

Lengnick-Hall, M.L. and Moritz, S. (2003) 'The Impact of e-HR on the HRM Function', *Journal of Labour Research*, 24(3): 365–79.

National Statistical Service of Greece (2002) *Register of Greek Enterprises*. Athens: National Statistical Service of Greece.

National Statistical Service of Greece (2005) *Greece in Figures*. Athens: National Statistical Service of Greece.

Panayotopoulou, L., Vakola, M., and Galanaki, E. (2007) 'E-HR Adoption and the Role of HRM: Evidence from Greece', *Personnel Review*, 36(2): 277–94.

Papalexandris, N. (1986) 'Management Development Practices in Manufacturing Firms in Greece', PhD Thesis, University of Bath.

Papalexandris, N. (1988) 'Factors Affecting Management Staffing and Development: The Case of Greek Firms', *European Management Journal*, 6(1): 67–72.

Papalexandris, N. (1991) 'A Comparative Study of Human Resource Management in Selected Greek and Foreign-owned Subsidiaries in Greece', in Brewster, C. and Tyson, S. (eds), *International Comparisons in Human Resource Management*. London: Pitman Publishing, pp. 145–58.

Papalexandris, N. (1995) 'Greece', in I. Brunstein (ed.) *Human Resource Management in Western Europe*. Berlin: Walter de Gruyter, pp. 113–34.

Papalexandris, N., and Chalikias, J. (2002) 'Changes in Training, Performance Management and Communication Issues among Greek Firms in the 1990s: Intercountry and Intracountry Comparisons', *Journal of European Industrial Training*, 26(7): 342–52.

Price-Waterhouse Cranfield Project (1993) *Survey on HRM in Greece*, Research monograph. Athens: Athens University of Economics and Business.

Prouska, R. (2006) 'Outsourcing Human Resource Activities: An Analysis of Firms in Greece', PhD Thesis, University of Manchester.

Psychogios, A., and Wood, G. (2010) 'Human Resource Management in Comparative Perspective: Alternative Institutionalist Perspectives and Empirical Realities', *International Journal of Human Resource Management*, 21(14): 2614–30.

Staikouras, P.K. (2004) 'Structural Reform Policy: Privatisation and Beyond: The Case of Greece',. *European Journal of Law and Economics*, 17(3): 373–97.

Stamati, A. (2004) *First Survey of Sexual Harassment in the Workplace*, European Industrial Relations Observatory. http://www.eurofound.europa.eu/eiro/2004/07/feature/gr0407103f.htm.

Tikos, S. (2007) *More Progress in Gender Equality Needed*, Institute of Greek General Confederation of Labour. http://www.eurofound.europa.eu/ewco/2007/03/GR0703049I.htm.

Winqvist, K. (2002) 'Women and Men beyond Retirement', *Statistics in Focus – Population and Social Conditions*, Theme 3-21, 2002. http://epp.eurostat.ec.europa.eu/cache/ITY_OFFPUB/KS-NK-02-021/EN/KS-NK-02-021-EN.PDF.

Xirotiri-Kufidu, S. (1993) 'Management Staffing and Training Development Policies in Selected Multinational Enterprises: The Case of Greece', *Management Education and Development*, 24(1): 58–70.

10
Marketing

Panagiotis Ballas

Overview

This chapter continues the exploration of the business environment in Greece, by focusing on marketing practices. It starts with the presentation of the environment within which marketing agencies operate and marketing professionals offer their services. Trying to provide as comprehensive a picture as possible of the situation in Greece, the first section provides details of the advertising spending among different media. Bearing in mind that the majority of companies in Greece are either small or medium in size, the discussion moves on to the problems that marketing agencies face as a result of the peculiarities of the marketing environment in Greece. At the same time, practices which marketing agencies could follow in order to transform these challenges into competitive advantages are identified. Further sections refer to innovative marketing practices for the Greek market, namely, e-marketing and mobile marketing activities. The chapter ends with a discussion of the corporate social responsibility of marketing activities in Greek companies.

The marketing environment in Greece

According to marketing literature, marketing practices involve the organized and systematic analysis of a product or service before the choice of specific marketing activities is made. The use of statistics, the study of the product's marketing mix, its brand strategy and so on contribute to this objective. Ideally, there should be a direct relationship between the marketing practices followed and the company's marketing strategy and a company should be confident that this will result in a positive outcome. In other words, marketing spending should be seen as an investment for the future.

However, the situation in Greece is far from ideal. The special characteristics of the market, the characteristics of the entrepreneurs and the performance of the economy shape the environment in which marketing agencies offer their services. First of all, there is a widespread scepticism in part of the market about the need to spend money on marketing activities. There are a number of entrepreneurs who own small or medium-sized companies (SMEs), who believe that personal relationships are the key to the success of a company and that marketing strategy, even though helpful, is not worth spending money on. Owners of SMEs are not deeply interested in studying and analyzing the marketing practices they follow. Even though marketing agents collect details about marketing practices, their clients (SMEs) are seldom really interested in analyzing this feedback. This section examines the reasons for this behaviour on the part of companies.

A first point for consideration is the size of the companies which operate in Greece. EU regulations define a small enterprise as one employing fewer than 50 people and with an annual turnover and/or an annual balance of not more than €10 million (Commission Recommendation, 2003). A medium-sized enterprise employs a maximum of 250 people; either its annual turnover does not exceed €50 million or its annual balance sheet total is less than €43 million (Commission Recommendation, 2003). According to the definitions of the Hellenic Organization of Small and Medium Enterprises and Handicraft, SMEs have employed an average of up to 100 salaried workers in the preceding three years and have an average turnover up to €2.4 million, unless they are capital-intensive in which case the maximum number of employees is 50 (EOMMEX, 2010). The latter type of organization is the most popular in Greece, accounting for 99.55 per cent of the total number of firms and employing 74 per cent of the total workforce in the private sector (EOMMEX, 2010). In 2009, Greece had more than 600,000 such companies (accounting for more than 95 per cent of the total number of Greek companies). A marketing agency that offers its services in the Greek territory should take particular account of the special characteristics of SMEs. First of all, these companies have *limited financial resources*. This is a major constraint when searching for sources of finance not only for future investments, but also in some cases for day-to-day operations too. These companies are continuously looking for funds and the amount of money they spend on marketing activities is limited. The client's budget is definitely a limitation on any decisions. During a period of recession such as the one the world economy has been going through since 2008, financial difficulties are severe and may occasion SMEs to have second thoughts when it comes to spending money on activities like marketing. Financial difficulties have negatively affected SMEs' receptiveness to marketing experts' ideas and suggestions. SMEs contact a marketing agency asking for specific marketing activities to be undertaken and delivered. Under these circumstances, marketing agencies seem to be given limited scope to apply their creative thinking and expertise.

Second, SMEs *cannot benefit from economies of scale*, a fact which negatively affects their liquidity. A close corollary of the above is that SMEs have low productivity as a result of *not taking (or not being able to take) full advantage of contemporary methods of management*. Bearing in mind the above characteristics, it is logical that even though SMEs follow some marketing principles, they apply them in a different way to larger firms (Carson and Gilmore, 2000). A key difference is that in SMEs, marketing decisions are inseparable from other daily decisions and are usually taken by a small number of people, or frequently, by the owner. Thus, it is the owner's competencies, knowledge and intuition that determine these marketing decisions.

Third, *marketing is not a top priority function* for SMEs and is not undertaken in a systematic way, which is why, in times of recession, marketing expenditure is among the first to be cut. SMEs feel that they do not actually need a stand-alone marketing department since they equate marketing with advertisement. It is also common for the sales manager (in the case of a medium-sized company) or the owner of the business (in the case of a small company) to be responsible for 'marketing management'. Hence, the logic of SMEs is to offer whatever they have already decided to produce or which they perceive gives them a competitive advantage, without really caring about what customers believe and want.

Consumer research is thus non-existent in this type of company. Small entrepreneurs in Greece do not realize that marketing requires listening to customers instead of believing you know (or following your instinct about) what they really want. Offering good quality (as perceived by the owner) products and services, or spending some money on advertisement is far from an effective marketing management approach. Unfortunately, few Greek companies adopt integrated marketing strategies, having conducted systematic consumer research in order to offer what their target customers actually want or even predict the situation in the future. As a result, it is not surprising that SMEs feel they do not actually need to spend money on establishing and maintaining an in-house marketing department.

Under these circumstances, SMEs follow what are known as push marketing approaches. Marketing agencies are also forced to follow push strategies to sell their services. Marketing experts take the initiative by contacting potential clients, proposing attractive marketing activities to convince them of the benefits of marketing and the advantages of a potential future co-operation. Such an approach has advantages for both agents and SMEs. Companies are exposed to ideas about how to improve their business or overcome a problem without any effort or cost, and marketing agents build up a data bank with information about different companies and sectors of the economy while improving their brand awareness. Of course agents are careful about the extent to which they reveal their ideas to companies. Marketing agencies are for-profit organizations that aim to sell their services to clients and, of course, get paid for it. They know that SMEs do not have the expertise to implement the marketing activities they propose, and this is where they come in.

What marketing agents also do in order to attract customers is to propose 'safe' solutions, that is, solutions with the lowest risks as perceived by clients. This strategy gives marketing agents an alibi in case something goes wrong. If a marketing agent proposed an innovative marketing activity to promote a product or service and it did not perform as expected, he/she would be heavily criticized for selecting such a 'high-risk' solution. A TV advertisement, on the other hand, is regarded as a less risky (although expensive) solution, limiting the scope for major criticism by the client. It is not surprising that around 32 per cent of advertising expenditure goes on TV, which is characteristic of a country that is underdeveloped in terms of media. Nowadays, major potential target groups do not watch TV enough to justify such high spending (the young, for example, watch less TV than the old), but there is still quite a high level of expenditure on TV advertising, because it leaves both marketers and their clients satisfied.

Marketing agencies in Greece mainly deal with promotion strategies. In very few cases do clients ask for an integrated marketing strategy plan, and they are usually large companies. The SMEs that form the vast majority of companies in Greece tend to evaluate any marketing action taken on the basis of its short-term profit. In some sectors, entrepreneurs' marketing decisions are significantly influenced by what the competitions is doing, with SME owners feeling they have no option but to copy without actually knowing if the practices in question are suitable for them. Restaurants provide a typical example. The majority of restaurant owners advertise their services regularly by distributing flyers in the neighbourhoods where they operate, since it is a practice which is followed by the vast majority of competitors.

Distribution of flyers is quite a common promotional activity for Greek SMEs. Marketing agencies design and distribute the appropriate number of flyers to cover particular geographical areas. The distribution may also be accompanied by a verbal promotion of the product or service in an attempt to increase the effectiveness of that particular marketing activity. Besides the door-to-door distribution of flyers, there are promotions in supermarkets, large shopping centres, cafés, on underground trains and generally in places where Greeks spend most of their time. A highly attractive distribution channel for flyers is the Sunday press, due to the increased number of newspapers sold on that day.

Quite often large marketing companies co-operate with smaller agencies especially in cases when the latter have the expertise in designing and implementing certain practices in certain places. Suppose that a marketing agency agrees to design the marketing strategy of a large company. Let us assume that one of a set of marketing activities is the distribution of a number of flyers in a particular geographical area. This action may be assigned to a small marketing agency with appropriate expertise. This expertise could be in the form of knowledge of a particular area, which could lead to the selection of the optimum number of flyers in order to cover it. These are very important decisions since they could lead to reduced marketing costs for the client. It is also possible that a large marketing company may not have the required number of flyer distributors to do it, or their distributors may not have the skills required to undertake a particular promotional activity (for example, fluency in a specific language, experience, adequate numbers to cover a particular area). Another reason for the involvement of many separate marketing agents is risk reduction: the more parties are involved, the greater the dispersion of potential risks for the client. Apart from the difficulty of finding the proper personnel to participate in a promotional activity, another risk may be the inability of a single agency to organize the whole process within a very short time. So it is a common practice in Greece for large marketing companies to divide up major marketing campaigns, hiring smaller agencies to help in the implementation phase, and besides, this approach is commonly followed by multinational marketing agencies, which act like middlemen between local agencies and the multinational clients. There is thus scope for many small marketing agencies with in-depth knowledge and expertise in particular sectors or marketing practices to support the services that larger marketing agents offer.

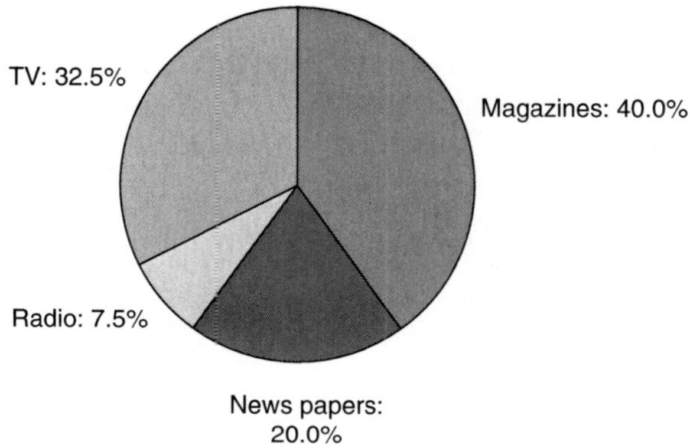

Figure 10.1 Advertising expenditure by various media 2009
Source: Based on data from Media Services SA.

According to data collected by Media Services SA,[1] advertising expenditure on both printed and electronic media in 2009 was reduced by around 17 per cent due to the economic crisis. The total amount spent was around €2.21 billion. €1.33 billion was absorbed by magazines (40 per cent, or €880 million) and newspapers (20 per cent) a reduction of around 20.07 per cent compared to 2008. TV (32.5 per cent of all advertising spending) was the sole medium that attracted more expenditure compared to 2008. The largest reduction was in spending on radio advertising, which at €166.1 million was 24 per cent less than in 2008 (see Figure 10.1).

Of all TV stations broadcasting in Greece, Mega Channel and Anti TV attracted the majority of advertising spending, earning around €226 million and €154 million respectively, among radio stations, Rythmos FM earned around €29 million and Lampsi FM around €24 million (data from Media Services SA). Table 10.1 shows the media that attracted the most advertising spending in 2009.

Challenges faced by marketing agencies in Greece

The discussion so far has implied that marketing in Greece mainly takes the form of advertising. An indication of the importance of advertising in marketing campaigns in Greece is the name of one association of marketing agencies – the Association of Advertising and Communication Agencies in Greece, established in 1968.[2] The member

Table 10.1 Top advertising revenue earners 2009

Name	Type	Euros earned
Mega Channel	TV	226,209,213
Ant1 TV	TV	154,602,370
City Press	Free daily newspapers	41,224,904
To Vima tis Kiriakis	Sunday newspaper	33,616,845
Proto Thema	Sunday newspaper	32,214,474
Rythmos FM	Radio station	28,934,481
Elle	Monthly magazine	26,463,693
Lampsi FM	Radio station	24,784,891
Sport Day	Daily sports newspaper	20,721,300
Auto Triti	Weekly magazine	20,409,694
Ta Nea	Daily evening newspaper	20,140,068
InStyle	Monthly magazine	20,014,748
Down Town	Weekly magazine	19,605,159
BHMAdonna	Weekly newspaper insert	18,877,585
Epsilon	Weekly newspaper insert	18,466,903
Athinorama	Weekly magazine	18,249,121
Goal News	Daily sports newspaper	13,607,853
Moto Triti	Weekly magazine	12,668,226
7 Imeres TV	Weekly TV magazine	12,628,134
Eleftherotipia	Daily evening newspaper	11,532,029
Teletheatis	Weekly TV magazine	11,059,335
Kosmos tou Ependiti	Weekly newspaper	11,017,680
Imerisia	Financial newspaper	10,700,171
Kathimerini	Daily morning newspaper	5,444,825
Nautemporiki	Financial newspaper	4,402,232
Isotimia	Weekly newspaper	3,509,554

Source: Based on data from Media Services SA.

companies offer services in the area of advertising, public relations, media, promotion and one-to-one marketing and market research. According to the most up-to-date directory of marketing agencies in Greece, there are around 5,000 companies which operate in this sector (Boussias Communications, 2010). Large companies in Greece have their own marketing departments even though they may not be called as such. 'Sales department' is often a substitute term for the marketing department. As discussed earlier, large companies may request external marketing agents to help in the implementation phase of a particular marketing activity. This decision requires close and effective co-operation between the marketing department of the company and the external agent. However, this relationship is not always without its problems. Company marketing departments, confident that they have an in-depth knowledge of the market, may ignore an expert opinion from a marketing agency. For example, the marketing department might contact a marketing agent asking for very specific activities, such as distribution of flyers, confident that this is the appropriate activity. This could lead to increased spending and jeopardize the effectiveness of the marketing for various reasons, such as the number of flyers distributed (for example, too many for a given geographical area), improper design of the flyer, unsuitable approach (for example, verbal communication instead of sole distribution), and so on. A number of problems are particularly in evidence in SMEs. Firstly, implementation of a particular marketing decision may proceed rather hesitantly because the company has not realized the benefits of the activity. The challenge for marketing agents, especially in a period of a recession when entrepreneurs are trying to minimize their spending, is to persuade companies to proceed with particular marketing campaigns that focus on short- and long-term benefits. Secondly, people responsible for marketing decisions do not necessarily have the required training and/or experience in the field. In small companies, decisions are usually taken by a single entrepreneur, and in medium-sized companies by people who also have other responsibilities (for example, sales manager, production manager). Even after the decision, these individuals may not fully understand or be able to justify their selection of a particular marketing practice. They often decide to undertake the same promotional activity as their competitors without questioning whether it is the appropriate action for the type of problem that their company faces.

Thirdly, a systematic approach to monitoring marketing activities is often lacking. It is even more difficult to persuade SME entrepreneurs who do not actually believe in market research to spend money on detailed analysis and feedback. They tend to believe that they know their market well and feel it is almost impossible for a marketing research company to propose something they have not already thought of.

Greek companies, irrespective of size, have neglected the meaning and the role of marketing, with the marketing department mainly managing the advertising budget, preparing advertising briefings and performing market research focusing on brand awareness and advertising impact (Spyropoulos 2007). Yet these are tactics which should follow on from strategic marketing decisions. Unfortunately, Greek companies underestimate the importance of fundamental marketing questions such as:

- Who are our customers?
- Which customer segment is valuable for the organization?

- Which needs does the customer satisfy when buying a product/ service?
- Who are our competitors?
- What is the competitive advantage?
- How much are customers willing to spend in order to buy a product/ service?

These questions are of particular importance for SMEs, because they strive to achieve maximum results with few resources.

The challenge for marketing companies in Greece is to offer as integrated a service as possible to SMEs, which are in the majority, but unfortunately, SMEs in general have not yet realized the power of marketing strategy, and the marketing budget is among the first to be cut in cases of a downturn in the market or a widespread economic crisis. Inevitably, marketing agencies succumb to what the customers (that is, SMEs) want and offer it in the way they want it, a situation that benefits neither clients nor companies. Typically, marketing agents propose marketing activities using familiar media in order to reduce entrepreneurs' perception of risk. Greek entrepreneurs feel comfortable when they see their marketing campaign in a local newspaper or on TV, whether or not it is ideal and effective for their company. They feel that the campaign is successful – or at least less risky – when their friends and relatives tell them that they saw their advertisement on TV.

Large companies, on the other hand, have their own marketing departments that undertake various forms of analysis which are used as indicators in the evaluation of their marketing activities. These large companies tend not to be receptive to freelance marketing agencies' proposals and use them for a limited range of very specific activities, such as distribution of flyers or shooting of an advertisement Maintaining good public relations with key market players (for example, key points of sale) is pivotal in Greece, but this poses a major barrier to entry for new marketing agencies. Thus, it is not surprising that new marketing agencies mainly deal with the implementation of small marketing activities instead of designing integrated and large marketing programmes.

The recent economic crisis has made the relationship between marketing agencies and clients more difficult and companies more reluctant to spend money on marketing campaigns. Clients evaluate the value of marketing activities on the basis of cost since it is the only measurable parameter. Marketing effectiveness is not visible in advance and is by no means guaranteed. Thus, clients usually ask questions about the cost per rating (CPR), which indicates how cheaply an advertisement can be bought. Clients also care about the return on investment (ROI) of the marketing activity undertaken. In effect, advertising has become a commodity and each decision is made on the basis of how cheaply a client can buy it.

The challenges faced by marketing agencies vary in different parts of Greece. First of all, there are differences in infrastructure, for example, in internet penetration rates. Second, the mentality of entrepreneurs differs: those in small villages, for example, are not as receptive to marketing consultation as their peers in large cities. Third, customers in urban and rural areas have different characteristics. Marketing agents should expect to make adjustments to marketing campaigns accordingly. Detailed local knowledge is a valuable resource, which local marketing agents could take advantage of by, for example, co-operating with larger counterparts in the implementation of major marketing campaigns.

The function of marketing is applicable not only to the private, but also to the public sector, and companies should follow appropriate marketing strategies (for example, acknowledging that profitability is not the prime objective in the public sector). In Greece public sector marketing mainly takes the form of advertisements. This is particularly evident in the Ministry of Tourism, which designs marketing campaigns to promote the country as a unique destination for tourists.[3] In the rest of the public sector, however, the government does not follow a systematic and co-ordinated approach to constructing the appropriate marketing strategy for each of the services it offers to its citizens.

E-marketing and mobile marketing

Another challenge faced by today's marketing agencies relates to new communication media. Internet penetration rates increase year after year, and Greece has a very high mobile phone ownership rate. E-marketing and mobile marketing are the new 'hype', and Greece has made some progress in exploiting the capabilities of the internet. In the early days of e-commerce (the late 1990s), Greek consumers were keen to buy standard products such as books, electronic gadgets and computer software online. The main problem with buying other types of products was the perceived risk, not only financial, but also in relation to the overall buying process.[4] Consumers were afraid of losing money through unfamiliar electronic distribution channels and unknown, distant providers, and anxious about the quality of the product and its actual delivery. Another major concern was the issue of guarantee.

Postal services were not well-equipped to deal with the delivery of products ordered online and it was common in large cities (where most online shopping took place) for many orders never to reach their destination or to arrive in bad condition. Finally, consumers in Greece enjoy window shopping, and they like to make the most of good weather conditions, and take the opportunity to socialize while going shopping. These conditions made companies quite reluctant choose online distribution channels. The pioneers maintained a physical presence on the high street to reduce consumers' perception of risk. They were established providers and consumers knew that they could physically visit them in case of a problem. E-commerce began to grow steadily by 2007, and the pace had increased quite rapidly by the end of 2009. Greek consumers' familiarity with the internet and online shopping created a promising critical mass, which made providers realize the need to take the internet into very serious consideration when designing their marketing strategies. Consumers started buying less standard products online too, such as clothes, shoes, jewellery and fashion accessories. The financial distress that started at the end of 2008 made consumers in Greece even more price-sensitive. Electronic distribution channels benefit both consumers and providers. Consumers could find cheaper products and services, while at the same time providers could reduce their fixed costs (rent, utilities, staffing, and so on). Large companies in Greece were the first to realize this, but gradually many smaller providers decided to go down the online route, taking advantage not only of the cost reduction, but also the ability to attract distant customers. Taking into consideration the morphology of Greece,[5] online distribution channels could be beneficial for the development of e-commerce in this country. Both the Greek government and the European Union provide funds to finance investments that relate to the development of e-commerce.[6] It is remarkable that more than 70 per cent of National Strategic Reference Framework (NSRF) funds for the period 2000–2006 were invested in e-commerce companies.

Greek consumers' willingness to use online distribution channels has increased Greek companies' interest in using new advertising practices too. The telecommunications sector was the first to experiment with mobile phone marketing practices benefiting from the telecommunication companies' expertise. Moreover, these companies could benefit from economies of scale by utilizing details they possessed about their customers. With the high rate of mobile phone ownership in Greece,[7] each of the telecommunications companies has the personal details of a significant number of Greek citizens. New regulations oblige 'pay as you go' customers to provide their details, mainly for security reasons, by 31 July 2010 (Law 3783/2009).[8] Telecommunication providers , with a bigger database of consumers, will be able to target their advertisements at the desired and appropriate focus groups each time.

Two of the four mobile communication operators in Greece (Vodafone and WIND Hellas) already offer mobile marketing services. At the beginning of 2010 a third one, COSMOTE, facing reduced profits mainly due to fierce competition and increased taxation on the use of mobile phones, widened the scope of its services to include mobile advertising.[9] These companies provide incentives such as discounts to participating customers who are willing to receive advertisements on their mobile phones. The practice of sending advertising SMSs has already started in Greece. In national elections in 2009, politicians took advantage of the power of mobile marketing and used mobile phones as part of their election campaigns, promoting their ideas via text messages. Clients express some concerns, however, about the destinations of messages. Although the marketing agency informs the client company that it is sending the messages to specific target groups and in particular volumes, it is very difficult for the client to verify this. Also, sending text messages may be quite irritating for the recipients and companies are afraid of not achieving the desired goals.

An important step forward for the development of innovative marketing practices occurred at the end of 2009 when the publishing sector in Greece realized the benefits of mobile marketing and decided to make changes. Specifically, Imako Media agreed to co-operate with Velti (one of the largest mobile marketing and advertising companies) and together they plan to offer a wide variety of mobile marketing strategies in Greece that include competitions via SMS, the creation of mobile communities, various types of alerts, and information 'on the go'. This type of co-operation indicates that Greek companies want to benefit from the convergence between traditional (printed media, radio) and innovative (mobile phones and internet) mass media. For example, electronic advertising panels in key sites around the country, controlled via the internet, allow advertising agencies to be much more creative, taking advantage of the power of video instead of still photos In effect, clients in future will be buying broadcasting time and the advertisement will come to look like a TV commercial instead of a frozen picture.

Social networking is a new trend, with sites such as Facebook, MySpace, Hi5, Secondlife (to name the most well-known) attracting a large number of visitors/potential consumers every day worldwide. The situation is not significantly different in Greece. A survey in 2010

(Kerdos, 2010) found that there are 2.6 million Greek Facebook users out of a total population of 10.5 million. Marketing agents could take advantage of this huge potential market to design promotional and advertising campaigns, for example by creating a fan page. An important advantage would be that companies could collect valuable information about customers, building a database with their habits, hobbies, favourite restaurants, travel destinations, lifestyle and beliefs. Companies could even benefit by promoting their services/products to the contacts of a particular Facebook user, quickly and cheaply attracting a wider section of the population. Marketers in Greece should take social networking websites very seriously when designing marketing campaigns.

Finally, marketing agents in Greece should bear in mind that there are some organizations that do not design traditional marketing campaigns. For example, one of the largest supermarket chains in Greece, Sklavenitis, very seldom advertises in the way its competitors do (mainly flyers). Its marketing department prefers to invest the funds back into the organization, reducing prices and increasing the value offered to its customers accordingly. Online marketing campaigns might benefit organizations that have not pursued traditional advertising strategies in the past. The internet opens up new possibilities that could be creatively exploited by marketing experts.

Corporate Social Responsibility

Since the beginning of the new millennium some of the largest Greek companies have been following the trend towards Corporate Social Responsibility (CSR), gradually trying to inculcate into the wider community a belief in their philanthropic and environmentally sensitive behaviour. Companies try to persuade consumers about their responsible attitude towards society and the environment by promoting their environmentally friendly and/or socially responsible actions. There are also particular sectors in which Greek consumers expect organizations to undertake a more active role in society and to pursue policies that positively contribute to environmental sustainability. Such behaviour is not without its critics. There are consumers who feel that CSR is nothing more than an artificial concept generated by marketing departments for companies to use in their advertisements to improve their brand image. However, there is a large body of consumers who care very much about the protection of the environment, participate in various events organized by socially responsible companies and organizations, and reward organizations that take social issues seriously when offering their products/services. According to the Institute of Social Innovation (2010), 19 per cent of the largest companies in Greece (based on income) published CSR and/or sustainability reports in 2009; 35 per cent made extensive reference to such issues without publishing a separate report. Moreover, 62 per cent of the largest Greek companies used the terms 'CSR' or 'accountability' in their official reports and 31 per cent referred to 'sustainability' and 'viable development'.

In recent research about consumers' attitude towards issue-related marketing in Greece,[10] researchers found that young consumers with a high level of education (around 53 per cent of participants) knew many details about organizations that pursued issue-related marketing practices. One in ten was positive, whereas six out of ten had a negative perception of companies pursuing this type of strategy. Almost half the participants (49 per cent) revealed that they did not very often buy products from companies with these policies, whereas 22.8 per cent of participants said the opposite. In effect, when companies report these kinds of activities, consumers are concerned about the 'purity of their intentions'. Older people with lower educational attainment are also more sceptical about these practices. The study revealed that Greeks are more positive when there is a non-governmental organization involved. Specifically, 53.4 per cent of participants believed that companies should donate to specific activities undertaken by a non-governmental organization.

Two types of CSR activities can be identified in Greece. First, a brand connects the sales of a product with a 'fair purpose' (for example, donations to charities, sustainable forestry, and investment in specific sectors such as healthcare or education). Second, a company may design a product or product line under the name of a for-profit or not-for-profit organization and make donations directly related to the volume of sales. (known as cause branding). The challenge for the marketing department or agent, however, is to determine the most appropriate 'cause'. With the globalization of economies and the evolution of technology, and given the massive amounts of information consumers receive every day from various sources about production procedures and their consequences to the environment, companies should be very careful about what they do and how they present it to the wider community in order for their campaigns to have the desired results.

As recently as a few years ago, the terms 'sustainability', 'CSR', 'viable development' and 'accountability' were unknown in the lexicon of companies in Greece, but now these companies are making significant progress in this area. As a result, they can be more confident when managing various operational crises and can contribute to society, the environment, or the economic life of the country in which they are based.

Summary

The discussion in this chapter has shown that business culture affects marketing strategies. This culture is quite traditional or 'mainstream' for Greek SMEs, whereas it becomes more cutting-edge in the case of large or multinational companies, and this follows logically, considering the people who run such organizations as well as their target groups . With the majority of companies in the category of small or medium-sized, marketing practices are mainly limited to advertisements and promotional activities. Large companies, however, are influenced by how marketing works abroad and are trying to introduce new practices within the existing infrastructure. It is encouraging to see that marketers are attempting to leave their own stamp on the market by designing their own individual marketing practices (examples include international jewellery shop Folli-Follie, toy retailer Jumbo, Goody's fast food chain). Much of this is the result of the improving quality of marketers in Greece, many of whom have studied this specific area and have experience of what happens abroad. Both marketing agents and the new generation of Greek consumers have travelled more than previous generations, acquiring a cosmopolitan lifestyle, and increasing numbers of Greek consumers have either personally (by visiting foreign countries) or visually (from information collected online) experienced marketing practices followed by companies abroad. The increasing penetration of new technologies in the Greek market has also had an effect. Although traditional media will always be of interest to marketers, the internet is a 'tube' that will filter everything in the future. Moreover, the next generation of consumers is being born into the internet era, and the critical mass of new digital technologies will be the basis of the innovative marketing practices of the future.

In an economic downturn, advertising budgets are among the first to be cut in Greece. Reducing advertising expenses can improve performance indicators, especially for traded companies. In addition, marketing managers' decisions tend to have a short-term horizon since they do not see themselves remaining in their post for many years and do not really have a vested interest in the long-term impact of their actions on the brand name of a company. Hence, the whole marketing system in Greece operates quite opportunistically, driven to a great extent by short-term financial performance. This was evident during the economic crisis of 2008–09, when marketing expenditure in Greece shrank and companies were mainly interested in the impact on their financial performance rather than in strengthening their brand names in the long term. What is encouraging, though, is the increasing rate of spending on e-marketing. Even during the economic crisis, when all mass media spending reduced, there was significant progress in the area of internet marketing. Thus the future challenge for the marketing profession in Greece is to persuade small and medium-sized companies that it can help them to achieve their short-term goals while at the same time ensuring their long-term viability.

Notes

1. Media Services SA is an organization which does research on advertising spending in printed, electronic, indoor or outdoor media (for more information see http://media.mediaservices.gr).
2. For more information see the Association of Advertising and Communication Agencies in Greece (http://www.edee.gr).
3. See Greek National Tourism Organisation (http:www.minitour.gr).
4. There is extensive literature on perception of risk (for example, Jacoby and Kaplan, 1972) in online settings (for example, Mitchell, 1999).
5. It is remarkable that Greece has around 150 inhabited islands.
6. This refers to the National Strategic Reference Framework (NSRF). Its first phase referred to the period 2000–06, and the second is from 2007 to 2013. The idea is to direct European Union Funds to investments that are in line with the strategic plans of the member states (for further details see: http://www.espa.gr).
7. It is more than 150 per cent, which means that every Greek citizen possesses more than one SIM card (see http://www.investingreece.com – the official agency which facilitates private investment in Greece).
8. In Greece 'pay as you go' customers were not obliged to provide their personal details in order to use their mobile phones until 2010.
9. The fourth provider (Q Telecom) did not announce mobile marketing services until the beginning of 2010.
10. This was a research project on consumers' stance towards issue-related marketing carried out by the Athens University of Economics and Business (Laboratory of Research in Marketing) at the end of 2008.

References

Boussias Communications (2010) *Marketing Guide 2010*. http://www.marketing-guide.gr.

Carson, D. and Gilmore, A. (2000) 'Marketing at the Interface: Not "what" but "how"', *Journal of Marketing: Theory and Practice*, pp. 1–7.

Commission Recommendation (2003) 2003/361/EC of 6 May 2003 concerning the definition of micro, small and medium-sized enterprises, Official Journal L 124 of 20.05.2003.

EOMMEX (2010) *The SMEs sector in Greece*. http://www.eommex.gr/Article.aspx?id=11771.

Institute of Social Innovation (2010). http://www.isi.org.gr.

Jacoby, J. and Kaplan, L. (1972) 'The components of perceived risk', in Venkatesan, M. (ed.), *Proceedings 3rd Annual Conference Association for Consumer Research*. Chicago: IL, 383–416.

Kerdos (2010) 'Online marketing: How can companies take advantage of social networking websites', 1 April 2010, p. A6.

Mitchell, V.W. (1999) 'Consumer perceived risk: conceptualizations and models', *European Journal of Marketing*, 33(1/2): 163–95.

National Statistical Service of Greece (2002) *Register of Greek Enterprises*. Athens: National Statistical Service of Greece.

Spyropoulos, G. (2007) 'The meaning and role of strategic marketing is neglected in Greece', *Express* financial newspaper, 23 December 2007, p. 32.

11
Sales

Ioannis Gedeon

Overview

This chapter presents the sales field in Greece from a practitioner's point of view, and is mostly based on the author's professional experience working with Greek organizations, rather than on academic literature on the field. However, it is important to note that academic literature focusing on sales practices of Greek firms is scarce. An attempt has been made to incorporate relevant literature where possible; however, even this mostly originates from comparative work which covers Greece to some extent, and not work focusing solely on Greece. The modern sales field in Greece started developing in the 1970s, as in the case of other management practices explored in this book. It was a when the Greek economy was enjoying an upturn as a result of joining the EEC. This resulted in the creation of new firms and in the further expansion of existing organizations. In addition, the entry of MNCs to the Greek market meant the introduction of new sales practices that were perhaps absent from local firms at that time. The introduction of these new practices by MNCs meant that local firms had to evolve their sales thinking and approach in order to survive in an increasingly competitive market.

The chapter explores the Greek sales force, focusing on sales representatives, Greek customer relationship management and the development of e-advertising and e-sales in Greece. It also incorporates two case studies, one of a local firm and one of a multinational one, in order to illustrate differences in their approach to the sales function.

The sales force

Salespeople in Greece today are quite different from their predecessors. In the 1980s and 1990s, sales people were simply executing a 'pitch' that had little to do with the prospect's needs and more with the company's need to sell a specific product to the target market. Companies expected the product to sell itself and believed that there was no need for sales management or sales expertise. However, several external environmental changes have influenced the sales field and the sales force (Jones *et al.*, 2005) and have resulted, in some cases, in changes in internal structures and processes (Dyer and Singh, 1998; Eisenhardt, 2002; Harrigan, 2001).

According to Jones *et al.* (2005), these dimensions of change can be represented in four categories of influence: customers, competitors, technology, and the ethical and regulatory environment. Firstly, customer expectations of salespeople and of the organizations they represent are constantly increasing, while at the same time, customer expectations constantly change, making it imperative for organizations to adapt and respond accordingly. On top of the need for salespeople to have technological expertise and product knowledge, customers also expect them to be familiar with information available about themselves and their company prior to making contact. In addition, although new technologies have facilitated communications, they have also increased customer expectations regarding response time to requests and enquiries. Furthermore, salespeople must now be able to effectively manage organizational resources, as well as influence dynamics and decision-making processes in client organizations. Secondly, given the fierce competition that currently exists in global markets, salespeople also need to constantly update their market knowledge of competition and products/services, and be able to effectively perform in this intensely competitive environment. Thirdly, salespeople need to adopt technology in their day-to-day communications with customers, as well as in their search for market knowledge. Finally, the ethical and legal environment can constrain an organization's ability to pursue some marketing activities, and salespeople therefore need to be aware of such issues and act accordingly.

These dimensions of change are also evident in the Greek market. Today, salespeople in Greece are armed with higher quality information, made possible through the internet, are better educated and trained, and are more astute than earlier generations of salespeople. This new attitude to selling is supported by sales managers who encourage their sales force to perform to high standards in order to reach sales targets. Sales professionals in Greece are now trying to interact with customers and build a long-term relationship with them, rather than just sell the product. The focus has turned to the consumer. Firms that isolate themselves from their customers have no place in today's market. On the contrary, firms that take advantage of their environment have a chance of adapting to their customers' needs and becoming more successful through increased sales.

Sales representatives in Greece hold an important role in organizations. They not only achieve sales, but also build a long-term relationship with their customers. The saying 'people buy people and not products' is quite well known in the sales field. This is especially the case when the purchase involves expensive products/services or those with a high level of involvement, regardless of whether they are sold through a face-to-face or telemarketing technique.

Sales job activities include selling, teamwork, sales presentations, sales planning, and sales support (Behrman and Perreault, 1984). The activities may be directly related to sales generation or may involve sales support. A typical day of a sales representative in Greece would include contacting existing clients, booking appointments with prospective clients, keeping track of statistics from meetings with clients and sales, and making him/herself available to customers for any further support needed. In addition, the duties of the Greek sales representative do not stop at the actual sale. For example, in the Greek car industry, sale managers advocate that the actual sale begins when the customer leaves the showroom in his/her brand new car, since dealerships survive through their service and after-sales departments rather than directly from selling cars. It is therefore expected that sales representatives will not only ensure new customers, but also secure more revenue from existing ones. Greek sales representatives are expected to listen carefully to customers and be able to identify their needs. They are also expected to use their knowledge of product characteristics to give advice to customers on products/services which fit their needs, while at the same time converting product characteristics into benefits for the customer. It is also just as important that they know exactly what competitors offer. In other words, sales representatives need to prove that they are specialists in the Greek market.

Piercy *et al.* (2004) categorized Greece as a 'developing country' (although the author would prefer to consider it as a 'less developed EU country') and placed it together with India and Malaysia in an analysis of the sales representative's role. Greek participants in this research were selected through local business directories, contacts and respondents' recommendations. The survey yielded a 40 per cent response rate, with 120 responses from sales managers. The research found that 59 per cent of Greek sales managers were described as 'generalists', 31 per cent as 'product specialists', and only 10 per cent as 'customer specialists'. These findings can be explained if one considers that, in Greece, most (if not all) small and medium-sized enterprises (SMEs) have a limited number of employees in charge of the various business functions. These firms, which constitute the majority of firms in the country (National Statistical Service of Greece, 2002), make their employees (sales managers or sales representatives) multitask between selling, building customer relationships, providing product specialist advice, monitoring sales targets and so on. Product specialists are, therefore, more likely to be employed in MNCs. MNCs in Greece have more advanced sales practices in place since they are following strategies produced by the parent company. They also invest in staff training and provide regular seminars on new products/services, as well as specialized seminars on sales techniques. It is important to note that, in Greece, salespeople are expected to be customer- focused (or 'customer specialists') as part of their daily duties even if professional training is not provided.

Another important point concerns the strategies used by Greek organizations to conduct performance evaluations of their sales force. It is common practice to evaluate sales staff based on sales outcomes. However, although sales outcomes are essential, behaviours (inputs) that lead to sales outcomes are even more important. The behaviour dimension of performance consists of the activities and strategies that salespeople use in meeting their job responsibilities (Jaworski and Kohli, 1991). Anderson and Oliver (1987) predict that behaviour-based control is positively related to behaviour performance. In applying behaviour-based management control, sales managers are closely involved with salespeople. Managers monitor, direct, evaluate, coach, and assist salespeople in various ways to improve performance. Anderson and Oliver (1987) propose that a behaviour-based sales management control strategy has a positive impact on behaviour performance of sales staff. This kind of strategy for managing salespeoples' performance is currently lacking in Greek organizations.

Customer relationship management

Every year, Greek firms spend large sums on advertising and promoting their products and services (see Chapter 10) in order to further improve their profitability and position in the competitive marketplace. However, current economic conditions are putting pressure on Greek organizations to also focus on providing high quality customer service if they wish to remain competitive in the marketplace. Firms need, therefore, to have a strategy in place to effectively manage their relationship with customers.

Customer feedback is valued by Greek organizations as a way of evaluating levels of customer satisfaction. They do so because they understand that continuous customer satisfaction can lead to customer loyalty. Large Greek manufacturing firms which sell through dealerships usually post a pre-paid customer satisfaction questionnaire to their customers a few weeks after the purchase of the product. The responses to this questionnaire are then analyzed in order to improve products and services accordingly. Although organizations use this feedback to build on their strengths, particular attention is paid to responses indicating customer dissatisfaction. Great emphasis is placed on identifying and dealing with dissatisfied customers, since customers will not necessarily share their positive experiences with a company, but will, most likely, mention it to people in their immediate environment or even post it on the internet.

In Greek firms, priority is also given to having regular contact with customers and developing in-depth knowledge and understanding of their needs. Salespeople are expected to be 'proactively', meaning able to identify customer needs and to attempt to satisfy these needs before a specific demand by a customer is made. In the Greek business-to-business sector, it is not uncommon for some marketing departments to recruit people with the role of providing 'business intelligence'. Their job is to inform and advise the sales team on customer/market needs. This information can assist the sales team to identify needs prior to a sales meeting.

With so many companies offering the same products, the responsibility to create brand loyalty, one of the key elements to succeed in a competitive environment, has been transferred to sales people. It is sales people that have to keep in contact with customers and provide after sales support.

E-advertising and e-sales

This section highlights some issues relating to the implementation of e-advertising and e-sales in Greece. The internet constitutes a daily tool for millions of people serving informational, sales and communicative purposes. In 2000, 400 million people worldwide were connected to the internet. In 2003, 43.5 per cent of the EU population were users of the internet (Garitaonandia, 2004).

According to the Greek IS Observatory (2010), the number of internet broadband connections in Greece showed a significant increase in 2007, with 30 per cent of people in the country connected, a 7 per cent increase from 2005. People with higher incomes are more frequent users of the internet. Students are an exception, with a higher rate of access to the internet than any other category, but that is based most on the free time available. The data from the Greek IS Observatory (2010) show that most Greeks have internet access at home (74 per cent), in their workplace (37 per cent), or local internet café (16 per cent). In more detail, 76 per cent of 16-20-yearolds and 72 per cent of 21-24-year-olds use the internet frequently, while young people aged16 to 24 use the internet more frequently that those aged over 24. Older people do not use the internet frequently (10 per cent of people aged 55 to 64 and 3 per cent of those aged 65 to 74). The following discussion explores e-advertising in the Greek market, with particular reference to the way in which it can enhance product promotion.

According to Selhofer *et al.* (2008), 80 per cent of large organizations in Greece think that e-business is vital for their daily operations, and around 70 per cent of SMEs think that it plays an important role in gaining competitive advantage and meeting customer needs. In the last decade, two of the most promising media for advertising products/services have been the internet and mobile phones. Focusing on the use of the internet as an advertising tool, there are three different ways in which companies can advertise on the Web: webpages, web banners/links, and direct e-mail campaigns.

According to Nowak *et al.* (1999), for many marketers, advertising involves homepages on the World Wide Web. *Web pages* quite often include multimedia applications in order to better communicate necessary information to users (Brill, 1999). *Web banner* advertisements are located at the top, sides or bottom of a webpage. In *direct e-mail campaigns,* internet users receive e-mails from companies about new products/services and offers. This medium is very similar to the traditional direct mail medium of earlier decades. Instead of creating leaflets or brochures, companies create rich HTML e-mails and send them directly to their prospect's e-mail address. Unlike direct mail, consumers can protect themselves from e-mail campaigns by redirecting all these mails to a different storage area or a secondary e-mail address.

E-advertising (or on-line/internet advertising) can also target specific groups of consumers. For example, Facebook is a well-known social networking site with more than 200 million active users. It operates on the principle of selling databases of users to advertising firms. Advertising firms can, therefore, target particular groups based on the user's demographics (age, sex and so on) or interests. Google also uses Google ads where a company can use metatags and keywords in order to promote messages to users seeking specific keywords in the search engine. If an internet user types a keyword in the search engine then the sponsored message will appear in the first three results of the Google result page, which are then tagged as sponsored.

One of the drawbacks of e-advertising is the fact that citizens in many countries have restricted access to the internet. For example, in Greece, only 30 per cent of the population had access to the internet in 2007, making e-advertising not so popular or effective, despite the fact that there has been an increase in internet users in the past few years. In 2010, the Greek government proposed a new law that would introduce a 21.5 per cent tax on e-advertising, payable to the journalists' pension fund. The tax would apply to online advertisements on news portals that are legally registered in Greece and produce their own news (but not other portals or forums). Despite these challenges, the fact that there is an increase in internet users in the EU, including Greece, suggests that e-advertising is a tool with a lot of potential.

The latest developments in e-sales in Greece can best be illustrated by the success story of E-Shop (Cosmo.gr, 2010), a company that started its activities through the internet and then expanded into the market with physical buildings. Following the business model of Amazon.com, E-shop started in 1998 as an online bookshop. A few years later the company decided to add a build-on-demand service, enabling customers to customize a PC or laptop based on their preferences. This idea quickly brought revenue to the company, and led it to expand its product range with CDs, more books and technology products. At the same time, it decided to open a business-to-business department. Following these successful decisions, the company started opening shops all over Greece. These shops could be used as central points, where local customers could go to collect their products instead of having them delivered. Today, despite the 70 shops operating nationally, E-shop has 120,000 individual visitors per day, more than 5,500 online orders daily, and more than 500,000 satisfied customers. E-shop's online sales process is accurate, efficient and reliable, while at the same time the company offers excellent online customer service combining online and offline solutions to customers.

The E-shop example shows that e-sales do occur in Greece, and more importantly, occur successfully. Although e-sales are not widespread as a way of selling products/services to consumers, they are gaining momentum as technology continues to develop in the country.

Comparison of sales practices in a local and a multinational firm

This section examines sales practices in two case studies by analyzing the role of the sales representative. The first case study is a local car dealership (referred to as CarCo), and the second is a multinational telecommunications company (referred to as TeleCo). The information in this section is drawn from the author's professional experience and is intended to be presented in such a way as to illustrate the differences in the approach to the sales function between local and multinational firms. It will demonstrate the lack of sophisticated sales practices in local firms and the greater strategic direction exhibited by multinational organizations.

CarCo is a well known family business that has been operating in Athens since the 1960s. It is a car dealership with a very strong portfolio of known car brands, a good reputation in the market and loyal customers. It recently opened a new dealership just outside Athens, close to Athens International Airport. The new dealership focused on selling two well-known car brands. When a sales representative arrives at the company premises for his/her first day of work, there is no employee induction in place to provide information on the organization and the role; new recruits have to find out about the organization's operating units (commercial car sales, enterprise fleet sales, service, rent-a-car leasing services) on their own without guidance from management. In addition, sales training is not provided to new sales representatives, who are expected to become knowledgeable about the products/services offered by the dealership by studying car prospectuses and other company documents. The sales manager informally provides the new recruits with information about the company approach to handling a prospective customer. Strategy meetings are not common practice, they are used as a short-term expedient for dealing with weekly or monthly decreases in sales and rather than strategically to drive the organization forward in terms of sales volume. The sales representative's duties vary each day. In addition to focusing purely on sales, duties also include car washing, car parking, can transfers between dealerships, after-sales support, and customer service (dealing with general enquiries and so on). Working hours are exhausting: twelve hours a day on weekdays and six hours on Saturdays, a total of sixty-six hours per week. Furthermore, there are only two sales representatives employed in a three-story building and often customers have to wait 30 to 40 minutes for a sales representative to become available. There is a six-month delay in the payment of bonuses.

TeleCo is a branch of a very well-known multinational telecommunications company, located in Athens. When a new sales representative joins the organization, he/she undertakes a one-week induction programme, which includes a welcomes and a tour of the offices and the local store within which they will be based by the sales manager, and a three-day training programme on the company's products and services. The sales representative's duties vary from selling mobile devices, lines and internet connections to dealing with corporate clients and providing customer support. During their first few days, new sales representatives are not given too many responsibilities. Instead, they have daily meetings with the sales manager at which they discuss their progress. Extensive training is also provided by the sales manager on how to approach customers and on how to deal with various customer situations. Colleagues assist the new sales representatives by sharing their experiences and helping them with their day-to-day work. Finally, remuneration is clearly explained and always paid on time.

The two case studies presented here illustrate the principal differences in the approaches of local and multinational firms towards the sales function. The local firm (family-owned) is characterized by an authoritative management style focusing around a cost-cutting strategy (which affects resourcing, provision of induction, training and development, employee working hours and remuneration). Strategic direction is lacking, the approach to strategy is reactive rather than proactive, and decisions seem to be based on intuition rather than on a calculated plan to drive the organization forward. On the other hand, the MNC presented here exhibits greater levels of strategic direction (stemming from the parent company), while the HR strategy implemented is in line with this direction (hence the investment in resourcing, induction, training/development, remuneration and so on). Although these two case studies cannot fairly represent the all companies, the comments made here corroborate the findings of other chapters in Part II of this book, in which major differences between local and multinational firms are discussed. It is important to remember here, however, that the vast majority of Greek firms are micro in size. Hence one can conclude that, although MNCs in the market implement more sophisticated and strategic sales practices, the majority of Greek firms are not investing much in this business function, nor do they see how it can strategically be used to drive the organization forward in the future.

Summary

This chapter has highlighted some main issues surrounding the sales profession and sales practices from a practitioner's point of view, including the role of the sales force in Greek firms, the importance of customer relationship management and the development of e-advertising and e-sales in Greece. It also incorporated case studies of a local and a multinational firm. These two case studies showed the different levels of sophistication in sales practices and approaches to sales, complementing the discussion on the differences between national and multinational firms in Greece that is a feature of this book.

References

Anderson, E. and Oliver, R.L. (1987) 'Perspectives on behaviour-based versus outcome-based salesforce control systems', *Journal of Marketing*, 51(4): 76–88.

Behrman, D.N. and Perreault, D. (1984) 'A role stress model of the performance and satisfaction of industrial salespersons', *Journal of Marketing*, 48(4): 9–21.

Brill, A.M. (1999) 'Online newspaper advertising: A study of format and integration with news content', in Schumann, D. W. and Thorson, E. (eds), *Advertising and World Wide Web*. New Jersey: Lawrence Erlbaum, pp.159–74.

Cosmo.gr (2010) E-shop.gr. http://www.cosmo.gr/SciTech/Hellas/274741.html.

Dyer, J.H., and Singh, H. (1998) 'The relational view: Cooperative strategy and sources of inter-organizational competitive advantage', *Academy of Management Review*, 23(4): 660–79.

Eisenhardt, K.M. (2002) 'Has strategy changed?', *Sloan Management Review*, 43(2): 88–91.

Garitaonandia, C. (2004) 'To be or not to be interactive – that is the question – interactivity on digital television and on the net.' Proceedings ESA-International Conference New Directions in European Media, 5–7 November 2004, Thessaloniki.

Greek IS Observatory (2010) 'Internet users in Greece', www.observatory.gr.

Harrigan, K.R. (2001) 'Strategic flexibility in the old and new economies', in Hitt, M.A., Freeman, R.E. and Harrison, J.S. (eds), *Handbook of Strategic Management*. Oxford: Blackwell.

Jaworski, B.J. and Kohli, A.K. (1991) 'Supervisory feedback: Alternative types and their impact on salespeople's performance and satisfaction', *Journal of Marketing Research*, 28(2): 190–201.

Jones, E., Brown, S.P., Zoltners, A.A. and Weitz, B.A. (2005) 'The changing environment of selling and sales management', *Journal of Personal Selling and Sales Management*, XXV(2): 105–11.

National Statistical Service of Greece (2002) *Register of Greek enterprises*. Athens: National Statistical Service of Greece.

Nowak, G.J., Shamp, S., Hollander, B. and Cameron, G.T. (1999) 'Interactive media: A means for more meaningful advertising?', in Schumann, D.W. and Thorson, E. (eds), *Advertising and World Wide Web*. New Jersey: Lawrence Erlbaum, 99–118.

Piercy, N.F., Low, G.S. and Cravens, D.W. (2004) 'Examining the effectiveness of sales management control practices in developing countries', *Journal of World Business*, 39(3): 255–67.

Selhofer, H., Lilischkis, S., Woerndl, M., Alkas, H. and O'Donnell, P. (2008) *The European e-Business report 2008: The impact of ICT and e-business on firms, sectors and the economy*. Luxembourg: Office for Official Publications of the European Communities.

12
Total Quality Management

Alexandros Psychogios

Overview

Total Quality Management (TQM) was initially developed in Japan and developed in the USA and the UK, influencing other business systems during the 1980s and 1990s. The Greek business system appears quite enthusiastic towards the adoption of this management approach. However, since it is widely accepted that TQM, as a management philosophy, sets a challenge for the organizational agendas in all business environments, it is important to understand how this initiative has been applied in Greece.

According to management literature, TQM is not a single entity, but it can be interpreted differently by different national business cultures in different national environments. The Greek environment differs from those in which TQM emerged and developed. The purpose of this chapter, therefore, is to explore the application of TQM in Greece. In particular, it investigates the rationale for TQM, as well as cultural and institutional factors which influence its application. The chapter is based on a series of empirical studies that support the adoption of a two-fold theoretical framework to understand and explain the conditions under which TQM can be applied in the Greek national business system. The components of this framework can be categorized in two major groups, the cultural and the institutional aspects. Both create pressures that either inhibit or promote TQM implementation within organizations. In this context, the tension between traditional business culture and modernization logic is the key to the evolution of TQM.

The chapter is structured in four sections. The first analyzes the context of the Greek management system and explains the need for modernization and therefore the adoption of sophisticated management practices such as TQM. The second section focuses on aspects of the emergence and development of the quality movement in the Greek system by focusing on both public and private employment sectors. The third section reviews a series of studies of current trends in TQM application and its impact on both managers and organizations. The final section develops the rationale and potential implications of the future application of TQM.

The nature of the Greek management system

According to Minoglou (1993), since World War II, Greece has evolved from a poor and semi-commercial business system to a middle-income semi-industrial one. The main feature of the system is its low effectiveness and efficiency. The small size of the country and of the market have led to economic growth but not the development of a business system supporting it (Minoglou, 1993). Moreover, management practices have not been used as the basis for designing and developing the system for both sectors of the economy, at least until recently (Psychogios and Szamosi, 2007). This has encouraged the development of a centralized system with a powerful state and relatively large public sector and a lack of co-ordination between industrial policies and other areas of fiscal policy. Also, the limited number of investments in general, and foreign direct investment (FDI) in particular, led to the unbalanced development of the business system. Finally, it can be argued that, while there are specific pressures for the system to evolve, at the same time there are specific resistors to reform.

The origins of this situation can be found in the Greek political system. According to Mouzelis (1978), it can be characterized as *constitutional parliamentarism*, meaning that Greece is among those countries in which a parliamentary political system was introduced before the beginning of the industrialization process, while in several western countries democratic regimes followed the industrial revolution. This encouraged a centralized system, in which the state was represented by a large public sector. The public sector was seen as the biggest and, sometimes, the only employer. This situation created what was later called *clientelism* between politicians and voters, under which politicians, in return for people's vote, promise jobs in the public domain. The political system also influenced management practices. Management of organizations in Greece can be seen to have a strong preference for central planning, monopolization, and political reliability.

Moreover, according to Diamantouros (2000), the Greek political system is bipolar: *reformism* versus *conservatism*. The former supports the view that the system needs to be modernized and reformed, attempting to follow international, and mainly European Union (EU), developments in social, political and economic trends. The latter resists any structural change of the system. For instance, new management methods have attracted the attention of the reformist group that argues in favour of adopting such practices. CEOs in both public and private sectors of employment emphasize the introduction of new management initiatives (Psychogios and Szamosi, 2007). On the other hand, there are people in senior positions who strongly resist these trends, because they threaten traditional sources of power and other interests (Diamantouros, 2000). These two long-established antithetical groups divide Greek business society and its institutions. At the beginning of the 1990s a reformist group appeared to dominate the system (Psychogios and Szamosi, 2007). This was mainly due to two inter-related reasons. The first was full membership of the EU, while the second related to the pressures emerging from the globalization of the economy (more competition, labour market flexibility, and so on). Therefore, state intervention became weaker and new management methods were adopted (Minoglou, 1995).

Beyond this socio-political explanation of how the Greek management system has been formed, it is important to understand how and to what extent management methods have been adopted. It is said that management, as an art and a science, is a relatively new item on the Greek business agenda (Psychogios and Szamosi, 2007). This reality has led many researchers to argue that there is a managerial gap in most Greek public and private organizations (Bourantas *et al.,* 1990) since organizational culture is characterized by high levels of formalization and low levels of decentralization (Joiner, 2000). There are other reasons explaining the managerial gap in Greece. According to Papadakis (2006), Greek companies tend to be centrally controlled and dominated by powerful individuals. Also, since the majority of firms are small and family-owned, management practices are mainly exercised by the owners, and sometimes by other members of their families. Moreover, the management culture is based more on emotion than on rationality and reflects a more autocratic style of leadership. According to Psychogios and Szamosi (2007), several Greek companies have been successfully created and developed by males with strong personalities, who are intimately involved in all aspects of the business operations, rarely delegating decision-making authority to subordinates. Finally, the managerial gap can be also demonstrated by the limited development of human resource management (HRM) practices in Greek organizations (Vouzas, 2004).

The fragmented nature of the Greek management system is also evidenced by the limited overall application of management methods in the public domain. An analysis of the historical context in which Greek public administration has been formed can lead to the conclusion that it is characterized by three specific pathologies: organizational/structural, personnel and operational (Psychogios and Szamosi, 2007). The organizational/structural refers to the lack of management sophistication in Greek public services (KEPE, 1991), whereby public organizations are dominated by bureaucratic forms of work which inhibit the adoption and application of new practices. For instance, the system is highly centralized and lacks the ability to delegate decision-making authority to other administrative levels (Makridimitris and Michalopoulos, 2000). The personnel pathology relates to the huge number of Greek civil servants who are unequally distributed in various public bodies (Makridimitris 2001). Further, employees in managerial positions lack managerial skills and this reduces their effectiveness (Makridimitris and Michalopoulos, 2000; Makridimitris, 2001). This is also associated with the limited application of HRM practices in the public sector which clearly reflects the operational pathology of public administration, since there is a lack of basic management methods such as strategic planning, evaluation and co-ordination of processes (Makridimitris and Michalopoulos, 2000; Michalopoulos 2001, 2002; Michalopoulos and Psychogios, 2003). Finally, the limited use of information technology is part of the pathological nature of the public management system.

Nevertheless, in the last 15 years, there has been some change in terms of management practices applied, confirming their increasing importance, and clearly related to the process of modernization (Psychogios and Szamosi, 2007). It can therefore be argued that there is a modernization agenda in the Greek management system that clearly sets a challenge for both private and public organizations attempting to adopt new management methods. The most important reasons for modernization are the country's full membership of the EU (Makridimitris, 1996; Kritsantonis, 1999; Makridimitris and Michalopoulos, 2000) and globalization pressures. The implications of the modernization movement can be seen in a variety of circumstances, including privatization, mergers, professionalization, promotion of entrepreneurship and innovation, and new patterns of employment. Beyond these implications, another significant aspect of the modernization movement can be found in the introduction of new management practices in many different industries and sectors. For instance, substantive changes to management practices have been identified in the banking sector (Glaveli and

Kufidu, 2005). According to Psychogios and Szamosi (2007) the application of new management methods seeks to make the system achieve additional quality results. For this reason, the most significant management item on the modernization agenda may be quality management in general, and TQM in particular (Vouzas and Gotzamani, 2005). The following sections examine the application of quality management initiatives in Greece.

The quality movement in Greece

The TQM movement has strongly infiltrated the Greek management system. In fact, TQM has been a management 'fad' for the last 15 years. The Ministry of Internal Affairs, Public Administration & Decentralization (MIAPAD) nominated the year 1998 the 'quality year' for both sectors of employment (MIAPAD, 17 March 1998).

Historically, there were specific points in time during which quality management practices were promoted. The need for quality outcomes first appeared in the late 1950s. It was the period after World War II, when rapid industrialization took place. After 1944, a series of Greek government policies, initiated by the Ministry of Industry (Kefis, 2005), attempted to financially support a variety of different companies in less developed geographical areas of the country. In addition, during this period, many foreign companies, in both the manufacturing and services industries, contributed to an increase in customer awareness of quality products and services (Dervitsiotis, 1999). Nevertheless, progress was rather slow because of the barriers associated with high import tariffs and customs duties, as well as a highly bureaucratic and inefficient public sector (Dervitsiotis, 1999).

In 1960, quality control processes became a significant issue on organizational agendas (Kefis, 2005)and it was realized that there was a lack of quality standards for Greek industries. At the beginning of the 1970s, there were some attempts to develop and implement standardization procedures (Kefis, 2005). During the same decade, the Chamber of Engineering attempted to develop a series of standards for Greek manufacturing industry, while at the same time, the Ministry of Agriculture tried to standardize agricultural products. Finally, in 1978, the Greek Organization for Standardization (ELOT) was established. Its main role was to monitor the quality of products and services.

A substantial turning point, however, was Greece's entrance to the EU in 1981. This resulted in the removal of trade barriers and intensified competition, creating strong pressures for performance improvement in every single industry (Dervitsiotis, 1999). According to Mandaraka and Kormentza (2000), Greek companies needed to shift their strategies towards meeting new legislation that emerged from the EU. Moreover, new government policies established by the Ministry of Development between 1997 and 2000 funded many companies attempting to implement quality assurance systems such as ISO 9001 and ISO 9002 (Kefis, 2005).

To sum up, there are specific factors which led to the development and enhancement of quality management methods in the Greek business system. The first factor is the industrialization process that occurred in the post-war period. This enhanced a series of government business support programmes especially in less developed areas, which can be considered the second factor. A third one is the operation of European and American companies in Greece which emphasize the superiority of quality products and services. A fourth factor is Greece's EU membership, which changed business regulations and drove them to place particular emphasis on quality improvement. A final factor is the rapid development of a variety of different organizations and consultancies responsible for supporting, evaluating and certifying industries with quality management systems and awards. These companies are mainly local partners of foreign institutions, such as TUV, Bureau Veritas, and so on.

Beyond these developments, however, there was little evidence of quality improvement efforts among Greek organizations. The majority of quality achievements have occurred in more recent years and are mainly observed in the private sector, as explained in the next section.

Aspects of TQM in the private sector

The single European market increased the demand for quality outcomes and, therefore, competition among firms. This created the need for more effective and efficient management practices in companies, in order to survive in the EU market. This challenge altered the thinking in most Greek private organizations, which adopted new managerial techniques, such as quality improvement initiatives. Large national companies have established quality management departments, with relative autonomy in decision making. These departments apply a wide range of quality tools, systems and techniques (Vouzas, 1997). Nevertheless, quality was, and still is, perceived by organizations as a peripheral function and the main role of the quality department is to monitor quality and maintain an acceptable quality level of products and/or services. In contrast, as Vouzas (1997: 164) argues, 'co-operation among departments on quality issues is nonexistent and conflicts between production and quality departments is a common phenomenon'.

At the same time, multinationals operating in Greece seem to be more interested in the quality management notion. Kufidu and Vouzas (1998), for instance, have shown that European multinationals operate in Greece on the basis of a productivity and quality mentality covering almost all departments. Moreover, the role of the trade unions in these organizations was a catalyst for the successful application of quality management programmes. They fully supported management efforts towards quality improvements and helped minimize employee resistance to these ideas (Kufidu and Vouzas, 1998).

Another factor is the increasingly important role of quality assurance systems, such as ISO 9000, in the majority of Greek private firms (Psychogios and Szamosi, 2007). According to Lamprecht (1992), the ISO 9000 system contributes to companies' competitiveness through the application of particular standards in managing operations. According to Tsiotras and Gotzamani (1996), the ISO 9000 series is well established in the Greek private sector. It has the great advantage of being a structured process with a clear end point, 'which is the certification of the quality assurance system' (Tsiotras and Gotzamani, 1996: 75). In practice, their adoption and application is considered the first step towards a total quality approach and philosophy (Vouzas, 1997; Psychogios and Wilkinson, 2007). However, TQM is a 'never-ending story'. It seeks to continuously improve the quality of products and/or services by satisfying customer needs. This is something that confuses Greek organizations (Tsiotras and Gotzzamani, 1996). Thus, the majority of Greek firms are not taking further steps towards TQM (Georgiadou and Tsiotras, 1998). They believe the adoption of an ISO 9000 system fulfils all the appropriate criteria for their transformation into TQM organizations (Lipovatz, 1998).

This conclusion is confirmed by various recent research studies. A study by Lazari and Kanellopoulos (2007) argues that TQM is still far from fully integrated into the process of Greek SMEs such as restaurants. It seems that managers, although they understand its importance, are not familiar with TQM methods. A problem that this study reveals is the lack of education about quality management tools, techniques and practices. Melidonioti and Gotzamani (2008) conducted a research study on the banking sector in Greece. They support the view that financial institutions are in general aware of the necessity for quality management practices. They are also familiar with TQM methods, but they shy away from the full adoption of the concept.

This arguably confirms Dervitsiotis' (1999: 2) view that there are 'only "islands of TQM" in Greek firms'. The same conclusion can be drawn if the application of TQM in public services is explored.

Aspects of TQM in the public sector

TQM was not even on the public sector agenda until recently. During the last ten years there have been many voices (politicians, scientists and specialists as well as the public) arguing for better public service delivery. This has made the total quality idea attractive to many central and local government agencies (Psychogios and Szamosi, 2007). A first official attempt to adopt TQM in the Greek public sector was undertaken by the National Bank of Greece (NBG) in 1998, when it published a report called *Quality for Public Administration*, attempting to introduce several management methods and ideas that had been previously applied in private industry. Management by objective (MBO), job design and job specification, and monitoring, were just a few of the practices proposed in this report. At the same time, the report supported the view that public administration in Greece should adopt a process targeted at minimizing the quantity of legislation. This effort resulted, a few years later, in the new (restructured) Code for Civil Servants. Finally, the same report emphasized the need for management specialists to contribute to the implementation of promising management practices in public organizations (NBG, 1998).

The NBG's report mainly influenced the MIAPAD policy outcome regarding the application of TQM in Greek public administration. A White Paper, *Quality for the Citizen*, was produced in an attempt to improve the services provided for citizens (MIAPAD, 17 March 1998), its main purpose being to improve several aspects of state–citizen relations (Michalopoulos, 2000, 2002). According to Psychogios *et al.* (2008), this policy paper was seeking to deliver improved communications between the state and the citizens; a managerial culture based on the satisfaction of citizen's requirements; an effective and efficient civil service through the application of performance indicators and other managerial techniques; and finally, a climate of partnership, trust and involvement between the state and society. MIAPAD (1998) designed a strategy in order to achieve these targets. The strategy included several key factors: free access to public services for citizens, the establishment of a new system of administrative control, improved transparency in public services, the improvement of technological infrastructure as well as the support of e-government programmes, the introduction of performance-based pay, the reduction of the number of public organizations and the development of a lean organizational structure based on fewer departments and more project-oriented teams.

A second stage of policy action occurred two years later. The new Minister, wishing to continue public administration reform efforts, introduced a new white paper entitled *Politia,*[1] which attempted to shift the operation of public administration in Greece, by improving the quality outcome. This report analytically presented a national business plan for the necessary changes in public services (Psychogios *et al.*, 2008). It also emphasized the adoption of specific management practices from the private sector (such as MBO, performance measurement, and so on). Finally, it supported the need for a new appraisal system for public sector employees.

Despite the fact that there was top-down pressure to improve the quality outcome of service delivery in the public sector, little changed in practice (Michalopoulos, 2002). This evidence seems to agree with Vouzas's (1997) argument that there were no encouraging steps towards TQM in the Greek public domain. According to Vouzas (1997: 167), the reason is that 'everything is coming through government regulations' and public services 'are not yet ready for such an evolutionary approach'.

Above and beyond this, though, there is evidence that TQM ideas and practices are impacting on both managers and organizations that seem to either inhibit or facilitate its implementation in the Greek business system.

Driving TQM application: barriers and facilitators

Although TQM is a critical aspect of organizational reform in the Greek private and public sectors, there is still limited evidence of its impact on both organizational processes and managers. The absence of evidence is mainly related to the adoption process of TQM methods in Greece. The main assumption is that TQM often fails because it is imported directly from the country of origin (Psychogios, 2010). It is therefore important to explore the conditions under which both principles and practices of TQM can be implemented in business systems that are different from those where it first emerged and developed (Psychogios and Wilkinson, 2007; Psychogios *et al.*, 2007, 2009). Although TQM originated in Japan, the USA and the UK (Cole, 1999), globalization pressures created an international TQM agenda widely applied in many organizations all over the world. and other countries are keen to adopt this kind of management philosophy. The business systems in these countries, however, represent a challenge for TQM application (Psychogios *et al.*, 2008, Psychogios, 2010). In other words, as Noronha (2003) argues, it is quite difficult to apply TQM values in every single national context. Greece is a prime example of a business system that differs culturally and institutionally from those in which TQM emerged. For instance, in the Anglo-Saxon model there are *ad hoc* and market-driven inter-firm relationships with strong financial control (Ferner and Quintanilla, 1998). Moreover, the majority of Anglo-Saxon organizations are characterized by leaner structures, as well as centralized policy-making (Ferner and Quintanilla, 1998). In addition, emphasis is laid on the generalist management career progression rather than the specialist one (Evans *et al.*, 1989). Finally, delegation of authority and responsibility from managers to subordinates is more usual. Furthermore, there are more flexible employee relations (Whittaker, 1990). In contrast, Greek political, economical and legislative factors and a series of cultural factors make the business system inflexible and promote individualism, as well as more rigid control of subordinates. These factors inhibit TQM application. However, there are other factors that can contribute positively.

Empirical evidence of TQM drivers in Greece is based on a series of investigations between 2002 and 2008 that have been published in a variety of academic journals, and have demonstrated an impact on both managers and organizations.

The business literature on TQM application in Greece is quite limited, with the majority of research focused on CEOs and their relationship to TQM. According to a study conducted by Koufopoulos and Chryssochoidis (2000), Greek CEOs' involvement in strategic planning is critical and extensive. By contrast, middle-level managers' involvement in decision-making and strategic planning seems to be very limited (Michalopoulos and Psychogios, 2003). Middle-level managers mainly concentrate on facilitating and executing decisions that have been made at the upper level. These studies confirm that senior executives seem to be the only 'driving force' of Greek organizations towards the application of management methods such as TQM. Nevertheless, they seem not to fully understand its concepts and practices (Vouzas, 1997). According to Lipovatz (1998), there are two important factors that positively and negatively influence Greek CEOs' leadership performance. The first is an institutional factor and is associated with the wide use of quality assurance systems, such as the ISO 9000 series. Its international reputation makes it currently a coercive isomorphic aspect of the business system, since it is regulated and required in many EU countries. The application of such a system is also considered by senior managers to complete TQM requirements. The second factor relates to the culture of company attempts to introduce a TQM approach sometimes 'reducing the freedom for the development of own activities' (Lipovatz 1998: 11).

There is more evidence on middle managers and their relationship with TQM. According to Vouzas (1997: 168), in a total quality context, middle managers in Greek organizations identify themselves 'as supervisors, with formalised lines of authority and a less autonomous role... they are acting as guardians of well-kept territories'. Therefore, their role is limited with respect to TQM application. The same conclusion can be drawn about public sector managers, who are mainly 'engaged in routine administrative tasks at the expense of managerial ones' (Kufidu *et al.,* 1997: 100). More specifically, their managerial activities are very much limited 'by their lack of authority in setting rewards, imposing penalties and participating in departmental planning and organizing'. The research participants blamed the public organization's culture as the most important factor determining the 'what' and 'how' of management in the Greek public domain (Kufidu *et al.,* 1997). Finally, they point out that, in a public organizational environment that lacks new technology and motivation towards better performance, it might be difficult for managers to adopt new practices in their daily work in order to meet citizen-customers' needs as required by TQM.

In short, according to these studies, management practices in both sectors of employment (private and public) are seen as presenting problems for the adoption and successful implementation of the TQM approach. More recent research evidence, confirms these conclusions, but at the same time shows that, at least at middle management level, there are also some positive elements that can be considered as TQM facilitators in the Greek business system.

In particular, a series of studies has been carried out between 2002 and 2008 (Psychogios and Wilkinson, 2007; Vouzas and Psychogios, 2007; Psychogios and Priporas, 2007; Psychogios *et al.,* 2008; Psychogios *et al.,* 2009), which demonstrate that TQM has become a significant issue on the Greek managerial agenda with a clear impact on both managers and organizations. More specifically, Table 12.1 summarizes the responses of 241 managers working in the Greek services industry. These findings are based on the analysis of a series of multivariate models developed for a variety of individual aspects of work and controlled for the whole sample of managers, as well as for those referring to the public and private sectors. Information about measurement of the TQM approach can be found in Vouzas and Psychogios (2007).

Table 12.1 Effects of 'soft' and 'hard' aspects of TQM on the nature of managers' work

Soft TQM aspects	**Whole sample N:241**			**Public sector N:108**			**Private sector N:133**		
	Effect +	**No effect**	**Effect –**	**Effect +**	**No effect**	**Effect –**	**Effect +**	**No effect**	**Effect –**
Autonomy	√			√			√		
Monitoring		√			√			√	
Stress levels			√		√			√	
Work effort	√				√		√		
Job security		√			√			√	
Career development		√			√			√	
Loyalty	√			√			√		
Hard TQM aspects	**Effect +**	**No effect**	**Effect –**	**Effect +**	**No effect**	**Effect –**	**Effect +**	**No effect**	**Effect –**
Autonomy	√			√			√		
Monitoring		√			√			√	
Stress levels	√			√				√	
Work effort	√				√		√		
Job security			√		√				√
Career development	√				√		√		
Loyalty	√				√		√		

Source: Adapted from Psychogios (2003: 151).

It can be argued that what really matters is the 'hard' side of TQM. 'Soft' principles of TQM play a less important role in the reported effects on managers' work. By contrast, TQM techniques and systems affect most managers' professional life. Furthermore, autonomy and loyalty are the only aspects that have been positively influenced by both sides of TQM, and no effect has been reported on the levels of top management's monitoring of subordinates. Other aspects show a variety of effects. Views on the levels of stress and work effort seem to be negatively influenced by particular 'soft' TQM concepts. In addition, managers' familiarity with TQM tools seems to influence the high levels of stress and work effort reported. Finally, their familiarity with 'hard' TQM practices indicates that they view their career prospects positively. If we divide the sample of managers according to employment sector, Table 12.1 confirms that familiarity with 'hard' TQM aspects influences both public and private managers' opinions about their jobs. However, the effect is much stronger among private sector managers, who report that they work harder, enjoy more autonomy and have been promoted. In addition, their counterparts in public organizations stating that they enjoy more autonomy and feel more stress are also those with the more developed views and understanding of TQM. In short, the results indicate there is evidence that TQM has affected the nature of managers' work both positively and negatively.

More qualitative studies confirm this conclusion. For instance, Psychogios and Wilkinson (2007) argue that there is no specific resistance to TQM in the Greek business system. Many managers understand that it is a part of a series of practices aimed at developing the management system further. However, 'the TQM paradigm has not cut very deep into organizations in general and managers in particular and it could not be said to be a core organising principle' (Psychogios and Wilkinson, 2007: 1057). In addition, Psychogios and Priporas (2007) suggest that, although there is evidence that TQM has affected several aspects of managers' daily work, this is mainly associated with the 'hard' version of TQM that includes techniques, tools and systems. In other words, it seems that Greek managers do believe in TQM results insofar as these are emerging from the application of statistical tools and other quality assurance practices. At the same time they understand but neglect its 'soft' side (Psychogios and Wilkinson, 2007; Psychogios and Priporas, 2007; Psychogios *et al.*, 2008). According to Psychogios and Wilkinson (2007: 1057) this attitude 'suggests that managers hold a realistic view of TQM', since 'according to their view, although the "soft" side of TQM is something "good" and useful, it has little to do with their organisational reality'. This attitude is characterized by high levels of control. Centralized decision-making systems seems to inhibit TQM further, since there is little evidence of delegation of authority and autonomy in decision-making, both of which are vital for total quality.

A general conclusion drawn from these arguments would be that TQM has started to enter managers' consciousness. It seems that – at least through the adoption of new 'hard' management quality improvement practices – their role has begun to widen as the nature of their work is reported to be changing. This suggests that Greek managers are slowly moving towards adopting the TQM agenda. Another question that now emerges is whether organizations are moving in the same direction.

Table 12.2 summarizes additional findings referring to organizational processes and the potential influence on them of TQM methods. The overall conclusion is that the TQM approach has a, mainly positive, impact on most of these aspects. Organizational performance is mainly affected by the 'hard' side of TQM and less by the 'soft' side, but organizational processes seem to be mainly influenced by 'soft' TQM. The awareness of 'soft' TQM concepts seems to be more significant for organizational processes, such as trust, communication, teamwork, training and empowerment, than familiarity with 'hard' TQM practices. Nevertheless, an observation of the results for each employment sector reveals a clear emphasis on the 'hard' side of TQM. It seems that awareness of the 'soft' side of TQM has less influence upon public sector managers' responses to most organizational aspects. Thus, what is important for public managers is the knowledge and use of TQM techniques and tools rather the awareness of TQM principles. One possible explanation relates to the fact that management techniques and tools are quite new practices for public sector managers which have recently started to affect organizational aspects of their jobs. By contrast, private services have longer experience of the use of 'hard' management practices. Therefore, their impact on changes to organizational processes is weaker.

A core question that emerges from the evidence presented here is: under what conditions can the Greek management system adopt TQM-oriented principles, concepts and tools? In other words, what are the special issues in the Greek business system facilitating or inhibiting the introduction of TQM? The research evidence concerning TQM application in both sectors of economy (Psychogios and Wilkinson, 2007; Psychogios *et al.*, 2007) suggests that there is a *Two-Fold Contingency Model* (see Figure 12.1) under which TQM should be seen in the specific national business environment (Psychogios and Wilkinson, 2007; Psychogios *et al.*, 2008).

Table 12.2 Effects of 'soft' and 'hard' aspects of TQM on organizational performance and process

Soft TQM organizational aspects	Whole sample N:241			Public sector N:108			Private sector N:133		
	Effect +	No effect	Effect −	Effect +	No effect	Effect −	Effect +	No effect	Effect −
Organizational performance									
Performance improvement	√				√		√		
Senior management commitment and support to employees		√			√			√	
Customer satisfaction		√			√			√	
Organizational process									
Trust	√			√					√
Communication	√				√		√		
Empowerment	√			√				√	
Teamwork Effectiveness	√				√		√		
Training Effectiveness	√			√			√		

Hard TQM organizational aspects	Effect +	No effect	Effect –	Effect +	No effect	Effect –	Effect +	No effect	Effect –
Organizational performance									
Performance improvement		√			√			√	
Senior management commitment and support to employees	√			√			√		
Customer satisfaction	√			√			√		
Organizational process									
Trust	√			√			√		
Communication	√			√				√	
Empowerment		√		√				√	
Teamwork Effectiveness		√			√			√	
Training Effectiveness		√			√			√	

Source: Adapted from Psychogios (2003: 180).

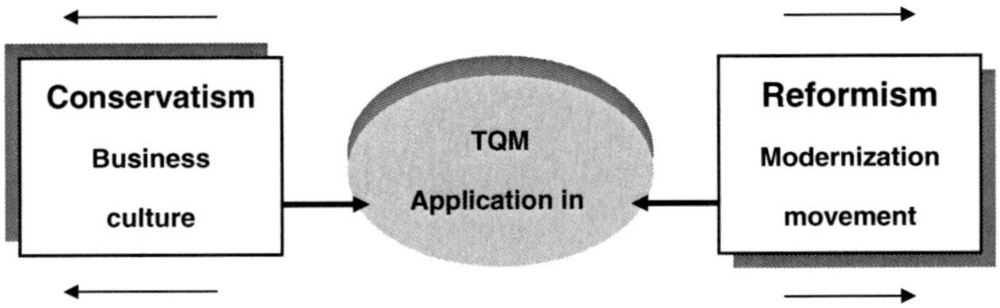

Figure 12.1 Two antithetical forces in the application of TQM to the Greek business system
Sources: Adapted from Psychogios and Wilkinson (2007) and Psychogios *et al.* (2008).

In addition, according to Diamantouros' (2000) view, two kinds of forces affect the application of TQM in the Greek business system: *conservatism* and *reformism*. The former can be seen as a barrier to TQM ideas since it tends to resist structural changes of the system. According to Psychogios and Wilkinson (2007), there are four major conservative elements determining TQM application: first, senior managers' dominance over the system (Liponatz, 1998); second, the existence of an autocratic or authoritarian management style (Burantas *et al.,* 1990; Psychogios and Szamosi, 2007); third, a trust gap within organizations (Bourantas *et al.,* 1990; Psychogios and Szamosi, 2007); fourth, the lack of open and clear communication among organizational members (Joiner, 2000; Papadakis, 2006). These cultural elements hold back the system, creating resistance to change. There are also questions about the reception of any new management approach like TQM. On the other hand, reformative cultural 'force' tends to support the modernization of the system. The reformative forces seem to facilitate TQM application. The assumption is that the pressures of globalization, EU membership and increased competition have altered the way Greece operates (Dervitsiotis, 1999; Mandaraka and Kormentza, 2000). The business system is therefore attempting to change by modernizing several aspects of its operations. This change process can be observed in the adoption of sophisticated management concepts, such as TQM. As Psychogios *et al.* (2008: 167) argue, 'the existence of these two "forces" intersects transversely the Greek public administration causing controversies and conflicts. Thus, under the pressures of the traditional "force" the application of TQM seems to be influenced by fixed and monolithic cultural values while under the reformative agenda TQM is not seen as mechanist and closed approach with set implications, but as a positive change aspect of the system'.

Beyond these conclusions, it can be argued that TQM has not cut very deeply into the face of Greek organizational realities. Although TQM can be seen as a modest but useful set of techniques and practices to improve organizational process and performance, in parallel, it can hardly be seen as a means of cultural transformation within organizations. One major argument supporting this conclusion relates to conservative forces. A second argument is associated with the suggestive but insubstantial linkages between awareness of TQM and managers' responses to aspects of organizational performance and process. It could be argued, therefore, that the Greek business system is only slowly moving towards total quality setting.

Summary

One overall conclusion is that, despite Greek managers' awareness of TQM concepts and ideas, their level of understanding and knowledge of these concepts is superficial. Without doubt TQM has become a substantial issue on the Greek managerial agenda. Nevertheless, Greek organizations have to undertake many steps towards the TQM approach before it can be said to be a core organizing principle. Moreover, there is evidence that TQM has made some progress with Greek managers, affecting several aspects of their day-to-day work, such as autonomy and work effort. However, this effect was mainly a result of their familiarity with 'hard' management practices rather than their awareness of 'soft' concepts. This suggests that managers have a more pragmatic view of TQM. According to their view, although the 'soft' side of TQM is something good and useful in their minds, it has little to do with organizational reality. The one that really matters is the 'hard' side. At the same time, senior managers are committed to TQM since it can accomplish targets and promote organizational effectiveness and competitiveness. In other words, senior executives are perceived as willing to promote total quality ideas, such as like greater autonomy. However, research evidence indicates that, in exchange for giving more autonomy and responsibility to employees, management expects them to work harder, to achieve quality results and to subscribe to decisions taken at higher levels.

In general, it can be concluded that TQM, as a whole new management philosophy with a set of concepts and tools, has started to enter the Greek business system. There is no particular opposition to the adoption of TQM. Most people seem to accept it and see it as part of a modernization package for the Greek management system. Nevertheless, the TQM paradigm has not made deep inroads into organizations in general and managers in particular. It has not yet become a driving force towards organizational management. Managers see TQM from a more realistic point of view insofar as firstly, they focus on the importance of its 'hard' side and secondly, they are sceptical about the actual implications and effectiveness of several 'soft' concepts (like trust or empowerment).

This chapter addressed the past and present drivers of TQM application in Greece. Having understood the background to TQM in Greece, it is important to discuss a number of possible future scenarios (Psychogios and Wilkinson, 2007; Psychogios *et al.,* 2008). The first scenario is the *pessimistic* one which supports a potential rejection of TQM by the Greek management system. According to Makridimitris and Michalopoulos (2000), there have been many examples of rejection of management practices. The special features of traditional cultural forces might prove to be an obstacle to the implementation of TQM. In other words, several special characteristics of the Greek national political economy continue to play a quite substantial role in the implementation of globalized policies and practices (Vernon and Rees, 2001). A second scenario – more *optimistic* – would suggest that continuous pressures from globalization and international competition lead to the dominance of the modernization agenda. This scenario would entail the adoption of globalized management approaches such as TQM. It would also mean pressure on the system to implement approaches that are still relatively novel (Psychogios *et al.,* 2008).

However, the current situation in both the global and the Greek economy suggests that a *contingency scenario* is more likely to occur. According to this scenario, TQM has some potential for successful implementation in Greek organizations, as both traditionalism and reformism are considered in its application. For instance, a synthesis of some features of conservatism with those of reformism could be useful. In other words, one can argue that the modernization agenda is not about adopting a whole package, but the selective use of certain elements. Some specific parts of the 'soft' TQM agenda may be consistent with modernization, but they might need a more developed HRM contribution to realise their potential (Simmons *et al.,* 1995).

Above and beyond these future scenarios, more research is needed in order to investigate the implementation of TQM in the Greek business system, and in particular the potential application of specific management approaches as well as whether these kinds of practices can actually contribute to changing the system. For instance, have specific features of the Greek management culture, such as the authoritarian style, been affected by such approaches? TQM ideas may have begun to encourage and facilitate these changes.

Note

1. From the Greek word *polis* (city). This meaning is similar to the Aristotelian view and includes the concept of government (administration).

References

Bourantas, D., Anagnostelis, J., Mantes, Y. and Kefalas, A. (1990) 'Culture gap in Greek management', *Organisation Studies*, 11(2): 261–283.

Cole, R. (1999) *Managing quality fads: How American business learned to play the quality game*. New York: Oxford University Press.

Dervitsiotis, N.K. (1999) 'Quality in Greece: past and present', *The TQM Magazine*, 11(2): 84–87.

Diamantouros, N. (2000) *Political Dualism and Political Change in Greece after the Dictatorship*. Athens: Alexandria (in Greek).

Evans, P., Lank, E. and Farquhar, A. (1989) 'Managing Human Resource in the international Firm: Lessons from Practice', in Evans, P., Doz, Y. and Laurent, A. (eds) *Human Resource Management in International Firms: Change, Globalization, Innovation*. Basingstoke: Macmillan.

Ferner, A. and Quintanilla, J. (1998) 'Multinationals, national business systems and HRM: the enduring influence of national identity or a process of Anglo-Saxonization', *The International Journal of Human Resource Management*, 9(4): 710–31.

Georgiadou, M. and Tsiotras, G. (1998) 'Environmental management systems: a new challenge for Greek industry', *International Journal of Quality & Reliability Management*, 15(13): 286–302.

Glaveli, N. and Kufidu, S. (2005) 'The Old, The Young and the Restless: A Comparative Analysis of the Impact of Environmental Change on Training in Four Greek Banks', *European Business Review*, 17(5): 441–59.

Joiner, T.A. (2000) 'The Influence of National Culture and Organizational Culture Alignment on Job Stress and Performance: Evidence From Greece', *Journal of Managerial Psychology*, 16(3): 229–42.

KEPE (1991) *Study for the Weaknesses of Greek Public Administration*. Athens: KEPE: Research Centre for Social Sciences (in Greek).

Kefis, A. (2005) *Total Quality Management*. Athens: Kritiki.

Koufopoulos, N.D. and Chryssochoidis, M.G. (2000) 'The effects of an uncertain business environment upon leadership and strategic planning practices', *Strategic Change*, 9(6): 379–95.

Kritsantonis, N. (1999) 'Greece: The Maturing of the System', in Ferner, A. and Hyman, R. (eds), *Changing Industrial Relations in Europe*. Oxford: Blackwell-Business.

Kufidu, S., Petridou, E. and Mihail, D. (1997) 'Upgrading managerial work in the Greek civil service', *International Journal of Public Sector Management*, 10(4): 244–53.

Kufidu, S. and Vouzas, F. (1998) 'Human resource aspects of quality management: evidence from MNEs operating in Greece', *The International Journal of Human Resource Management*, 9(5): 818–30.

Lamprecht, L.J. (1992) *ISO 9000: Preparing for Registration*, ASQC Quality Press, Marcel Dekker Inc.

Lazari, C. and Kanellopoulos, D. (2007) 'Total Quality Management in Hotel Restaurants: A case study in Greece', *Journal of Engineering and Applied Sciences*, 2(3): 546–71.

Lipovatz, D. (1998) 'Leadership performance in Greek enterprises using the EQA framework', *The TQM Magazine*, 10(3).

Mandaraka, M. and Kormentza, I. (2000) 'Greece faces up to the EU packaging regulation: Businesses reveal their plans to meet the new legislative environment', *Environmental Management and Health*, 11(1): 7–19.

Makridimitris, A. (1996) *Administration in Crisis*. Athens: Livanis (in Greek).

Makridimitris, A. and Michalopoulos, N. (2000) *Scientific Reports for Greek Public Administration: 1950 – 1998*. Athens: Papazisis (in Greek).

Makridimitris, A. (2001) 'Public Administration in the political system: The Government, the Prime Minister, the Ministers', in Spiliotopoulos, P.E. and Makridimitris, A. (eds), *Public Administration in Greece*, Athens: Sakkoulas.

Melidonioti, M. and Gotzamani, K. (2008) 'Standardization and Quality in Greek Banking Sector', National Conference of Business Administration & Economics, Technological Educational Institution (TEI) of Larisa, Faculty of Business Administration & Economics, 4–5 July 2008, Larisa, Greece.

Michalopoulos, N. (2001) 'Methods of management and organisation of state-citizen relations', in Spiliotopoulos, P.E. and Makridimitris, A. (eds), *Public Administration in Greece*, Athens: Sakkoulas.

Michalopoulos, N. (2002) 'Aspects of Citizen–Public Services Relationships: The Case of Greece', *Chinese Public Administration Review*, 1(2):177–184

Michalopoulos, N., and Psychogios, A.G. (2003) 'Knowledge management and public organisations: How well does the model apply to Greece?', *Chinese Public Administration Review*, 2(1/2):64–80.

Ministry of Internal Affairs, Public Administration & Decentralization (MIAPAD), (1998) Programme: 'POLITIA', *Journal: Dimosiografika*, 17 March 1998 (in Greek).

Minoglou, I. (1993) 'The Greek state and the international financial community, 1922-1932: Demystifying the foreign factor', PhD Thesis, London School of Economics and Political Sciences.

Minoglou, I. (1995) 'Political factors shaping the role of foreign finance in Greece', in Harriss, J., Hunter, J. and Lewis, C. (eds), *The New Institutional Economics and the Third World Development*, London: Routledge.

Mouzelis, N. (1978) *Modern Greece: Facets of Underdevelopment*. London: Macmillan.

National Bank of Greece (1998) *Quality in Public Administration*, Research Report. Athens: National Bank of Greece (in Greek).

Noronha, C. (2003) 'National Culture and Total Quality Management: Empirical Assessment of a Theoretical Model', *The TQM Magazine*, 15(5): 351–56.

Papadakis, V.M. (2006) 'Do CEOs Shape the Process of Making Strategic Decisions? Evidence from Greece', *Management Decision*, 44(3): 367–94.

Psychogios, G.A. (2003) 'Towards the adoption of new management methods in a modernising national business system? A study of the responses of middle managers to Total Quality Management in Greek service industry', PhD thesis, University of Warwick.

Psychogios, A. (2010) 'A Four-Fold Regional-Specific Approach to TQM: The case of South Eastern Europe', *International Journal of Quality and Reliability Management*, 27(9): 1036–53.

Psychogios, G.A, Michalopoulos, N. and Szamosi L. (2008) 'Anglo-Saxon Change in a Non-Anglo-Saxon Cultural Context: Lessons from TQM application in Greek Public Organizations', *International Journal of Learning & Intellectual Capital*. 5(2): 153–71.

Psychogios, G.A. and Priporas, K. (2007) 'Understanding Total Quality Management in Context: Qualitative Research on Managers' Awareness of TQM Aspects in the Greek Service Industry', *The Qualitative Report*, 12(1): 40–66.

Psychogios, G.A. and Szamosi, L. (2007) 'Exploring the Greek National Business System: Towards a Modernization Agenda', *Euro Med Journal of Business*, 2(1): 7–22.

Psychogios, G.A. and Wilkinson, A. (2007) 'Exploring TQM awareness in the Greek national business context: between conservatism and reformism cultural determinants of TQM', *International Journal of Human Resource Management*, 18(6): 1042–62.

Psychogios, G.A., Wilkinson, A. and Szamosi, L. (2009) 'Getting to the Heart of the Debate: 'Hard' Versus 'Soft' Side Effects of TQM on Middle Manager Autonomy', *TQM & Business Excellence* , 20(4): 445–66.

Simmons, D.E., Shadur, M.A., and Preston, A.P. (1995) 'Integrating TQM and HRM', *Employee Relations*, 17(3): 75–86.

Tsiotras, G. and Gotzamani, K. (1996) 'ISO 9000 as an entry key to TQM: the case of Greek industry', *International Journal of Quality and Reliability Management*, 13(4): 64–76.

Vernon, G. and Rees, C. (2001) 'Transnational capital and the end of national social settlements? Recent developments in Sweden', paper presented at IREC Network Conference on Globalisation, Competitiveness and the Government of Employment in Europe: Structures, Strategies and Actors, 26–28 April 2001, Madrid.

Vouzas, F. (1997) 'Middle Management and Quality Improvement: Evidence from five countries', in Livian, Y.F. and Burgoyone, G.J. (eds), *Middle Managers in Europe*, Routledge Advances in Management and Business Studies, Routledge.

Vouzas, F. (2004) 'HR utilization and quality improvement: the reality and the rhetoric – the case of Greek industry', *The TQM Magazine*, 16(2): 125–35.

Vouzas, F.K. and Gotzamani, K.D. (2005) 'Best practices of selected Greek organizations on their road to business excellence', *The TQM Magazine*, 17(3): 259–66.

Vouzas, F. and Psychogios, G.A. (2007) 'Assessing Managers' Awareness of Total Quality Management', *The TQM Magazine*, 19(1): 62–75.

Whittaker, D.H. (1990) 'The End of Japanese-Style Employment?', *Work, Employment and Society*, 4: 321–47.

13
Accounting and Auditing Practices

Constantinos Caramanis and Emmanouil Dedoulis

Overview

Accounting and auditing are integral parts of wider management and business practices. Accounting provides the necessary information for making rational economic and business decisions, while auditing adds credibility to that information. The historical development of the institutions of accounting and auditing reflects the social, economic and political environment in each country and Greece is no exception.

Greece has undergone a series of significant changes over the past few decades, starting with the country's entry to the European Union (EU). However, features of her traditional governance system exhibit remarkable resilience, often leading to conflicts and ineffective arrangements and structures. This situation has had significant implications for Greek accounting and audit practices and institutions, as this chapter will illustrate. The breadth and depth of these reforms is such that accounting and auditing practices in Greece have been in a state of flux, as more traditional arrangements are increasingly challenged by the EU-endorsed Anglo-American model.

To make sense of the complexities of the current Greek accounting and auditing practices, as well as future perspectives, this chapter employs the theoretical model of Puxty *et al.* (1987) for the study of accounting (including auditing) in modern economies. The model draws attention to the interaction of market and state agencies and the role of supra-national (EU) institutions.

In addition to the introduction, this chapter is organized into five sections. Section two gives a brief account of the politico-economic history of modern Greece to provide the background for understanding the development of Greek accounting and auditing practices. Section three explains the origins of accounting and auditing practices from the 1920s to the early 1980s. Section four is divided into three sub-sections. The first refers to the early 'europeanization' of Greek accounting practice through the transposition of the EEC (European Economic Community, renamed the EU in 1992) accounting directives in the late 1980s. The second explains the adoption of the International Financial Reporting Standards (IFRSs) in the 2000s and the third sub-section describes developments in the auditing profession since the 1980s. Section five presents brief summary results of a survey of auditors and financial executives about the state of Greek accounting and audit practice and regulation, following the adoption of the IFRSs. Finally, section six presents the concluding remarks.

A brief account of the politico-economic history of modern Greece

This section provides a brief account of the economic and socio-political history of the country to help the reader understand the developments in the accounting domain. As will be explained, accounting and auditing in Greece did not emerge as a market need; rather, developments in the field were largely the result of state intervention, as accounting was seen as a tool in the service of wider state policy objectives.

Greece, which gained her independence from the Ottoman Empire in the late 1820s, remained an overwhelmingly agrarian economy during the nineteenth century, burdened by a huge war debt and political instability. There was no industrial revolution in the country during this period, as in other Balkan states that had been under Ottoman rule. Very few small, family-owned commercial firms operated and these kept hardly any kind of accounting records (Ministry of Co-ordination, 1952; Anagnostopoulos, 1937). The industrialization of Greece began in earnest during the 1870s when the state embarked on an extensive developmental and modernization effort (Tsoukalas, 1969; Mouzelis, 1986). Several companies were set up before the turn of the twentieth century through public subscription and the first massive frauds occurred (Dertilis, 1980). The effort to construct an industrial infrastructure continued during the early twentieth century and received a boost after the military defeat of Greece in Asia Minor in 1922. During the 1940s economic development was derailed by the Second World War, the German occupation, and the five-year civil war which followed, resulting in unprecedented destruction of the economy. With the assistance of massive American aid and very favourable investment terms, post-war economic recovery was rapid, especially following Greece's association with the Common Market in 1961 (Mouzelis, 1986).

Eventually, Greece became a member of the EEC in 1980, participated in the signing of the Maastricht Treaty in 1992 and became a full member of the monetary union in 2001. This appeared to seal the country's commitment to transform itself into a market economy.

Over the last three decades, Greece's membership of the EEC/EU has been a major factor in institutional and other reforms in the country (Mouzelis, 1995). In fact, all major institutional reforms have arguably been the outcome of European integration. The EU's strategy for the creation of a single market, in particular, has had important implications as regards the institutional and legal framework for accounting and audit practices in the country. This has involved modernizing corporate legislation, the adoption of International Financial Reporting Standards and of International Standards on Auditing, not to mention the adoption of EU directives for the operation of the financial sector (banking and insurance) and the capital markets.

However, in general, Greece's performance regarding the implementation of EU-inspired reforms has been notably poor. Indeed, while Greece may adopt EU-inspired policies, it often appears that such reforms remain largely on paper, producing rather limited real results. For instance, in assessing the progress of reforms in member states based on the 2000 Lisbon Strategy Plan,[1] the World Economic Forum shows that Greece has been the weakest performing country: 'Greece consistently receives the lowest scores in all dimensions' (World Economic Forum, 2002: 7; similar comments were also made in the 2004 and 2006 reports). Featherstone and Papadimitriou (2008) have examined Greece's 'Europeanization'[2] project and have identified a serious 'reform capacity' problem.[3] This poor performance in introducing real reforms is certainly related to the country's significant, long-term structural economic problems (for example, high budget deficit and fiscal imbalances, high public debt, low competitiveness, lack of transparency, institutional deficiencies, and so on, see OECD, 2009, 2010 and European Commission, 2010). Such problems have become acute during the current global economic crisis and are unquestionably related to the country's system of governance, known for its strong clientelistic and populist overtones (Mouzelis, 1986).

Origins and development of accounting and auditing up to the 1970s: a conservative, state-oriented mentality

Early development of accounting practice and regulation

The development of accounting and auditing in the modern world is associated with the industrial revolution and the institution of the limited liability company. In Greece noticeable industrial and commercial activity by limited liability companies[4] first appeared in the early part of the twentieth century. At that time, following a series of corporate scandals, the state, in an attempt to steer economic development, started increasingly to intervene in accounting and auditing matters, ending an almost century-long *laissez-faire* period (1830 to 1920). The first major state intervention was company Law 2190/1920[5] which was carefully framed and included some basic legal provisions[6] and a few accounting rules. Despite its limited scope, Law 2190/1920 constituted a basic regulatory framework for its time and is still considered a milestone in the development of Greek corporate legislation. Before the transposition of the EEC directives in the 1980s, Law 2190/1920 had received relatively minor amendments.

Besides corporate legislation, another way traditionally used by the Greek state to intervene in accounting matters has been through tax legislation, ostensibly for the purpose of curbing rampant tax evasion. The Code of Corporate Books and Documents, known in Greece by the acronym KVS, was enacted in 1952 and concerned the organization of book-keeping by companies and other forms of business enterprise. Its most fundamental provision was the requirement that companies maintain appropriate books and records. As the late Professor Tsimaras has noted: 'for many (companies) the maintenance of books of account is a very burdensome state intervention of a tax nature. If it were not legally enforceable, accounting would be limited to keeping a few creditor and debtor accounts' (Tsimaras,1958: 37, trans.). KVS has received numerous amendments and supplements and today, along with the relevant ministerial circulars, comprises an overly-voluminous set of detailed regulations (see Presidential Decree 186/1992). It contains excessive procedural detail and provides for hefty fines, even for breaches of rules that lack economic substance. It is widely perceived as an ineffective means of combating tax evasion and as an unnecessary burden by professionals and firms alike, although it appears to enjoy support from key individuals from the services[7] of the Ministry of Economy. In addition to KVS, income tax legislation (Law 3323/1955 and Law 3843/1958) also included accounting provisions and requirements that often deviate, as is the case with KVS, from applicable accounting rules.

The limited (almost rudimentary) accounting rules initially enshrined in Law 2190/1920, and the nature of the provisions included in KVS and other tax legislation, along with the severity of penalties, have helped to establish among accounting practitioners a 'tax mentality' or rather, a preoccupation with keeping to the letter of the tax law, so much so that tax requirements are often given priority over proper accounting for financial reporting purposes. In short, the origins of Greek accounting are clearly conservative and tax-oriented, focusing on serving the needs of state policies, rather than the needs of investors.

The inception of corporate auditing

The audit of the annual balance sheet of joint-stock companies was first introduced in Greece in 1920 under article 36 of Law 2190/1920, which, on paper, gave significant powers to would-be practitioners. However, the law failed to prescribe any qualifications for auditors and there were no auditing standards available at the time. In addition, the vast majority of Greek companies were family-owned and there was little, if any, separation between ownership and management. In other words, auditing did not emerge as a market need, but rather as an attempt by the state to impose standards of corporate governance and accountability. Due to these limitations, auditing under Law 2190/1920 was largely ineffective and attracted trenchant criticism from many eminent professors of commercial law, following a series of corporate scandals and collapses in the 1920s. In response, Law 5076/1931 was passed through parliament in 1931, despite strong resistance, even from the government benches. Article 31 of Law 5076/1931 provided for the establishment, under the supervision of the Ministry of National Economy, of an Institute of Certified Accountants. However, even this attempt failed to institute a system of effective corporate auditing and the provisions of Law 5076/1931 remained on paper only (Dedoulis and Caramanis, 2007).

The attempt to introduce effective corporate auditing eventually proved successful in the mid-1950s when the Institute of Sworn-in Accountants, known in Greece by the acronym SOL, was established[8] by Law 3329/1955 (Dedoulis and Caramanis, 2007). SOL was instituted as an auditing organization with centralized control over audit assignments and enjoyed a legally sanctioned monopoly in the market for statutory audits. In return, auditor members of SOL were explicitly required by law to always act in the public interest and were considered public functionaries. The essence of SOL's organization was that auditor appointment and fee determination for statutory company audits were controlled by SOL's state-appointed Supervisory Council. In summary, the organizational and remunerative arrangements[9] of SOL were such that individual certified auditors of SOL had no direct economic interest in securing audit appointments, and there was no competition between auditors under SOL. It eventually became an apparently widely held perception among SOL's members that as long as SOL acted as a public watchdog, the status of the profession was strengthened and the chances of government interference to impair its monopolistic position in the market were reduced.[10]

In its first years, SOL mostly audited public sector organizations and social security funds. It also performed a few private sector audits on a voluntary basis. Its jurisdiction was expanded in 1960 when all listed companies were subjected to statutory audit by law. By 1980, SOL was conducting about 250 statutory company financial statement audits and over 400 voluntary and public sector audits annually, employing about 250 audit personnel.

This analysis shows that accounting as well as auditing practices and institutions in Greece did not really emerge as a market need. Rather, they were created and used by the state in order to accommodate wider policy objectives, namely to curb tax evasion and to exercise discipline over corporate behaviour, arguably with questionable results.

The 'Europeanization' era: 1980 to date

The first attempt at 'europeanizing' accounting practice in the 1980s

The distinctive characteristics (tax mentality and preoccupation with the letter of the law rather than its substance) of early Greek accounting and auditing as developed up to the 1960s and 1970s survived, and in certain respects were even reinforced, during two major developments in the 1980s: the introduction of the Greek General Accounting Plan (GAP) and the transposition of EEC accounting and auditing directives. These two developments, along with the continuing influence of tax legislation, have essentially shaped the very nature of today's Greek accounting.

Importing and localizing the continental European accounting tradition

The preparation of the GAP was launched in the 1960s but the project was only completed in 1980. The GAP draws heavily on its French counterpart – reflecting continental European accounting ideas – and has been gradually implemented[11] since the late 1980s, almost concurrently with the first application of the Fourth Directive. It includes a set of basic accounting rules (for example, valuation rules), definition of accounting terms, model financial statements and detailed provisions for drawing up annual financial statements. In addition, it provides for a uniform chart of accounts for all companies, the use of which is compulsory. Many accounting textbooks are based on the GAP, which forms part of the curriculum of several teaching institutions. In addition, corporate and tax legislation require its application, although there are instances where tax legislation may be in conflict with certain provisions in the GAP. The accounting rules included in the GAP are generally in line with the provisions of the Fourth Directive, as transposed in Greek legislation (see below).

The GAP has had a significant impact as it helped create a basic accounting infrastructure and a common language for practitioners. However, the accounting rules initially included in the GAP have not been kept up-to-date with international developments. In addition, the GAP is often over-procedural and unnecessarily costly.[12]

The transposition of the EEC accounting directives in the 1980s

Whereas the introduction of the GAP reflected continental European accounting, the transposition of EEC directives presented an opportunity for the country to move towards the Anglo-American accounting tradition. Three key accounting and auditing EEC directives were transposed into the Greek legal and regulatory system during the 1980s. The Fourth Directive (78/660/EEC) on (separate) annual financial statements of companies was transposed in 1986 (see Presidential Decrees 409/1986 and 419/1986) and became effective from 1987; the Seventh Directive (83/349/EEC) on consolidated financial statements was transposed in 1987 (see Presidential Decree 498/1987) and became effective from 1992. The newly enacted legislation discarded many of the anachronistic and deficient provisions of Law 2190/1920 which had governed the drawing up of annual financial statements, and significantly improved the level of the country's financial reporting system[13] and regulatory framework.

However, the details of the new rules were not problem-free. During the transposition of the Fourth Directive, which largely reflects continental European accounting ideas, (and to a lesser extent the Seventh Directive, which reflects the Anglo-American accounting tradition), Greece opted[14] for the most conservative options available. More importantly, the text adopted in Greek was sometimes in clear violation of the provision in the original text of the directive, reducing the usefulness of financial reporting for decision making. Some examples are listed below:

1. Whereas under the Fourth Directive (Article 39), inventory at year end is valued at the lower of purchase price (production cost) and market value, Article 43 of Law 2190/1920 prescribed that inventory is valued at the lower of purchase price (production cost) and (current) replacement cost.
2. The recognition of exchange differences (gains) from the valuation of certain current assets and current liabilities (accounts receivable

and payable) is deferred and the relevant amounts are shown as a provision in the balance sheet (as if it were a liability).
3. Deferred tax accounting was altogether ignored as an unnecessary complicating accounting treatment (see Grigorakos, 2007), although this issue is provided for in the Fourth Directive (Article 43.11 of the directive).
4. Held to maturity fixed financial assets, such as government bonds, are valued (Article 43 of Law 2190/1920) at the lower of cost and current value, whereas under the Fourth Directive[15] (Article 35) such assets may[16] be carried at cost.

At the same time, the Greek interpretation of the Fourth Directive, as enshrined in the Greek regulatory framework, seems to allow or encourage companies to show increased accounting profitability and a stronger balance sheet, which is in contrast with the principle of conservatism that, on paper, Greek accounting regulation recognizes as its fundamental principle (for example, see Grigorakos, 2007). Examples include:

1. Income tax is not treated as an expense in the income statement; rather, it is treated as part of the appropriation of annual profits.
2. Provisions are instituted for the capitalization of various expenses (for example, formation expenses, research and development, and so on) which are less strict than required or warranted.

In addition, existing legislation renders the distribution of a minimum dividend out of annual profits compulsory. More specifically, Article 3 of Law 148/1967 requires that at least 35 per cent of annual profits, reduced by any amount for legal reserve, be distributed[17] as cash dividend, unless a qualifying majority of 70 per cent at the annual general meeting decides otherwise. Thus, it appears that Greek accounting in practice is actually a mixture of conservatism, as dictated by Article 43 (para. 1b) of Law 2190/1920, and 'optimism'. The modernization of Greek accounting has been further undermined by the government's frequent interventions in accounting and financial reporting issues on an ad hoc basis, as matters arise. Such intervention, often the apparent result of successful lobbying by corporate interests, is as a rule in direct violation of existing legally enforced accounting rules, not to mention EU directives and common business sense. For example, when the stock exchange bubble broke in 1999 and many companies incurred huge losses from the sale or valuation of listed shares in their portfolio (see ASE, 2001), a new law (2874/2000, Article 37) was passed which provided that such losses may be capitalized and amortized over a five-year period or written off against reserves, without reducing (!) distributable profits. Another significant distortion in accounting numbers is caused by regular fixed asset revaluation required under tax legislation (Law 2065/1992). Under this law, fixed assets (land and buildings) are revalued using tax-determined factors every four years. The new (increased) values of these assets are also used for financial reporting purposes while the resulting revaluation reserve is mandatorily used to offset any losses carried forward. Hence, when a company carries losses forward, the track record of its operating performance (losses carried forward) disappears from the balance sheet and the company is legally free to distribute dividends!

The introduction of International Financial Reporting Standards (IFRSs) in the 2000s

In the late 1990s, the Athens Stock Exchange experienced unprecedented growth followed by an intensive downward spiral, as the General Index fell from 6,355 to 1,800 points within the space of a few months in the last quarter of 1999. Soon, public concerns emerged about the role of politicians and key public institutions, including the auditing profession (*Kathimerini*, 17 June 2001; *Imerisia*, 17 May 2002; *To Vima*, 7 May 2003). In an apparent move to reduce criticism and restore public trust in the stock market, the government employed a legitimation strategy with two main objectives: early introduction of the IFRSs and the establishment of an Independent Oversight Board over accounting and audit practice (examined in the following sub-section).

Law 2992/2002 was passed in 2002 and prescribed that, from 1 January 2003, all listed companies would have to prepare their financial statements according to the IFRSs (Government Gazette, 2002). However, despite initial wide-spread public enthusiasm for the idea, it was soon realized that the switch to IFRSs was an over-optimistic objective, as no appropriate preparatory measures had been taken (for example, conflict with other legislation, lack of training, and so on). It was formally announced in July 2003 that the early application of IFRSs would be optional and a new law, Law 3229/2004 was enacted in January 2004 to regulate various important issues for the application of IFRSs from 1 January 2005, in line with the deadline set by EU Regulation 1606/2002.

The introduction of IFRSs has certainly ushered in a new era in Greek accounting. It has also revealed the weakness of the local accounting standards as well as the inappropriateness of legal provisions in corporate legislation, even of those introduced in conjunction with the switch to IFRSs. A recent example of problematic legislation is Article

12 of Law 3453/2006 which stipulates that losses recognized from the first-time adoption of IFRSs[18] (1 January 2004) are not taken into consideration with regard to the distribution[19] of profits.

Following the introduction of IFRSs, Law 2190/1920 contains both legal (corporate law) and accounting provisions, for both separate and group financial statements. The legal provisions apply to every joint-stock company while the accounting provisions of the law, as well as the rules in the Greek GAP, only relate to those that do not apply IFRSs. Thus, as far as accounting practice is concerned, two markedly different accounting models are currently in use in Greece: IFRSs (the Anglo-American model) and Greek accounting rules (Law 2190/1920 and the GAP) which draw on a deep-rooted, tax-oriented tradition.

Developments in auditing: from state control to short-lived 'liberalization'

In the 1980s, the profession, in the form of SOL, strengthened its ties with the state and effectively operated as an extension of the state apparatus. For example, Article 17 of Law 1563/1985 required auditors to blow the whistle: 'a certified public auditor, who during his (her) audit discovers a breach of tax legislation, should report it immediately to the tax evasion department of the Ministry of Public Finance'. It seems that this provision made a significant contribution to creating a tax-centric mentality among SOL's members, who saw themselves as the guardians of the law (Caramanis, 1996; Grigorakos, 1989). In practice, tax authorities relied on the audit report and related remarks for assessing taxable income and for imposing tax fines. Further important developments occurred in Greek auditing during the 1980s as a result of EU legislation. In 1986, all companies exceeding the size criteria of Article 11 of the Fourth EEC Directive (1978L0660) were subjected to statutory financial statement audit[20] by members of SOL (Presidential Decree 409/1986). As a result of this expansion, SOL conducted almost 2,000 statutory audit assignments and had around 600 auditor members at various ranks as of 1990. More importantly, the Eighth Directive (84/253/EEC) on statutory audits was transposed in 1989 (see Presidential Decree 15/1989). The Eighth Directive apparently presented an immediate threat to SOL's monopoly over statutory audits, as it gave SELE,[21] SOL's main rival group, the opportunity to gain professional recognition via legislation. However, Presidential Decree 15/1989 maintained the status quo, leaving SOL's monopoly in place, although the new legislation was unsuccessfully challenged in the courts (Caramanis, 1996: 106).

The liberalization of the Greek auditing profession eventually took place in 1992 following an intense intra-professional struggle between

SOL and SELE (Caramanis, 1999). The essence of the reform was to introduce competition between auditors in the market for statutory audits. Auditor appointment and fee determination became a matter to be negotiated freely between auditors and audited companies. In addition, members of SELE gained access to the statutory audits market. The legislative reform of 1992 also abolished SOL and established the Institute of Certified Public Accountants of Greece, known in Greece by the acronym SOEL, a new largely self-regulated professional institute.

As of 2009, the profession (SOEL) had over 2,000 members employed in 24 audit firms. In terms of revenue, the market was worth about € 190min 2008. Detailed data are presented in Table 13.1.

The era of self-regulation for the liberalized profession soon came to an end in the aftermath of the 1999 stock exchange scandal. Law 3148/2003 was passed in 2003 and established an independent Accounting and Auditing Oversight Board, known by the Greek acronym ELTE. The establishment of ELTE took place at a time when the EU had announced its plans to introduce some form of independent oversight over accounting and auditing for its members (European Commission, 2001). ELTE operates as a public sector legal entity, is supervised directly by the Minister of Economy and is funded largely by a 1 per cent levy on total audit fees.[22] ELTE's seven-member Administrative Council is essentially controlled by the government. Its mission is to 'promote transparency in the operation of business

Table 13.1 The Greek audit market by numbers in 2009

	Number of members of the profession				**Audit fee revenue (in € m)**	
	CAs	**Trainees**	**Total**	**Per cent (on total)**	**Amount**	**Per cent**
SOL	347	272	619	30.6%	46.5	24.5%
PWC	16	276	292	14.5%	30.7	16.2%
Ernst& Young	31	122	153	7.6%	22.6	11.9%
Deloitte	24	200	224	11.1%	20.1	10.6%
BDO	50	109	159	7.9%	16.5	8.7%
Grant Thornton	23	190	213	10.5%	14.5	7.7%
KPMG	25	118	143	7.1%	13.8	7.3%
Sub-total	*516*	*1287*	*1803*	*89.3%*	*164.9*	*87.0%*
Other	104	113	217	10.7%	24.7	13.0%
TOTAL	620	1400	2020	100.0%	189.6	100.0%

Source: Author; data provided by SOEL (March 2010).

firms through accounting standardization and to ensure the quality of corporate audits' (Article 1 of Law 3148/2003). For example, ELTE's competences under the legislation include the performance of quality inspections on audit files and the exercise of disciplinary action. Further changes in the Greek accounting and auditing architecture occurred in 2008 during the transposition of the new Eighth Directive 2006/43/EC via Law 3693/2008 (Government Gazette, 2008). The new law provides for the transfer of almost all the remaining regulatory and oversight powers of SOEL to ELTE, including the organization of professional qualifying exams and the keeping of the public register of certified auditors and audit firms.

However, ELTE, apparently entrapped since its inception within the bureaucratic, ineffective and clientelistic Greek political system (Caramanis *et al.*, 2010), has been largely inactive and has failed, at least until now, to produce any significant impact. Following public criticism (for example, Caramanis and Papadakis, 2008, articles in the press and two parliamentary questions), a new leadership for ELTE was installed in spring 2009 which seems much more active. For example, the first audit quality inspections commenced in autumn 2009.[23] However, it remains to be seen whether the Greek Accounting and Auditing Oversight Board will succeed in playing the vital role necessary, if the level of Greek accounting and audit practice is to improve.

The intrinsic characteristics of Greek accounting and auditing practice as described so far, coupled with weak public oversight, create conditions favourable for creative accounting and earnings management to grow, if not to prosper or thrive. In fact, according to Leuz *et al.* (2003), Greece is top of the league in earnings management among 31 countries. The results of their study of extensive earnings management are confirmed by a survey of auditors and corporate financial executives presented later in this chapter.

Accounting and auditing following the adoption of IFRSs: the view of financial executives and auditors

A survey of certified auditors and corporate financial executives of listed companies (Caramanis and Papadakis, 2008) examined the current state of affairs of Greek accounting and auditing practice and institutions. The survey[24] focused on the impact and problems associated with the switch from the traditional accounting system to IFRSs and the role of public oversight authorities in the change. The main findings of the survey are summarized under six headings below.

Evaluation of IFRSs and comparison with local accounting rules

- The overwhelming majority of both groups of respondents appear to take a very positive view of IFRSs.
- IFRSs clearly outperform Greek accounting rules on a number of criteria (understandability, relevance, reliability, comparability, true and fair presentation, exercise of economic thought, protection of the interests of shareholders and creditors, and so on).
- The application of IFRSs has improved the overall quality of financial reporting in Greece.
- Financial executives tend to have more positive views than auditors.

Problems in the application of IFRSs

- Lack of timely and complete adjustments to the institutional and legal framework required for the proper application of IFRSs.
- Lack of business accountants and auditors sufficiently trained in the application/audit of IFRSs.
- The professional judgement inherent in IFRSs leaves scope for the manipulation of accounting numbers. The frequent re-statement of published financial statements at the request of the Greek Capital Markets Commission provides evidence of problems in the application of IFRSs.
- The concurrent application of two distinctly different accounting models for listed (IFRSs) and unlisted (Greek accounting rules) companies causes significant costs and problems, including lack of comparability of financial statements and unfair competition, obstacles to job mobility for accountants and auditors, increase in the cost of professional education, and so on.
- An average of 90 per cent of respondents believe that irrespective of cost, the introduction of IFRSs is a useful step in the improvement of management systems and the incorporation of Greece into the EU and the international economic system.

Preferred financial reporting framework

- An average of 95 per cent of respondents reject Greek accounting standards in their existing form as the applicable financial reporting framework.
- A majority of 55 per cent of business accountants and 40 per cent of auditors state their preference for IFRSs, while 49 per cent of auditors and 35 per cent of business accountants would prefer a modernized version of Greek accounting standards to bring them closer to IFRSs.

Public oversight

- Oversight authorities have not played the instrumental role required for the successful transition to IFRSs. In particular, oversight authorities have not provided timely and sufficient guidance, and have not acted swiftly to resolve problems as they arise.
- Oversight authorities lack independence from political and economic centres of power, and need significant improvement in term of staffing and transparency in their operation.
- A system of effective, independent public oversight needs to be established, given the degree of judgement required in the preparation of IFRS financial statements.
- Auditors express the view that, given the level of competition in the market for audit services in Greece, the introduction of impartial, reliable and effective audit quality inspections will help to improve the credibility of financial reporting, protect the status of the profession and maintain audit fees at a level to allow the conduct of proper audits. Further, auditors seem to accept the cost of such a system of audit quality inspections.

The impact of IFRSs on the professions of auditor and business accountant

- The status and prospects of the profession (auditors and business accountants), as well as of accounting itself, have significantly improved following the introduction of IFRSs.
- A significant proportion of auditors (40 per cent) report increased professional income following the introduction of IFRSs (as do 23 per cent of business accountants).
- Following the introduction of IFRSs the profession is in a better position to attract the best graduates.
- Professionals (auditors and business accountants) with long experience in Greek accounting standards but lacking knowledge of IFRSs have suffered a significant negative effect.

The implications of IFRSs for companies

- Improvement/rationalization of the internal organization of companies.
- Benefits include providing useful information to individual business units within the company; identifying important issues, risks, strengths and weaknesses; supporting strategic decision making, and evaluating the results of strategic changes.

- Improvement in the status of the company and in its access to sources of finance, locally and internationally.
- Facilitation of the internationalization of Greek companies.
- The benefits derived from applying IFRSs are higher (positive association) when companies have established formal planning systems and formalized decision-making systems. By contrast, when environmental hostility is high, the perceived benefits of IFRSs appear lower.

Summary

The analysis in this chapter has identified a number of significant problems and deficiencies in Greek accounting and auditing practices, institutions and systems of public oversight, which have broader business and economic consequences or implications in an increasingly internationalized environment. The situation requires immediate attention, given the severity of the current economic crisis which has revealed Greece's weakness to introduce essential reforms. The analysis shows that participants in the market have already recognized the need for essential and widespread reforms as far as accounting and auditing practices are concerned. The most important issues for government action include the following.

The first requirement is the establishment of an efficient, truly independent (in substance, appearance and transparency of operation) system of public oversight over accounting and auditing, which entails reforming and strengthening ELTE. A key component is the immediate introduction of quality control inspections of audit work on a regular basis. Effective oversight is imperative for building public confidence in financial reporting and the operation of the capital market, against a volatile global environment and a local economy in deep crisis. The second issue is the need to modernize the tax-oriented and over-procedural accounting standards applied by unlisted companies, eliminating problems and costs to the economy such as lack of comparability of financial information and unfair competition; obstacles to job mobility for accountants and auditors; increase in the cost of education, and so on. Finally, modernization and simplification of corporate law and tax legislation are long-awaited reforms.

Action on the lines described would certainly facilitate the improvement of business and management practices and help the country improve its reputation as an investment destination. Questions remain, however, as to whether the government and other key actors have themselves truly recognized the importance of accounting for the economy and whether they will act promptly upon the issues raised, instead of delaying desperately needed reforms.

Notes

1. The Lisbon Strategy Plan aimed at bolstering economic growth and competitiveness among member states.
2. The term 'Europeanization' is used synonymously with 'modernization'. It is a powerful symbol enjoying widespread public appeal, despite its vagueness (Lavdas, 1997: 252; see also Ioakimidis, 2001).
3. Others have underlined that the country's membership of the EU has nurtured a latent modernization, leaving open the possibility for significant reforms in the future for the country's economy, society and politics (Diamantouros, 1993; Mouzelis, 1995).
4. The limited liability company (known as a joint-stock company or Société Anonyme – SA) was imported to Greece as early as 1822, via the adoption of the Napoleonic Commercial Code. However, most joint-stock companies – even today – are essentially family-controlled business adopting this particular legal form for tax and other reasons. This is a particular characteristic of Greek joint-stock companies and also applies to many corporations listed on the Athens Stock Exchange.
5. The number after the slash (/) indicates the year of enactment of the law.
6. Law 2190/1920 introduced regulations on issues such as the setting up of a joint-stock company, its management, the composition of the board of directors, and the annual general meeting. In addition, the law introduced basic accounting rules and provisions for the drawing up of annual financial statements, the appropriation of profits and, for the first time, the appointment of external auditors.
7. In February 2010 the government announced its decision to phase out this legislation. Similar announcements, or demands, have been made in the past, but instead KVS has been growing in size over the years.
8. The creation of an effective auditing infrastructure was a prerequisite for the flow of much needed international (US) reconstruction aid to the country (see also Balas, 1998; Dedoulis and Caramanis, 2007).
9. Essentially, individual members of SOL earned salaried income as opposed to professional fees and the level of their remuneration was comparable with most senior public servants.
10. It has been suggested (Caramanis, 1999) that auditor members of SOL used to eagerly undertake a watchdog role over auditees on a number of issues, including tax legislation and observing provisions for the protection of national currency, employment legislation, and so on.
11. In order to assist in the implementation of the GAP, Law 1819/1988 was passed in 1988 which provided for the establishment of the ESYL (National Accounting Council). Among the responsibilities of ESYL were to prepare any necessary amendment or revision to the GAP, and to issue any guidelines relating to its application.
12. One such example is the Cost and Management Accounting section of the GAP, known in Greek as *Analytiki Logistiki*. According to the detailed rules,

each company is required by law to prepare its various categories of cost using a complicated system of journal entries every month. Several books have been written on this subject, seminars are being organized and computer programmes sold. The application of the *Analytiki Logistiki* has been explicitly required by tax legislation, although the relevant requirement was implicitly abolished by Law 3522/2006 (it is still, however, required by Article 7 of Law 1882/1990). The Cost and Management Accounting system was essentially copied from the French accounting plan and implemented in Greece in the 1990s, while the French had never implemented it themselves in practice, apparently due to cost and effectiveness considerations. In fact, the French have since 1999 abolished any reference to cost and management accounting in their accounting plan (see Nobes and Parker, 2002: 219).

13. Particularly in terms of the quantity of published information.
14. The auditing professional organization, SOL, played a key role in the transposition of the accounting directives.
15. It is interesting to note that Greece has not to date rectified the problems identified above, although such problems have been brought to the attention of competent authorities on several occasions, for example, during the transposition of Directive 51/2003/EU and Directive 65/2001/EEC.
16. In the current severe financial crisis, this provision of the Greek legislation has created serious problems for banks and particularly insurance companies which hold significant investments in long-term Greek government bonds. Investors in these bonds have suffered huge losses, although their value may well recover in the longer term.
17. A qualified majority of 70 per cent of shares in the annual general meeting is required for the distribution not to take effect. The provision for the compulsory distribution of annual profits as dividends does not seem to be in common use in EU countries or elsewhere.
18. The losses recognized from the first-time adoption of IFRSs primarily relate to write down of inventory, impairment of receivables and intangible assets, and provision for post-employment benefits.
19. This provision renders ineffective Article 44a of Law 2190/1920 which prescribes that losses carried forward should first be offset, before any dividends are distributed.
20. Certain types of companies as well as public sector organizations had already come under SOL's jurisdiction by enabling legislation.
21. Association of Certified Accountants Auditors. SELE was established in 1979 by local branches of international accountancy firms which had become established in Greece since the mid-1960s. SELE offered consulting and voluntary audits to its clients which mostly consisted of local subsidiaries of multinational corporations. The main objective of SELE was to gain access to the market of statutory audits from which it was excluded by law.
22. This currently amounts to just under € 2m per annum in total revenue for ELTE.
23. ELTE's quality inspections focused on audit firms' quality control systems. The results of the survey (available in Greek at http://www.elte.org.gr) were publicly presented on 14 April 2010 and revealed significant weaknesses.
24. The research was a mail questionnaire survey. It achieved a response rate of over 40 per cent (340 useable questionnaires).

References

Anagnostopoulos, G. (1937) *The Legislation of the Joint-Stock Companies*. Athens (in Greek).

ASE (2001) *Athens Stock Exchange 125 years*. Athens Stock Exchange SA.

Caramanis, C. (1996) 'Intra-Professional Conflict in the Greek Auditing Profession: "Liberalisation" and its Impact on Auditor Behaviour.' Unpublished PhD Thesis, University of Edinburgh.

Caramanis, C. (1999) 'International Accounting Firms versus Indigenous Auditor: Intra-professional conflict in the Greek auditing profession, 1990–1993', *Critical Perspectives on* Accounting, 10: 153–96.

Caramanis, C. (2002) 'The Interplay between Professional Groups, the State and Supranational agents: Pax Americana in the Age of "Globalization"', *Accounting, Organizations and Society*, 27: 379–408.

Caramanis, C. (2005) 'Rationalisation, Charisma and Accounting Professionalization: Perspectives on the Intra-professional Conflict in Greece, 1993–2001', *Accounting, Organizations and Society*, 30(3): 195–221.

Caramanis, C., and Papadakis, V. (2008) *The Application of IASs(IFRSs) in Greece: Implications for Auditors, Business Accountants, Companies and Oversight Authorities*. Athens University of Economics and Business (in Greek).

Caramanis, C., Dedoulis, E., and Leventis, S. (2010) 'The Establishment of EU-Inspired 'Independent' Oversight Boards: Local Constrains and the Elusive Feat of Europeanization in Greece.' Paper to be presented at the 2010 European Accounting Association Congress, Istanbul.

Cooper, D., and Robson, K. (2006) 'Accounting, professions and regulation: Locating the sites of professionalization', *Accounting, Organizations and Society*, 31: 415–44.

Dedoulis, E., and Caramanis, C. (2007) 'Imperialism of influence and the state-profession relationship: The formation of the Greek auditing profession in the post WWII era', *Critical Perspectives on Accounting*, 18: 393–412.

Dertilis, G. (1980) *The Question of the Banks 1871–1873: Economic and Political Dispute in the Nineteenth Century Greece*. Athens: Educational Institute of the National Bank of Greece.

European Commission (2001) *Commission Recommendation of 15 November 2000 on quality assurance for the statutory audit in the European Union: minimum requirements*. Official Journal of the European Union L 091, 31 March 2001, pp. 91–7.

European Commission (2002). *Regulation of the European Parliament and of the Council No 1606/2002*. Official Journal of the European Union, L 243, 11 September 2002.

European Commission (2003) *Adopting certain international accounting standards in accordance with Regulation (EC) No 1606/2002 of the European Parliament and the Council*. Official Journal of the European Union, L 111, 17 April 2004.

European Commission (2010) *Commission assessment on Greece*. Press Release, IP/10/116 Brussels. http://europa.eu/rapid/pressReleasesAction.do?reference=IP/10/116.

European Parliament and Council (2003). *Directive 2003/51/EC of 18 June 2003, amending Directives 78/660/EEC, 83/349/EEC, 86/635/EEC and 91/674/EEC on the annual and consolidated accounts of certain types of companies, banks and other financial institutions and insurance undertaking*. Official Journal of the European Union, L 178/16, 17 July 2003.

European Parliament and Council (2006). *Directive 2006/43/EC of 17 May on statutory audits of annual accounts and consolidated accounts, amending Council Directives 78/660/EEC and 83/349/EEC and repealing Council Directive 84/253/ EEC.* Official Journal of the European Union, L 157, 9 June 2006.

Featherstone, K., and Papadimitriou, D. (2008) *The Limits of Europeanization: Reform Capacity and Policy Conflict in Greece*, Palgrave Macmillan.

Freris, A., F. (1986) *The Greek Economy in the 20th Century*. London & Sydney: Croom Helm.

Government Gazette (1955) *Law 3329/1955: On the Establishment of the Body of Sworn-in Auditors*. A' 230/1955, Athens: National Printing Office.

Government Gazette (1985) *Law 1563/1985*. A' 151/17.9.1985, Athens: National Printing Office.

Government Gazette (1992) *Law2065/1992: Reforming direct taxation and other provisions*. A' 113/30.06.1992, Athens: National Printing Office.

Government Gazette (2000) *Law 2874/2000: Facilitating employment and other provisions*. A' 286/29.12.2000, Athens: National Printing Office.

Government Gazette (2002) *Law 2992/2002: Measures for strengthening the Stock Market and other provisions*. A'54/20-3-2002, Athens: National Printing Office.

Government Gazette (2003) *Law 3148: The Establishment of the Accounting Standardization and Audits Committee and Other Provisions*. A'136/05-06-2003, Athens: National Printing Office.

Government Gazette (2004) *Law 3229/2004: Supervising private security funds, control on lotteries and application of International Accounting Standards and other provisions*. A' 38/10.02.2004, Athens: National Printing Office.

Government Gazette (2006) *Law 3522/2006: Changes in the income tax, simplifying the Code of Corporate Books and other provisions*. A' 276/22.12.2006, Athens: National Printing Office.

Government Gazette (2008) *Law 3693/2008: Transposition of Directive* 2006/43/ EC. A'174/25-08-08, Athens: National Printing Office.

Grigoracos, T. (1989) *The Provisions of Company Law which Have Been Brought in Line with the EEC Fourth Directive and their Basic Objective*. Athens: SOL (in Greek).

Grigorakos, T. (1964) *The Evolution of the Joint-Stock Company and the Question of the Capital Market*, Athens: Deltion Forologikis Nomothesias, pp. 325–27 (in Greek).

Grigorakos, T. (1989) *The Codification of the Legislation Regulating the Operation of SOL*. Athens: SOL (in Greek).

Grigorakos, T. (2007) *Analysis-Interpretation of the Greek General Accounting Plan*, (12th ed.) Athens: Sakoulas (in Greek).

Hanlon, G. (1994) *The Commercialization of Accountancy*. St Martin's Press.

Ioakimidis, P. (2001) 'The Europeanization of Greece: An Overall Assessment', in K. Featherstone and G. Kazamias (eds), *Europeanisation and the Southern Periphery*. London: Frank Cass.

Lavdas, K. (1997) *The Europeanization of Greece: Interest Politics and the Crises of Integration*. Macmillan.

Leuz, C., Nanda, D. and Wysocki, P. (2003) 'Earnings management and investor protection: an international comparison', *Journal of Financial Economics*, 69:(3): 505–27.

Ministry of Commerce (1988) *Law 2190/1920: on Joint-stock Companies*. Athens (in Greek).

Ministry of Co-ordination (1952) *Certified Accountants: A Collection of Laws, Decrees and Ministerial Decisions*. Athens (in Greek).

Ministry of National Economy (2002) Press Bulletins 9 July and 23 July. www3.mnec.gr (in Greek).

Mouzelis, N. (1978) *Modern Greece, Facets of Underdevelopment*. New York: Holmes and Meier Publishers.

Mouzelis, N. (1986) *Politics in the Semi-periphery - Early Parliamentarism and Late Industrialisation in the Balkans and Latin America*. London: Macmillan.

Mouzelis, N. (1995) 'Greece in the twenty-first century: institutions and political culture', in Constas, D. and Stavrou, T. (eds), *Greece prepares for the twenty-first century*. Washington: Woodrow Wilson Center Press.

Nobes, C., and Parker, R. (2002) *Comparative International* Accounting, 7th ed. Pearson Education.

OECD (2010) *Economic Outlook: Greece*, 2010/2: 171–173.

Papas, A. (1993) *European Financial Reporting: Greece*. London: Routledge.

Previts, J., and Merino, B. (1998) *A History of Accountancy in the United States*. Ohio State University Press.

Puxty, A., G., Willmott, H., Cooper, D., and Lowe, T. (1987) 'Modes of Regulation in Advanced Capitalist: Locating Accountancy in Four Countries', *Accounting Organizations and Society*, 12(3): 273–91.

Tsimaras, M., (1958) *Principles of General Accounting*, 2nd edn. Athens (in Greek).

Tsoukalas, C., (1969) *The Greek Tragedy*. Penguin Books: London.

World Economic Forum (2002) *The Lisbon Review 2002–2003: An Assessment of Policy and Reforms in Europe*. Geneva: World Economic Forum.

World Economic Forum (2006) *The Lisbon Review 2006: Measuring Europe's Process in Reform*. Geneva: World Economic Forum.

Part III

Conclusion: Summary, Comparison and Suggestions

14

The Business System and Management Practices in Greece

Rea Prouska and Maria Kapsali

Overview

We started this book with the intention of providing an outline, a succinct story describing the business system and management practices in Greece. It began as a simple categorization of contextual factors and managerial activities and ended in a rich tapestry of behavioural patterns, linking systemic elements and actions. In the process, we learnt more about how certain systemic structures and institutional contexts allowed for the development of the Greek business system, leading in turn to the emergence of certain managerial practices. The themes that surfaced in chapter after chapter revealed a complex mix of the above elements posing certain challenges to the system.

It is important to remember that Greece is not the only country to be affected in this way. Other EU peripheral countries (Italy, Spain, Portugal and Ireland) are all facing similar challenges, are experiencing an economic downturn and they are affected by the global crisis to a greater degree than the counties that caused the crisis. The recession is slowly revealing malfunctions in the systems of advanced economies too, such as the USA and the UK, which now face great deficits in the midst of political scandals that revealed corruption in their financial sectors and inefficiencies in their public structures, with consequences for less developed countries. We believe, therefore, that the example of Greece has educational value as a case study which can contribute to existing business systems literature. The contribution of this book is to complement the business systems paradigm with a sense of forward momentum and change.

The typology and classifications from business systems theory used in this book are ideal types. This means that categorization of the characteristics of management practices in firms and the Greek business system is approximate and a perfect match with any of these ideal types will not necessarily be found using the profiles originating from our research. It is our contention that business systems is a framework for abstracting the most prominent characteristics of the system, those that matter most for its major attributes and functions. This framework will be used in both chapters of the conclusion in which we describe the Greek business system and management practices and compare it with other countries' systems and practices.

We will therefore describe the Greek business system according to Whitley's theory of business systems (2007, 2005, 2002, 2001, 2000, 1999, 1997), using evidence from the research included in this book. Whitley suggests that different types of state construct different institutional frameworks that support the emergence of particular types of business systems, which subsequently accommodate certain firm characteristics and practices. State types are defined by the state's involvement in economic development and whether or how it intervenes in market structures and relations. Whitley's typology of six types of business systems (fragmented, co-ordinated industrial district, compartmentalized, collaborative, highly co-ordinated and state organized) categorizes them in terms of the linkages between state, credit and labour systems. Ownership patterns, governance structure, patterns of inter-firm relations, employment relations and organizational capabilities are complementary to the features of the state and business systems. The business system, in turn, impacts the types of managerial activities preferred by firms in terms of managerial autonomy, control systems and co-operative relations. Therefore the premise of this book is that the state type shapes the business system which affects managerial practice (see Figure 14.1).

Key dimensions linking the business system with managerial practices (Whitley, 1999) are first, the size and differentiation of markets; second, employers' flexibility in adjusting activity levels to changes in the employment market; third, functional flexibility achieved through training, task rotation, work reorganization and similar measures; fourth, availability of or constraints on gaining a suitable workforce; fifth, the level of institutional constraints on short-term economic opportunism; sixth, the availability of risk capital; seventh, the supply, availability and access to new scientific and technical knowledge; and eighth, the ease of modularizing the value chain and disintegrating production processes.

The firm's structure and practices are linked to the institutions that govern access to resources and dictate rules of conduct, which are often

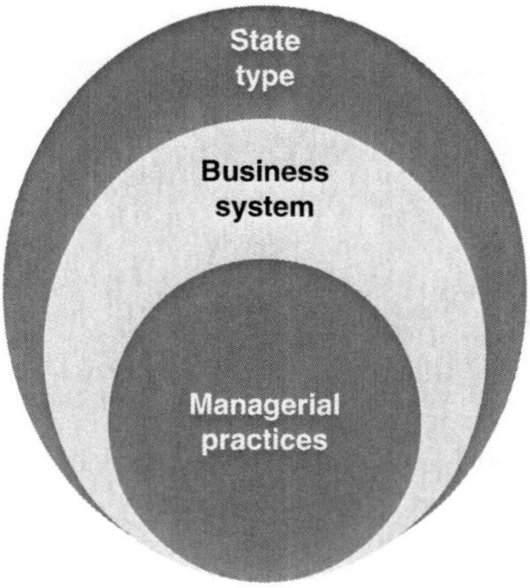

Figure 14.1 The relationship between state type, business system and managerial practices

distinctive and determined at a national level. Where these institutions are not established firmly or are weak, informal practices perform this function, which form the ways in which markets behave and risks are shared between firms and other actors, ownership and authority patterns, and access to resources. The interdependencies between the elements of a business system depend very much upon these institutions, which govern not only order but also change.

Part III is arranged in three chapters. The first, Chapter 14, summarizes the common themes found through most chapters. Part I of the book (Chapters 1 to 6) dealt with the structure of the business system: the country's political, economic, financial, development, innovation and legal structures. Causal factors stemming from within this business system describe the relations between the state (the power to make decisions and authority to implement them), the resource institutional infrastructure (knowledge and innovation, law, administration and finance in particular) and the labour market. Managerial practices are frequently explicitly attributed to these systemic causal factors within these chapters. These same factors have also appeared quite often throughout Part II of the book (Chapters 7 to 13), which looked at managerial practices within firms. Thus Parts I and II do not provide a clear-cut division between causality between the systemic parts and management practices, nor should they.

A summary of the links between practices and systems causes follows, using the micro type of firm as its principal reference point, because it is the dominant type of organization in the Greek business system (with references to larger organizations where appropriate).

The second part of the conclusion (Chapter 15) will provide a comparative brief based on data from European databases, as well as existing data in comparative academic literature. The chapter compares Greece with the other peripheral EU countries (Italy, Spain, Portugal and Ireland) and one developed core country, the UK. This concludes our holistic approach of providing comparative facts to aid understanding of the position of the national system within the larger supranational environment.

Finally, Chapter 16 concludes the book by outlining avenues for further research of particular interest to Greece.

Systemic factors in the Greek business system

The search for systemic factors began in Chapter 1 where, first, the discussion on the politico-economic history of Greece identified patterns of political and social divisions, where successive changes in policies had allowed for policy discontinuity. Second, the chapter explored the lack of development of solid financial, information and technological institutions and infrastructures to support business development. These two factors affected the implementation of policy, which is channelled through a large public administration structure. The need for centralized control over the business sector due to the lack of consistent policy and developed infrastructure led to the heavy bureaucratization and enlargement of the public sector. The public sector, therefore, became established as a political token for governments. For the private sector, it represents an institution of control and not of support and order. Public administration is one of the main reasons for the huge public debt, since it consumes double the amount of resources it produces. The cost of running such a huge public sector, in addition to heavy military expenses and conflicts, raised multiple debts which resulted in *de facto* economic bankruptcies. The last 30 years, however, with relatively fewer conflicts and the help of the EU, have seen a relatively calmer period, with more growth in infrastructures and business and a reduction in policy discontinuity. Ups and downs have been experienced, but this is because the public structure is outdated and expensive, and institutions are not well developed to sustain steady stimulation of business activity and productivity. Today, the economic results of sustaining such a structure are evident. Society, business and politics seem to be aware of the urgent need to restructure and change the public sector.

Stimulating business activity and productivity is not easy. Social divisions and the crisis of Fordism forced governments after the 1970s to use re-distributionary policies in attempts to reduce class inequalities and social divisions, but these policies only worsened the gap between productivity and debt. Although contractionary fiscal policies, in the form of heavy taxation and cutbacks, are the primary means of reducing the deficit during the current economic recession, they are not the way to recovery. Such policies can only lead to further tearing of the economic and social fabric by creating more recession and division. They cannot, by definition, act as a counterbalance to the gaps these re-distributionary policies have created in the economy in terms of economic productivity, performance and competitiveness. Although the Greek public sector is currently dependent on foreign lending, the economy will be able to recover and debt will be reduced only if productivity increases, and at the same time public sector waste is reduced.

The second chapter (on economics) made the above arguments more explicit by looking at productivity. The chapter described, amongst other things, the patterns of de-industrialization in the most recent period of economic history (since the 1970s), the uneven development of business sectors and the effect these have had on national convergence to EU productivity levels. In addition, the chapter discussed the need to rationalize state control mechanisms and revise several employment, tax, accounting, auditing and finance laws to address the real needs of firms, while at the same time offering protection to employees, employers and investors. The discussion on the unbalanced development of the primary, secondary and tertiary sectors revealed a continuous growth in service productivity and a sharp decline in manufacturing and agricultural productivity for the same period. The conclusion suggested a strategy: to develop institutional resources to support the manufacturing of high technology products, and not simply to depend on economies of scale and heavy industrialization; to compete in the knowledge economy in some sort of national flexible specialization, and avoid competing in the mass production of commodities. Productivity can therefore be further increased by financing, investing in and supporting the more promising industrial sectors. In effect, a prescription of 'dominant-developmental' state should spearhead growth in R&D and applied research productivity, creating the appropriate business system for this goal. The success of this strategy could be judged by efforts in other business systems (see Chapter 15).

But how can this be achieved in a national system that lacks certain types of infrastructures? Chapter 5 takes a 'helicopter view' of the

National Innovation System, using the theoretical framework of the Triple Helix. The development of R&D and applied research business sectors requires, first and foremost, interaction and exchange of resources between the public sector, academia and firms. A suitable infrastructure would include support networks for micro firms, with resources (mentoring, finance, training, information, contacts, legal rules) channelled through transparent processes. A cycle of co-investment and collaboration between actors in the system would be the basis for the creation of the modern Technopolis, through which business can invest in growth and development (therefore access to investment) and can accumulate information about markets and their development (through interaction, contacts and research). In reality, the interaction between public, academic and business actors is inhibited by the factional silos between these groups, which create barriers inhibiting mutual access to their resources. In addition, the underdevelopment of certain industrial sectors leaves an 'infrastructural gap' in terms of production know-how and innovation capabilities (the most significant of these is the absence of a system for basic research and the low levels of absorptive capacity). The system needs to develop an infrastructure that actively supports the strategic shift of firms towards producing innovative products through an effective, transparent and stable system of investment and systematic support for start-up companies.

The EU's structural and technological programmes have contributed to the basic development of a technical infrastructure. However, although this is ongoing, it is far from efficient. The example in Chapter 4 showed why the system has not yet been fully developed, by focusing on the role of the public sector in the implementation of EU cohesion policies. In this example, the administration of these EU programmes absorbs most of the resources through organizations and their administration, most of which are set up in the public sector, marginalizing the role of firms to sub-contracting. This discussion revealed the real structural obstacle which is endemic in the Greek system: the strict division between the public and the private sectors, exemplified by the way firms get marginalized in participating in these programmes. The cause of this structural weakness is rooted in the need for centralized control embedded in the public sector, and it is the real reason why, although governments try hard to modernize policies and adopt many of the EU's suggested procedures, these policies often fail to materialize. This example shows how successive governments rather than fulfil the 'systems designer' role have limited themselves to the administration of public funds, and have tried to imitate outside policy models, but without managing to direct interaction and collaboration between social partners.

Developing such infrastructures is more complicated than pouring resources and guidelines into agencies. Chapters 3 (on finance) and 6 (on law) bring some critical issues to light. The policy discontinuity which stems from the lack of consistent strategic direction at the policy level, such as changes in tax, audit, finance and company legislation, and the procedural difficulties of setting up a new business, discourages private investors (domestic or otherwise). This partly affects the levels of internal investment, that is, entrepreneurs' investments in new business, as well as the ability to attract FDI. This is achieved up to a point in the bank-led system in Greece; however, more rigorous control is needed to develop a stock market finance culture. Progress has been made in stabilizing and managing liquidity and creating rules for the adequate supervision of finance, including the liberalization of financial markets, the modernization of financial regulation to match EU standards and the implementation of a financial services action plan, as well as the increasing integration of European money markets and clearing services through the operation of Eurosystem and the introduction of the Euro. Financial markets, financial services law and banking regulation have been completely modernized since the 1990s. The Greek banking system has been gradually liberalized and this has led to significant competition, making banking a strong sector in the economy.

Management practices in Greek firms

Most micro firms in Greece are not influenced by foreign models of organization, with the exception of MNCs. This means that bureaucratic structures are not preferable because ownership and control are often not separated, work is organized by specialized tasks, largely trade and craft, with narrow lines of demarcation. Greek micro firms have limited access to resources, particularly market intelligence (information about market developments and competition), information about technological and operational developments, and collaborative networks. This limited access to information deprives them of the opportunity to develop absorptive capacity and create competitive advantages in a flexible and informed way. This limitation is linked to the barriers (limited interaction, collaboration and communication) between the public and private domains and the poor infrastructure. Knowledge of foreign markets beyond the firm's local environment is therefore limited, and the micro firms will not invest in reaching them, unless local or personal networking makes it possible. Instead, the micro firms gather intelligence through their networks. Personal communication with suppliers, traders or customers is the main source of information about local markets. Therefore, the way the micro firms will approach their markets is usually very individualistic. Personal contacts and networking are the preferred ways of establishing trust and getting first-hand information. The micro firms will have developed very specific creative and productive capacity and problem-solving skills, adjusting to change in particular local markets and achieving only a limited range of flexible specialization.

The market locality forces the micro firms to produce only the products or services absorbed by that particular market. Logically, the productive capacity of the firm will be focused on transforming the resources required for these specific products and services. Change and diversification will not come easily, as it is expensive and the final marketability of the product is uncertain. Therefore, the micro firms are cautious about further investment, and the competitive strategy is usually based on cost reduction and price. Medium-sized and larger firms, on the other hand, will expand, albeit in a conservative way (consolidating and protecting markets, expansion only in nearby markets, related diversification and cost reduction/price competition). Larger firms will be more active in their international activities, and they will expand in geographically close markets, diversifying their existing products and services to minimize risk, as they already know the needs of the target markets. Again, they will continue to compete on price and use cost reduction strategies, and although product quality is important to them, their strategies do not focus on developing innovation in their products and services, which will be imported or (less usually) copied, if necessary, from other systems. common misconception is that the critical mass of productivity is the main problem of the Greek private business system (this belief is valid for public sector productivity, not for the private sector), whereas in fact the principal issues are fragmentation, lack of innovation and the unbalanced way the industries have grown (and thus lack of a variety of infrastructures). When certain industrial infrastructures have not developed, it is difficult for firms to acquire the productive core and dynamic capabilities that are necessary to develop innovation. On the other hand, co-investment from strategic alliances is scarce; some horizontal integration is practised to internalize resources, but there is little vertical integration. It is rare for relationships to be developed between firms for co-design, co-contracting or co-manufacture to be built up through long-term transactions. This is important because alliances with high technology foreign partners would be another way to develop or imitate dynamic capabilities that cannot be drawn from the infrastructure, as occurs in developing countries like India. Internal investment is again preferred, and production remains generally conservative and focused on improving efficiency. The prevailing risk aversion means that high and long-term investment industrial sectors are not developed in this business system, despite the surplus of highly educated and underexploited labour. These factors affect internal organization and management practices in terms of operations, HRM and accounting. Micro firms develop a low-cost, agile production process (usually in services), which does not demand high levels of knowledge and is primarily focused on customer satisfaction and internal efficiency. This creates a demand for low-skilled workers who have a highly entrepreneurial attitude and strong customer relations skills but do not incur high staff development costs. The micro firms do not see management philosophies such as TQM as relevant to their operation, while their medium-sized and larger counterparts perceive them as an opportunity to ensure superior product quality and market reputation. Process improvement is seen in terms of cost reduction and other efficiencies; only a few firms have operational processes for producing high technology goods in place, since most production is of services. A paternalistic-idiosyncratic, controlling management style has developed in the micro firms' structure, based on informal interaction but with high power asymmetry. In a sense, SMEs have become mercurial in order to adjust to customer change and develop market flexibility, and, to compensate for this phenomenon, they have developed centralized control within a very strong entrepreneurial culture. In larger companies, the structures are a hybrid of role divisions based on professionalization and the control orientation inherited from their previous history as micro firms, which promote individualism and conformism in employees. Where middle management exists, it is restricted to administrative roles, focusing on maintaining control and consolidation of operations. This controlling attitude leads to suspicion and resistance to new management ideas and methods, whilst the small scale of everything (market demand, investment, operations and production) eliminates the need for more advanced management methods. This trend, however, could now be reversed, with a new generation of managers slowly replacing the old guard whose experiences during the controversial political and economic events prior to the 1980s led them to develop this attitude. The new generation of managers and employees are more educated in management methods and many have had experience of working abroad, or are working in MNCs, so there is already impetus for change. Management, however, is still control-oriented, especially as firms have to conform to strict and frequently complex and changing, tax and company laws.

All this is not as negative as it sounds. Firms in Greece have developed in this way to fit and grow in an environment with limited resources and high levels of change, and they have succeeded in surviving and competing. Greek firms are agile and have developed high levels of initiative, entrepreneurship and opportunism so as to survive in the most difficult of political and economic circumstances, as historical accounts show. They have therefore developed a major capability which helps them survive with limited access to resources in highly volatile environments. Based on our own research and a study of Greek business literature, we have formed the opinion that this element in Greek business has not been yet fully appreciated. Swift responses, combined with now highly educated human resources are the underexploited and overlooked assets in the Greek business system. The proof is in the fact that business has displayed highly dynamic levels of growth in the few spells of political and financial stability that have occurred in the past, and have succeeded in boosting the frequently systemically damaged economy and in competing internationally in certain sectors, which are themselves highly volatile (trade-shipping-hospitality services).

Therefore, we should not condemn this type of management practices. Organic and entrepreneurial forms of organization are highly successful in volatile environments and there is much academic literature in management science on this topic. The Greek management practices are fine in some ways but not in others, because no form of organization suits all situations, no matter what successive academic and consultancy fashions might advocate. Recently there has been an attempt to rationalize and improve management methods by imitating foreign practices which are held up as superior and highly desirable. This philosophy has entered, firstly, the Greek political system, and secondly, foreign MNCs, and spread to management circles. There is also a new educated generation in today's labour market, who support the development of more westernized standards in management. However, the value of this 'importing' approach is questionable, as is evidenced by cases of policies and programmes imported from the USA and the EU that do not fit the reality of domestic systems and, thus, quickly become obsolete. Greek management practices are currently in a period of transition, with the inevitable confusion that follows.

Confusion stems from the fact that practices do not change overnight; they neither spontaneously emerge from bottom-up nor are mechanically imposed by top-down pressures. Their emergence is the outcome of change that occurs when current habits and a mixture of endogenous and exogenous socioeconomic influences ferment and chemically react, and it is precisely this theme that we find in almost every chapter of this book. Business practices are constantly in between political power and control over resources throughout the history of the modern Greek state. Multiple windows of opportunity to modernize and create the infrastructural support for business were missed because of these patterns, which are uncannily mirrored within the firm, where there is confusion between ownership and control, and decision-making is centralized. This compulsion to keep control centralized is why, when firms get bigger, they tend to create bureaucracies, with the example of public bureaucracy mirrored in the private sector. This tendency stems not just from the form of organizations, but also from a wider social and political attitude. Centralized control concentrated in small informal hubs of power can be observed not only in the business sector, but more generally in life, and it is a pattern that is generally accepted as the only way to manage. This system of management leads to very dynamic results, where size remains small. In larger contexts, like the public sector, multiple hubs of power disorganize the system, because entropy and friction arise amongst them. This is why, for example in public organizations, there is low competitiveness, a stifling of entrepreneurship and little contribution to economic and social development.

It is important not to miss the fact that management does not really come in pre-packaged form. It is a practice, partly tacit, partly scientific and partly social, which is and should be tailored to different situations and contexts. It is necessary to improve (not to marginalize) the current management systems in Greece, but this cannot happen without some change in work habits which are sustained by a system of inappropriate formal and informal rules. Once more, importing practices will only lead to hybrid combinations and mutations of current practices, which will not necessarily be appropriate to the situation or serve the current needs of business. What needs to be done is to examine current management practices, find the systemic causes that sustain them, and intervene to incentivize change in work habits.

The bigger picture

Greece is a 'fragmented' business system influenced by a 'business corporatist' state, according to Whitley's typology (2000). We see a state system which is highly influenced by, and dependent on, exogenous institutions, lacking solid domestic institutional structures to support entrepreneurship and business activity. We understand that informal institutions (like cultural norms of informal exchange) are undertaking a 'regulating' role in this business system for precisely the same reason. In this society, trust in formal institutions is low, authority is personal, control is patriarchal and the state is either aloof from, or antagonistic to, private business, maintaining monopolies and placing firms under heavy regulatory control. Co-operation between firms is also rather rare, short-term and based on highly personal connections. Co-ordination of activities across firms is difficult to sustain due to the lack of rules or institutions that guarantee conduct and build trust. Inputs and outputs are traded as commodities in a highly volatile competitive market. Financial and other resources are typically not consistently available or accessible, therefore business is risk- averse and opportunistic in its pursuit of markets and possibilities. Firm structures are characterized by low ownership and poorly integrated production chains. These firms need the functional and market competences that derive from labour flexibility. The flexible use of resources to meet changes in customer demand is preferred to commitment to business partners and workers. Tools, technologies, routines and employees can be changed when necessary.

However, business continues to show initiative, despite its weak linkages with the infrastructure and the absence of institutions to support it. Firstly, Greek firms can choose from a large supply of skilled and educated labour. Greece does not lack talent and has the benefit of an underexploited, usually entrepreneurial and multilingual, skilled labour force. Secondly, the same geopolitical conditions that cause political disturbance are also a major advantage in terms of business. This key position allows Greek firms to expand very fast since they have first-hand knowledge of a multiplicity of markets. This position has enabled the Greek maritime industry to be one of the world's leaders and trade services to grow rapidly. Ideal location and a unique knowledge of diverse local environments enables Greek firms to easily access the emerging markets of South-east Europe and the eastern Mediterranean, for example, Albania, Bulgaria, Egypt, FYROM (the former Yugoslav Republic of Macedonia), Morocco, Romania, Serbia and Turkey. Greece's proximity to the Balkans enables Greek firms to outsource tasks in the region at much lower cost, increasing their competitiveness. Greece has been helping her Balkan neighbours to become members of the EU, and their introduction into the single market and uptake of EU laws and rules expands business further for domestic firms with the building of bilateral agreements and ties. In terms of infrastructure, the hosting of the 2004 Olympic Games was a major catalyst for a number of infrastructural improvements to transport (road, rail and underground networks and ports), logistics and telecommunications, which further enhanced this expansion of business. Several other promising developments are on the horizon, such as the Greece–China bilateral agreement (October 2010) on economic, industrial and technological co-operation in a wide range of areas. These are positive developments for business in Greece. It is certainly the case that tackling the core issues raised in this book will improve conditions for business and management practices and will increase productivity in sectors other than services, making the market more attractive to local and foreign investors. This troublesome period should be seen as a time not only of major challenges, but also of new opportunities, as is usually the case for business in recurring economic cycles of deconstruction and reconstruction.

References

Whitley, R. (1997) *Governance at Work: the social regulation of economic relations in Europe*. Oxford: Oxford University Press.

Whitley, R. (1999). *Divergent Capitalisms: the social structuring and change of business systems*. Oxford: Oxford University Press.

Whitley, R. (2000) *Developing Capitalisms: the comparative analysis of emerging business systems in the South*. London: Sage.

Whitley, R. (2001) *The Institutional Structuring of Business Transactions*. Oxford: Hart Publishing.

Whitley, R. (2002) *Competing Capitalisms: institutions and economies*. Elgar: Cheltenham.

Whitley, R. (2005) 'How national are business systems? The role of states and complementary institutions in standardising systems of economic co-ordination and control at the national level', in Morgan, G. *et al.* (eds) *Changing Capitalisms?*, pp. 190–231.

Whitley, R. (2007) *Business Systems and Organizational Capabilities: the institutional structuring of competitive competences*. Oxford: Oxford University Press.

15
Systems and Practices: Peripheral Countries Compared with the UK

Rea Prouska and Maria Kapsali

Overview

This chapter aims to aid understanding of the data presented in this book by presenting key themes in a comparative perspective. A selection of countries has been made: Portugal, Italy, Ireland and Spain are all considered comparable (especially in terms of debt) following the global financial crisis, and the UK has been chosen for comparison as a representative of the stronger economies in the EU in terms of productivity, political structure, innovation, and strong SME sector. These countries will be compared in terms of systemic elements and management practices that are related to competition models, according to Whitley (2005). The system also is compared in terms both of Whitley's typology of business systems (fragmented, coordinated industrial district, compartmentalized, collaborative, highly coordinated, state organized) and of the linkages between state, credit and labour systems, managerial autonomy, control systems and co-operative relations. Figure 15.1 illustrates the elements of the business system on which the analysis of this chapter will focus.

State, institutions and infrastructures in the peripheral and UK business systems

This part will compare briefly the development of the business systems in the peripheral countries along with the UK's starting from the start of industrialization. The purpose is to have an overview which will be the basis for comparing the key indicators of management practices in these systems in the next part. We start with the UK business system and follow with those of Greece, Ireland, Italy, Portugal and Spain. Regarding

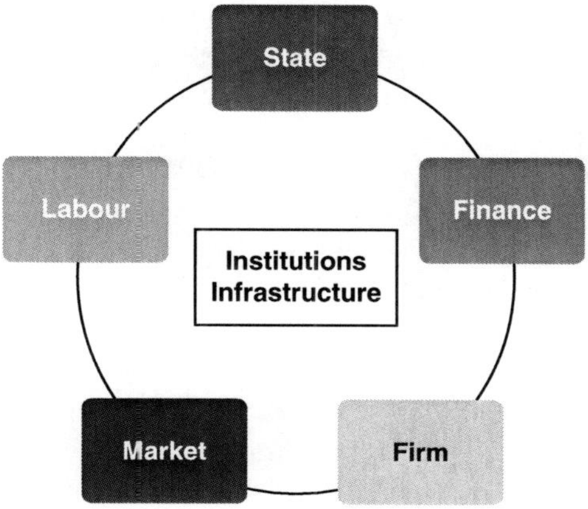

Figure 15.1 The business system
Source: Based on Whitley (2007, 2005, 2002, 2001, 2000, 1999, 1997).

the peripheral countries there are some similarities in the process of industrialization and modernisation of managerial practices, especially regarding high growth (often called economic miracles in popular press) and sharp decline periods which are much more dramatic that those happening in the UK.

Britain

The process of industrialization started from a mainly feudal agrarian system. The main components of industrialization in the UK were the freeing up of labour from agrarian employment, creating a pool of unskilled and readily available cheap labour, the widening of new markets in colonial areas, and the political empowerment of a middle class which developed a risk-taking investment mentality using legal means. A series of socioeconomic changes initiated this process, with the middle classes buying land from landowners and using it to grow wool instead of leasing to farmers. This middle class could influence the passing of progressive legislation through the parliament. In addition, a central national bank was in place with a stock exchange that was willing to back up ventures. Therefore, political and social restructuring led to the systemic factors that collided to ignite the process of industrialization, factors unique to Britain. The industrialization of England was 'unique and atypical ... mass production industry was cautious and protracted, far from complete by the 1840s when over 75 per cent of manufacturing remained in un-modernised industries, small in scale, little affected by the use of steam power' (Belchem, 1990: 9). The explosion in industrial production was determined, first, by the fact that the majority of labour was occupied in these industries (Belchem, 1990: 9; Hartwell, 1965: 18–19) and, second, by 'the clustering of technological innovations that occurred in Britain' (Hicks *et al.*, 2006: 143). Slowly, the fragmented business system consisting of small industries clustered and complemented (as well as competing with) each other into industrial clusters through cross-investment, planning and control systems. However, relatively few large companies were created and they continued to be structured like family firms using a holding company structure with little vertical integration and diversification. Managerial hierarchy and competence were low and these conditions prevented widespread organizational and technological innovation on a systematic scale. The main structural and managerial transformation came with the advent of large companies. Due to the lack of state involvement, manufacturing SMEs started to decline after the 1930s because they were left exposed to market forces without buffers. Consequently, a series of mergers leading to highly concentrated large firm sectors started after the 1960s and were followed by frequent structural modernization. Managerial capitalism started to dominate practice. Rapid radical change of this kind was confirmed by the imitation of American models of business and managerialism. Innovative firms and activities of an international orientation grew in number. Although the decline of industrial SMEs was reversed after the 1970s, the industrial structure remained unbalanced, affecting firm relationships and market organization (Whitley, 1997). Political changes led to several types of industrial restructuring including nationalizations, privatizations and hybrid structures with public–private sector partnerships. Business was less affected in Britain than in other countries by de-industrialization, with a shift in productivity from the industrial to the service sector.

Greece

In contrast to the evolution of the British 'arm's length' state and market-led business system, Greece developed a 'corporatist' state and bank-led, centrifugal business system. The labour force remained mainly agrarian, in small plots of land, limiting the industrial labour pool. The middle class were mainly occupied in trade and, without political influence, could not gain the financial resources to invest in industry. Industrialization was based on the resources of the state, which were consumed by war most of the time, while production levels were insufficient to compete in wider markets and local markets were not strong.

Business used the state to acquire resources through clientelism. During the first half of the nineteenth century, industrialization in Greece was based on the emergent efforts of a few individuals rather than being planned. Services, such as marine transport, trade and some small industries, such as weaving, became the main activities (Agriandonis, 1991). Industry, therefore, was isolated or marginalized in the economy. It did not complement the other types of economic activity, and did not acquire the critical mass needed for the development of industrial clusters and knowledge infrastructure. Industry was haphazard or opportunistic and remained small in size (Agriantonis, 1986: 56, Limberakis, 1991: 99). Greece tried to imitate the industrialization process, based on the northern European and American examples, but it never overcame the underdevelopment of domestic institutions and infrastructures that stigmatized its economic history especially during the period between 1922 and 1960 (Demiris, 1991: 19). However, some economically important industries began to develop after de-industrialization in the 1960s to 1980 (Polizos *et al.*, 1998: 32, 51). There was a pattern in which growth followed a disaster (for example between 1880 and 1920 when the Balkan Wars and the First World War took place) (Demiris 1991). There were fragmented attempts during these patterns to build the missing infrastructures by using the support of foreign institutions (due to the lack of domestic ones), for example, supranational organizations and their development programmes (e.g. Marshall Plan, EU funds). Such institutions and programmes, however, in combination with an elitist, bureaucratic state without long-term goals or resource allocation system, could not help build the infrastructures needed in this particular business system, because there was not continuous evolutionary trajectory in their development, fitted to the specific needs of the business. Business, therefore, remained small, and management methods did not need to modernize.

Ireland

Ireland, like Greece, has for much of its history lived under the rule of a colonial power. The division of the country between North and South creates two distinct business worlds. During the eighteenth- and nineteenth-century industrialization era, the economy in Ireland was mainly agrarian, characterized by small-holdings producing raw goods for British manufacturing, and few substantially developed industries. A series of events (famines, wars with Britain and internal conflicts) led, firstly, to successive mass emigration and subsequent and continuous haemorrhaging of the labour pool and, secondly, to sharp economic booms and busts. The major economic and business development took place after the partitioning of the country between North and South in 1921, which had severe economic effects on the border areas but did not actually solve the real issue of dependence on Britain. Although the North was directly dependent on Britain, it became industrialized (shipbuilding, ropes, clothing and textiles); the South, although politically independent, still relied on exports to Britain for its economic existence, remained mainly agricultural and was weaker than the North. By continuing to use the pound sterling, it also remained monetarily dependent on Britain. Protectionist policies in the 1930s led to further economic isolation followed by mass emigration. De-industrialization hit the North in the 1960 and 1970s, ending the unfulfilled promise of full industrialization. The turning point for Ireland was its entry to the EU. The southern economy benefited from the European Structural Funds system between 1973 and 2002. The so-called Celtic Tiger economy grew rapidly in the 1990s in high technology industries and continued until 2007, but no corrective policy measures were taken to control the process, which led to the 2008 crisis. Ireland became the perfect example of a 'dominant-developmental' state which attracted much foreign direct investment (FDI) with its lower corporate taxes, limited government intervention in business, state agencies and incentives to promote entrepreneurship, transfer payments from EU membership, its cheap and educated labour force and expert accounting, law and finance sectors. The boom was fuelled by offshore investment unlike any other in the EU and it became a well publicized phenomenon (Foster, 2008). However, the Tiger collapsed due to a combination of poor investment decisions, because of its propensity of government to interfere business in, by a lack of investment in proper public services that would create more innovative infrastructure (White, 2010), and a series of events like foot and mouth disease and recession in the USA.

Certain trends appear in this economic history. Ireland has sprung from the poorest to the fastest or highest economic growth, only to plummet again, and these gaps are quite noticeable (Armstrong, 1999). A second trend is the continuous emigration and urbanization centred on the major industries during the boom periods. There is no unified system in the whole country due to politico-economic partition and social division. The difference in governance between North and South is distinctive, which exposes it to decision-making based on influence. Ollerenshaw (1985, 1991) states that from 1920 to 1972, Ireland was governed by one party, facing little opposition, and unless industrial leaders were integrated into the government, they had little chance of a sympathetic hearing. The system had not built institutional structures to support bottom-up business development and the state adopted a high-risk 'dominant development' strategy, turning to foreign investment favouring only certain industries. The main characteristic of this business system, which proved both a strength in the rapid booms and a weakness in the frequent busts, is that it is one of the most globalized in the world and, therefore, externally driven and dependent in terms of both markets and operations on other systems to a greater extent than other business systems. Although Irish business appears to take advantage of opportunities and has developed a strong labour force despite thinning through emigration, this international orientation creates a dependence which means that international trade recovery is the only route for national recovery from the current crisis. Without it, there is insufficient investment to sustain business growth. In addition, a new obstacle is that, this time, new members of the EU are competing to provide a flexible and well trained workforce with lower costs than Ireland, so foreign investment may no longer be at the levels experienced before. The promotion of domestic entrepreneurship, given the knowledgeable labour force that now exists, is the only solution, but the dependence on foreign markets will remain since domestic ones are not large enough.

Italy

Italy, by contrast, went from being an agricultural country to one of the world's most powerful modern economies in a more consistent way. Before the two world wars, Italy experienced a breakdown of feudalism and redistribution of land which led to the now common phenomenon of the small-plot, fragmented agrarian economy with uncoordinated production. This led to mass emigration, mainly from the south, from the beginning of the 1800s to World War I. However during the 1930s, the government became corporatist and the economy grew strongly from the mid-1950s until the mid-1960s, owing to Marshall Plan aid, the relatively minor war damage that Italy had suffered, a generation of talented business leaders, natural resources (gas in the Po valley), a 'reservoir of cheap labour', and membership of the EC (Duggan, 2008). There were two types of government intervention during this period: strict control of labour costs and a strict monetary policy, and investment in industrialization through state holding companies. This system collapsed and a series of heterogeneous and internally contradictory reform processes emerged, resulting in large government debt.

Until then, however, a strong economy had emerged based on two types of institutions: collaborative regional clusters of SMEs and flexible specialization production methods based on rich inter-sector and inter-firm connections within strong economic industrial triangles in the north (Bianchi *et al.*, 1997). This business system seemed to successfully overcome the structural weaknesses observed in the Greek and Irish business systems. Since, however, the system was supply-driven and income-based, the government soon realized that it had to develop a national industrial policy to initiate economic planning and reform public firms. The policies they created were basic imitations of foreign institutions (French, Scandinavian and US), but their implementation was ineffective due the structural weaknesses of the system – it is regionally fragmented, has multiple and competing centres of economic decision making and locality pervades the procedures, processes and practices of institutions. The policies thus had different effects depending on whether various firms and regions processed the resources necessary to take advantage of them (Locke, 1997). The system has high levels of corruption, uneven development between north and south, heavy taxation and high public spending with high public deficit and low spending on innovation, a sizable black economy (which according to some estimates accounts for as much as 15 per cent of GDP), tax evasion and clientelistic resource allocation practices (Eisenhardt and Roniger, 1984). The economy has a diversified industrial structure, which is concentrated in regional clusters in the developed industrial north. Division remains between the north and a less-developed, welfare-dependent, agricultural south, with high unemployment. In this 'co-ordinated industrial district' business system, and in contrast to other EU countries, neither the market nor the banks have a monopoly on a relevant implementation and governance system. Firms favour certainty of control at the expense of shareholder protection. In most cases, the main shareholders exercise control through block holdings. Therefore, there is seldom division between ownership and control, and for this reason firms seldom receive funds from the stock market. The system is bank-led (Melis, 2000) with well-known consequences for management practices. It is for these reasons that Italy has a smaller number of world-class firms than other countries of comparable size, and it has a very high proportion of micro firms-SMEs (Bianchi *et al.*, 1997) which can adjust rapidly to new forms of specialization (Rabellotti and Carabelli, 2007).

Spain

Spain could have become an industrial power early, but like Portugal (and unlike Britain) it used its colonies, not to create industries and markets, but to accumulate rents and resources from their estates in a semi-feudal system. Moreover, due to political and economic problems, Spain had little military or economic control over commercial marine routes. She retreated into a backward-looking agrarian economy after the loss of her colonies and, like the other peripheral countries, she suffered from internal political conflicts before World War II that led to a dictatorial regime. But unlike the other countries, Spain did not gain the entrepreneurial and human capital to start business early. Consequently, she was the last peripheral country to industrialize fully, starting during the 1950s, peaking in the 1960s, and intensifying after the death of dictator Franco in 1975, when she became a constitutional democratic monarchy. The economy quickly overcame the gap with other European countries and this growth was regarded as an 'economic miracle', similar to that of Italy in the 1950s and 1960s. Industrialization began with the creation of a labour pool for industrial development in the major Spanish citiesin heavy industries selected by the state (steel, oil refineries and shipyards) (Tusell, 2007). Liberalization measures introduced by Franco in 1957 included the devaluation of the peseta; the introduction of a single exchange rate; allowing foreign investors and banks from other countries to become established in Spain; a programme of monetary and fiscal restraint; and a liberalization of price controls and trade restrictions. The economy grew fast but conservatively due to the regime's fear of the loss of control entailed by full industrialization, and also because the inward-looking and defensive attitude of the regime towards its own labour force inhibited FDI (Pierson, 1999; Shubert, 1990). Simpson (1997) described the situation as one of 'slow growth', although it seems more likely to have been 'cautious growth', since Franco's regime was actually inspired by technocratic ideas of modernizing the economy through liberalization.

Initially the state had a very strong 'dominant- development' role with the explicit intention of transforming the fragmented agrarian business system into one of co-ordinated industrial districts, very much following Italy's example but without the regional clusters. Industrialization in Spain did not take as strong a foothold in firm practice as in Italy because fewer industries were 'developed', with hardly any inter-sector connections (co-ordinated regionally or by firms) established between them and between firms. The economy recovered from 'slow growth' only after 1985, and especially after Spain joined the EC in 1986, spurred on by the privatizations and liberalizations of new socialist governments after 1990, which promoted growth in markets such as vehicle production, ICT, shipbuilding, food, medical products, pharmaceuticals, cosmetics, construction and the alternative energy industry). Spain has thus successfully undergone a dramatic political and economic transformation from relative underdevelopment and authoritarianism to wealth and pluralist democracy, although with certain omissions which led to structural weaknesses (Carr, 2001; Shubert, 1990; Tusell, 2007).

These weaknesses seem to be shared with the other peripheral countries: recent socialist governments have overspent and debt and deficit have soared (11.4 per cent of Spanish GDP in 2009) (Kern, 2010), while the recession has hit the construction market and the green economy. The main weaknesses in this business system are a combination of labour factors. Spain's economy has persistently experienced high unemployment at rates of close to 20 per cent, which fell only between 1998 and 2001 (30 per cent for women and 45 per cent for young people in the 1990s) (Boix, 2004) because there were no labour policies during the industrialization period under Franco. The regime at the time encouraged urbanization of labour from agrarian occupations and created a pool of 5 million unskilled workers. However, they deprived them of labour rights and abandoned modern educational practices, using religious education for propaganda instead. Later governmental reforms have sought to make the labour market more flexible and skilled, decreasing the unemployment rate by almost 4 per cent by 2001, but it rose again to nearly 20 per cent with the credit crisis in western markets causing the collapse of the construction industry (Moya, 2010). In addition, immigration has a particularly large impact on the agricultural labour market of southern Spain, and terrorism has a disturbing impact on production and investment. Many economists fear that the unemployment high rate has contributed to the expansion of the black market, although there are no firm and credible estimates of what percentage of the economy this actually constitutes. Governments have only recently dealt with issues of regional autonomy, and have managed to create a pluralist state. Division between the richer north and poorer south remains evident, however, along with the remains of the old politico-social divisions between republicans and francoists (Carr, 2001; Pierson, 1999; Shubert, 1990; Tusell, 2007). All these issues are linked with the development of human capital.

Other structural issues refer to investment and structural change. Apart from Catalonia and the Basque country, which had industrialized in the nineteenth century, Spain lacked a large 'bourgeois' middle class with financial and political power, since it simply consisted of civil servants, military officers and professionals (such as doctors and lawyers), very much like Greece. Firms relied on financial credit subject to stringent regulations and channelled only to certain sectors by the state, since foreign investment was artificially restricted to 25 per cent of each venture. This economic framework was a natural legacy of dictatorship and had an extraordinarily stifling effect on entrepreneurial activity. Despite the fact that the Spanish economy experienced significant growth throughout the latter part of the century, it did so in a very volatile manner which was constrained by important supply bottlenecks (Boix, 2004). Secondary causes of low performance include low levels of aggregate demand, scarcity of cheap energy, low levels of human capital and entrepreneurship, and relatively lower internationalization due to an inwardly-focused business community with poor differentiation strategies and poor export activity in SMEs (Harrison and Corkill, 2004). Recent governments are in the process of acknowledging these structural faults; however, the state has transformed its role to a more inclusive business corporatist one, and in order for its interventions to work, more interaction and specialization at the firm level need to be developed.

In spite of relocation to industrial settings, the lack of appropriate labour force and the unmodernized education system, in addition to lower levels of investment and structural change (Molinas and Escodura, 1989), were the main structural problems that compromised the momentum of competitiveness and performance which had started declining as early as the 1970s, had an upturn in the 1980s, reached its peak and then declined again.

Portugal

The Portuguese business system has many similarities to the Greek system, as it was forged under a series of class struggles and a strong corporatist state which has turned to democracy only in the past 30 years. The main characteristic of these struggles was a competition to concentrate power, in terms of ownership of the means of production, whether this was land or finance. Industrialization was initially mostly ignored in Portugal, mainly because it did not compete with the industrialized products of Britain in its own markets (colonies). The whole system was underperforming for many reasons: the state had exhausted its resources to sustain its empire (the country was twice declared bankrupt, on June 14 1892 and May 10 1902); the French and Spanish wars led to a prolonged period of foreign political interference; the loss of colonies shrank traditional markets (the loss of Brazil alone deprived Portugal of 60 to 80 per cent of her exports) and its own deflated markets; and the agrarian population could not be transformed into a skilled or unskilled industrial labour force. Most significant of all, however, was the failure to liberalize infrastructure and raise capital, in the hands of an upper middle class controlling the banking sector. This factor caused much political disturbance (coups and dictatorships), and inhibited the development of entrepreneurship among the economically deprived lower and lower middle classes. Portugal's private sector was dominated by 40 prominent industrial dynasties, which had intermarried with the traditional landowning families of the nobility, gained access to state office and exercised extensive authority over private investment decisions and the wage levels.

During the four waves of industrialization (1670–90, 1769–78, 1820–23 and 1835) in Portugal's recent history, the business system achieved very slow agrarian reform which led to fragmented, small-plot agricultural production and an equally slow mechanization of industry, since investment was directed by the elite class towards commercial business activities and firms preferring easy, short-term returns. Investment to fund the modernization of the infrastructure came, not from a risk-taking middle class through a stock market, but from a tax squeeze on the lower classes, which, however, did not produce direct industrialization plans (Corkill, 1999). However, commercial and other types of service activity allowed the economy to grow during the late 1950s, and some liberalization occurred. Despite the concentration of the means of production in the hands of a small number of family-based financial-industrial groups, Portuguese business culture permitted the upward mobility of university-educated individuals with middle-class backgrounds into professional management careers. There were several political attempts at democratization and the liberalization of the Portuguese economy, the latest one turning into a 'revolution' that forced an abrupt stop to the business growth that had been achieved during the Salazar regime (Baer and Leite, 1991; Gallagher, 1983). Nationalizations, the break-up of traditional markets and the chaos involved in the regime change from dictatorship to left-wing socialism resulted in the slowdown of heavy industry and all sectors collapsed, with the exception of the commercial banking and insurance industries which were left with a degree of competition. Portugal quickly went from the country with the highest to the lowest growth rate in Europe, and experienced several years of negative growth (Magone, 2004; Chislett, 1997; Gallagher, 1983). The result was economic migration of successful economic actors and an industrial system driven by subsidy, although it is competitive in terms of value added (Corkill, 1999).

The downward trends started to be reversed after the 1989 revisions of the constitution and the introduction of democracy and subsequent involvement with the EU. An inefficient public sector and rigidity inherited in the system have raised concerns of further downturn since the current crisis began (Syrett, 2002; France-Presse, 2009), since it will take some time for privatizations, the upgrade of the stock market in 1997, and the streamlining of public services to effect positive changes in the system (Magone, 2004; *The Economist,* 2007). The role of the corporatist state was neither capitalist nor communist, but it combined two salient characteristics: predominantly private ownership (for the most part until the communist regime of 1974) in an institutional and infrastructural framework tightly controlled by extensive state regulation. In general, Portugal has the same pattern of business sectors as Greece – big service sector, small primary and secondary sectors. The industrialized system is characterized by small-size firms, a small pool of labour, capital and raw resources and poor government. Both labour and capital – and indeed the entire institutional network – were subordinate to the central state. Financiers and industrialists accepted extensive bureaucratic controls in return for minimal public ownership and certain monopolistic privileges.

A comparison of finance, market, firm and labour figures in the peripheral countries' and UK business systems

This section highlights the rest of the business system elements in terms of figures relating to the peripheral countries (Greece, Spain, Italy, Ireland, and Portugal) and the UK. It focuses only on an analysis of main figures relating to 1) firms (number of firms, turnover, value added, operating expenditure); 2) market (imports, exports, largest/specialized activities); 3) finance (gross tangible investment, investment rate); and 4) labour (people employed, labour costs, apparent labour productivity, average gross annual earnings, minimum wage). These are displayed in Table 15.1.

Market

The figures show that Italy, Ireland, Spain, Portugal and the UK have as their largest activity business services, and all of them, except Ireland, are much involved in construction. In specialized activities, Ireland, Spain and Portugal are involved in light industry, Italy and Ireland share some other manufacturing activities, and the UK has more heavy industrial activities and also innovation. Greece serves these markets through wholesale and retail trade and water transport. The specialization of production requires a different kind of market and firm organization. In terms of imports, Ireland is in the lead, followed by Portugal, the UK, Spain, Greece and Italy, while Ireland is the leading exporter, followed

Table 15.1 Main indicators of the non-financial business economy 2006

Indicators	Greece	Italy	Ireland	Spain	Portugal	UK
Firms						
Number of enterprises (% of EU-27)	4.1	19.1	0.5	13.1	4.3	8.0
Turnover (% of EU-27)	1.3	12.4	1.5	9.2	1.4	15.9
Value added (% of EU-27)	1.2	11.2	1.6	9.5	1.3	19.0
Operating expenditure (% of EU-27)	13.0	12.8	:	15.6	14.0	18.8
Market						
Largest activities	Wholesale trade; retail trade & repair	Business services; construction	Business services; fuel processing & chemicals	Construction; business services	Construction; business services	Business services; construction
Specialist activities	Wholesale trade; retail trade & repair	Textiles, clothing, leather & footwear; furniture & other manufacturing	Electrical machinery & operating equipment; food, beverages & tobacco	Construction; other non-metallic mineral production	Wood & paper; other non-metallic mineral production	Mining and quarrying; R&D
Imports (% of GDP)	25.1	23.8	74.5	25.7	35.2	30.1
Exports (% of GDP)	20.3	23.5	90.3	23.7	27.7	27.7

Finance						
Gross tangible investment (non-financial business economy) (% of EU-27)	1.5	10.8	:	10.7	1.9	15.1
Investment rate (non-financial business economy) (% of EU-27)	22.6	17.7	:	20.7	28.3	14.6
Labour						
People employed (% of EU-27)	2.0	11.7	0.8	10.7	2.5	13.7
Labour productivity (€ thousand/person employed)	26.9	41.6	83.5	38.6	21.6	60.5
Labour costs (€ thousand/employee)	21.9	31.2	:	26.1	13.3	33.9
Average gross annual earnings* industry and services (2007), €	16,738.5 (latest in 2003)	:	39,858.0	21,890.7	15,345.2	46,050.5
Minimum wage (2008), €	681	:	1462	700	497	1223

Sources: Eurostat (2010b, c) and Czech (2009).

by Portugal/UK, Spain, Italy and Greece. In all countries, except Ireland and Italy (marginally), imports are higher than exports.

Finance

In terms of gross tangible investment, the UK is the leader, followed by Italy, Spain, Portugal and Greece (ten per cent of UK). Portugal leads in investment rate, followed by Spain, Greece, Italy and the UK. What this means is that Greece needs to invest in her specialized services less, however, the rate of this investment is more than that of UK, with Portugal and Spain following the same trend.

Labour

The UK employs the greatest number of people, followed by Italy, Spain, Portugal, Greece and Ireland. Employment productivity is highest in Ireland, followed by the UK, Italy, Spain, Greece and Portugal. Note that Ireland has the lowest levels of employment and the highest labour productivity of all. The cost of labour is highest in the UK, followed by Italy, and Spain, while the UK and Italy come second and third in productivity. Greece and Portugal have the cheapest labour of all and they have similar lower levels of productivity. In terms of employee remuneration, the highest annual salaries are in the UK and Ireland. The lowest-paid employees are in Portugal and Greece. The lowest minimum wage is in Portugal, followed by Greece and Spain. Remuneration is 2.9 times higher in Ireland (highest minimum wage) than in Portugal, and 2.2 times that of Greece.

Firms

In terms of the number of firms, Italy is in the lead with Spain, the UK, Portugal, Greece and Ireland following. However, the UK comes first in turnover, followed by Italy, Spain, Ireland, Greece and Portugal. The UK still leads in value added, followed by Italy, Spain, Ireland, Portugal and Greece. Finally, the UK exhibits the highest percentage in operating expenditure, followed by Spain, Portugal, Italy and Greece. Although the UK has only half as many firms as the leader, Italy, (but 50 per cent large companies compared with 28 per cent for Italy), the competitiveness of UK firms is obviously higher since they lead on performance indicators, with almost double the value added. Greece is more comparable to Portugal in most indicators.

The most important factor in terms of all these indicators is the size of firms. SMEs are the backbone of the European economy. According to the 2010 Eurostat Yearbook (Eurostat, 2010a), there were an estimated 20.2 million firms within the EU-27 non-financial business economy (defined

Table 15.2 Value added by enterprise type, non-financial business economy 2006 (€ billion)

Country	Total	Micro (1–9)	Small (10–49)	Medium (50–249)	Large (250+)
EU-27	*5,650.00*	*20.2*	*18.8*	*17.8*	*43.1*
Greece	69.56	35.1	:	17.1	:
Portugal	76.79	:	22.8	21.4	:
Ireland	90.91	:	:	:	:
Spain	536.80	26.5	24.1	17.3	32.1
Italy	631.33	32.7	23.0	16.1	28.3
UK	1,072.55	18.5	15.5	16.6	49.3

Source: Eurostat (2010a).

as industry, construction, distributive trades and services, but excluding financial services) in 2006. It is important to note that, although SMEs in the EU-27 employ an average of 4.3 persons (2005), there are great variations between member states – from 12 employees per SME in Slovakia, 10 in the UK, more than 7 in Estonia, Ireland, Latvia and Germany, approximately 4 in Portugal, Italy and Spain, to less than 3 in the Czech Republic and Greece (Schmiemann, 2008; see Table 15.2).

SMEs are of great importance to the EU-27 countries, as 67.1 per cent of the non-financial business economy workforce is employed by SMEs, while 57.6 per cent of the non-financial business economy's value added is generated by SMEs (Schmiemann, 2008). Almost a fifth of all value added to the European economy is contributed by UK firms. Italy, Spain, Ireland and Portugal follow, while Greece has the lowest score of the countries under study in terms of added value (see Table 15.2). In the case of the UK, almost half of this value added is contributed by SMEs and the other half by large organizations. The UK economy appears to rely more on large organizations than that of other EU countries, in which SMEs seem to primarily add value to the economy (for example, Spain shows 67.9 per cent of the value created by SMEs compared with 32.1 per cent by large organizations).

The figures show that SMEs are the predominant form in all cases; the next section therefore explores the obstacles they face.

Challenges faced by SMEs in the EU

According to a Flash Eurobarometer survey (2007), the challenges and constraints faced by SMEs in the EU are bureaucracy, lack of skilled labour, problems accessing finance, and difficulties with new technology, organization and regulations. In addition, SMEs in the EU are characterized by risk aversion, which may hinder growth, and lack of entrepreneurial spirit. Overall, SMEs in Greece, Portugal and new member states (Czech Republic, Slovakia, Slovenia, Lithuania, Poland and Romania) report that they are more constrained than the EU average but that their situation has not been deteriorating further. The most advantaged SMEs, facing few obstacles, belong to the Nordic countries (Norway, Denmark, Iceland, Finland and Sweden), along with the UK, Spain and the Netherlands. Turkey reports a number of problem incidences and lack of promising changes. A relatively low proportion of SMEs in Luxembourg and Cyprus (marginally) face challenges and report a worsening situation. The most disadvantaged SMEs reporting various constraints with further deterioration in their situation are from France, Belgium, Italy, Hungary and Malta. The following constraints are cited:

(1) 25 per cent of SMEs in Greece report *limited access to finance,* in comparison to 24 per cent in Portugal, 28 per cent in Italy, 19 per cent in the UK, 18 per cent in Ireland and 11per cent in Spain.
(2) 33 per cent of SMEs in Greece report that the *labour force is too expensive,* in comparison to 45 per cent in Italy, 36 per cent in Ireland, 33 per cent in Portugal, 25 per cent in the UK and 23 per cent in Spain.
(3) 54 per cent of SMEs in Greece report that there is a *lack of skilled labour* (particularly in the construction and manufacturing sectors), compared with 42 per cent in Portugal, 37 per cent in Italy, 37 percent in Spain, 32 per cent in Ireland and 28 per cent in the UK.
(4) 19 per cent of SMEs in Greece report that they face *challenges in implementing new technology,* compared with 31 per cent in Portugal, 19 per cent in Spain, 18 per cent in the UK, 15 per cent in Italy and 14 per cent in Ireland. Greece, therefore, faces a similar challenge to the UK in this respect.
(5) 24 per cent of SMEs in Greece report *challenges with implementing new forms of organization* (in particular implementing new organizational solutions, restructuring, or other organizational changes) in comparison to 26 per cent in Portugal, 20 per cent in Italy, 16 per cent in the UK, 16 per cent in Spain and 13 per cent in Ireland.
(6) 19 per cent of SMEs in Greece report a *lack of quality management.* The figures are 13 per cent for Portugal, 12 per cent for Spain, 12 per cent for Ireland, 11 per cent for the UK and 11 per cent for Italy.

(7) 29 per cent of SMEs in Greece report *problems with administrative regulations* (excessive or inappropriate regulations). The other countries report as follows: Italy 45per cent, Portugal 42 per cent, the UK 34 per cent, Ireland 28 per cent and Spain 11 per cent. The most unfavourable reports originate from the healthcare and the financial sectors.

(8) Greek SMEs rank first in the EU-27 on *problems with infrastructure* (for example, roads, gas, electricity and communications), with 47 per cent reporting problems in comparison to 41 per cent in Ireland, 36 per cent in Portugal, 23 per cent in Italy, 22 per cent in the UK, 21 per cent in Italy and 15 per cent in Spain.

(9) Greek SMEs rank first in the EU-27 for *problems with the purchasing power of customers,* 77 per cent reporting problems in comparison to 74 per cent in Portugal, 54 per cent in Italy, 33 per cent in Spain, 25 per cent in Ireland and 23 per cent in the UK.

(10) In terms of *problems with understanding/implementing governmental regulations* (if the firms think that the regulations that apply to them are appropriate to achieve governmental goals), 41% of Greek SMEs believe that regulations are appropriate, in comparison to 56 per cent in Ireland, 33 per cent in the UK and 21 per cent in Italy. An important 24 per cent of Greek SMEs report that regulations go clearly too far, in comparison to 38 per cent in Italy, 28 per cent in the UK and 15 per cent in Ireland. A small proportion of Greek SMEs report that regulations go slightly too far (9 per cent). This is in comparison to 21 per cent in Italy and 18 per cent in the UK. Finally, 13 per cent of Greek SMEs report that regulations could be more ambitious, in comparison to 16 per cent in Ireland and 11 per cent in the UK (see Table 15.3).

Table 15.3 Problems with government regulations (% responses per country)

	Greece	**Portugal**	**Italy**	**Ireland**	**Spain**	**UK**
Yes, regulations are appropriate	41%	29%	21%	**56%**	44%	33%
No, regulations go clearly too far	24%	31%	**38%**	15%	20%	28%
No, regulations go slightly too far	9%	12%	**21%**	9%	7%	18%
No, regulations could be more ambitious	13%	10%	11%	**16%**	11%	11%

Source: Flash Eurobarometer report (2007).

(11) In terms of *time spent on administrative requirements*, Greek SMEs spent on average 51 working days dealing with activities needed in order to comply to legislation requirements, compared with 139 days in Spain, 106 days in Portugal, 96 days in Italy, 42 days in the UK and 42 days in Ireland.

(12) *Innovation in SMEs*. According to the Flash Eurobarometer report (2007), almost four in ten SMEs in the EU report that they do not have new products or that they do not have income from new products. The EU-27 average of firms reporting no revenue from innovation stands at 37 per cent. Spain and Italy rank among the highest in the EU with 46 per cent, followed by Portugal (40 per cent), Greece (31 per cent), Ireland (28 per cent) and the UK (27 per cent). However, some firms did report a percentage of turnover coming from new/improved products/services: Ireland (16 per cent), Greece (16 per cent), the UK (14 per cent), Portugal (13 per cent), Italy (12 per cent) and Spain (10 per cent). The EU-27 average stands at 12 per cent. It is important to note that among the old member states, the highest proportion of 'innovative income' was reported in Greece and Ireland, while the lowest proportion was reported in Bulgaria and Denmark (both 6 per cent). A main constraint on innovation is that fact that a large proportion of SMEs (38 per cent) do not plan to introduce innovations to their products or technology. However, of the overall number of firms in the EU, 38.9 per cent are considered as 'innovative' (Eurostat, 2010a). The highest propensity to innovate is recorded in Germany (62.6 per cent). Greece comes after Ireland and Portugal, and before the UK, Italy and Spain. Other major constraints on innovation include problems with access to finance, other than interest rates, (10 per cent), expensive human resources (9 per cent), lack of skilled human resources (8 per cent), lack of market demand for innovation (8 per cent), high interest rates (6 per cent), lack of ability to use new technologies (3 per cent) and difficulty in protecting intellectual property (3 per cent).

Management practices in the peripheral countries and the UK

Having compared the business systems of the peripheral countries and the UK, and the structure, significance and challenges for SMEs in these systems, we will now turn our attention to management practices in the firms in these systems. This section does not compare the different systems *per se*, as in the previous section, but discusses the practices individually.

Strategic management

Flash Eurobarometer (2007) reports increased business competition in Europe for SMEs. Strategies that firms follow to address this increase in competition include the following.

Increasing quality of products/services is the most frequently mentioned strategy with the average percentage in EU-27 standing at 64 per cent. Estonia (86 per cent) and Greece (83 per cent) show the highest percentages in the EU in terms of applying this strategy to address pressures from competition, followed by Ireland (75 per cent), Italy (71 per cent), the UK (64 per cent), Portugal (59 per cent), and Spain (48 per cent).

Increasing marketing activity is the second most frequently used strategy reported with an EU-27 average of 61 per cent. Turkey (83 per cent) and Greece (82 per cent) have the highest percentages in the EU, followed by Ireland (77 per cent), the UK (72 per cent), Spain (62 per cent), Italy (57 per cent) and Portugal (55 per cent).

Increasing product differentiation is the third most commonly used strategy. The EU-27 average stands at 62 per cent, while Ireland (81 per cent) holds the first place, followed by the UK (73 per cent), Portugal (63 per cent), Italy (62 per cent), Greece (61 per cent) and Spain (45 per cent).

Reducing costs is the fourth most popular strategy used. The EU-27 average stands at 53 per cent. Ireland (69 per cent) shows one of the highest percentages in the EU, followed by Greece (66 per cent), the UK (54 per cent), Portugal (52 per cent), Spain (45 per cent) and Italy (45 per cent).

Forming strategic partnerships is another strategy used. The EU-27 average for this strategy stands at 38 per cent, with Greece (61 per cent) one of the highest in the EU. Portugal (39 per cent), Italy (36 per cent), Spain (35 per cent), Ireland (35 per cent) and the UK (33 per cent) follow.

Other strategies less frequently used include *reducing prices*, which can be a risky strategy in the long term and is less frequently used by SMEs in the EU. The EU-27 average is 36 per cent for this strategy. Greece (54 per cent) holds one of the highest places in the EU, followed by Ireland (54 per cent), Portugal (45 per cent), the UK (41 per cent), Spain (35 per cent) and Italy (30 per cent). *Increasing working hours* (EU-27 = 28 per cent), is used by Greece (45 per cent), Ireland (36 per cent), the UK (33 per cent), Portugal (29 per cent), Italy (23 per cent) and Spain (22 per cent). In addition, *looking for new foreign markets* (EU-27 = 26 per cent), is used by Greece (49 per cent), Ireland (40 per cent), Portugal (31 per cent), Spain (28 per cent), the UK (26 per cent) and Italy (22 per cent). Finally, *reducing production* (EU-27 = 11 per cent), is used by Portugal (21 per cent), Ireland (18 per cent), Greece (14 per cent), the UK (13 per cent), Spain (13 per cent) and Italy (8 per cent).

International business

According to Flash Eurobarometer (2007), less than one in ten SMEs in the EU is directly involved in exports (EU-27 average 8 per cent). Some of the largest EU countries are not particularly involved in cross-border trade. For example, the proportion of firms with any revenue from exports was 23 per cent for Estonia (highest percentage in the EU), followed by 11 per cent in Ireland, 9 per cent in the UK, 9 per cent in Portugal, 9 per cent in Greece, 7 per cent in Italy and 3 per cent in Spain.

In terms of export's share in SMEs revenue, there is great variation across the EU, with Belgium (15 per cent) and Estonia (12 per cent) having the highest percentages of export's share in revenue, followed by Portugal (5 per cent), Ireland (4 per cent), Spain (4 per cent), the UK (4 per cent), Italy (3 per cent) and Greece (2 per cent). It is important to note that the EU average is 4.6 per cent. Main constraints for exports were identified as lack of knowledge of foreign markets, reduced price competitiveness due to import tariffs in destination countries and difficulties caused by the different regulations that still prevail within the EU's single internal market.

In addition, the proportion of foreign business partnerships gaining any revenue from foreign subsidiary or joint venture abroad stands at 4.8 per cent for the EU-27. The highest percentages are seen by SMEs in Turkey (14 per cent), Belgium (13 per cent) and Portugal (10 per cent), followed by Ireland (10 per cent), the UK (7 per cent), Greece (6 per cent), Spain (2 per cent) and Italy (2 per cent).

Human Resource Management

In terms of comparative HRM practices in Europe, the Cranet study provides a longitudinal framework exploring trends and changes in HRM issues in eighteen European countries. Nikandrou *et al.* (2005) used this study to categorize countries following a North-west/South-east distinction. This research concluded that there is no indication of convergence between the major clusters.

The north-western cluster is sub-categorized into a western sub-cluster (the UK, Switzerland, Sweden, the Netherlands, Belgium, Germany, France and Spain) and the northern sub-cluster (Denmark, Norway and Finland). The south-eastern cluster is sub-categorized into (i) Eastern Germany, Czechoslovakia, Italy; and (ii) Turkey, Ireland, Greece and Bulgaria.

The north-western cluster exhibits the following characteristics in toa greater extent than the south-eastern cluster: a significant role for HRM in the organization; more formalised HR policies in place; less involvement of managers and more involvement of employees in HRM;

more external labour market orientation (although internal training has recently increased); more employment flexibility; more emphasis on training; more centralized HR policies; more briefing of managers about organizational issues; more frequent recruitment of HR managers from outside the organization; more flexible working practices. In addition, in the north-western cluster, the head of HR is on the board of directors in more cases than in the south-eastern cluster. The south-eastern cluster shows a decreasing role for HR, more unwritten HR policies and strategies, more investment in training in terms of days spent by managers on training, and more involvement of managers in performance appraisals than in the north-western cluster.

Marketing and sales

There is great variety in the marketing practices of SMEs. Reijonen's research (2010) in eastern Finland found that marketing practices in SMEs are not uniform and that they depend on firm size and types of customer. The industry and product/service offered is therefore an important differentiator of marketing practices in SMEs. The business context does not matter as much, although the marketing practices of competitors are an important influence. In addition, O'Dwyer's research (2009) on innovative marketing in SMEs found that innovative marketing in SMEs was specific to the context and needs of the enterprise and related to products/services, new product and technology development, as well as in other marketing-related activities and decisions. Gilmore's research (2007) on e-marketing practices in Northern Ireland found that it is still in its infancy and not used to its full potential.

According to Flash Eurobarometer (2007), the EU average for the proportion of revenue spent on marketing stands at 3.4 per cent (EU-27). Spain holds the second highest position in the EU with 9 per cent, followed by the UK, Greece and Ireland (all 4 per cent), Italy (3 per cent) and Portugal (2 per cent). Furthermore, this report found that there is no significant relationship between the perception of increased competition and the relative size of the marketing budget in each country, implying that the size of the marketing budget is a matter of overall business strategy and not an ad hoc response to changing market conditions.

Total Quality Management

There are plenty examples of successful TQM implementation in both the East and West (Maccoby, 1994). It is true that a lot of US, European and Japanese organizations seem very keen on the implementation of TQM practices (Aspinwall and Magana-Campos, 2003). However, this does not mean that all organizations in all countries perceive TQM in the same manner.

Drew (1998, 2006) found heightened TQM awareness since the mid-1990s by Irish firms in the manufacturing and services sectors, although service organizations have been slower in adopting TQM practices. Furthermore, research conducted by Walsh *et al.* (2002) concluded that TQM activities are practised throughout Irish industries and that TQM is adopted in a comprehensive manner with evidence of long-term commitment to TQM programmes. Furthermore, their research found that TQM practices are suitable for adoption by Irish organizations and can offer increased competitiveness to firms that adopt them.

On the other hand, research by Soltani and Lai (2007) on UK-based firms found that, although ISO and TQM models attracted a lot of interest and were seen as tools that can help organizations improve their performance, a major discrepancy existed between the rhetoric of these systems and the reality of their practice. This piece of research found little evidence that UK-based organizations adopted a strategic approach to managing the soft aspects of TQM. In addition, research by Antony *et al.* (2008) into UK-based SMEs in the manufacturing sector found that SMEs are not aware of TQM strategies such as Six Sigma and Lean Sigma, nor do they have the resources to implement such projects. Firms in the UK therefore seem to be facing similar issues to Greek firms in terms of TQM adoption, particularly in embracing the softer side of this management philosophy.

Psychogios (2010) further argues that cultural and structural features of the business systems in South-eastern Europe (SEE) create pressures which either promote or inhibit TQM adoption by organizations. His research uses data from Romania, Serbia, Bulgaria and Greece and argues that organizations in the SEE region adopt a pragmatic view of TQM application that mostly focuses on its hard elements and often ignores the softer side of this management philosophy. So it seems that Greece is following an international trend that, although the majority of countries are keen to adopt TQM practices, at the same time they face critical challenges in their adoption.

Accounting and auditing

A comparative study of accounting shows that there is currently great inconsistency in practices between countries. Although standardization is impossible due to the fact that accounting is embedded in cultural environments that differ greatly, harmonization efforts (that is, reducing the differences in reporting between countries) are taking place (Walton *et al.,* 2002; Nobes and Parker, 2008). National cultures, legal systems, the providers of finance, taxation, the status of the accountancy profession and other external influences are all elements that make up for the difference in accounting practices (Nobes and Parker, 2008).

According to McLeay (1999), accounting regulation in most European countries is primarily based on commercial law. In Spain (the *Codigo Commercio* of 1829), Portugal (the *Codigo Comercial* of 1888) and Italy (the *Codice Commerciale* of 1882), codified law is revised at regular intervals. In the UK, Ireland and Greece, parliamentary law in the form of statute law is the main form of legislation regulating company activities. The first Acts bearing substantially on company affairs were the 1844 Joint Stock Companies Act in the UK and Ireland, and the Companies Law of 1920 in Greece. In Spain, Portugal and Greece, there is also a general (national) accounting plan that acts as a supplement to codified commercial law. These national accounting plans provide detailed regulations on the way in which accounts are maintained and records of transactions kept, on ways of valuing assets and liabilities, and on the form and content of financial statements. The national accounting plans were greatly influenced by the 1957 version of the *Plan Comptable Général* (a French version of a German national accounting model), and led to Spain's *Plan General de Contabilidad* of 1973 (revised 1990), Portugal's *Plano Oficial de Contabilidade* of 1977 (revised in 1989, 1991), and Greece's General Accounting Plan of 1980. In Italy, where there is no national accounting plan, standardized charts of accounts are published by professional or industrial associations and are often adopted by companies.

Decrees and ministerial orders are also frequently used in Italy, Spain, Portugal and Greece, in order to increase flexibility in their legal systems of accounting regulation. However, there is still evidence that despite flexible legislative instruments, accounting regulation appears to fit uneasily with law in a number of countries.

In terms of the status of standard-setting bodies, a legal status following approval by the government is required in Spain[1] and Portugal. In the UK and Greece, the law requires compliance, while in Italy and Ireland, the only recognition is that the stock exchange requires listed companies to comply.

According to Walton *et al.* (2002), Greece, together with Belgium, Germany, France, Italy, Japan, Portugal and Switzerland belongs to the set of countries implementing continental European accounting systems. Some characteristics of the socioeconomic environment of these countries are: (i) capital is mainly provided by the banking sector; (ii) the culture is state-focused; (iii) the legal system is dominated by codified law (providing detailed accounting rules); and (iv) the fiscal system is based on the close connection of financial accounting and taxation. On the other hand, countries such as Australia, the UK, Ireland, Canada, New Zealand, the Netherlands, Singapore and the USA belong to the set of countries implementing Anglo-Saxon accounting systems. Main characteristics of these systems include: (i) capital is mainly raised through stock markets; (ii) the culture is individualistic; (iii) the legal system is dominated by case law (accounting rules developed by private standard setting bodies); and (iv) within the fiscal system, tax rules do not influence financial accounting practice.

As far as auditing is concerned, the functions of auditors differ between countries. Nobes and Parker (2008) provide useful information on comparative auditing practices. According to their work, it is common practice in the USA and other Anglo-Saxon countries to include the opinion of the external independent auditor with the published financial statements to add credibility to the financial statements for investors and creditors. In Germany, on the other hand, where financial reporting for legal purposes and tax reporting are closely connected, audits are focused more on legal acceptability and acceptability for tax purposes and less on the true and fair presentation for the benefit of external stakeholders.

Furthermore, within the European Union, the Council of the European Communities has issued directives (the Fourth and Seventh) on the preparation, publication and audit of annual reports, with the aim of harmonizing legislation within the EU. Factors that have contributed to the harmonization of auditing practices include the emergence of MNCs, the increasing globalization of capital markets, the growth of international accounting firms (which share approaches to audit methodology, training and quality review), and the convergence around common international frameworks for accounting and audit. The Eighth Directive also provides a set of qualifications and education criteria for auditors, in order to ensure standards in the auditing profession. Other documents continue to be published by the EU in an attempt to modernize the Eighth Directive and to achieve public oversight of the auditing profession and establish an appropriate regulatory structure at EU level.

Summary

This second concluding chapter aimed at putting the Greek case in a comparative context. It did so by, firstly, discussing the state, institutions and infrastructures in the peripheral (Portugal, Italy, Ireland and Spain) and UK business systems. The analysis here included a historical reference to the industrialization process of each country in order to illustrate major similarities and differences with Greece's industrialization process and explain similarities and differences in the current business systems of these countries. Secondly, the chapter provided a comparison of finance, market, firm and labour figures in the peripheral countries and the UK business systems. A main issue that arose from this analysis concerned the dominant form of SMEs in these countries. This led, thirdly, to a discussion on the main obstacles that these firms face in the EU. Fourthly, the chapter provided an overview of business and management practices (strategic management, international business, human resource management, marketing and sales, total quality management, accounting and auditing) in peripheral countries and the UK. The next, and final, chapter of this book provides some avenues for further research specific to Greece.

Note

1. In Spain, an independent body (AECA) issues standards.

References

Antony, J., Kumar, M., and Labib, A. (2008) 'Gearing Six Sigma into UK Manufacturing SMEs: Results from a Pilot Study', *Journal of the Operational Research Society*, 59: 482–93.

Armstrong, D.L. (1999) *The Growth of Industry in Northern Ireland*. Oxford University Press.

Aspinwall, E. and Magana-Campos, A.J. (2003) 'Comparative study of Western and Japanese improvement systems', *Total Quality Management*, 14(4): 423–36.

Baer, W., Leite, A. (1991) 'The peripheral economy, its performance in isolation and in integration: the case of Portugal' Working Paper 176. Universita Nova de Lisboa.

Bianchi, P. Miller, L.M. and Bertini S. (1997) *The Italian SME Experience and Possible Lessons for Emerging Countries*. Executive Summary, NOMISMA.

Boix, C. (2004) 'Spain: Development, Democracy and Equity. Equity and Development', World Development Report 2006 Background Papers.

Carr, R. (ed.) (2001) *Spain: A History*. Oxford University Press: USA.

Chislett, W. (1997) *Portugal: investment and growth*. Euromoney in association with Banco Espírito Santo.

Corkill, D. (1999) *The development of the Portuguese economy: a case of Europeanization*. London: Routledge.

Duggan, C. (2008) *The Force of Destiny: A history of Italy since 1796*. Penguin Books.

Eileen, D. (1998) 'In pursuit of excellence: total quality approaches in Irish organisations', *The TQM Magazine*, 10(6): 452–7.

Eileen, D. and Catherine Healy (2006) 'Quality management approaches in Irish organisations', *The TQM Magazine*, 18(4): 358–71.

Eisenhardt, S.N. and Roniger, L. (1984) *Patrons, Clients and Friends: Interpersonal Relationsand the Structure of Trust in Society*. Cambridge: Cambridge University Press.

Eurostat (2010a) *Eurostat Yearbook 2010 – Europe in Figures*. European Commission.

Eurostat (2010b) *Key Figures on European Business*. Luxembourg: Publications Office of the European Union.

Flash Eurobarometer (2007) *No. 196 – Observatory of European SMEs*. European Commission.

France-Presse, A. (2009) 'Standard and Poor's pessimistic on Portugal', *MSN News*, 12 June 2009. http://news.ph.msn.com/business/article.aspx?cp-documentid=3737721.

Foster, R.F. (2008) *Luck and the Irish: A brief history of change 1970–2000*. Harmondsworth: Penguin Books.

Gallagher, T. (1983) *Portugal: a twentieth-century interpretation*. Manchester University Press.

Gilmore A., Gallagher, D. and Henry S. (2007) 'E-marketing and SMEs: operational lessons for the future', *European Business Review*, 19(3): 234–47.

Harrison, J. and Corkill, D. (2004) *Spain: a modern European economy*. Ashgate Publishing.

Kern, S. (2010) 'Spain: A Political Risk Analysis' *Euroasia Review News and Analysis*, 14 June 2010.

Locke, R.M. (1997) *Remaking the Italian economy*. Cornell University Press.

Maccoby, M. (1994) 'Creating quality cultures in the East and the West', *Research Technology Management*, 37(1): 57–9.

Magone, J.M. (2004) *The developing place of Portugal in the European Union*. Transaction Publishers.

McLeay, S. (ed.) (1999) *Accounting Regulation in Europe*. London: Macmillan.

Melis, A. (2000) 'Corporate Governance in Italy' *Empirical Research-based and theory-building papers*, 8(4): 347–55.

Molinas, C. and Escodura, L.P. (1989) 'Was Spain different? Spanish historical backwardness revisited', *Explorations in economic history*, 26(4): 385.

Moya, E. (2010) 'Spain battles to convince financial markets it is a 'solid' country.' *The Guardian*, 7 February 2010. http://www.guardian.co.uk/business/2010/feb/07/spain-greece-market-turmoil.

Nikandrou, I., Apospori, E. and Papalexandris, N. (2005) 'Changes in HRM in Europe: A longitudinal comparative study among 18 European countries', *Journal of European Industrial Training*, 29(7): 541–60.

Nobes, C. and Parker, R. (2008) *Comparative International Accounting*, 10th edn. Essex: Prentice Hall.

O'Dwyer, M., Gilmore, A. and Carson, D. (2009) Innovative marketing in SMEs. *European Journal of Marketing*, 43(1/2): 46–61.

Ollerenshaw, P. (1985) 'Industry 1820–1914', in Kennedy, L. and Ollerenshaw, P. *An Economic History of Ulster 1820–1939*, Manchester: Manchester University Press p. 83.

Ollerenshaw, P. (1991) 'Textiles and regional economic decline; Northern Ireland 1914–1970', in Holmes, C. and Booth, A. (eds), *Economy and Society; European Industrialisation and its social consequences*, Leicester: Leicester University Press, pp. 68–72.

Pierson, P. (1999) *The History of Spain*. Greenwood Publishing Group.

Psychogios, A.G. (2010) 'A Four-fold Regional-specific Approach to TQM: The Case of South Eastern Europe', *International Journal of Quality & Reliability Management*, 27(9): 1036–53.

Rabellotti, R., Carabelli, A. and Hirsch, G. (2007) 'Italian SMEs and industrial districts on the move: Where are they going?' Working Papers 115, SEMEQ Department, Faculty of Economics, University of Eastern Piedmont.

Reijonen, H. (2010) 'Do all SMEs practise same kind of marketing?' *Journal of Small Business and Enterprise Development*, 17(2): 279–93.

Schmiemann, M. (2008) *Eurostat: Statistics in Focus – Enterprises by Size Class – Overview of SMEs in the EU*, European Commission.

Shubert, A. (1990) *A Social History of Modern Spain*. Routledge.

Simpson, J. (1997) 'Economic Development in Spain, 1850–1936', *The Economic History Review*, 50(2): 348–59.

Soltani, E. and Lai, P.C. (2007) 'Approaches to quality management in the UK: survey evidence and implications', *Benchmarking: An International Journal*, 14(4): 429–54.

Syrett, S. (ed.) (2002) *Contemporary Portugal: Dimensions of Economic and Political Change*. Ashgate: Aldershot.

The Economist (2007) 'A new sick man of Europe', 14 April 2007. http://www.economist.com/world/europe/displaystory.cfm?story_id=9009032.

Tusell, J. (2007) *Spain: From Dictatorship to Democracy, 1939 to the Present*. Wiley-Blackwell.

Walsh, A., Hughes, H., Maddox, D.P. (2002) 'Total quality management continuous improvement: is the philosophy a reality?', *Journal of European Industrial Training*, 26(6): 299–307.

Walton, P., Haller, A. and Raffournier, B. (eds) (2002) *International Accounting*, 2nd ed. London: Thompson Learning.

White, R. (2010) 'Fruits of boom largely wasted, says Davy report', *The Irish Times*, 10 February 2010. http://www.irishtimes.com/newspaper/finance/2010/0220/1224264879149.html.

16
Suggestion for Further Research on the Business System and Practices in Greece

Rea Prouska and Maria Kapsali

As most research focuses on developed 'core' economies, such as the USA, the UK and Germany, research in peripheral and semi-peripheral ones is usually neglected and the smaller the country, the fewer the sources of information. This book has bridged this gap by drawing together the latest research related to the business system and management practices in Greece in order to create a holistic picture. Subsequently, by providing an example of a peripheral country, it was possible to compare Greece to other peripheral countries (Italy, Ireland, Spain and Portugal) and to contrast it to a core one (UK). We contend that this can be an illustrative and useful case study for looking into peripheral systems.

Even though this book has initiated this new perspective, this type of research could be further enhanced and perfected, as no picture is perfect and no research is without its limitations. Further research could thus look into more aspects of the business system (for instance, it could analyze labour, industrial relations, consumer markets and the function of a SME in more detail) and of other management practices (operations and project management, administration practices and forms). The comparison could be further expanded to include more peripheral EU and non-EU countries. This book is a useful resource as a basis for understanding the business system and research areas of further interest. The editors and contributors believe it is important at this point to offer some suggestions as to the focus of future research into management practices in the case of Greece.

Strategic management

In light of the recent crisis faced by the Greek business system, the implications for strategic management in organizations are numerous. Since the disposable income of Greek citizens is diminishing, almost all organizations now focus on cost leadership as the basis of their competitive strategy. This poses a problem with regard to customer satisfaction, since Greek consumers are used to high quality products and services and have been willing until now even to pay a premium for them. Consequently, a business opportunity and challenge is arising for organizations to pursue a hybrid strategy, offering high-quality products at lower prices. Future research in the strategy of Greek organizations should thus incorporate new forms of competitive strategies and specifically, how to achieve these two seemingly contradictory targets: to maintain high product and service quality while at the same time reducing prices. Organizations that are able to meet this challenge will also be able to achieve sustainable competitive advantage under difficult circumstances, namely an idiosyncratic market.

International business

Research on international business in or from Greece emerges as particularly interesting, given the phenomenal fiscal hardships of the country in 2010. Thus, investigating how international or aspiring international Greek firms cope with the challenges of the economic crisis is a key avenue for further research. It is expected that the decline of local economic activity will lead a number of firms to identify new innovative ways of conducting international business and especially cause local firms to adopt a new approach towards international markets. More specifically, future research topics may include: Do local firms consider internationalization as a response to decline in local demand? Has the new economic landscape influenced the way multinational firms conduct business in Greece? Shedding more light on such issues will contribute much-needed knowledge of firms' performance in the era of economic crisis, a crisis which is responsible for the loss of employment and the declining productivity and prosperity of societies and individuals.

Human Resource Management

There is a variety of potential areas for further research on HRM practices in Greece , but three stand most urgently in need of attention. Firstly, given the dominance of micro firms in the market, there is need for further research on the practices these firms use to manage people, in terms of employee resourcing, training/development, rewards and monitoring, employee and industrial relations, and managing performance. Secondly, comparative research between MNCs and local firms can shed light on similarities and differences in HR practices, particularly on the degree of sophistication of HR strategies, and establish the extent to which local firms can benefit from the use of more advanced practices. Thirdly, there is a need to focus research on such critical issues as, for example, the ageing population of Greece, and controversial employee and industrial relations. The latter issue is of critical importance to the country's employment policies on redundancy, harassment, equality and retirement.

Total Quality Management

Further research is needed on new trends in TQM practice and their potential application in the Greek business system. The most indicative example is Lean Six Sigma. New ways of adapting and applying TQM within the Greek firm should be explored, rather than copying quality practices without understanding their potential and implications for the firm. It is imperative that public sector management should be at the forefront of this type of investigation, since it is in urgent need of reform. The wider application of the Common Assessment Framework (CAF), for example, can be placed as a priority issue on the academic research agenda. Another urgent theme that has been neglected in research is the application of TQM practices in Greek micro firms. There is need to find ways of improving their productivity and performance through the introduction of specific techniques and practices like Lean Six Sigma, 5S, and so on. Overall, there is a need to understand the aspects of the Greek business system which may support or inhibit TQM application.

Marketing and sales

Future research in marketing should seriously consider the situation of the Greek business system in light of the current economic conditions. The increase in the rate of unemployment makes the situation worse, especially in the younger age groups (20-to-30-year-olds) and so is the stringency in consumer credit. This is discouraging Greek consumers and affecting their consumption patterns. Hence, companies should be very careful when targeting their markets and positioning their products and services. On the other hand, there are some consumer segments which are not much affected by the economic downturn. The changes in the spending behaviour of different consumer segments under conditions of social instability and economic uncertainty can therefore usefully be investigated.

Marketing and advertising spending are among the first to be reduced in times of recession, and it would be interesting to research the extent to which the current financial crisis has affected marketing and advertising budgets. In addition, a common practice for companies in a period of recession is to reduce their prices in order to boost sales. Adding value to a brand is extremely difficult, requiring careful scrutiny of marketing strategies by organizations. Future research should include the potential implications for the brand of price reductions.

Accounting and auditing

Given the importance of accounting and auditing systems for broader management and business practices and the urgent need of significant improvement to them, further research in the area is warranted at two levels. At one level, the institutional settings of accounting and auditing following the adoption of the IFRSs should be critically examined using an institutional approach to accounting research, in order to identify issues that may impede the development of practice. At another level, market-based accounting research could focus on issues such as earnings management in the periods preceding and following the adoption of IFRSs, the impact of IFRSs on audit fees, or the information content of IFRSs compared to local GAP financial statements.

Comparative research

As a final note, in order to further improve the systemic picture initiated in this book, and in addition to more research in aspects of the business system and management practices in Greece, there is an equal need to conduct further comparative study involving deeper variable analysis. Many of the issues raised in this book are not unique to Greece; their causes and frames should be sought in similar peripheral and semi-peripheral national business systems and not just in the European context. It is, therefore, important to compare within a wider framework in order to better understand the business system and management practices in Greece.

Index